REPRESENTATIVE MAN

REPRESENTATIVE MAN

Ralph Waldo Emerson in His Time

JOEL PORTE

Columbia University Press
New York   1988

Columbia University Press Morningside Edition 1988
Columbia University Press, New York
Copyright © 1979 Oxford University Press
Preface to the Morningside Edition copyright © 1988
Columbia University Press

LIBRARY OF CONGRESS
Library of Congress Cataloging-in-Publication Data

Porte, Joel.
Representative man : Ralph Waldo Emerson in his time / Joel
Porte.
—Columbia University Press Morningside ed.
p. cm.
Reprint. Originally published: New York : Oxford University Press,
1979. With new pref.
Bibliography: p.
Includes index.
ISBN 0-231-06740-2.   ISBN 0-231-06741-0 (pbk.)
1. Emerson, Ralph Waldo, 1803–1882.   2. Authors, American—
19th century—Biography.   I. Title.
[PS1631.P65 1988]
814'.3—dc19   88-829
[B]   CIP

Publication of this edition has been aided
by a grant from the
Hyder E. Rollins Fund

for Daniel Aaron

Contents

Contents

IV: THE FALL OF MAN

V: A WINTER'S TALE: THE ELDER EMERSON

EPILOGUE: REPRESENTATIVES

Preface to the
Morningside Edition

Since this book was first published a decade ago much useful work devoted to Emerson and his circle has appeared. Gay Wilson Allen, Stanley Cavell, Eric Cheyfitz, Denis Donoghue, Julie Ellison, William Gass, Irving Howe, Jerome Loving, John McAleer, Barbara Packer, Richard Poirier, David Robinson, and others, have made substantial contributions to an Emerson "revival" that shows no signs of abating. I have not attempted to incorporate the findings of such recent scholarship into this paperback edition of *Representative Man*. To do so would have demanded a thorough rewriting of a book that still has value, I hope, in its own terms as a critical introduction to Emerson's life and work.

The essentially Eriksonian frame that I designed for this study ten years ago was intended to identify crisis points in Emerson's career that were at once individual and representative of cultural conditions generally. These include the reinvestment of religious faith and energy into more diverse forms of imaginative expression, innovative solutions to problems of vocation, the integration of both mercantile and sexual economies into literary discourse, and, most especially, the formation of intellectual identity in an American nineteenth century that was at once raw and overrefined (Santayana observed years ago that America was a young nation with an old head on its shoulders).

Emerson's work as a figure in literary culture was that of finding ways to wed new forms of energy with inherited modes of discourse. In doing this, of course, he proved to be not only a pioneer in practice but also a substantial provocation to other talents. What I want to stress, however, is the importance of viewing Emerson as a figure *in culture*. No writer of his time was more sensitively attuned to his environment than was Emerson nor more concerned to define both the virtues and the vices of singularity as a literary posture. Emerson, that is, at the inception of a truly national culture helped both to set the terms of cultural debate and to provide a language for the work of critical reflection.

The strength as well as the polemical and strategical diversity of the current wave of Emerson criticism should make clear to what extent Emerson succeeded in the double task of cultural invention and reevaluation. If I may appropriate Denis Donoghue's terms from a stimulating recent essay entitled "Emerson At First," it is the "presence of . . . contradictory perceptions" that marks the richly representative nature of Emerson's work and helps to justify calling him "the founding father of nearly everything we think of as American in the modern world." That was and is the informing premise of this book.

Cornell University, 1988

Textual Note

In quoting from *JMN*, I have generally used a simplified text of my own for the sake of clarity and ease of reading. This means that I have silently omitted the textual apparatus, employed to reproduce Emerson's manuscript as accurately as possible, which indicates his cancellations, revisions, insertions, variants, manuscript page numbers, and the like. In every case, my own version represents Emerson's final judgment on his text according to editorial indications. Where I have wished the reader to see Emerson's first thoughts, revisions, or variants, I have adopted the apparatus of the Harvard text as follows: < > cancellation; ↑ ↓ insertion; / / variant. Volume and page references are supplied for readers who wish to check my quotations against the Harvard text.

ABBREVIATIONS

For convenience, the following abbreviations are used in the text to identify sources of material quoted from Emerson's writings:

CW   *The Collected Works of Ralph Waldo Emerson,* Vol. 1: *Nature, Addresses, and Lectures,* ed. Robert E. Spiller and Alfred R. Ferguson. Cambridge: Harvard University Press, 1971.

EL   *The Early Lectures of Ralph Waldo Emerson,* ed. Stephen E. Whicher, Robert E. Spiller, and Wallace E. Williams. 3 vols. Cambridge: Harvard University Press, 1959, 1964, 1972.

J   *The Journals of Ralph Waldo Emerson,* ed. Edward Waldo Emerson and Waldo Emerson Forbes. 10 vols. Boston and New York: Houghton Mifflin, 1909–14.

JMN   *The Journals and Miscellaneous Notebooks of Ralph Waldo Emerson,* ed. William H. Gilman, Alfred R. Ferguson, George P. Clark, Merrell R. Davis, Merton M. Sealts, Harrison Hayford, Ralph H. Orth, J. E. Parsons, A. W. Plumstead, Linda Allardt, and Susan Sutton Smith. 14 vols. Cambridge: Harvard University Press, 1960–.

L   *The Letters of Ralph Waldo Emerson,* ed. Ralph L. Rusk. 6 vols. New York and London: Columbia University Press, 1939.

W   *The Complete Works of Ralph Waldo Emerson,* Centenary Edition. 12 vols. Boston and New York: Houghton Mifflin, 1903.

It is only a very great mind, seasoned by large wisdom, that can lend such an accent and such a carrying-power to a few facts as to make them representative of all reality.

George Santayana

REPRESENTATIVE MAN

INTRODUCTION: EMERSON
AND HIS CIRCLE

Emerson has long been a popular subject of academic study, and college catalogues from the past frequently yield such course titles as "Emerson and His Circle." Though a rubric of this kind may seem merely old-fashioned, suggesting the pleasantly antiquarian aspect of such an investigation (the study of Emerson and other literary venerabilities of his time and place who may be arranged around him in a design symbolizing a principal cultural configuration of mid-nineteenth-century America), it can be put to more critical use. Emerson provided a new impetus and direction for thought and writing in his time and definitively changed the shape of our literary history. In order to understand that history as it now appears to us, we must make an effort to reconstruct the rise and growth of this seminal figure and trace the lines of his influence. Emerson was *the* central figure in an ever-widening cultural circle which has been called the American Renaissance but—following Irving Howe—should perhaps simply be termed the American Newness.[1] The circles that move out from his center represent a series of remarkably individualistic self-creators who were inspired by his example to put themselves and their world, in Whitman's words, "freely, fully and truly on record." But as a result of their appropriately Emersonian rejection of any notion of imitation or discipleship, we find that the base of the design so traced, as Wallace Stevens would say, is eccentric. We find arranged around Emerson, that is, not a neat circle of little Emersons but rather a loose association of resolutely self-defined figures who shaped their careers as much in reaction to Emerson as in emulation of him.

Emerson's "circle" was in fact subject to some odd topological distortions. We have only to glance at Henry Thoreau, whose insistence on *"extra vagance"* and the paradoxical manipulation of symbols both pleased and perplexed his mentor, who quickly came to realize that this presumed satellite was determined to move in a curious orbit of his own design. Another sometime Emersonian planet, the formidable and fascinating Margaret Fuller, would wander off to revolutionary Italy in search of a more thrilling destiny than provincial Concord could provide. But she never passed entirely out of Emerson's solar system. If her aphelion was the dangerous world of Mazzini's and Garibaldi's Italy, circumstance or desire nevertheless drew her back to America and death by drowning off the shores of Fire Island in 1850. That tragic event, as Perry Miller has remarked, may have caused timorous intellectuals in New England to breathe a secret sigh of relief,[2] but it left Emerson desolate. "I have lost in her my audience," he noted in his journal; "I hurry now to my work admonished that I have few days left" (*JMN* 11:258). Emerson's true inner circle was composed of such extraordinary figures; and whether he represented their center or simply an indispensable point on their unpredictable circumferences cannot be stated with precision. The design, as I say, was triumphantly eccentric.

Have I, then, demolished the notion of Emerson's "circle"? Only verbally and temporarily, for of course I have been playing with a figure of speech by way of introduction to Emerson's world and his own imaginative habits. Let us go around in a few more circles. Fundamentally, I want to suggest that the only circle of which Emerson is the true center is his own. Emerson's circle, that is, is best represented by the shape of his career and the design of his own discourse. The adequate expansion of this proposition will occupy many of the pages that follow in his book; but let us take a few pages now to examine one of the best and most engaging specimen bricks from the Emersonian edifice—to observe our "circular philosopher" in a characteristic flight of his curvilinear imagination. Here is the opening paragraph of "Circles" (1841):

> The eye is the first circle; the horizon which it forms is the second; and throughout nature this primary figure is repeated without end. It is the highest emblem in the cipher of the world. St. Augustine described the nature of God as a circle whose centre was everywhere and its circumference nowhere. We are all our lifetime reading the copious sense of this first of forms. One moral we have already deduced in considering the circular or compensatory character of every human action. Another analogy we shall now trace, that every action admits of being outdone. Our life is an apprenticeship to the truth that around every circle another can be drawn; that there is no end in nature, but every end is a beginning; that there is always another dawn risen on mid-noon, and under every deep a lower deep opens. (W 2:301)

This passage is an epitome of Emerson's thought—or rather, I should say, an epitome of that fundamentally poetic imagination which thinks in figures, providing not so much ideas as tropical notations for the structures of ideas.[3] Emerson says that "the eye is the first circle," and we are presented with a crucial homophonic pun—the primary metaphor or equivalence in Emerson's view of experience. The "eye" *is* the "I"; he conceives of himself as a process of vision; he is what he sees. The self is both the fundamental nucleus of creation and the act of envisioning that creation. (As a footnote, I might add that in one of Emerson's earliest extant letters—a rebus-note to his brother William, written when he was eleven—he anticipated Christopher Cranch's well-known caricature by using a picture of the eye to represent the first person singular.)[4] And, of course, we might well pause here to cast a glance at this familiar passage in *Nature*:

> Standing on the bare ground,—my head bathed by the blithe air, and uplifted into infinite space,—all mean egotism vanishes. I become a transparent eye-ball. I am nothing. I see all. (CW 1:10)

Emerson's insistence on the radical identity of "I" and "eye" seems so thoroughly assimilated to his speech patterns here that the very sounds chime with the burden of his equation ("eye-ball," "I . . . all").

The "eye," then, comes first; the horizon which *it* forms (*forms*, not simply sees; Emerson's epistemology in this essay is still resolutely idealistic) is second; and thereafter, "throughout nature this primary figure is repeated without end." Emerson's sequence is interesting: one, two, without end. It is as if he began, for convenience, with a linear enumeration but then quickly obliterated such distinctions as first and second by moving us into a universe where things are "repeated without end"—a universe, that is, which works not according to any sequential scheme but rather in terms of an endless metamorphic process that has neither beginning nor end.[5]

By "primary figure," accordingly, Emerson means to imply a fundamental figure in nature: which is to say, the way in which nature works. "It is the highest emblem in the cipher of the world." Shall we pause for a moment to savor this bit of verbal wit? In which sense does Emerson intend us to take "cipher"? Evidently, in several at once. The world is a cipher, or puzzle, to us. We must *figure it out*. We achieve such a figuring-out by starting with the Emersonially idealistic notion that the world is indeed a *cipher*—an absence or zero—which we need to fill in, or give meaning to, through precisely that imaginative process that Emerson is enacting. We figure the world out by putting it in figures—slicking it "up in types," as the Puritan poet Edward Taylor says.[6] The world remains an empty circle until each of us determines its boundaries and fills it with substance. The world is thus seen as a paradoxical object—everything or nothing, depending on the strength of our own imaginative processes. If God may be described as a circle which is all center and no circumference, so may each of us. As Emerson says a few pages further on, "there is no outside, no inclosing wall, no circumference to us" (W 2:304). We are being invited to think of ourselves not as a completed design but as the center of a never-ending process. We are never finished, for "every action admits of being outdone" (W 2:301).

4

Introduction: Emerson and His Circle

Emerson's "circle," then, *can* be said never to exist, for it is always being drawn and redrawn. We are manifestly not—at least, not in this essay—in the world of John Donne's compasses, where people define, contain, and enclose one another ("Thy firmness draws my circle just, / And makes me end, where I begun").[7] Emerson refuses to be detained, contained, or engaged. He is "a self-evolving circle" (W 2:304) perpetually giving birth to himself out of the womb of his own fertile imagination. If Emerson had no circle, socially speaking, it was because this strenuous ideal of Faustian expansion tended to be destructive of normal social relations, as the idealistic epistemology that underlies it sometimes weakened Emerson's faith in a world of real objects permanently fixed in space. "Men cease to interest us when we find their limitations," he writes further on in the essay:

> The only sin is limitation. As soon as you once come up with a man's limitations, it is all over with him. Has he talents? has he enterprise? has he knowledge? It boots not. Infinitely alluring and attractive was he to you yesterday, a great hope, a sea to swim in; now, you have found his shores, found it a pond, and you care not if you never see it again. (W 2:307–8)

One may take those as fairly brutal remarks, but they represent Emerson in only one mood—and an extreme one at that. It is a mood that we may all be expected to share, at least fitfully. Settling in to things and people requires a certain compromise of our freedom and aspirations. Limitation may in fact be necessary, but it also hurts; it wounds that omnipotent ego we all carry within us that hungers to devour another and newer piece of experience. "I want, I want," cries Saul Bellow's Henderson the Rain King.

The Emersonian ego is a lonely one and longs to embrace and be embraced; but it is also proud and experimental and needs to free itself from that embrace when it feels itself trapped. "I am not the man you take me for," Emerson wrote his wife Lidian in 1842, describing what he had felt like saying to some reformers in New

York who had tried to pin him, wriggling, as J. Alfred Prufrock would say, on the "formulated phrase" called the Transcendental Movement (*L* 3:18). "I am not the man you take me for." Which elicited the following dry comment from Henry James, Jr.: "He was never the man anyone took him for, for the simple reason that no one could possibly take him for the elusive, irreducible, merely gustatory spirit for which he took himself."[8] Emerson wanted merely to be tasted, not swallowed and comprehended. How could he possibly be comprehended? He himself claimed to be not comprehensive and definite, but rather a center that was as wobbling and uncertain as the circumference he could never quite draw.

Emerson's career, in fact, is one of the best examples we have of the American literary character in the process, perpetually, of defining and redefining itself. It is utterly appropriate that Emerson's preferred mode of expression should have turned out to be the essay—that tentative and fragmentary record of the mind in search of its meaning. Such a collection, as Emerson wrote of Bacon's *Essays*, frequently has "the order of a shop and not that of a tree or an animal where perfect assimilation has taken place and all the parts have a perfect unity." Though Emerson at his best certainly achieves far more than simply displaying his intellectual wares helter-skelter, he actually intended his remark about Bacon's literary habits as a kind of praise, and we may take it as a pregnant anticipation of Emerson's own evolving intent. "So loose a method," he continues, "had this advantage,"

> that it allowed of perpetual amendment and addition. And every one of his works was a gradual growth. . . . Works of this sort which consist of detached observations and to which the mind has not imparted a system of its own, are never ended. Each of Shakspear's dramas is perfect, hath an immortal integrity. To make Bacon's works complete, he must live to the end of the world. (*EL* 1:335)[9]

Though I would claim more integrity for Emerson's best pieces than he was willing to allow Bacon, the emphasis here is in the right place for a student of Emerson—namely, on the *process* of self-creation and self-discovery. We shall keep our eyes not so much on Emerson the finished thinker as on Emerson in the act of thinking, working his way indefatigably to that land's end which was always just disappearing over the horizon of his thought.

"All life is an experiment," he noted in 1842; "the more experiments you make, the better" (*JMN* 8:255–56). Emerson believed that the "species of architecture" that he studied and practiced should be called "the Building of Discourse." He would patiently erect his rhetorical towers without quite knowing what their shape would be in advance, pleased with his occasional successes but undismayed if what he had accomplished proved to be only the building material for a new attempt. "A man," he continued, "may find his words mean more than he thought when he uttered them & be glad to employ them again in a new sense" (*JMN* 5:409). We ourselves may locate here precisely the source of Emerson's literary vitality in his willingness to make one moment's circumference the next moment's center, as he redrew the circle of his meaning and thus reshaped the configurations of his existence. "All my life is a sort of College Examination," he lamented to his brother William in 1847; "I shall never graduate" (*L* 3:416). How could he possibly graduate, since the course he had enrolled in was "Emerson and His Circle"? Perhaps Emerson's greatest gift to his readers is that the example he provides can inspire us to conduct our own examinations as we try to make new sense of his.

[11]

Harold Clarke Goddard noted many years ago that "the finest and most heroic elements of the old New England culminated in Ralph Waldo Emerson. He is the representative man of one of the world's most memorable experiments in living." [10] Under the assumption not only that Goddard's assessment of Emerson is correct but also that the experiment is still in progress, in New England and far beyond its borders, I have long wanted to draw my own circle of the Emersonian seasons, believing as I do that Emerson continues to provide one of our best models of the American spirit in letters.

The seasonal metaphor I have used to structure this book is not meant to be merely quaint or gimmicky, but rather to follow the contours of Emerson's own experience and to exemplify the way his mind worked. Emerson's lifelong belief in putting the world "under the mind for verb and noun" (W 3:20) not only suggests that he was an irrepressible symbol-hunter in the manner of his forebears in old New England; it also tells us, or should tell us, that he was philosophizing, to use Susanne K. Langer's familiar term, "in a new key." When Emerson brought himself to say "we are symbols and inhabit symbols," he had finally entered fully into that post-Kantian universe built, to cite Mrs. Langer again, on "the surprising truth that our *sense-data are primarily symbols.*"[11] Which is emphatically *not* to say that Emerson believed that the world is not real, but rather that we are necessarily always the victims of our own concepts. For good or ill, we live in the mind. Life, Emerson liked to say, "consists in what a man is thinking of all day" (*JMN* 10:146).

I am not, therefore, suggesting simply that Emerson appropriated the cycle of the seasons as a "metaphor" because it is a convenient figure for the stages of a human life, particularly a rural life such as he mostly led. Rather, he understood (and built his philosophy on the understanding) that nature and the human mind exist necessarily in a reciprocal relationship. As he writes in his first book, *Nature,* "is there no intent of an analogy between man's life and the seasons? And do the seasons gain no grandeur or pathos from that analogy?" (*CW* 1:19). All of our symbols are *natural,* and all nature is symbolic, because the very act of making verb and noun, by means of which we take possession of the world, is constitutive of reality for us. The "metaphor" of the seasons is as true a representation of the way our lives move, and the way we think about that movement, as it is of the natural processes it images. All of these things are contained in a system of equivalences which we may call *verbal,* from the human perspective. The notion is suggested well by Frost in his fine lines to his "window tree":

> That day she put our heads together,
> Fate had her imagination about her,
> Your head so much concerned with outer
> Mine with inner, weather.[12]

Emerson considered himself to be a "a very indifferent botanist," but he particularly loved that perennial "four petalled flower, which science much neglects. One grey petal it has, one green, one red, & one white" (*W* 12:150; *JMN* 13:447). Botanists might view it as no more than a flower of the mind, but Emerson—in line with what I have argued above—would make no such distinctions. The year was both a concept and a fact for him. It was his boutonnière, the truest emblem of his experience. He lived in it and through it, often measuring his moods by the conjunction, or disparity, between inner and outer weather, and notching its seasons on his stick. " 'Tis very certain," he wrote in 1848, "that this almanack of the soul may be written as well as that of Greenwich. We have had our heights of sun & depths of shade, & it would be easy in the soul's year to recall & fix its 21 of June" (*JMN* 11:52). He went on to say that "there is a sort of climate in every man's speech running from hot noon, when words flow like steam & perfume, —to cold night, when they are frozen." Some years before, in his lecture "The Conservative," he had anticipated these jottings, and perhaps adumbrated the shape of his own career, when he wrote: "We are reformers in spring and summer, in autumn and winter we stand by the old" (*CW* 1:186).[13]

Emerson's life has been written many times in the traditional way—that is, with an emphasis on factual detail and chronology—and the existence of such books (particularly Ralph Rusk's standard *Life of Emerson*) can liberate the aspiring biographer to attempt the sort of treatment suggested by the sub-title of Maurice

Gonnaud's fine work, "an essay in spiritual biography."[14] Emerson's life was largely devoid of what Henry James would call "incident" and is not marked by the flamboyant gestures that have helped to mythologize and popularize some of his fellow Romantic authors. He did not live in a cabin by the shores of Walden Pond or spend a night in jail; nor did he pass over Harvard College in favor of a whaling ship, nor take to wearing white and speaking to his visitors from an adjoining room. The drama and interest of his life lie fundamentally in the development of his extraordinary mind and spirit, as recorded in his journals, notebooks, letters, and published writings. His career was profoundly literary, in the best sense of that word. In order to demonstrate the enormous richness of Emerson's life, one must necessarily write a biography of his works. But I believe we must never lose sight of the fact that those works issued from, and constitute the record of, a *life*—an exemplary American life unsurpassed for the intensity of purpose and meaning with which it was lived. I have therefore provided a biographical headnote for each of the four major sections of this book, both as a guide for those readers unfamiliar with Emerson's story and as a historical frame and counterpoint to the more sharply focused and interpretive version of the Emersonian "season" that follows.

Emerson himself seemed to think that the story of his life would not make very interesting reading for the usual kind of devotees of biography. When an English admirer proposed to sketch his life in her journal in 1847 and wrote for information. Emerson replied as follows: "With regard to the very flattering proposition you make me of giving my name & poor history a place in your Journal it has my thanks but no such thing can be gravely considered [.] I am concerned to say I have no history no anecdotes no connexions no fortunes that would make the smallest figure in a narrative. my course of life has been so routinary, that the keenest eye for all its point or picture would be at fault before such remediless commonplace. We will really say no more on a topic so sterile" (*L* 3:418). Although Emerson was being extremely self-effacing (and un-

doubtedly also purposely secretive) about his biography, the truth
is that he had a theory of literary biography with which these
remarks are perfectly consistent. In 1845 he noted in his journal:

> We are very clumsy writers of history. We tell the chronicle of
> parentage, birth, birthplace, schooling, companions, acquisition of
> property, marriage, publication of books, celebrity, & death, and
> when we have come to an end of this external history, the reader is
> no whit instructed, no ray of relation appears between all this
> lumber & the goddess-born, and it really appears as if, had we
> dipped at random into the modern Plutarch or Universal Biogra-
> phy, & read any other life there, it would have fitted to the poems
> quite as well. (*JMN* 9:314–15)

It thus appears that Emerson put off his inquisitive correspondent
not so much because nothing of interest had happened to him as
because he believed that the ordinary "chronicle" of a literary life
for which he was being asked to supply facts would tell the reader
little about the qualities of mind and spirit that informed his work.
Why read such a chronicle, he seems to be asking, when you have
the poems themselves? The only narrative in which an author cuts
even the "smallest figure" is the one he himself composes.

"Plato & the great intellects have no biography," Emerson
writes. "As a good chimney burns up all its own smoke, so a good
philosopher consumes all his own events in his extraordinary intellectual performances" (*JMN* 9:266). Life, as Emerson would say
in *Representative Men*, "is eating us up. We shall be fables presently" (*W* 4:154). An artist anticipates that inevitable fate, and in
a sense disarms it, by turning his life into fable beforehand. "The
old writers," Emerson notes, "such as Montaigne, Milton, Browne,
when they had put down their thoughts, jumped into their book
bodily themselves, so that we have all that is left of them in our
shelves; there is not a pinch of dust beside" (*JMN* 10:350). The
macabre humor of Emerson's elliptical joke reinforces his point:
the only dust of the literary past worth stirring up is that which

has settled on our authors' books. Emerson was in striking agreement with Keats when the latter wrote: "Shakespeare led a life of allegory; his works are the comments on it." [15] His own formulations are very close to such a notion. "The life of Rafaello is the Catalogue of his works. The life of a great artist always is thus inward, a life of no events. Shakespeare has no biography worth seeking" (*JMN* 7:248–49):

> What can any biography biographize the wonderful world into which the Midsummer Night's dream admits me? Did Shakspeare confide to any Notary or Parish Recorder, sacristan or surrogate in Stratford upon Avon, the genesis of that delicate creation? The forest of Arden, the air of Scone Castle, the moonlight of Portia's villa; where is the third cousin or grandnephew, the prompter's book or private letter that has heard one word of those transcendant secrets? Shakspeare is the only biographer of Shakspeare. (*JMN* 9:315)

Emerson himself, in humorous—or grim—exemplification of these remarks, frequently tried his hand at mini-allegories of his own life that suggest both his impatience with "external history" and his desire to shape fact into fable. One such is set down under the date of October 24, 1841:

> Life in Boston: A play in two acts, Youth & Age. Toys, dancing school, *Sets,* parties, picture galleries, sleighrides, Nahant, Saratoga Springs, lectures, concerts, *sets* through them all, solitude & poetry, friendship, ennui, desolation, decline, meanness, plausibility, old age, death. (*JMN* 8:114)

Those critics who continue to argue that Emerson lacked the tragic sense of life, or did not develop such a sense until after the death of his son in 1842, simply have not read well or deeply enough in Emerson's writings. He saw himself, as here, dancing his way to death in a drama too familiar, and painful, to require more than the laconic notations he has himself provided. Another little autobiographical fable written the following year provides the humor which is more characteristic of Emerson's ventures in this genre:

> I was a little chubby boy trundling a hoop in Chauncey Place and spouting poetry from Scott & Campbell at the Latin School. But Time the little grey man has taken out of his vest pocket a great aukward house (in a corner of which I sit & write of him) some acres of land, several fullgrown & several very young persons, & seated them close beside me; then he has taken that chubbiness & that hoop quite away (to be sure he has left the declamation & the poetry) and here left a long lean person threatening soon to be a little grey man, like himself. (*JMN* 8:258)

Life in Boston (and Concord) does not seem here to be a tragically linear play in two acts, but rather a compensatory circle figured by the hoop of Emerson's boyhood in Chauncy Place, which leaves some things behind, provides replacements for others, and in the endless turnings of its comedy produces an Emerson who is an incarnation of the very power that is running his show. If fate appears to be unkind, Emerson might be saying, we have mostly ourselves to blame.

Emerson's interest in fables of the self, especially of the comic variety, might fruitfully be considered, as F. O. Matthiessen suggests, in the context of native American humor, and particularly in the folkloric tradition of the tall tale, best exemplified perhaps by the Crockett almanacs.[16] In such material, as both Matthiessen and Constance Rourke point out, humor and something akin to lyric poetry, often tinged with a strain of melancholy, unite in the service of creating national myths of self-definition. Emerson was manifestly encouraged by these attempts of the American muse, in both primitive and more sophisticated forms, to express that peculiar propensity in the national character to extract American fables from American facts.[17] That metaphysical passion (to paraphrase Santayana) which drove the Puritans to these shores had its comic as well as its serious avatars in the nineteenth century, and Emerson paid attention to both kinds. In 1849, he copied into his journal a wonderful sentence that he found in a review of William Starbuck Mayo's popular comic allegorical fantasy *Kaloolah*, which purported to be the autobiography of an archetypal American traveler named "Jonathan Romer": "The Kentuckian said, his country 'was bounded on the east by the rising sun, on the north by the aurora borealis, on the west by the precession of the equinoxes, & on the south by the Day of Judgment' " (*JMN* 11:130–31). Emerson undoubtedly liked this spoofing description of the "boundaries" of his country because it at once exemplified and questioned the familiar belief that geography and eschatology were inseparable categories for the American mind.[18]

The seasons of Emerson's life were equally charged with meaning, and I have simply tried to follow his lead by filling in the outlines of a fable suggested to me by the contours of his own career and writing. Thus, boxing Emerson's compass in the other direction, I might say he was bounded on the east by his regenerative trip to Europe in 1832, on the south by the Book of Jeremiah, on the west by his visionary America, and on the north by the prudential economies of old age. Whether or not this structure seems factitious I must leave to the judgment of readers willing to consider, in a somewhat Transcendental spirit, the materials I have gathered in this study. And though I hesitate to anticipate an objection where none may exist, or to be so arrogant as to associate myself with the fine audacities of Emerson's own literary practice, I cannot resist the temptation to quote this passage from a journal entry of 1846: "Men quarrel with your rhetoric. Society chokes with a trope, like a child with the croup. They much prefer Mr Prose, & Mr Hoarse-as-Crows, to the dangerous conversation of Gabriel and the archangel Michael perverting all rules, & bounding continually from earth to heaven" (*JMN* 9:395). I offer that not as a justification for what I have myself done but rather as an illustration of what I mean by willingness to consider Emerson's life and works in a "Transcendental spirit."

No account of Emerson's career can be adequate unless it rises to the challenge of what Richard Poirier has recently termed Emerson's "troping."[19] To paraphrase Frost, a true literary life is inherently poetic or metaphoric; to step on its first rung is equivalent to stepping on Jacob's ladder, for we will find ourselves "bounding continually from earth to heaven." Which is to say finally that Emerson's "circle" is essentially hermeneutic—an invitation to interpretation that has no real beginning or ending, and that equally offers no clear demarcation between the literal and the figurative. I should remind the reader at the outset that Emerson regularly used the word "representative" to mean *symbolic* or *emblematic*. When Emerson wrote, in "The Poet," that "the man is only half himself, the other half is his expression" (W 3:5), I believe he intended to suggest that "expression" is the figurative "half" that completes and gives value to the literal fact of our existence. In that sense, we can all be, or hope to be, "representative" men and women. The circle of Emerson's seasons accordingly provides a prime example that may serve essentially to implement or illustrate the process.

I

LEGENDS OF AN
AMERICAN SAINT

Hagiography

The canonization of Ralph Waldo Emerson undoubtedly began long before his death in the exalted impression he left on many fervent nineteenth-century souls filled with secularized millennial yearnings. It was, such people seemed to agree, more a question of the transcendent aura that appeared to surround him than of the orphic and uplifting nature of his pronouncements. Even prior to his having published anything of note, Emerson began to be thought of in unearthly terms. Jane Carlyle claimed that the young Emerson who arrived at the farm in Craigenputtock on an August day in 1833 descended "on us, out of the clouds, as it were, and made one day there look like enchantment for us, and left me weeping that it was only *one* day." Her husband thought their guest "a beautiful transparent soul" and watched him, on his departure, vanish at the summit of a hill like an "angel."[1] Carlyle would complain, to be sure, in the correspondence that ensued in 1834 and lasted almost forty years, that Emerson and his utterances never quite descended from that mountain—that the ethereal spirit of Concord hardly deigned to body itself in flesh and blood and be clothed in the ordinary garments of corrupt humanity. As time wore on, Carlyle would seem less and less disposed to praise the literary angel's food he received from his presumably otherworldly American friend.

Immediately following Emerson's death, his friends and disciples intensified the process of translating New England's Reformer of the Reformation to that higher status of quasi-apotheosization as the patron saint of America's spiritual life that he would hold for many years to come. In 1882, for example, Moncure D. Conway, a southern radical whom Emerson led up from the bondage first of religious orthodoxy and then from the pale negations of Harvard Divinity College, published his worshipful remembrance, *Emerson at Home and Abroad*, the first chapter of which, "A Vigil," begins as follows:

> It is the vigil of Emerson. To-morrow (May 25, 1882) he will be seventy-nine years of age. I cannot bear to write "he would be." This day, gazing on a picture of Emerson's funeral, picking out from beneath their grey hairs faces of some with whom I have sat at his feet, there comes home to me the secret of that longing out of which were born myths of men that never died, of Yami and Arthur, of Enoch and Saint John. The love of a Madonna is in his own interpretation. "The fable of the Wandering Jew is agreeable to men because they want more time and land in which to execute their thoughts. But a higher poetic use must be made of the legend. Take us as we are with our experience, and transfer us to a new planet, and let us digest for its inhabitants what we could of the wisdom of this. After we have found our depth there, and assimilated what we could of the wisdom of the new experience, transfer us to a new scene. In each transfer we shall have acquired, by seeing them at a distance, a new mastery of the old thoughts, in which we were too much immersed. In short, all our intellectual action not promises, but bestows a feeling of absolute existence. We are taken out of time and breathe a purer air."
>
> Such duration did Emerson devise; but one source of the longing for immortality he could not know so fully as we who cannot leave his grave. It needed this night to bring out the star of that hope.[2]

For Conway, this deathless being who had passed into myth, even while he lived, was not simply one more star in the firmament of Christian hagiography, but rather part of that larger universe where the exalted names of all times and religions shine together in bright intergalactic splendor. "I was taken to Emerson by his children," he recalls, "and gave him my note of introduction":

> He remembered, and said, "Surely you are my Virginian correspondent." With that he extended his hand and welcomed me with a smile—his smile, not to be lightly lost by one it has warmed. . . . I could not answer. Many years after I read that one in paradise was asked how he got there and replied, "One day as Buddha passed by he smiled upon me." [3]

Other commentators on Emerson followed suit, though usually not with the hyperbolic adoration that characterizes Conway's response. Oliver Wendell Holmes, who knew Emerson well and could observe him with a dispassionate eye, semi-seriously dubbed the great man in 1885 "our Saint Radulphus." [4] Young intellectuals, such as John Jay Chapman, who struggled valiantly to come to terms with Emerson's daunting presence, could comment, as Chapman did in 1897, on the irony that the great New England radical who believed that "piety is a crime" should have been "calmly canonized and embalmed in amber by the very forces he braved. He is become a tradition and a sacred relic. You must speak of him under your breath, and you may not laugh near his shrine." [5] Though the older, more conservative critics of the period, such as George Woodberry or W. C. Brownell, could describe Emerson as "a shining figure as on some Mount of Transfiguration," or as "some new kind of saint—perhaps Unitarian," [6] the young Turks, especially at Harvard, reacted more ambivalently to the near-deification of a figure whom they took to represent the stultifying orthodoxies of the genteel tradition. By 1919 T. S. Eliot, while praising Hawthorne, would pronounce the essays of Emerson "already an encumbrance," [7] and Eliot's language suggests not so much a literary burden as a *monumental* physical weight—the lares and penates of Victorian culture which the brave new Aeneases of the twenties were determined to jettison:

Matthew and Waldo, guardians of the faith,
The army of unalterable law.[8]

The Unitarian saint seemed to keep watch over outmoded standards of conduct, not over the new canons of literature. As a result, "in those days [the twenties]," asserts Malcolm Cowley, "hardly anyone read Emerson."[9] Such a quirky exception as D. H. Lawrence only proved the general rule, for this self-admitted "spiritual drug-fiend," despite an odd personal taste for Emerson that he could not totally exorcise, summarized the temper of the times when he argued in 1923 that "all those gorgeous inrushes of exaltation and spiritual energy which made Emerson a great man now make us sick. . . . When Professor [Stuart] Sherman urges us in Ralph Waldo's footsteps, he is really driving us nauseously astray."[10] With a *"Sic transeunt Dei hominorum,"* Lawrence reluctantly ushered the tarnished deity from his niche. The devils—Melville and Poe—were in, and the leading saint went marching out (or at least into the reverent halls of genteel academia).

Emerson himself would surely have appreciated this divine comedy. His own beloved Aunt Mary Moody pronounced herself "never patient with the faults of the good."[11] And the iconoclastic saint seems to have written his own epitaph for the twenties when he noted in *Representative Men* that "every hero becomes a bore at last" (W 4:27). Though the Emerson of "The Transcendentalist" might like to insist that "a saint should be as dear as the apple of the eye" (CW 1:214), he also knew enough about the temptations of forbidden fruit to consider all human notions about divinity somewhat ridiculous: "I believe that if an angel should come to chant the chorus of the moral law, he would eat too much gingerbread, or take liberties with private letters, or do some precious atrocity" (W 3:227). As skeptical as Chaucer about the authenticity or value of the "pigges bones" frequently displayed as the sacred relics of the saints, Emerson insisted that the figures in his own literary pantheon were of value not for the details of their lives but for the force and universality of their words and spirit.

Emerson would have agreed, for example, with Milton, that the essence of Shakespeare lay not in his "honored bones" and other "hallowed reliques" but in the dissemination of his genius throughout the human intellect. When Emerson thought of Shakespeare as a saint, it was not as one whose garments might be preserved and worshipped in a local shrine but rather "like some saint whose history is to be rendered into all languages, into verse and prose, into songs and pictures, and cut up into proverbs" (*W* 4:210).

Even as he himself prepared to set off to meet the great men of European letters in 1832, Emerson wrote: "I would draw characters, not write lives. I would evoke the spirit of each and their relics might rot. Luther, Milton, Newton, Shakspear. Alfred a light of the world. Adams. I would walk among the dry bones & wherever on the face of the earth I found a living man I would say here is life & life is communicable" (*JMN* 4:35). What Emerson valued was not the legends and leavings of these great commanding figures but the possibility of a vital communication with the spirit that informed them. Those whom Emerson conceived to be "great men" he found "yoked together by the accidents of their lives" not into a community of saints whose examples might be imitated, but rather into a "genial constellation" of creative power the light of which would help to further the growth of his own spirit (*JMN* 4:88).

Still, Emerson's own desire to "make Milton shine" in his countenance, to "mourn for Bacon" and "fly in the face of every cockered prejudice, feudal or vulgar, & speak as Christ of their good & evil" (*JMN* 4:35–36) harbors a tendency toward the universalizing of his individual history into suprapersonal fables. He could therefore provide models for precisely the sort of translation of his own life to the level of quasi-divine legend that he would undoubtedly have found offensive. Would Emerson have been completely surprised to hear Oliver Wendell Holmes saying, "Emerson's earthly existence was in the estimate of his own philosophy so slight an occurrence in his career of being that his relations to the accidents of time and space seem quite secondary matters to one who has been long living in the companionship of his thought," [12] when he himself could write:

> For this was I born & came into the world to deliver the self of myself to the Universe from the Universe; to do a certain benefit which Nature could not forego, not I be discharged from rendering & then immerge again into the holy silence & eternity, out of which as a man I arose. God is rich & many more men than I, he harbors in his bosom, biding their time & the needs & the beauty of all. Or, when I wish, it is permitted me to say, these hands, this body, this history of Waldo Emerson are profane & wearisome, but I, I descend not to mix myself with that or with any man. Above his life, above all creatures I flow down forever a sea of benefit into races of individuals. Nor can the stream ever roll backward or the sin or death of man taint the immutable energy which distributes itself into men as the sun into rays or the sea into drops. (*JMN* 7:435)

This seems to be a good example of what Emerson called "biography above biography" (*JMN* 12:574), whereby, through a species of cosmic consciousness, he could be enabled to elevate the odious facts of his personal existence to the level of something approximating divine myth. Of course, Emerson could see both the danger and the comic aspect of such rarefied talk, and tell Margaret Fuller that "if you do not quit the high chair, lie quite down, & roll on the ground a good deal, you become nervous & heavyhearted"; whereupon he promised to gossip of "chenangoes" and a "new garden spout," the acquisition of a pig and the planting of forty-four pine trees (*L* 2:135). But when the muse of timeless legend once again took possession of his soul. Emerson would leave the pigs and chenangoes far behind and compose little allegories of his secular sainthood:

> Yet it seemed to him as if gladly he would dedicate himself to such a god, be a fakeer of the intellect, fast & pray, spend & be spent, wear its colors, wear the infirmities, were it pallor, sterility,

celibacy, poverty, insignificance, were these the livery of its troop ... so that he be rewarded by conquest of principles; or by being purified & admitted into the immortalities, mount & ride on the backs of these thoughts, steeds which course forever the ethereal plains. (*JMN* 13:455)

When she was around fourteen, Gertrude Stein reports, she used to say to herself, "May I be one of those immortal something or other."[13] Later on, told that she resembled a saint, she wrote herself into *Four Saints in Three Acts,* announced, "My country 'tis of thee sweet land of liberty of thee I sing,"[14] and portrayed Ulysses S. Grant as "a religious leader who was to become a saint" in *Four in America.*[15] Perhaps all of this helps to explain why she once became "very eloquent" with Bertrand Russell "on the disembodied abstract quality of the american character and cited examples, mingling automobiles with Emerson."[16] American religion, Stein says, is "remarkable in not separating anything from anything";[17] the whole country is one enormous camp meeting. Why, then, shouldn't all the great American personalities tend to apotheosize themselves? Saint U. S. Grant and Saint Gertrude and Saint Radulphus (and perhaps even Saint Gatsby) can therefore plausibly rub shoulders under the universal revival tent that inspires the American tendency toward abstract self-conceptions. Saint Radulphus, however, may be said to have founded that religion. It is therefore appropriate that the canonization of Ralph Waldo Emerson should have been initiated by his own fertile Transcendental imagination.

Henry James' "Fine Adumbration"

Though Henry James was not one to be skeptical about saints and other spiritual apparitions, in his treatment of Emerson he tended to approximate Dr. Holmes' urbane familiarity more than Moncure Conway's reverent genuflections. Emerson had, indeed, bestowed his blessings on both William and the young Harry James, but as an intimate of the family and an occasional presence in their Manhattan house, not as the religious leader of Transcendental Concord and Boston. In time, James himself came to know Emerson on more or less familiar terms, and that familiarity may have helped to breed the affectionately ironical tone that James tended to adopt in writing about his father's good friend. James himself, for example, had the privilege, if not the pleasure, of conducting the seventy-year-old sage around the Louvre and the Vatican Museum in 1872–73, and was far from impressed by the great man's reactions. He could only conclude, humorously, that on the Emersonian piano "certain chords . . . did not vibrate at all."[18] James might speak, as in his 1883 review of the Emerson-Carlyle *Correspondence,* of that "united pair" of nineteenth-century giants as presenting themselves "in something of the uplifted relief of a group on canvas or in marble,"[19] but his marmorealizing of the American demi-god ended there.

This review was not, of course, the first opportunity James took to open up the large subject of Emerson, but it did reiterate the dominant note that James had struck in his comments on Emerson, four years previous, in his book on Hawthorne. "His letters," James remarked in the review, "are especially interesting for the impression they give us of what we may call the thinness of the New England atmosphere in those days."[20] In his *Hawthorne,* James had already argued that the Emersonian "doctrine of the supremacy of the individual to himself" found the ready response it did in the New England of the time because there was so little to feed on, culturally, *outside* of the self.[21] Emerson's doctrine, James insists, "must have had a great charm for people living in a society in which introspection, thanks to the want of other entertainment, played almost the part of a social resource."[22] ("I am not alone," Thoreau says with ironic bravado, "if I stand by myself.")[23] As a symbol of the fact that "small things were made to do large service," James picks out a detail from George Lathrop's *Study of Hawthorne,* which describes how an evening's entertainment was provided for the Hawthornes at Elizabeth Peabody's house by the arrival of Flaxman's illustrations for Dante's *Divine Comedy.* Meditating on this scene, James has "a vision of a little unadorned parlor, with the snow-drifts of a Massachusetts winter piled up about its windows, and a group of sensitive and serious people, modest votaries of opportunity, fixing their eyes upon a bookful of Flaxman's attenuated outlines."[24]

That last phrase may stand as a sufficient indication of how James tended to view Emerson as a representative of his cultural milieu. Finding little opportunity in the bareness of the American scene, the Emersonian mind turns inward and invents its own opportunities. Whether or not there is truly anything there depends on one's point of view and, as Hawthorne would say, the brightness of the light in which one examines one's creations. *Twice-Told Tales,* Hawthorne warns us, "requires to be read in the clear, brown, twilight atmosphere in which it was written; if opened in the sunshine, it is apt to look exceedingly like a volume of blank pages."[25] James' own eyes, accustomed to the unlimited visual opportunities of Europe, sometimes had trouble adjusting themselves to the attenuated adumbrations which they found in Emerson's world.

Typical, perhaps, is this sentence from a letter written by James to a friend in September 1870: "I spent lately a couple of days with Mr. Emerson at Concord—pleasantly but with slender profit."[26] Such is the situation more amply, and amusingly, described in James' early novella, *The Europeans* (1878), where the brother and sister pair of the title, Felix Young and the Baroness Eugenia Munster, receive little return on their investment in Boston society. Reporting to Eugenia on his initial visit to his American cousins, Felix notes that their *ton* is that of the "golden age":

> "And have they nothing golden but their *ton?* Are there no symptoms of wealth?"
>
> "I should say there was wealth without symptoms. A plain, homely way of life: nothing for show, and very little for—what shall I call it?—for the senses."

Eugenia perceives that the Wentworths are "Puritans" and that they are "anything but gay":

> "No they are not gay," Felix admitted. "They are sober; they are even severe. They are of a pensive cast; they take things hard. I think there is something the matter with them; they have some melancholy memory or some depressing expectation. It's not the epicurean temperament. My uncle, Mr. Wentworth, is a tremendously high-toned old fellow; he looks as if he were undergoing martyrdom, not by fire, but by freezing."

One's suspicion that the symptoms being displayed by the Wentworths are those of Emersonian idealism is strengthened by a parallel scene, in which Eugenia goes to meet Mrs. Acton, the mother of the New Englander who interests her:

> Mrs. Acton was an emaciated, sweet-faced woman of five and fifty, sitting with pillows behind her, and looking out on a clump of hemlocks. She was very modest, very timid, and very ill; she made

Eugenia feel grateful that she herself was not like that—neither so ill, nor, possibly, so modest. On a chair, beside her, lay a volume of Emerson's Essays.

Though Mrs. Acton's disease proves to be terminal, the other Americans not only endure but prevail, demonstrating, presumably, that the thin but morally bracing atmosphere in which they exist provides both its own protections and its own rewards.

In his old age, James would find more profit in Emerson, comparing him to Goethe and a "potful" of gold, and remembering Emerson as "an apparition sinuously and . . . elegantly slim, benevolently aquiline," who put him in touch for the first time with "the wonder of Boston." [27] But when he wrote his review in 1887 of James Elliot Cabot's *Memoir of Ralph Waldo Emerson,* he was more ambivalent about the Emersonian etiolations. Laying down the book "with a singular impression of paleness," James puzzled over how to come to terms with "the white tint of Emerson's career considered simply in itself." Though James pronounced himself "charmed by the image of Emerson's mind," that physiognomy was also "so fair, so uniform and impersonal, that its features are simply fine shades." The Emersonian surface presented in Cabot's book is "of the smoothest" and one "on which nothing was reflected with violence," but nevertheless it constituted a kind of Moby-Dick to James' imagination. [28]

As James continues to speak of Emerson's "rather bare and stern" situation with its "impression of a terrible paucity of alternatives"—of cultural nudity presented "in a kind of achromatic picture"—one begins to sense a sinister presence (or absence) despite James' familiar assurance that Emerson's "ripe unconsciousness of evil . . . is one of the most beautiful signs by which we know him." [29] In the use of *evil* as applied here to Emerson's lack, James undoubtedly meant what he would later call, speaking of himself, "the imagination of disaster." [30] Although that ferocious awareness of life's dark corners seems indeed to be missing from the portrait of Emerson, what one finds amply documented in

James' own presentation is that *privative* aspect of evil which Emerson would himself speak of. James is sketching for us, that is, without perhaps quite being aware of it, an Emerson whose heroism would consist in facing, with apparent lack of drama, the "undecorated walls" of his own denuded consciousness—stripped of tradition, religious assurance, cultural appurtenance, and the consolations of high passion. "We get the impression," James himself goes on to write, "of a conscience gasping in the void, panting for sensations, with something of the movement of the gills of a landed fish."[31]

The possibilities of exposing a darker side of Emerson's life are in fact clearly suggested when James comes to describe Emerson's "ladies" and his "strangely unfamiliar" way of dealing with love and death. "Courteous and humane to the furthest possible point," James writes, "to the point of an almost profligate surrender of his attention, there was no familiarity in him, no personal avidity." Yet James is not really praising Emerson:

> Even his letters to his wife are courtesies, they are not familiarities. He had only one style, one manner, and he had it for everything— even for himself, in his notes, in his journals. But he had it in perfection for Miss [Margaret] Fuller; he retreats, smiling and flattering, on tiptoe, as if he were advancing. "She ever seems to crave," he says in his journal, "something which I have not, or have not for her." What he had was doubtless not what she craved, but the letter in question should be read to see how the modicum was administered.[32]

Hinting at indirection and egotism, James nevertheless manages to skirt ironically the very issues he is raising, leaving the reader to fill in the tantalizing blanks. Yet James does go on to bring up—*only* to "bring up"—"the question of [Emerson's] inner reserves and skepticisms, his secret ennuis and ironies." It would be a long while before any modern biographer would venture to make a true response to James' muted appeal. James quotes Emerson's own "I am not the man you take me for," and then remarks, as we have noticed, "He was never the man anyone took him for, for the simple reason that no one could possibly take him for the elusive, irreducible, merely gustatory spirit for which he took himself." [33] More than a half-century later, after writing an *inner life* of Emerson, Stephen E. Whicher would note, in apparent perplexity, "The more we know him, the less we know him." [34] James' "fine adumbration" was only partially out of the shadows.

SANTAYANA'S EMERSON:
ULTIMATE PURITANISM

When George Santayana came to write his "Preface" to the Triton edition of *The Last Puritan* in 1937, he claimed that he had lived with the book's characters for forty-five years.[35] He was undoubtedly referring to his friendships, in the 1890s, with the Harvard undergraduates who served as models for Oliver Alden and Mario Van de Weyer.[36] But in view of the true underlying subject of the book, Santayana might have extended his time span for the genesis of that "Memoir in the form of a novel" back at least to 1886, when he submitted his own undergraduate essay, "The Optimism of Ralph Waldo Emerson," in an unsuccessful bid for Harvard's Bowdoin Prize. *The Last Puritan,* one student of the subject notes, "is really a novel about Santayana's own . . . semitranscendental ambivalence toward Emerson and transcendentalism"; and he suggested that someone ought to write a chapter in Santayana's life entitled "*The Last Puritan* and the Ghost of Emerson" or "*The Last Puritan* as an Exercise in Loving Exorcism."[37]

If such was Santayana's intent, then he seems to have failed in laying the ghost to rest. At the end of his life, writing the last volume of his autobiography, Santayana invoked both the spirit and the letter of Emerson to explain the *metanoia,* or "change of heart," which led him "through darkness . . . into the pure starlight that transports without dazzling" of his disillusioned mature philosophy.[38] The Emerson that Santayana quotes is represented by the best lines from "Threnody" ("This losing is true dying, /

Santayana's Emerson: Ultimate Puritanism

This is lordly man's down-lying, / This his true and sure declining, / Star by star his world resigning"),[39] but the drama of renunciation enacted here recapitulates another Emersonian moment—Oliver's last chapter in Santayana's novel. His proposal of marriage turned down by Rose Darnley, "his earthly person ... rejected, his earthly plan defeated," Oliver feels "wonderfully liberated" as he walks away from "the burning city of our vanity." Love is finished, and both the Vicar and his son Jim, the two people Oliver cared about most, are dead, yet Oliver thinks: "The strain is relaxed. The play is over, the doors open, and after all those unnecessary thrills and anxieties, I am walking out into the night, into my true life. . . . I am falling back upon my deeper self. I may hardly be able to see the stars, after the blinding light of the theatre, but there they are; and gradually they will become visible again, I shall recognize them, I shall call each of them by its name."[40] And the name that Oliver gives to the feeling that exalts him is pure Emerson: "self-recovery."[41]

Santayana's attitude toward Emerson has usually been measured by the essay he wrote for *Interpretations of Poetry and Religion* in 1900, which is largely informed by the same tone of ironic detachment that James had employed in 1887. In Santayana's case, the note of gentle satire struck at the beginning of the piece served to undercut the hagiographic tradition which was already firmly in place in the Harvard of Santayana's day:

> Those who knew Emerson, or who stood so near to his time and to his circle that they caught some echo of his personal influence, did not judge him merely as a poet or philosopher, nor identify his efficacy with that of his writings. His friends and neighbours, the congregations he preached to in his younger days, the audiences that afterward listened to his lectures, all agreed in a veneration for his person which had nothing to do with their understanding or acceptance of his opinions. They flocked to him and listened to his word, not so much for the sake of its absolute meaning as for the atmosphere of candour, purity, and serenity that hung about it, as about a sort of sacred music. They felt

themselves in the presence of a rare and beautiful spirit, who was in communion with a higher world.[42]

That Santayana himself was not disposed to speak in only reverent tones of New England's saint is clear from other evidence of the period. In some comments recorded in the back of a copy of Santayana's *Lucifer,* Wallace Stevens describes an evening spent with Santayana in the spring of 1900 when, over whisky and cigarettes, they "discussed the Emerson essay" in *Interpretations* (as well as a "decidedly unpleasant—and shallow" criticism in the *Nation*) and "laughed at Emerson's habit of eating pie for breakfast etc."[43] Another student of Santayana's, Baker Brownell, reports on Santayana's reaction to the statue of Emerson that presides over Harvard's philosophy building:

> Once on his way down the hall, he paused before the bronze, seated Emerson for whom the hall is named. He looked at it a moment and turned to me standing nearby. "How do you like it?" he asked me; and to my rather indefinite reply, he said, "The upper part is all right, but those shanks are too prominent."[44]

If Santayana was suggesting that the statue made Emerson look more like a long-legged Yankee preacher or schoolmaster, such as Ichabod Crane, than a candidate for canonization, such a debunking view might have adumbrated Jim Darnley's acerbic response to Oliver Alden's calling Emerson a "saint" who loved nature and humanity: "An old barebones like Emerson doesn't *love;* he isn't a *saint.* He's simply a distinguished-looking old cleric with a sweet smile and a white tie: he's just honourable and bland and as cold as ice."[45]

Such a pronouncement, decidedly not characteristic of Santayana's later attitude toward Emerson, does in fact capture some of the sharpness of tone discernible in the "Emerson" of 1900:

> A Puritan whose religion was all poetry, a poet whose only pleasure was thought, he showed in his life and personality the meagerness,

the constraint, the frigid and conscious consecration which belonged to his clerical ancestors, while his inmost impersonal spirit ranged abroad over the fields of history and Nature, gathering what ideas it might, and singing its little snatches of inspired song.[46]

Santayana's animus is obvious, and the reason for it should be equally so—and familiar in Emerson criticism. Beneath Emerson's "occasional thin paradoxes and guileless whims," Santayana thought he detected a cruel indifference, or imperviousness, to pain and suffering.[47] Granting—importantly—that imagination was clearly Emerson's "single theme," Santayana nonetheless felt that Emerson's insistence on the power of imaginative thought "first to make the world, then to understand it, and finally to rise above it" was rather too facile and chillingly mystical, though it moved in the direction of a philosophical attitude which Santayana himself was ambivalently attracted to:

While the conflict of life and the shocks of experience seem to bring us face to face with an alien and overwhelming power, reflection can humanize and rationalize that power by conceiving its laws; and with this recognition of the rationality of all things comes the sense of their beauty and order. The destruction which Nature seems to prepare for our special hopes is thus seen to be the victory of our impersonal interests. To awaken in us this spiritual insight, an elevation of mind which is at once an act of comprehension and of worship, to substitute it for lower passions and more servile forms of intelligence—that is Emerson's constant effort. All his resources of illustration, observation, and rhetoric are used to deepen and clarify this sort of wisdom.[48]

This was the sort of wisdom which Santayana was almost—but not quite—prepared to accept in 1900, as he contemplated renouncing his youthful impulses in the name of spiritual peace. But in 1886, when he wrote his Bowdoin essay, Santayana was even less disposed to accept an optimism based on "indifference to circumstances"—one, that is, which feels that all things are well because it has taken refuge in a frigid aestheticism that habitually, and heartlessly, distances itself from the inconveniences and tragedies of experience. "From optimism of this kind," Santayana notes (exposing, perhaps unconsciously, one of the darker paradoxes of Emerson's thought), "pessimism differs only in name."[49] In the second paragraph of his essay, calling Emerson a "champion of cheerfulness," Santayana claims that "he does not hesitate to surrender the field of experience to the weeping philosophers" because of his idealistic armor; whereupon Santayana, interestingly and significantly, quotes this passage from "Love":

> Each man sees his own life defaced and disfigured. . . . Let any man go back to those delicious relations which have given him sincerest instruction and nourishment, he will shrink and moan. Alas! I know not why, infinite compunctions embitter in mature life the remembrances of budding joy, and cover every beloved name. Everything is beautiful seen from the point of view of intellect, or as truth. But all is sour, if seen as experience. . . . In the actual world, the painful kingdom of time and place, dwell care, and canker, and fear. With thought, with the ideal, is immortal hilarity, the rose of joy. Round it all the Muses sing. But grief clings to names, and persons, and the partial interests of today and yesterday.[50]

The passage evidently broached issues that touched the young Santayana nearly; and we shall notice very shortly how he himself, struggling to clarify his own feelings, would turn Emerson's sentences and metaphors to good use as he developed the central figure of *The Last Puritan*.

But one other point is worth mentioning in a consideration of this early piece on Emerson. As he reached his conclusion, Santayana admitted that he still, somehow, found the "mystic turned dilettante" charming, even occasionally "delightful" in his "very indifference." Turning to his final paragraph, Santayana then made a pregnant concession: "To do justice to the personal element in

Emerson's optimism we should have to study his whole life. We should have to inquire whether he ever felt an emotion stronger than delight in the landscape, and decide whether his serenity was the result of discipline or of insensibility." Santayana, of course, did not have at his disposal the materials that would have enabled him to conduct such an investigation. But he did put his finger on *the* crucial issue in modern Emerson studies and presciently suggest the direction they might take. "He is never a philosopher," Santayana noted, "but always Emerson philosophizing."[51]

Beginning perhaps with Henry Nash Smith's essay, "Emerson's Problem of Vocation," in 1939, a highly influential group of scholars and critics, notably sensitive to Emerson's human complexity, would return to his writings with the hope of discovering a living personality beneath the bland (or pompous, or smug) official portrait. An unfamiliar Emerson thus would begin to emerge—one whose painful struggle for self-realization belied that older image of an optimistic aphorist appropriately cherished by captains of industry, genteel professors of literature, and hopeful preachers in search of suitably uplifting remarks. Like other great writers of the American Renaissance—Hawthorne, Melville, Dickinson—Emerson was on the way to being considered a richly evasive and enigmatic figure whose interest would more and more turn on that "personal element" which Santayana had pointed to in his Bowdoin essay.

Santayana's third significant piece of writing on Emerson in his own Harvard period, delivered on May 22, 1903, during the centennial celebrations, is entitled "Emerson the Poet" and marks a dramatic departure in Santayana's continuing effort to clarify his own philosophy by struggling with Emerson's. The tone and posture of this address are markedly different from those of the essays that precede it. For one thing, Santayana had now moved away from clichéd references to Puritan "constraint" and begun to talk about Emerson's ancestral religion in more nearly tragic terms: "The dogmas which Calvinism had chosen for interpretation were the most sombre and disquieting in the Christian system, those which marked most clearly a broken life and a faith rising out of profound despair." What despair, Santayana goes on to ask, could a young American of Emerson's hopeful time have felt to justify sharing such "spectral traditions"? Emerson, indeed, was one of the first fully to throw off the "incubus" of this "ancestral dream" and spring wholeheartedly into "the world of nature."[52]

Associating Emerson with Spinoza, Shakespeare, and Goethe, Santayana argues that this "born master at looking deep and at looking straight" discovered that the generative order of nature is not inclined to respect human feelings and inspire "transcendental conceit."[53] Although Santayana had claimed only a few years earlier that "reality eluded [Emerson],"[54] he now insists on precisely the opposite, namely, that Emerson saw [nature] as she really is and loved her in her indomitable and inhuman perfection":

> Not the least of his joys was the self-effacing one of being able to conceive, and therefore to share, a life which creates, animates, and destroys the human. He was charmed and comforted, quite without technical apparatus, by universal beauty. He yielded himself insensibly and placidly to that plastic stress which in breeding new forms out of his substance would never breed anything alien to those principles of harmony and rhythm which stand like sentinels at the gates of being and challenge the passage into existence of anything contradicting itself or incongruous with its natural conditions. His best lyric flights express this honest and noble acceptance of destiny, this imaginative delight in innumerable beauties which he should never see, but which would be the heirs of those he had loved and lost in their passage.[55]

As a kind of secular analogue to the Puritan faith's "rising out of profound despair," Santayana now posits Emerson's delight in the *forms* and *structures* which underlie human experience and persist despite the destruction of individual expressions of that "plastic stress." Particular lives may be "broken," but the glorious principles of metamorphosis move on unharmed.[56] Caught up by his own excited exegesis of the true Emersonian philosophy, Santayana now announces that he has arrived "at the frontiers of that province in Emerson's kingdom into which it is hardest to pene-trate—the forbidden Thibet, with its Grand Lama, behind his Himalayas," namely, Emerson's religion. It is not at bottom, San-tayana claims, "an account of credible facts producing, when duly reported, saving emotions in the soul. It is rather an expression of the soul's native emotions in symbols mistaken for facts, or in facts chosen for symbols." Emerson's interest, we are being told, has shifted to the *process* by which the soul generates its own symbols of belief. And "all the unction and sanctity of religion" that Emer-son has salvaged from his discarded dogmas he is now free to invest in a new, ultimate religion—the worship, not of particular existent *beings,* but of the multiform energy itself that perpetually builds new *shapes* of being. Santayana's exposition of this notion is filled with a true Emersonian afflatus:

> All ideas, we presently perceive, are fluid; and we are on the point of venturing the assertion that it matters very little what things exist or how long they endure, since the only reality is the perpetual motion that creates, transforms and exchanges them. We have seen how this perpetual motion, observable in nature, fascinated Emer-son; but while the poet could justify and communicate his delight by dwelling on the forms and beauties of things in transition, the metaphysician would fain sink deeper. In his desperate attempt to seize upon the real and permanent he would fain grasp and hold fast the disembodied principle of change itself.[57]

This idea is "loaded with religious passion," Santayana tells us. And he goes on to cite the conclusion to "Threnody," Emerson's lamentation and testament of acceptance in the face of the crushing loss of his young son. Emerson's poems, Santayana concludes, "proclaim the divinity of nature, her kinship with man, and her immortal fecundity in all things which the human spirit might recognize to be beautiful and good if keyed to heroism and rapt in contemplation." Such beauty, Santayana concedes, "involves cruelty" and the optimism preached by Emerson's poetry is a difficult one that "demands abnegation." The ability to sing "nature's fluid harmonies" is not given to all—indeed, only to that man with "a long civilization behind him who has learned to love nature for her own sake."[58] James had claimed, in writing of Hawthorne, "that the flower of art blooms only where the soil is deep, that it takes a great deal of history to produce a little literature, that it needs a complex social machinery to set a writer in motion."[59] The claim that Santayana now seemed prepared to make for Emerson was perhaps more fundamental and obviated the need to apologize for America: only a man with a long experience of reality could truly come to accept that deeper soil out of which spring the forms of both society and art.

The Last Puritan represents Santayana's most serious and sustained engagement with Emerson's ultimate refinement of Puritanism. On the surface, at least, the presence of Emerson is not difficult to detect in the book. Oliver Alden's mentality is more than once described as "transcendental," and he is frequently associated with Emerson (stopping one day to feed his "idealism" on Concord's meagre sights, Oliver finds that "unseen things loomed all the larger and nearer in that visible desolation"; he subsequently takes up residence in Emerson's room in Divinity Hall, and when he moves on to Oxford his lodgings remind him somehow of that room).[60] Verbal echoes of Emerson's writings abound in the book, and may be sufficiently exemplified through a glance at the first chapter of Part V. Oliver's "journey round the world had taught [him] little except how inevitably centered and miserably caged he was in himself" ("Travelling is a fool's paradise" [*W* 2:81]). Meditating on Goethe (Oliver had been taught in school that "Emerson served up Goethe's philosophy in ice-water"), he follows Emerson in pronouncing the great man insufficiently idealistic and asserts, "I won't be the slave of my circumstances" ("You think me the child of my circumstances: I make my circumstance" [*CW* 1:204]). Whereupon, Santayana tells us, Oliver felt "confirmed in his spiritual self-reliance."[61]

Santayana's Emerson: Ultimate Puritanism

But such allusions really constitute the least of Santayana's Emersonianism in *The Last Puritan*. A much more complex and significant instance may be seen in the many pages Santayana devotes to an exposition of "the vision of Jacob's ladder," which is presented to us in the form of a debate between Oliver and his father, Peter. The notion, we are told, is a favorite one of Peter's (meaning of Santayana's), and the father tries to explain:

> "Jacob's ladder, you will say, what do I mean by that? Let me try to tell you. Do you remember Cousin Caleb Weatherbee and his opinion about Goethe? Yes, and you naturally continued to think Goethe a great, wise, and good man, even if a heathen and not a gentleman. Well, Jacob's ladder is the fabulous moral order imposed on the universe by the imagination of Cousin Caleb and Plato and conservative Anglican gentlemen; but the heathen imagination in Goethe and Emerson and you and me, and in your liberal British intellectuals and philosophers, has outgrown that image. Instead, either we impose no moral order on the universe at all—which I think would be safer—or else a moral order such as we expected to find in our own lives when we were young and romantic. I suppose, as a matter of fact, there is an obscure natural order in the universe, controlling morality as it controls health: an order which we don't need to impose, because we are all obeying it willynilly. But this half-deciphered natural order leaves us, morally, in all our natural heathen darkness and liberty: and we are probably little inclined to devote ourselves to ascending and descending the particular Jacob's ladder imagined by Platonists and Catholics and Conservative English Gentlemen." [62]

Santayana is here offering us, in terms of the familiar fable, a continuation and amplification of the central issue which he had isolated in his discussions of Emerson—an issue of crucial importance in his own philosophy: namely, the extent to which a disillusioned thinker, having jettisoned all the traditional (Platonic, Judeo-Christian) "machinery" of transcendence, may reasonably place his reconstituted faith in a moral order which is purely naturalistic.

It is fundamentally a question of adequately defining a spiritual life, and spiritual discipline, which might truly be called humanistic as opposed to the supernaturalistic systems symbolized by the traditional idea of Jacob's ladder. Is Emerson really in the dark, morally, Santayana seems to be asking; or is his passionate belief in the unshakable natural structures of the universe—"the spires of form" (*CW*, 1:7)—a credible substitute for the discarded harmonies of Jacob's ladder?

Oliver responds that he believes in Jacob's ladder even less than his father does, rejecting all hierarchical systems, social as well as metaphysical. Peter continues:

> "Why have we free Americans a certain sneaking tendency to be snobs? Proud, romantic heathens that we are, like Nietzsche, or like Walt Whitman, why do we feel an unavowed inclination to worship the archangel in a light blue cap—or a pink one, if he is elderly—standing at the top of Jacob's ladder? Because, my dear Oliver, our heathenism is still green and bashful. We are imperfectly weaned from feudalism and Christianity. Our pride in freedom is a mere affectation: we put it on in order to stifle our deeper conscience which still believes in Jacob's ladder."[63]

It is as if Santayana were saying that Emerson can afford to be so defiantly antinomian in his naturalism only because in his heart he still half believes in the Christianity he claims to have discarded. Some lingering vestiges of faith still buttress his heathen pride or console him in his moments of self-doubt. Peter, in fact, goes on to argue that the elements of traditional religious discipline (humility, penance, suffering, mortification—and the thrashing practiced at Eton!) may actually function as "rungs in Jacob's ladder" to lead the soul to a higher state, even though the religious system of which they form a part can be considered an illusion.

> All of this seemed to Oliver rather in the air. Why dwell on the consequences of a false hypothesis? Or was the hypothesis possibly true? And he broke in rather impatiently:

Santayana's Emerson: Ultimate Puritanism

"But do you believe in Jacob's ladder yourself?"

"Believe?" Peter answered, as if bewildered. "Dear me, I don't believe in anything nowadays, if I can help it. Didn't I say that Jacob's ladder was a myth? It's a picture of what the universe would be if the moral nature of man had made it. I suppose in the universe at large the moral nature of man is a minor affair, like the moral nature of the ant or the mosquito. But our moral nature is everything *to us;* to us the universe itself is of no consequence apart from the life we are able to live in it. Jacob's ladder is a picture of the degrees which this moral life of our might attain, in so far as we can imagine them. It is a poetic image. Those who mistake it for an account of the universe or of history or of destiny seem to me simply mad; but like all good poetry, such an image marks the pitch to which moral culture has risen at some moment. To the morally cultivated, Jacob's ladder shines distinct and clear: it becomes vague and broken to the morally barbarous."[64]

Peter Alden is speaking now in the accents, not only of Santayana, but of Emerson and Wallace Stevens. All knowledge and experience—and especially the moral side of life—are mediated to us by means of poetic symbols, the fictions which enable us to imagine our lives. And though we may lose Jacob's ladder as literal religious truth, it can still—perhaps *must* still—be retained as a viable part of our imaginative vocabulary. It is what Stevens calls a "transcendent analogue."[65] A life in which transcendence has ceased to be possible, a life without *degrees,* is morally bankrupt. And we shall see more precisely, in the case of Emerson, how his own "vague and broken" mood in "Experience" is figured in the collapse of Jacob's ladder; whereas to the ultimately reconstituted self of "Threnody," the ladder begins again to shine "distinct and clear." As Daniel B. Shea has argued well, and as Santayana intuited, Emerson's career may be viewed in terms of an "alternation between regressive and progressive metamorphosis."[66]

Oliver Alden's own ultimate lesson in the possibility of self-transcendence is emblemized by Santayana in the conflation of two symbols, everywhere to be found in *The Last Puritan,* which seem

clearly to recall the Platonic ladder of love, in Emerson's essay
"Love," with the ideal "rose of joy" perched at its top.[67] Even
before he has been denied by the crimson rose—his cousin Edith
—and the white one—Rose Darnley—Oliver senses that he has a
sterner destiny reserved for himself:

> All these images are shifty and misty and treacherous. What en-
> dures is only this spirit, this perpetual witness, wondering at these
> apparitions, enjoying one, suffering at another, and questioning
> them all. If I keep this spirit free, if I keep it pure, let roses be red
> or white as they will, let there be no end of wars of the roses; let
> me wear the rose of Lancaster or the rose of York; neither will
> taint my soul or dye it of a party colour.[68]

He turns away form the worldly advice he finds in an old volume
of verse ("Stripling, rifle now the rose, / tempt the perils of a kiss"),
and ultimately walks by choice into the heaven that Santayana has
prepared for him, believing that the feeling he had of being in love
was only a mirage created by his own aspirations:

> They may drop out, they may change, they may prove to be the sad
> opposite of what I thought them: but my image of them in being
> detached from their accidental persons, will be clarified in itself,
> will become truer to my profound desire; and the inspiration of a
> profound desire, fixed upon some lovely image, is what is called
> love. And the true lover's tragedy is not being jilted; it is being
> accepted.[69]

Though this may strike modern ears as representing a rather chilly
brand of Platonism, it is unquestionably characteristic of both
Santayana and Emerson in their most exalted moods.

Perhaps, however, one can respond more sympathetically to
the philosophical point that Santayana has embodied in his theme
of "pure" love whereby we come closer to the speculative essence
of this story of the "purification of puritanism." The holocaust
which Oliver suffered, Santayana tells us, was "real enough":

> . . . it was the endless fire of irrational life always devouring itself;
> yet somehow the spirit rose from that flame, and surveyed the
> spectacle with some tears, certainly, but with no little curiosity and
> satisfaction. Oliver hardly got so far as to feel at home in this
> absurd world: I could never convince him that reason and goodness
> are necessarily secondary and accidental. His absolutist conscience
> remained a pretender, asserting in exile its divine right to the
> crown.[70]

We note in this adumbration of his theme in the "Prologue" how
the verbal texture of Santayana's symbols informs his abstract
formulation. Leaving its earthly flowers behind, Oliver's spirit itself
"rose," as it inevitably had to, up the ladder of being from suffering to the vantage point of pure idea. And we may be sure that that
which Santayana claims he could not convince Oliver of continued
to pain him also as the central problem of existence: the thwarting
of every rational ideal in the mixed currents of experience. The
only true satisfaction that remains for the human spirit, according
to Santayana, is the possibility of surveying "the spectacle" from
the level of pure contemplation. This notion is stated more eloquently on the last page of the book, where Mario is allowed to
paraphrase Santayana's very own sentiments from *Platonism and
the Spiritual Life:*

> After life is over and the world has gone up in smoke, what realities
> might the spirit in us still call its own without illusion save the
> form of those very illusions which have made up our story?[71]

Ultimate Puritanism, then, is equivalent to total disillusionment, the ability to see that what persists through every disappointment and death in a world of incessant and inexorable change, the
only reality, is the form or principle which *creates* our illusions.
That divinity, which might be called the *order* of created things,
informs the human imagination no less than it does the natural
world which generates human beings. Such a formulation returns
us directly to Emerson's "religion" and suggests, perhaps, that

Santayana's text for his novelistic sermon might well have been the concluding paragraph of "Illusions" in Emerson's *The Conduct of Life:*

> There is no chance and no anarchy in the universe. All is system and gradation. Every god is there sitting in his sphere. The young mortal enters the hall of the firmament; there is he alone with them alone, they pouring on him benedictions and gifts, and beckoning him up to their thrones. On the instant, and incessantly, fall snowstorms of illusions. He fancies himself in a vast crowd which sways this way and that and whose movement and doings he must obey: he fancies himself poor, orphaned, insignificant. The mad crowd drives hither and thither, now furiously commanding this thing to be done, now that. What is he that he should resist their will, and think or act for himself? Every moment new changes and new showers of deceptions to baffle and distract him. And when, by and by, for an instant, the air clears and the cloud lifts a little, there are the gods still sitting around him on their thrones,—they alone with him alone. (W 6:325)

Four seasons fill the measure of the year;
There are four seasons in the mind of man:
He has his lusty Spring, when fancy clear
Takes in all beauty with an easy span:
He has his Summer, when luxuriously
Spring's honied cud of youthful thought he loves
To ruminate, and by such dreaming nigh
His nearest unto heaven: quiet coves
His soul has in its Autumn, when his wings
He furleth close; contented so to look
On mists in idleness—to let fair things
Pass by unheeded as a threshold brook.
He has his Winter too of pale misfeature,
Or else he would forego his mortal nature.

KEATS,
"The Human Seasons"

II

RITES OF SPRING

1803–1836

Born in Boston on Election Day, May 25, 1803, Ralph Waldo Emerson was the fourth child of William and Ruth Haskins Emerson. His mother was the daughter of a successful distiller; his father was a liberally inclined minister, pastor of Boston's oldest church (the First). Ralph's paternal grandfather, also named William, built the Old Manse at Concord and was himself a minister and graduate of Harvard College (1761); known for his ardent patriotism, he died, aged thirty-three, at Ticonderoga, where he had gone to serve as chaplain to the army. The Emerson line could claim descent in America from the Reverend Peter Bulkeley, who left Bedfordshire, England, in 1634 and settled in Musketaquid (the original name of Concord). Ralph, who lost his father when he was eight, seemed destined to continue the ministerial line, and passed in due course through Boston Latin School, Harvard College (1821), and a year of divinity studies at Harvard (which were interrupted by eye trouble). Approbated to preach in the fall of 1826, he became pastor of Boston's Second Church two and a half years later, but left that post in the fall of 1832 because he could no longer serve the Lord's Supper (communion) in good conscience. This disturbance in Emerson's professional life was preceded by personal tragedy—the death from consumption, in February 1831, of his nineteen-year-old bride Ellen (Tucker). Critically in need of recuperation (he, too, had a "mouse" in his chest), Emerson sailed for Europe on December 25, 1832. He landed in Malta in early February and enthusiastically worked his way north through Italy, Switzerland, France, England, and Scotland. Eager to meet great men, he sought out Walter Savage Landor in Florence, saw Lafayette in Paris, and visited John Stuart Mill in London, Coleridge in Highgate, and Wordsworth at Rydal Mount. But the one lasting friendship he established was with Thomas Carlyle. Returning to America in the fall of 1833, Emerson immediately initiated his new career as a lecturer with a series on science. He also continued to preach sporadically while he wrote more lectures and planned his first book, Nature *(published in September 1836). Emerson settled in Concord in the fall of 1834, married Lydia (whom he renamed Lidian) Jackson the following year, and became a householder. Their first son, Waldo, was born shortly after* Nature *made its appearance. Emerson had a new vocation, a family, and the expectation of about $1200 in annual income from the settlement of his first wife's estate.*

EASTERING

[I]

It has always seemed worthy of note to students of Emerson that he left Boston harbor, bound for his first European journey, on Christmas day in 1832. By merest chance—but it is the sort of thing Emerson himself would have appreciated for its symbolic value, he anticipated the narrator of Melville's *Moby-Dick,* who, finding himself "growing grim about the mouth" in a "damp drizzly November in his [soul]," shipped aboard the *Pequod* on another Christmas day in expectation of finding "meads and glades so eternally vernal, that the grass shot up by the spring, untrodden, unwilted, remains at midsummer." [1]

Emerson undoubtedly would have associated himself both with Ishmael's low spirits and with his high hopes. He had lost his young wife Ellen to tuberculosis in February 1831, and on the first of April felt that his "spring [was] wearing into summer & life . . . into death" (*JMN* 3:238). By the summer of 1832 he had determined to leave the ministry and—another coincidence—on July 15, precisely six years to the day before the delivery of his momentous Divinity School Address, he announced himself at "the hour of decision" and the crisis of his fate (*JMN* 4:29–30). With an appropriate Lutheran flourish (in his journal, at least), [2] Emerson resigned his pastorate on October 28 and entered the drizzly November of his thirtieth year. That year, as Emerson's friend and biographer Cabot observes, "proved fatal to [his brother] Edward" and was not quite attained by the beloved youngest brother, Charles; it "was the critical period for him too." [3] On the 24th of the month, Ellen's sister Margaret died, and Emerson lamented with "sinking spirit" over her "cold November grave" (*JMN* 4:62). Disheartened, disoccupied, and sick—himself threatened with the ubiquitous consumption that carried off so many of his friends and relations—Emerson proposed at first "to make a modest trip to the West Indies" to be with Edward. But on December 10 he wrote his brother William that "in a few hours the dream changed into a purpureal vision of Naples & Italy" (*L* 1:359). The Italienische-Reise that loomed before Emerson seemed to promise not the "hooded phantom, like a snow hill in the air," of Ishmael's wildest conceits, but rather the rebirth and perpetual spring that Melville's narrator dreamed of on December 25.

In view of Emerson's celebrated dictum that "travelling is a fool's paradise," whereby we carry "ruins to ruins" (*W* 2:81), the reader may well wonder at his manifest excitement as he contemplated his first trip to the Old World. To be sure, we are here dealing with the same Emerson who prided himself on contradiction and who, to cite only one example, though obsessively bookish and a scholar to the tips of his toes, could blandly insist that "books are for the scholar's idle times" (*CW* 1:57). Perhaps it is worth noting that the sentence quoted above about traveling represents Emerson's own version of a familiar Horatian utterance (*"caelum non animum mutant qui trans mare currunt")* [4] and that, in his more Olympian moods, Emerson frequently liked to affect the Augustan virtues of detachment and self-sufficiency.

But the truth is that he was as exercised by the great question of the relative virtues of America and Europe as were Cooper, Hawthorne, and James, to cite only the most obvious names. He, too, could worry about the lack in America of a rich history and social structure, and complain that the atmosphere was not conducive to heroism or daring exploits. Yet at the same time, he felt unbounded pride in his nation's spiritual and imaginative potentialities. Thus, in May 1843, he would write: "Our American lives are somewhat poor & pallid, Franklins & Washingtons, no fiery grain. Staid men like our pale & timid Flora. . . . The young men complain that here in America is no past, no traditions; only shopkeeping, no ghost, no god in the landscape, no stimulus." The complaint, however, immediately provokes the expected Emersonian response: "But why go to Europe? Best swallow this pill of America which Fate brings you & sing a land unsung. Here stars, here birds, here trees, here hills abound and the vast tendencies concur of a new Order" (*JMN* 8:398).

Admittedly, the response sounds a bit mechanical, falling back at the end, as it seems to, on another Augustan commonplace (from Virgil's "Messianic" *Eclogue: "Magnus ab integro saeclorum nascitur ordo"*) or at least on its redaction, as found in the Great Seal of the United States *("Novus ordo saeclorum").*[5] America here seems little better than a dose of tough medicine; whereas Europe, characteristically for Emerson in times of crisis or torpor, could hold out the promise of a needed "stimulus." By the fall of 1847, when he was preparing to set off on his second trip to England and France, Emerson reached an insight about the obligatory Grand Tour that seems to anticipate the point of view of a Henry James: "We go to Europe to . . . be Americanized, to import what we can. This country has its proper glory, though now shrouded & unknown" (*JMN* 10:161). Like James' Christopher Newman, whose name is a sufficient indication of his role as the archetypal American, Emerson was to find that the most valuable thing he could import from Europe would be a renewed sense of himself as at least potentially the Adam of the West. Christopher's French interlocutress, in the first chapter of *The American,* wittily observes that his "patron-saint" was the great man who "invented America." Both James' hero and Emerson could be said to have returned to the Old World for the purpose of finding out what their forebear had had in mind.

Predictably, in fact, Emerson had that very forebear in his own mind as he commenced his maiden voyage across the Atlantic, and his comment suggests that he was very close to seeing in that first

American the earliest representation of that self-reliance which would become his major personal criterion:

> I do not find much attraction in the seaman yet I can discern that the naval hero is a hero. It takes all the thousand thousand European voyages that have been made to stablish our faith in the practicability of this our hodiurnal voyage. But to be Columbus, to steer WEST steadily day after day, week after week, for the first time, and wholly alone in his opinion, shows a mind as solitary & self-subsistent as any that ever lived. (*JMN* 4:107)

Emerson's Columbus seems to have mainly *himself* in mind—his resolute sense of purpose and fierce determination to vindicate that purpose. Though his intention is to realize a visionary East, he has paradoxically convinced himself, as Thoreau would say, that "the farthest west is but the farthest east."[6] Such was the extent of Columbus' faith. And Emerson himself seems almost on the brink of affirming that his own Eastern adventure was undertaken for the purpose of rediscovering his "proper glory" as a Western man and thereby reestablishing his tarnished faith in himself.

Fortunately, however, idle speculation about Emerson's sense of the intent and probable result of his journey east is rendered superfluous by a long entry which he inscribed beginning on the third page of his newly purchased pocket notebook. This fine paragraph seems to amount to a species of hymn to the new year as well as to the emerging self:

> 3 Jan. I rose at sunrise & under the lee of the spencer sheet had a solitary thoughtful hour. All right thought is devout. "The clouds were touched & in their silent faces might be read unutterable love." They shone with light that shines on Europe, Afric, & the Nile, & I opened my spirit's ear to their most ancient hymn. What, they said to me, goest thou so far to seek—painted canvass, carved marble, renowned towns? But fresh from us, new evermore, is the creative efflux from whence these works spring. You now feel in gazing at our fleecy arch of light the motions that express them-

selves in Arts. You get no nearer to the principle in Europe. It animates man. It is the America of America. It spans the ocean like a handbreadth. It smiles at Time & Space. Yet welcome young man! the Universe is hospitable. The great God who is Love hath made you aware of the forms & breeding of his wide house. We greet you well to the place of History as you please to style it; to the mighty Lilliput or ant hill of your genealogy, if, instructed as you have been, you must still be the dupe of shows, & count it much, the three or four bubbles of foam that preceded your own on the Sea of Time. This strong-winged sea gull & striped sheer-water that you have watched as they skimmed the waves under our vault—they are works of art better worth your enthusiasm, mas-terpieces of Eternal power strictly eternal because now active & ye need not go so far to seek what ye would not seek at all if it were not within you. Yet welcome & hail! So sang in my ear the silver grey mists & the winds & the sea said Amen. (*JMN* 4:104)

Perhaps we may see here some sort of fertile resolution of Emerson's ambivalent attitude toward the value of travel. Though the principle that he is going so far to seek is within, and therefore presumably need not be sought at all, Emerson's impulse to search it out by means of this reanimating sea voyage to the east gives him the truest evidence he has had of its existence. The voyage is thus, at the same time, both unnecessary and vitally necessary! The light that inspires Emerson's "ancient hymn" is light from the east ("light that shines on Europe, Afric, & the Nile"), and it expresses precisely that principle of "creative efflux" which Emerson so badly needs to find, or find again. Of course, he will "get no nearer to the principle in Europe." But he was even farther away from it before he left home. The "spring" he is in search of is the *true* idea of America—"the America of America." Paradoxically, Emerson can realize *that*—the fulfillment of his Western destiny—only be resolutely facing east.

He finds himself welcomed simultaneously to this new universe of energy and beauty *and* to Europe—the "place of History." Are they linked or not? Emerson seems driven to apologize for and justify his voyage even while he is filled with pleasure at the emerging prospect. He has clearly received a blessing from the mists, echoed by the "Amen" of the winds and sea. The omens are auspicious. Though Emerson may be embarked on searching for a fool's paradise, he seems also to feel that if he persists in his folly he may become wise. Years later, in his chapter on "Plato," he would come to understand that "our strength is transitional, alternating," and that therefore "the experience of poetic creativeness . . . is not found in staying home, nor yet in traveling, but in transitions from one to the other, which must therefore be adroitly managed to present as much transitional surface as possible" (*W* 4:55–56). It is that "transitional surface" which Emerson—like the "strong-winged sea gull" he sees skimming the waves—is here moving over and celebrating. The value of Emerson's European trip would lie in managing to repeat the experience as often as possible, so that he might have convincing assurance that his ability to change was alive and active.

On January 14, a week before he was to see the Rock of Gibraltar and already impatient for that vision, Emerson made another journal entry that suggests how great was the cultural baggage—both assumptions and expectations—which he was carrying along with his purely personal objectives:

> Peeps up old Europe yet out of his eastern main? hospitably ho! Nay the slumberous old giant cannot bestir himself in these his chair days to loom up for the pastime of his upstart grandchildren as now they come shoal after shoal to salute their old Progenitor, the old Adam of all. Sleep on, old Sire, there is muscle & nerve & enterprise now in us your poor spawn who have sucked the air & ripened in the sunshine of the cold West to steer our ships to your very ports & thrust our inquisitive American eyes into your towns & towers & keeping-rooms. Here we come & mean to be welcome. So be good now, clever old gentleman. (*JMN* 4:109)

Anticipating the conclusion he would reach in *English Traits,* "that England, an old and exhausted island, must one day be contented, like other parents, to be strong only in her children" (W 5:275–76), Emerson here humorously sees himself as a representative of the "poor spawn" who have unexpectedly gathered strength and courage in the bracing Western air, and are returning to strut defiantly in the face of "their old Progenitor." The American, that is, is returning not only to *see* Europe but to possess and assert his manhood. Emerson's clear determination to assume this role and to be accepted on these terms is further amplified by another entry made some two months later as he entered Naples: "And what if it is Naples ... I won't be imposed upon by a name ... Baiae & Misenum & Vesuvius, Procida & Pausilippo & Villa Reale sound so big that we are ready to surrender at discretion & not stickle for our private opinion against what seems the human race. Who cares? Here's for the plain old Adam, the simple genuine Self against the whole world" (*JMN* 4:141). Emerson presumes to speak for "the plain old Adam" of America who refuses to be imposed on by European culture—"the old Adam of all"—even though it represents the combined experience of the whole human race and the weight of history. If that experience and that weight do not tend to help Emerson verify his own being, they will not interest him very much. Traveling through Catania, Emerson notices a famous monument and writes: "Passed the trophy of Marcellus, a pile of broken masonry and yet it answers its purpose as well as Marcellus could have hoped. Did he think that Mr Emerson would be reminded of his existence & victory this fine spring day 2047 years to come?" (*JMN* 4:128–29).

For all of Emerson's admittedly comic bravado (and surely the comedy is a measure of how rapidly Emerson's spirits were rising), it was impossible for him not to feel imposed upon by Rome. Faced with the seemingly infinite riches of art and history that he found there, Emerson's straitened New England consciousness expanded in that cultural sun like corn and melons:

> I went to the Capitoline hill then to its Museum & saw the Dying Gladiator, The Antinous, the Venus.—to the Gallery. then to the Tarpeian Rock. then to the vast & splendid museum of the Vati-

can. A wilderness of marble. After traversing many a shining chamber & gallery I came to the Apollo & soon after to the Laocoon. . . . Here too was the Torso Hercules, as familiar to the eyes as some old revolutionary cripple. On we went from chamber to chamber through galleries of statues & vases & sarcophagi & bas reliefs & busts & candelabra—through all forms of beauty & richest materials—till the eye was dazzled & glutted with this triumph of the arts. Go & see it, whoever you are. It is the wealth of the civilized world. It is a contribution from all ages & nations of what is most rich & rare. He who has not seen it does not know what beautiful stones there are in the planet. . . . (*JMN* 4:150)

Though Emerson may have felt obliged to write his brother William, "I hate travelling. Happy they that sit still! How glad I shall be to get home again," he could tell another correspondent on the same day that "though travelling is a poor profession—bad food, it may be good medicine. It is good, like seasickness, to break up a morbid habit, & I sometimes fancy it is a very wholesome shaking for me" (*L* 1:370–71). Shaken indeed he was, especially by the Vatican Museum and its wilderness of statues. Rome "is a grand town," he wrote his brother Charles, "& works mightily upon the senses & upon the soul. It fashions my dreams even, & all night I visit Vaticans. I am in better health than ever since I was a boy." Sounding more like the young Henry James than Waldo Emerson, he exploded: "Ah great great Rome! it is a majestic city, & satisfies this craving imagination" (*L* 1:373–74).[7] Over twenty years later, he would write a friend who was traveling abroad, using language that suggests how paradisaic the visit to Rome had been for him: "How gladly go to Paris & to Rome[.] I seem to have been driven away from Rome by unseen Angel with sword or whip for nothing would have served me so well & dearly as Rome & I have never been able to recall any reason I had for returning." Whereupon he warned his friend, "be sure, you do not make the mistake of coming back too quickly. No man goes but once to Europe, or but once with the right appetite" (*L* 4:461–62).

Perhaps the high point of Emerson's stay in Rome was the

opportunity he had to observe Pope Gregory XVI celebrate the festivities of Easter Week. This surely represents a pivotal cultural confrontation: America's ultimate Protestant exposing himself to the forms and pageants of Europe's ancient Roman Catholic Church. Here, if anywhere in Europe, was *the* experience designed to raise the New English hackles of this freshly (but barely) unchurched Unitarian minister. One is reminded of the sometime traveling companion whom James' Christopher Newman meets abroad, the Reverend Benjamin Babcock, "a young Unitarian minister . . . with a strikingly candid physiognomy" from Dorchester, Massachusetts, whose weak digestion ("he lived chiefly on Graham bread and hominy") forces him to eschew all of the Old World's culinary delights. Though Mr. Babcock, like Emerson, is a great reader of Goethe and "extremely devoted to 'culture,' " James informs us that "nevertheless in his secret soul he detested Europe," finding it, if not "utterly bad," at best "very bad indeed." Though we are not given the chance to follow Benjamin Babcock around Rome, it is possible to recognize his spirit in some of Emerson's reactions— as, for example, this one of Thursday, April 4, 1833: "Gregory XVI is a learned & able man; he was a monk & is reputed of pure life. Why should he not leave one moment this formal service of fifty generations & speak out of his own heart?" (*JMN* 4:155). One could scarcely ask for a better expression of the Reformation speaking in a nineteenth-century American accent, proud of having jettisoned fifty generations of history in the name of simplicity and truth.[8]

But Emerson, of course, is no Reverend Babcock; he is much closer, as I have suggested, to Christopher Newman (who, though both exhilarated and awed by Babcock's "tender conscience," suspects that it has led his friend into a sad muddle). Like Newman, Emerson had gone to Europe expressly to change his life, to open himself to new experience. One measure of his ability to do so is his impressive reaction to Easter Sunday at St. Peter's. Though Emerson felt that there was "not much to be said for the service," other aspects of the day's events were clearly not lost on him:

It is Easter & the curtains are withdrawn from the pictures & statues to my great joy & the Pope wears his triple crown instead of a mitre.

At twelve o'clock the benediction was given. A canopy was hung over the great window that is above the principal door of St Peter's & there sat the Pope. The troops were all under arms & in uniform in the piazza below, & all Rome & much of England & Germany & France & America was gathered there also. The great bell of the Church tolled, drums beat, & trumpets sounded over the vast congregation.

Presently, at a signal, there was silence and a book was brought to the Pope, out of which he read a moment & then rose & spread out his hands & blessed the people. All knelt as one man. He repeated his action (for no words could be heard,) stretching his arms gracefully to the north & south & east & west—pronouncing a benediction on the whole world. It was a sublime spectacle. Then sounded drums & trumpets, then rose the people, & every one went his way. (*JMN* 4:156–57)

Emerson seems more than willing to feel himself part of this great universal congregation, kneeling "as one man" (did Emerson actually do so himself, or only in spirit?) to receive a benediction from which none are excluded—including, obviously, our American pilgrim himself, whose Protestant dislike of pomp and tradition has, at least for the moment, been vanquished by his craving imagination. It is amusing to note that, twenty-five years later, Nathaniel Hawthorne would take his son Julian to see the same spectacle but with a very different result: "I ought to have waited to witness the papal benediction from the balcony in front of the church; or, at least, to hear the famous silver trumpets, sounding from the dome; but Julian grew weary (to say the truth, so did I), and we went on a long walk, out of the nearest city gate." Going homeward over the Ponte Rotto, Hawthorne stopped to observe "the arch of the Cloaca Maxima, close by the Temple of Vesta, with the water rising within two or three feet of its keystone."[9] That certainly could not have been a sublime spectacle, though

62

given Hawthorne's professed interest in secret sin, one can understand his fascination with the outlet of Rome's great sewer.

Emerson, however, had come to Rome at a different time of life with very different needs, and Easter at St. Peter's was not an experience he could be expected to miss or forget. Shortly after the event, he wrote in his journal: "I love St Peter's Church. It grieves me that after a few days I shall see it no more. It has a peculiar smell from the quantity of incense burned in it. The music that is heard in it is always good & the eye is always charmed. It is an ornament of the earth" (*JMN* 4:157). Oddly enough—or perhaps it is an indication that the Roman experience was turning Emerson into a kind of Proustian aesthete [10]—it was the *odor* of St. Peter's that stayed with him most. Some ten years later, writing Margaret Fuller from Baltimore, he described his visit to the Cathedral: "I went to the Cathedral to hear mass with much content. . . . The chanting priest, the pictured walls, the lighted altar, the surpliced boys, the swinging censer every whiff of which I inhaled, brought all Rome again to mind. And Rome can smell so far! It is a dear old church, the Roman I mean, & today I detest the Unitarians and Martin Luther and all the parliament of Barebones" (*L* 3:116). Of course, Emerson is not repudiating his long Protestant heritage but rather just taking a brief holiday, as it were, from the responsibilities of being the most distinguished descendant of all the "Barebones." For our present purpose, however, his remarks here suggest how durable was the experience of that Easter Week at St. Peter's.

After receiving Pope Gregory's Easter benediction, Emerson might well have felt that the rest of his Italian journey, from the spiritual point of view at least, was bound to be somewhat of an anticlimax. But he had, in fact, another festival to celebrate. Traveling on to Florence, he continued in high spirits, comparing the Duomo to "an archangel's tent," marveling at the Venus de Medici, and pronouncing himself (echoing Byron) "dazzled & drunk with beauty" from the splendors of the Pitti Palace (*JMN* 4:168). On the human side, he was particularly pleased to make the acquaintance of the English author Walter Savage Landor, whom he would remember, along with Carlyle, as one of the few great men he encountered on his trip. But the student of Emerson's development, paying special attention to his personal reactions in this critical thirtieth year of his life, will be interested to note—as Emerson manifestly was—how he celebrated his thirtieth birthday. The following journal entry is dated May 25, 1833:

> It is the Festa of San Zenobio once bishop of Florence. And at the churches, the priests bless the roses & other flowers which the people bring them, & they are then esteemed good for the cure of head ache & are laid by for that purpose. Last night in the Duomo I saw a priest carrying a silver bust of San Zenobio which he put upon the head of each person in turn who came up to the barrier. This ceremony also protects him from the head ache for a year. But, asked I of my landlady, do you believe that the bust or the roses do really cure the head ache of any person? "Secondo alla fede di ciascuno," she replied. It is my Festa also. (*JMN* 4:178)

Once again, Emerson has received a blessing, willy-nilly. And despite his healthy Protestant skepticism about the superstitious value of the rite he had seen performed on his own birthday, it seems clear that he was also touched somehow by the whole business. The lesson he has learned from his landlady—"it depends on one's faith"—would point forward to a central Emersonian tenet, as, for example, in the essay "Experience": "it is not what we believe concerning the immortality of the soul or the like, but *the universal impulse to believe,* that is the material circumstance and is the principal fact in the history of the globe" (*W* 3:74). Ten years after the event, Emerson would copy that crucial Italian sentence into his journal again, followed by a line from Proclus which is clearly related to the story about San Zenobio's headache cure: "And whatever soul has perceived anything of truth, shall be safe from harm until another period" (*JMN* 8:350). Now, however, the pith of the anecdote has expanded into a much more serious notion about the great virtue of this "truth" *(the universal impulse to believe);* and, indeed, Emerson uses a version of the sentence from Proclus to conclude the penultimate paragraph of "Experience" ("I hear always the law of Adrastia, 'that every soul which had acquired any truth, should be safe from harm until another period' " [W 3:84]).[11] So, in a manner of speaking, Emerson had made San Zenobio his patron saint, and he could henceforth hope to celebrate May 25, not simply as a birthday, but as part of his liturgical calendar, marking an article of private faith. It is perhaps a measure of the wry disillusionment which frequently marks the wit of his later years that Emerson in 1850 could appear to switch his faith from San Zenobio to the acerbic medical wisdom of his brother-in-law when he noted in his journal: "Dr. Jackson's remedy for the headache is amputation" (*JMN* 11:288).

[11]

If it is reasonable to speculate about the fundamental meaning (or result) of Emerson's eastern journey as he himself perceived it, I find myself, following Emerson's lead, inevitably drawn to the notion of his having discovered a *process* of self-recovery—a way of reanimating and re*orienting* the self—which he hoped he might make perpetual. The principle is finely articulated, I believe, in this journal entry for May 13, 1835: "What a benefit if a rule could be given whereby the mind could at any moment *east* itself, & find the sun. . . . Perpetually must we East ourselves" (*JMN* 5:38). Merton M. Sealts, Jr., provides an illuminating footnote on this passage in which he directs our attention to a sentence in Coleridge's *The Friend* that undoubtedly helped Emerson to this formulation. Coleridge speaks of "that preparatory process, which the French language so happily expresses by *s'orienter,* i.e. to find out the east for one's self." Although Emerson's pilgrimage to Highgate in August 1833 to seek out Coleridge had been a disappointment ("he was old and preoccupied, and could not bend to a new companion and think with him" [W 5:14]), Coleridge's writings assumed great importance in the years immediately following his return from Europe.[12] Emerson's notion about *easting* himself was, it seems, linked for him with the crucial Coleridgean distinction between *fancy* and *imagination:* "The Fancy aggregates; the Imagination animates. The Fancy takes the world as it stands & selects pleasing groups by apparent relations. The Imagination is Vision." Emerson made that journal entry in the evening of August 1, 1835; and it clearly constitutes the continuation, or conclusion, to an entry begun earlier in the day in which Emerson expressed his enthusiasm over Jacob Böhme's *Aurora:* "Jacob Behme is the best helper to a theory of Isaiah & Jeremiah. You were sure he was in earnest & could you get into his point of view the world would be what he describes. He is all imagination." As an indication, presumably, of *where* that point of view lies, Emerson then copied into his journal part of the title page of Böhme's book: "Aurora i e the Dayspring or dawning of the day in the Orient or Morning Redness in the rising of the sun i e the root or mother of Philosophy, Astrology, & Theology" (*JMN* 5:75–76).[13]

This first book of the mystical shoemaker seems to have embodied and symbolized for Emerson that understanding of the process of *easting* the self which was at least partially the fruit of his own eastern journey. He had learned to trust his imagination —to believe in its power to animate and transform experience. His new *orientation* lay in the direction of incessant imaginative rebirth. His "Prospects"—to use the title of the last section of *Nature*— were to be seen, as he says there, in "a continual self-recovery" and a divine awareness which he calls "morning knowledge, *matutina cognitio.*" Such an awareness, Emerson would argue, might help us to realize the sacramental quality of ordinary facts and experiences—"to see the miraculous in the common" (*CW* 1:39– 44). Life would then be a perpetual blessing or benediction. For Emerson, one might say, *easting* and *eastering* were therefore equivalent. And he would probably have felt some sort of kinship with the Jesuit priest who could write at the conclusion of his

Eastering

"Wreck of The Deutschland": "Let him easter in us, be a dayspring to the dimness of us, be a crimson-cresseted east."

But the British author whose name is most closely linked with Emerson's pilgrimage to Europe is, of course, not Hopkins but Carlyle. Of all the thinkers and writers whom Emerson sought out, Carlyle alone seemed truly to understand what Emerson was after and what his function would be. "These voices of yours," Carlyle would write Emerson in 1841, "are light-rays darting upwards in the East. . . . You are a new era, my man, in your new huge country."[14] And in 1843: "My friend Emerson, alone of all voices out of America . . . is a prophecy and sure dayspring in the East."[15] Lest we take the metaphor that Carlyle applied to Emerson as a mere commonplace, or accident, it is worth noting that it has a history in the Emerson-Carlyle relationship. In 1839, the Carlyles sent the Emersons a "memorial" of the bond between the two families "to be hung up in the Concord drawing room. The two Households, divided by wide seas," Carlyle explained, "are to understand always that they are united nevertheless." The gift was a print of Guido Reni's *Aurora,* which Carlyle described in an inscription as an "Italian sun-chariot."[16] Emerson was immensely pleased with the "noble Italian print" and wrote Carlyle: "It is a right morning thought, full of health and flowing genius, and I rejoice in it."[17] In his journal for June 9, Emerson noted: "Guido's Aurora for a morning prayer, so wills & so loves us Thomas Carlyle" (*JMN* 7:209). And later on, in November, he entered a fuller appreciation:

> In Guido's Aurora I enjoy the distinct expression of morning health & earnestness. It breathes the dawn. What profound health these Hours have, & how firmly they tread the clouds. With the most masculine force in every part of the picture, there is no convulsion, no straining, no foam, no ado, but the most flowing grace & ease. What fine propriety in all the details, in the arrangement of the horses, in the disposition of the group, in the variation of the attitude & drapery of the two figures in the foreground. Then the

horse is nothing but a morning cloud. The little sea landscape in the corner is matutinal also. (*JMN* 7:314–15)

That may be the most extended criticism Emerson ever wrote of a single work of art, which is perhaps an indication of how significant and apposite he found Carlyle's gift. It was a perfect symbol of the needs and aspirations that had sent Emerson to Europe, and he would continue to associate it with the first flowering of youthful genius. Thus, he writes in another journal entry from 1839: "Last night came to me a beautiful poem from Henry Thoreau, 'Sympathy.' The purest strain & the loftiest, I think, that has yet pealed from this unpoetic American forest. I hear his verses with as much triumph as I point to my Guido when they praise half poets & half painters" (*JMN* 7:230–31). (Thoreau would humorously, and dubiously, return the compliment in his first book, where he describes Emerson as "That Phaeton of our day, / Who'd make another milky way, / And burn the world up with his ray.")[18] And one senses the presence of Carlyle's gift, with all its complex weight of meaning for Emerson, in his description, in "The Poet," of the arrival of a new bard:

> . . . the experience of each new age requires a new confession, and the world seems always waiting for its poet. I remember when I was young how much I was moved one morning by tidings that genius had appeared in a youth who sat near me at table. He had left his work and gone rambling none knew whither, and had written hundreds of lines, but could not tell whether that which was in him was therein told; he could tell nothing but that all was changed,—man, beast, heaven, earth and sea. How gladly we listened! how credulous! Society seemed to be compromised. We sat in the aurora of a sunrise which was to put out all the stars. (*W* 3:10)

Interestingly, in the same essay, Emerson distinguishes between the poet and the mystic by complaining that the latter mistakes "an accidental and individual symbol for an universal one," and he cites Böhme's *Aurora* as an example: "The morning-redness happens to be the favorite meteor to the eyes of Jacob Behmen, and comes to stand to him for truth and faith; and, he believes, should stand for the same realities to every reader" (W 3:34). Emersonially enough, the self-reliant sage chafes at receiving his symbols second-hand and insists that others will serve as well. Yet—contradiction, of course, is eminently Emersonian—Aurora continued to serve Emerson himself, even if only by chance. Forty years after his first European journey, Emerson would find himself traveling up the Nile in a dahabeah appropriately named *Aurora*. This was to be his ultimate journey east, and his goal was Philae and the temple of Osiris. If it is true that *easting* for Emerson fundamentally implied the attainment of a degree of self-realization that could be said to approximate experience of the divine, fate had somehow conspired to confirm Emerson's faith. In a manner of speaking, he became Osirified. "In the region of Assuan," Ralph Rusk tells us, Emerson came upon an Englishman named George Owen who "confessed that Emerson 'had been his idol and his guide from his earliest youth,' " and "heaped incense on his idol's shrine." Rusk concludes: "The river was now alive with travelers, and Emerson was inevitably cast in the role of a venerated idol."[19] Appropriately, the initial journey to the east—to the source of the "light that shines on Europe, Afric, & the Nile"—had finally culminated, albeit comically, in the long-desired apotheosis.

A LIVING LEAPING LOGOS

Emerson's budding sense of personal power was in the process of being buttressed by events at home just at the time when he was making his way to Rome. To the blessings of Pope Gregory and San Zenobio would be added two seemingly disparate advantages: a new idealistic epistemology and a financial windfall. Though such a conjunction may seem odd in the career of America's greatest Transcendentalist, it may serve to draw into sharp focus the dual nature of Emerson's genius (and perhaps to provide one illustration of the paradoxical mixture of idealism and materialism that Santayana would find characteristic of the American spirit). Admirers of Emerson were probably both puzzled and shocked in 1848 by this description of the master's character in James Russell Lowell's *Fable for Critics,* but it contains a large measure of truth:

> A Greek head on right Yankee shoulders,
>   whose range
> Has Olympus for one pole, for t'other
>   the Exchange.[20]

Emerson himself, as early as 1827, had noted in his journal among the *"Peculiarities of the present Age"* not only Transcendentalism ("Metaphysics & ethics look inwards") but also the prevalence of "paper currency" and "Joint stock companies" (*JMN* 3:70). It may indeed seem peculiar, but it is difficult to separate these two items entirely in any comprehensive consideration of Emerson's first fruits.

In March 1833, a young Unitarian minister named Frederic Henry Hedge published in *The Christian Examiner* ("the organ," as Perry Miller describes it, "of literate Unitarianism") [21] an article on "Coleridge's Literary Character" that would prove seminal for Emerson, as would Hedge himself. [22] Besides drawing the reader's attention to the important edition of Coleridge's *Aids to Reflection* that had been brought out by James Marsh in 1829, Hedge praised, and outlined, the "transcendental method" in philosophy — particularly in epistemology — which had been developed by Kant and his followers. The central emphasis was on "the interior consciousness" and its active power in the production of knowledge. The articulation of that principle was enough, Hedge argued, "to make us rejoice that such men have been, and that they have lived and spoken in our day." And he went on to specify "the sharp and rightly dividing lines that have been drawn within and around the kingdom of human knowledge; the strongly marked distinctions of subject and object, reason and understanding, phenomena and noumena; — the categories established by Kant; the moral liberty proclaimed by him as it had never been proclaimed by any before; the authority and evidence of law and duty set forth by Fichte; the universal harmony illustrated by Schelling." Here, especially in the crucial distinction between Reason (intuition; Coleridge's "Imagination") and Understanding (ratiocination; Coleridge's "Fancy"), were the "new views" that presumably would free Emerson from the empirical (Lockean) tradition upon which the Unitarianism of his teachers at Harvard had been built. Emerson would learn to despise tradition and, instead, "look inwards." [23]

All of this is well known to Emerson scholars, as are the two letters to his brother Edward in which Emerson, on his return from Europe, waxed enthusiastic over the new thought. What, however, has never received much attention is the curious connection one finds in both these letters between Emerson's burgeoning Transcendentalism and his financial expectations. In the first letter, written in late December 1833, about two and a half months after he docked at New York, Emerson praised Hedge as "an unfolding man" and cited his article as "a living leaping Logos" that might prove helpful. But before getting to Hedge, Emerson undertook to cheer Edward up by announcing that the family's financial prospects were likely to improve very soon: "One of these days if we may believe the lawyers I am to be the richer for Ellen's estate & whenever that day arrives I hope it will enable me to buy a hearth somewhere to which we pious Aeneases may return with our household gods from all the quarters of our dispersion" (*L* 1:401–2). Which is to say that fresh from his wanderings, and especially from Aeneas's Rome, Emerson was dreaming of imitating Virgil's hero and reaching a Lavinium of his own.

Emerson biographers and critics have been notably skittish about dealing with the circumstances and implications of Emerson's first marriage to Ellen Tucker, particularly on its financial side, as if the mere act of mentioning Ellen's prospective wealth were tantamount to suggesting that Emerson married her for her money.[24] Such a suggestion would indeed be unwarranted and crude. The sincerity of Emerson's love for Ellen, and his motives for marrying her when he did (at a time, that is, when she was already seriously ill from the tuberculosis that would carry her off, aged nineteen, after scarcely one and one-half years of marriage), are not legitimately open to question. The fact is, simply put, that Emerson had married an heiress. And what he had innocently written in 1827 while entertaining fantasies of his own death— "for one word that is spoken of your character ten twenty will be spoken of the settlement of your estate" (*JMN* 3:97)—would unfortunately turn out to be prophetic of Ellen's fate.[25] There was to be much legal maneuvering over her estate, and Emerson would expend a good deal of time and ink in behalf of his own interests.

Ellen died in February 1831, and it is difficult to know what to make of Emerson's state of mind, and emotions, in the period immediately subsequent to her death. Though his grief over the loss was clearly very real, he knew at the same time that her death was likely to prove a very great benefit to him. At some level of awareness, Emerson must have therefore been in considerable conflict over his reactions to the event. It would not be unreasonable to suggest that the breakdown in health and spirits that led Emerson to embark for Europe on Christmas day, 1832 (by coincidence, he had met Ellen on Christmas day five years before), was part of a crisis that was not only vocational but also profoundly psychological. Emerson's tendency to feel guilt-ridden, everywhere manifest in the early journals, must have been horribly exacerbated by the complex emotions stirred up by the death of Ellen.

At all events, about three months after Ellen's death, Emerson was capable of writing a letter to his brother William which gives no evidence of settled grief and can only be described, in fact, as rather cheerful. William himself had sent a letter indicating "low spirits," and Waldo's chatty note is clearly intended to improve those spirits:

> Bulkeley [their retarded brother] is a little better, but still at Charlestown. You asked of his expenses—they are 3.00 pr week & some new clothes & new shoes. If Edward should get employment & have no bills, I suppose I can pay for B. without difficulty. especially as it seems that Ellen is to continue to benefit her husband whenever hereafter the estate shall be settled. but at this present time I am going fast in arrears, I believe. I please myself that Ellen's work of mercy is not done on earth, but she shall continue to help Edward & B. & Charles. (*L* 1:323)

Although it would be cruel to suggest that Emerson's somewhat breezy and optimistic feeling about "Ellen's work of mercy" follows hard upon the funeral baked meats, it does seem nevertheless odd that her death could be so easily and quickly assimilated into Emerson's calculations of thrift. One month later he wrote William again, and this time Emerson spoke more circumstantially of the Tucker estate:

> Do you not die of the Jews to whom you pay usance? What is your debt? I dare not yet promise you any help, because I do not know what I am worth. Ellen's estate remains wholly unsettled but as much as I understood of a long legal opinion sent me by Mr Cutler the other day was favorable to my claims. I do not know what authority is to determine the questions, but I suppose the discretion of the Judge of Probate. If he should adopt the opinions of Mr Ashmun & Mr Washburn I think I shall be rich enough to help you. But some circumstances, to my mind make this quite uncertain. I may have legal rights which I shall not choose to enforce. Besides there are I am told many questions to be settled of serious difficulty, & they are very slow to take them up. (*L* 1:327)

The two sentences that immediately follow this paragraph—"Ellen's mother & Margaret [her sister] have gone to Bristol R.I. they will return presently. They comfort me with kindness"—read a little ironically, it must be said, after all the hard-headed talk about the more tangible comforts that seemed to be heading Emerson's way. But it would be fairer to say that Emerson was trying to assuage his own guilt feelings by alluding to his grief and his tender relations with Ellen's mother and sister.

Emerson himself could unquestionably already see the potential for ugly rumor and bad feelings implicit in this situation. By the following March, when Emerson's lawyer was preparing to take out letters of administration, Ellen's executor was vowing that the widower would see no money in his lifetime, and Emerson, clearly uneasy, wrote William that he would try "to adhere to ye right remembering y^t there are worse things y^n being defrauded to wit, defrauding, though there is no occasion for using either of these words" (*L* 1:345). Other people obviously did not agree about the absence of bad feeling, because one month later Emerson wrote: "Pestered was I sadly one day lately by a quoted conversation y^t

came to my ear y^t Mr E. had refused all compromise with his wifes friends & was gone to law with them.' For ye first time I saw to my sorrow yt ye thing admitted of y^t face." Emerson then stressed the mutuality of the petition to the Supreme Court and insisted that he took no step without consulting with Ellen's family. He concluded by saying that he hoped for a confirmation of his own side's legal opinions by "sometime next summer" (*L* 1:349). In view of the fact that it was precisely during that summer—the summer of 1832—that Emerson determined he could no longer in good conscience serve the Lord's Supper (communion) and therefore ensured his dismissal from the Second Church, it is difficult to avoid feeling that the immediate prospect of financial independence must certainly have helped him to make that decision.[26] To such an extent, perhaps, did Ellen Tucker's wealth help change the course of American intellectual history.

From the financial point of view, Emerson's resolution to give up the only sure vocation he knew was a miscalculation, since the summer did not bear any tangible legal fruit. His disappointment in this regard may have led to the further deepening of his personal crisis and his decision to turn in December toward Europe, where at least he would be out of earshot of the legal wrangling and any accompanying gossip, and could gird up his loins for future battles. He did, of course, return immeasurably stronger in both body and spirit in October 1833, and the following spring, in time for his thirty-first birthday, Emerson's "legal rights" brought him one-half of his inheritance from Ellen—stocks and cash amounting to about $11,600.

Which brings us to Emerson's second, and justly celebrated, letter to his brother Edward, dated May 31, 1834. Though the letter has frequently been cited in studies of Emerson as evidence of his firm adherence to the Transcendental epistemology of Kant and Coleridge, it has rarely been looked at in more prudential terms—mainly because its conclusion is ignored. The letter is a very merry one indeed, and Emerson's high spirits clearly have as

much to do with his new financial prospects as with the novel
world of thought Hedge and Marsh had introduced him to:

My dear brother,

Your last letter to mother postpones to a pretty distance our
prospect of seeing you but as some of our feet were shod with
quicksilver when we came into the world there is still an even
chance that you may slip in upon us in some of the revolutions of
Night & Morn. Here sit Mother & I among the pine trees still
almost as we shall lie by & by under them. Here we sit always
learning & never coming to the knowledge of.—The greatest part
of my virtue—that mustard seedlet that no man wots of—is Hope.
I am ever of good cheer & if the heaven asks no service at my
hands am reconciled to my insignificance yet keeping my eye open
upon the brave & the beautiful. Philosophy affirms that the outward world is only phenomenal & the whole concern of dinners of
tailors of gigs and balls whereof men make such account is a quite
relative & temporary one—an intricate dream—the exhalation of
the present state of the Soul—wherein the Understanding works
incessantly as if it were real but the eternal Reason when now &
then he is allowed to speak declares it is an accident a smoke
nowise related to his permanent attributes. Now that I have used
the words, let me ask you do you draw the distinction of Milton
Coleridge & the Germans between Reason & Understanding. I
think it a philosophy itself. & like all truth very practical. So now
lay away the letter & take up the following dissertation on Sunday.
Reason is the highest faculty of the soul—what we mean often by
the soul itself; it never *reasons,* never proves, it simply perceives; it
is vision. The Understanding toils all the time, compares, contrives,
adds, argues, near sighted but strong-sighted, dwelling in the present the expedient the customary. Beasts have some understanding
but no Reason. Reason is potentially perfect in every man—Understanding in very different degrees of strength. The thoughts of
youth, & "first thoughts," are the revelations of Reason. the love
of the beautiful & of Goodness as the highest beauty the belief in
the absolute & universal superiority of the Right & the True But
understanding that wrinkled calculator the steward of our house to

whom is committed the support of our animal life contradicts evermore these affirmations of Reason & points at Custom & Interest & persuades one man that the declarations of Reason are false & another that they are at least impracticable. Yet by & by after having denied our Master we come back to see at the end of years or of life that he was the Truth. . . . The manifold applications of the distinction to Literature to the Church to Life will show how good a key it is. So hallelujah to the Reason forevermore.

But glad should I be to hold academical questions with you here at Newton. Whenever you are tired of working at Porto Rico & want a vacation or whenever your strength or your weakness shall commend to you the high countenances of the Muses, come & live with me. The Tucker estate is so far settled that I am made sure of an income of about $1200. wherewith the Reason of Mother & you & I might defy the Understanding upon his own ground, for the rest of the few years in which we shall be subject to his insults. I need not say that what I speak in play I speak in earnest. If you will come we will retreat into Berkshire & make a little world of other stuff. Your brother

Waldo (*L* 1:412–14)

This is surely one of the most curious documents in the whole Emerson canon—and one of the most difficult to interpret. How is one to separate what is spoken "in play" from what is spoken "in earnest"? In many ways, the most important thing about the letter is Emerson's announcement that he had achieved relative financial independence—a goal which, for the son of an impecunious minister who prematurely widowed his wife and left her in straitened circumstances, was by no means insignificant. (Emerson was somewhat ashamed of his "prospects" when he met Ellen and had to be reassured by her avowal that his prospects were not important to her. Was his distaste for the ministry partly prompted by his disgust at the genteel poverty to which it relegated its adherents?)[27] Emerson sees his greatest virtue as hope, and that virtue has now been rewarded in pecuniary terms, with more promised. And although Emerson's interest in the high distinction between Reason and Understanding should by no means be discounted, it makes an odd bedfellow with his obvious pleasure over the financial windfall. Money unquestionably belongs to the phenomenal world, but it actually provides the basis for Emerson's excitement over the noumenal one. It is therefore hard to keep them firmly distinguished. Our Prospero needs his Caliban. For although money (understanding) may be no more than "that wrinkled calculator the steward of our house to whom is committed the support of our animal life," it does in fact support the Emerson household. Does it really, then, contradict the Reason? The "Reason" of all the Emersons, Waldo says, has now been enabled to "defy the Understanding upon his own ground." Whereby one must conclude that the Reason owes a good deal to the wrinkled calculator. Emerson's feet had indeed been shod with silver, allowing him to tread the highest reaches of the mind's empyrean. And although Reason was indubitably to be the Christ-Master of that new intellectual universe—Emerson's "living leaping Logos"—it would have a hard time totally denying its dependence on that very State Street whose contracts it was presumably sent into the world to annul.

THE BOOK OF REVELATION OF
ST. RADULPHUS

[1]

To judge by the dominant tone of his journal entries on the voyage home, Emerson's eastern journey had brought him to a considerable boil. Like the poet whom he would later celebrate in the second series of *Essays,* Emerson was in a mood to say, "By God it is in me and must go forth of me"; prepared, that is, to see his thought "ejaculated as Logos, or Word" (*W* 3:39–40). *Nature* was already germinating in some fashion, for as he left the coast of Ireland on September 6, 1833, he wrote: "I like my book about nature & wish I knew where & how I ought to live. God will show me" (*JMN* 4:237). Does this entry suggest that he was expecting a revelation or meditating one? Perhaps, however, the word to stress here is *like*—hinting at Emerson's nascent sense that a literary project must in some way be connected with a feeling of personal satisfaction, even pleasure. That had not been, one might say, a notable feature of the literary scene which had nurtured Emerson. Writing almost a half-century later of Hawthorne's youth, Henry James would opine that "there was no appreciable group of people in New England at that time proposing to itself to enjoy life; this was not an undertaking for which any provision had been made, or to which any encouragement was offered." The "idea of pleasure," James would insist, is necessarily connected with the life and work of an artist: "He proposes to give pleasure, and to give it he must first get it."[28]

As Emerson's journal entry indicates, he was not at all clear on *how* he "ought" to live. Does the *ought* refer to duty or desire? Those, in fact, seem to be the terms of the debate that was taking shape on this voyage home. On September 11, Emerson reported that he was "nihilizing as usual," but that gloomy habit appears to have been undermined by the end of the entry, when he says: "I tipple with all my heart here. May I not?" (*JMN* 4:239). It sounds as if Emerson had picked up some dubious habits in Europe which the long sea journey—that hiatus in ordinary existence—was further encouraging. But why not "tipple," if he felt like it? Was he not free to do exactly what he pleased, even if that included occasionally acting a bit like the devil's child? (Emerson might have remembered that he still presumably had San Zenobio's charm against the headache!) Wednesday's tippling was followed, perhaps penitentially (and even providentially), by a stormy Sunday which Emerson "kept . . . with Milton & a Presbyterian magazine." On Monday, puzzling, apparently, over the issue of whether it makes any sense to seek rules of conduct, or paradigms of right living, outside of oneself, Emerson hypothesized about a person who "reads in a book the praise of a wise man who could unbend & make merry & so he tosses off his glass," only to find that "round him are malicious eyes watching his guzzling & fat eating." Since he finds both the license to guzzle and criticism of that license in the world outside, clearly little help is to be looked for there. "The truth is," Emerson concludes, "you can't find any example that will suit you, nor could, if the whole family of Adam should pass in procession before you, for you are a new work of God" (*JMN* 4:240). That lesson, to paraphrase Wallace Stevens, was probably worth crossing seas to find, and would undoubtedly inform the opening of *Nature* with its call for an "original relation to the universe": "There are new lands, new men, new thoughts. Let us demand our own works and laws and worship" (*CW* 1:7).

Emerson's richest and most complex journal entry during the voyage was entered on the next day, the 17th, when he was no longer in the mood to feel that malt was more efficacious than Milton in helping him justify his ways to himself:

The Book of Revelation of Saint Radulphus

Milton describes himself in his letter to Diodati as enamoured of moral perfection. He did not love it more than I. That which I cannot yet declare has been my angel from childhood until now. It has separated me from men. It has watered my pillow; it has driven sleep from my bed. It has tortured me for my guilt. It has inspired me with hope. It cannot be defeated by my defeats. It cannot be questioned though all the martyrs apostatize. It is always the glory that shall be revealed; it is the "open secret" of the universe; & it is only the feebleness & dust of the observer that makes it future, the whole *is* now potentially in the bottom of his heart. It is the soul of religion. Keeping my eye on this I understand all heroism, the history of loyalty & of martyrdom & of bigotry, the heat of the methodist, the non-conformity of the dissenter, the patience of the Quaker. But what shall the hour say for distinctions such as these—this hour of southwest gales & rain dripping cabin? As the law of light is fits of easy transmission & reflexion such is also the soul's law. She is only superior at intervals to pain, to fear, to temptation, only in raptures unites herself to God and Wordsworth truly said

> Tis the most difficult of tasks to keep
> Heights which the soul is competent to gain.
> (*JMN* 4:87)

Emerson, it seems, already knew *how* to live: namely, with an unflagging love of "moral perfection." That last phrase is difficult, suggesting as it normally does a *moralistic* concern for right conduct. But that surely is not what Emerson intends here, since the sort of passion Emerson commends he finds equally in the martyr *and* the bigot, in loyalty as well as in dissent. Perhaps a fair gloss would be to say that he longs to achieve an integrity of being consonant with the integrity of the universe (God); to live, that is, totally *toward* being in its highest manifestation. The sign that one is approaching such an integrity would be *rapture*—total pleasure in being in the world. Emerson seems to be reaching for a definition of "moral perfection" that unites the notion of one's obligation as an ethical creature with the desire for a total *creaturely* satisfaction.

He has always had an inner life, he suggests, which he has never been able to "declare"—perhaps because the yearning for perfection, like the momentary attainment of it, is intrinsically ineffable. Perfection of what, one might ask? One's life? One's work? Or of some *Gestalt* that unites all things? The key term here—as indeed everywhere in Emerson—is *perfection;* and he yearns for an experience of it that will unite ethics, emotion, and expression, somewhat as he describes in this passage from an 1837 lecture, "The Eye and Ear," in the "Human Culture" series:

> The doctrine of Art is that the human soul is perfectly receptive of the external Universe, and every beam of beauty which radiates from nature finds a corresponding inlet into the soul. The soul is like a circle within the circle of the world and for every point of light on the outer sphere is a point of sight on the inner. When this correspondence of the soul to nature, of the Individual to the All is perfect, then the divine loveliness passes into the Mind which way soever it turns and the Artist never rests but toils with enthusiasm to express that which he beholds, to transfer to some visible or audible object the perfection he contemplates. (*EL* 2:266).

Since the design of the universe is perfect, the passion for perfection in a human creature is the key to the "glory" of the whole and indeed suggests that "the whole *is* now potentially in the bottom of his heart." Writing a sort of précis of the opening pages of *Nature* in this journal entry of September 17, Emerson calls for "a religion by revelation to us" (*CW* 1:7) and counsels himself to "trust the perfection of the creation" despite the blowing and dripping weather. Indeed, his experience of "perfection exhilaration" in *Nature* will occur "in snow puddles . . . under a clouded sky" and will not exclude the pain and fear mentioned in the entry, since he will find himself "glad to the brink of fear" (*CW* 1:288). His raptures have always coexisted with tears, sleeplessness, and anguish—"hope," too, is their bedfellow. He would later articulate the principle by saying that "Paradise is under the shadow of swords" (*W* 2:243).[29] For now, it is probably enough to say that

Emerson had learned to take risks, not the least of which was a willingness to open himself to pleasure.

Indeed, though it would never be easy for him totally to abandon his "nihilizing," other lessons in the simple joy of being were multiplying as Emerson worked his way to the ecstatic expressions of *Nature*. On April 11, 1834, he spent the day in Cambridge, mostly at the Mount Auburn Cemetery:

> After much wandering & seeing many things, four snakes gliding up & down a hollow for no purpose that I could see—not to eat, not for love, but only gliding; then a whole bed of Hepatica triloba, cousins of the Anemone all blue & beautiful but constrained by niggard Nature to wear their last year's faded jacket of leaves; then a black capped titmouse who came upon a tree & when I would know his name, sang *chick a dee dee;* then a far off tree full of clamorous birds, I know not what, but you might hear them half a mile. I forsook the tombs & found a sunny hollow where the east wind could not blow & lay down against the side of a tree to most happy beholdings. At least I opened my eyes & let what would pass through them into the soul. (*JMN* 4:272–73)

This afternoon odyssey through the Cambridge woods reads like a mini-allegory of Emerson's own life in this part of his career. If he felt obliged to justify his wanderings abroad (which had cost him, as Rusk says, "more than a year's salary at the Second Church at a time when he was no longer drawing a salary"),[30] he had the example of these four snakes, "only gliding." Patience in the face of constraint was counseled by the Hepatica triloba, in "their last year's faded jacket of leaves" (but Emerson would complain angrily in *Nature* about putting "the living generation into masquerade out of [the past's] faded wardrobe" [*CW* 1:7]). Invited and invigorated by the noisy birds with their "floods of life" (ibid.), Emerson forsakes the tombs ("the sepulchres of the fathers . . . the dry bones of the past," [ibid.]) and opens his eyes and soul to the pleasures of experience, in preview, as it were, of becoming a "transparent eye-ball" in *Nature*. Having done so, as he tells us, he

83

"heeded no more what minute or hour our Massachusetts clocks might indicate—I saw only the noble earth on which I was born, with the great Star which warms & enlightens it." As in the previous April at Rome, when he expanded in the universal sun of Pope Gregory's benediction, Emerson is fully alive to all experience. Now, however, he would read from his own Book of Revelation.

[II]

The student of Emerson's first book can hardly do better than to begin with Dr. Holmes. "It may be remembered," he writes, "that Calvin, in his Commentary on the New Testament, stopped when he came to the book of the 'Revelation.' He found it full of difficulties which he did not care to encounter. Yet, considered only as a poem, the vision of St. John is full of noble imagery and wonderful beauty. 'Nature' is the Book of Revelation of our Saint Radulphus. It has its obscurities, its extravagances, but as a poem it is noble and inspiring."[31] Not many of us are likely to remember much about Calvin's Commentaries, but it hard to forget Holmes' own description. Apart from the witty latinization and canonization of "Ralph," Holmes' sentence contains a useful hint about a way of approaching Emerson's sometimes difficult little treatise.

A "Revelation" (or "Apocalypse") means literally in Latin (or Greek) an *unveiling,* and this—the clarification of vision—is Emerson's fundamental desire in *Nature.* Let us recall that in the journal entry describing that Easter service in Rome, Emerson expressed "great joy" when "the curtains [were] withdrawn from the pictures & statues." Such a gesture embodied for Emerson the essential nature, and meaning, of a religious or philosophical revelation—that which was symbolized by the idea of rebirth at Easter. What he is aiming for is stated succinctly in the final two words of his book: "perfect sight" (*CW* 1:45).

This notion is a central one in Emerson's writings and naturally has a long history.[32] In his early journals, Emerson's sense of the actual powers of sight was limited ("our eyes are small, and can take in but a little at a glance"—1822 [*JMN* 2:25]), and his idea of "Revelation" was constricted within the doctrinal boundaries of his church, as when he praised William Ellery Channing, in 1823, for an eloquent sermon which "was a full view of the subject of the light of Revelation compared with Nature & to shew the insufficiency of the latter alone" (*L* 1:138). Here *Revelation* carries its traditional meaning of the truth exposed in the Bible and in Christian doctrine. By 1826, Emerson had advanced far enough to write his Aunt Mary in terms that must have brought her to the brink of apoplexy: "it is one of the *feelings* of modern philosophy, that it is wrong to regard ourselves so much in a *historical* light as we do, putting Time between God & us; and that it were fitter to account every moment of the existence of the Universe as a new Creation, and *all* as a revelation proceeding each moment from the Divinity to the mind of the observer" (*L* 1:174). That is fairly close to Emerson's fully unchurched position in *Nature*. "It is the office of the priest," he wrote in 1829, "to see the creation with a new eye" (*JMN* 3:152). At such a point, the priest and the poet are hardly distinguishable. When Emerson praised Sampson Reed's *Observations on the Growth of the Mind* in 1826 (and regularly thereafter) for having the "aspect of a revelation" (*JMN* 3:45), he undoubtedly intended the term as he himself would use it in *Nature* —with reference to the actual perfecting of vision—and might have had such a passage from Reed's book as the following in mind:

> The imagination will be refined into a chaste and sober view of unveiled nature. It will be confined within the bounds of reality. It will no longer lead the way to insanity and madness by transcending the works of creation and, as it were, wandering where God has no power to protect it; but finding a resting place in every created object, it will enter into it and explore its hidden treasures. . . . When there shall be a religion which shall see God in every-

thing, and at all times; and the natural sciences not less than nature itself shall be regarded in connection with Him, the fire of poetry will begin to be kindled in its immortal part and will burn without consuming. The inspiration so often feigned will become real, and the mind of the poet will feel the spark which passes from God to nature. The veil will be withdrawn and beauty and innocence displayed to the eye. . . .[33]

Setting out on his voyage westward in the fall of 1833, Emerson wrote in his journal, "The whole creation groaneth until now waiting for that which shall be revealed" (*JMN* 4:85). Although Emerson's language (leaning, as it does, on the New Testament) seems filled with the spirit of Apocalyptic expectation as we find it in biblical prophecy, his actual interest lay much closer to that expressed in the passage from Reed's *Observations*. As Emerson would say in the penultimate paragraph of *Nature:* "The invariable mark of wisdom is to see the miraculous in the common. What is a day? What is a year? What is summer? What is woman? What is a child? What is sleep? To our blindness, these things seem unaffecting" (*CW* 1:44).

In his seminal study, *Natural Supernaturalism,* M. H. Abrams has richly documented, in the total context of European Romanticism, the massive tendency, "grounded in texts of the New Testament itself, to internalize apocalypse by transferring the theater of events from the outer earth and heaven to the spirit of the single believer." Thus, "Shelley's ruling figure for the advent of the renovated world is that of an instantaneous and radical alteration of sight: man's imaginative vision, suddenly liberated, penetrates to the inner forms, both of man and his world, which had been there all the time, beneath the veil."[34] Such a formulation may be directly applied to the sixth section of *Nature,* for example, where Emerson, turning his attention to "the apocalypse of the mind" (*CW* 1:29), argues that "the eye of Reason" (Reason-Imagination; and let us recall Emerson's sentence of 1835: "The Imagination is Vision"), when it is "stimulated to more earnest vision," transforms surfaces so that they "become transparent" and "causes and spirits are seen through them" (ibid., p. 30). At the very highest reaches of his idealistic faith, Emerson insists that we can "behold unveiled the nature of Justice and Truth" (ibid., p. 35).

The central figure in Abrams' exposition is Wordsworth, whose apocalyptic vision, in Abrams' words, "is that of the awesome depths and height of the human mind, and of the power of that mind as in itself adequate, by consummating a holy marriage with the external universe, to create out of the world of all of us, in a quotidian and recurrent miracle, a new world which is the equivalent of paradise."[35] This summary of the Wordsworthian vision could serve as a fairly accurate précis of Reed's *Observations on the Growth of the Mind*, which is thoroughly informed by the spirit of Wordsworth (and, indeed, the first edition in 1826 bore an epigraph from *The Excursion*), as is Emerson's own first book. It is interesting to note that the Wordsworth text upon which Abrams builds his argument, the now familiar lines from Wordsworth's "Prospectus" to *The Recluse*, is in fact quoted by Emerson in that lecture of 1837, "The Eye and Ear," cited above as an illustration of Emerson's passionate desire for "perfection." Emerson writes:

> In the best moments of life, in moments of great peace we are susceptible to the beauty that fills and overflows nature. It is the song of a living poet,
>
> > Paradise and groves elysian
> > Fortunate fields like those of old
> > Sought in the Atlantic Main why should they be
> > A history only of departed things
> > Or a mere fiction of what never was?
> > For the discerning intellect of man
> > When wedded to this goodly Universe
> > In love and holy passion, shall find these
> > A simple produce of the common day.
>
> We divorce ourselves from nature . . . . (*EL* 2:273)

The always percipient Dr. Holmes noticed long ago that "no writer is more deeply imbued with the spirit of Wordsworth than Emerson," and went on to juxtapose Wordsworth's lines to the opening of *Nature:*

> The foregoing generations beheld God and nature face to face; we, through their eyes. Why should not we also enjoy an original relation to the universe? Why should not we have a poetry and philosophy of insight and not of tradition, and a religion by revelation to us, and not the history of theirs?[36]

It remains to add only that the final section of *Nature,* "Prospects," which provides the *volte-face* implied in the opening sentence of the essay ("Our age is retrospective"), owes not only its title but also much of its language and imagery to Wordsworth's "Prospectus." Perhaps he and not Bronson Alcott is the "Orphic poet" whom Emerson claims at least partially to be quoting:[37]

> A man is a god in ruins. When men are innocent, life shall be longer, and shall pass into the immortal, as gently as we awake from dreams. Now, the world would be insane and rabid, if these disorganizations should last for hundreds of years. It is kept in check by death and infancy. Infancy is the perpetual Messiah, which comes into the arms of fallen men, and pleads with them to return to paradise. . . .

> The problem of restoring to the world original and eternal beauty, is solved by the redemption of the soul. The ruin or the blank, that we see when we look at nature, is in our own eye. The axis of vision is not coincident with the axis of things, and so they appear not transparent but opake. The reason why the world lacks unity, and lies broken and in heaps, is, because man is disunited with himself. He cannot be a naturalist, until he satisfies all the demands of the spirit. Love is as much its demand, as perception. Indeed, neither can be perfect without the other. In the uttermost meaning of the words, thought is devout, and devotion is thought. Deep

calls unto deep. But in actual life, the marriage is not celebrated. (CW 1:42 and 43)

In this passage, Emerson actually provides our best gloss on that "moral perfection" which he tried to illuminate in his journal entry on Milton: the glory that is here revealed—"the 'open secret' of the universe"—is simply that perception and love can, and must, unite and thereby lead us to the perfection of our moral being. When we come to look at the world with the "new eyes" that Emerson provides, we shall find "the phenomenon perfect" and have "all that Adam had" (CW 1:44–45). This secularized program for the redemption of the soul is Emerson's great argument in this final survey of "Prospects" where, as Holmes puts it well, Emerson "dreams of Paradise regained."[38] Indeed, since the spirit —if not the theology—of Milton so thoroughly pervades the conclusion of Emerson's book (as it underlies Wordsworth's "Prospectus"), it is probably worth noting that book XI of *Paradise Lost* provides the model (and perhaps even some of the vocabulary) for Emerson's project here. We recall that the archangel Michael is sent down to Adam and Eve for the purpose, not only of removing them from paradise, but also of providing a preview of the history of salvation. To that end, Michael leads Adam up a mountain:

> So both ascend
> In the Visions of God: It was a Hill
> Of Paradise the highest, from whose top
> The hemisphere of Earth in clearest Ken
> Stretcht out to the amplest reach of prospect lay

Here, Milton tell us, "Michael from Adam's eyes the Film remov'd" and proceeded to unfold the Christian vision. Such is the function that Emerson now arrogates to himself, though he has lost his belief in its theological underpinnings. In the mid-1820s Emerson noted in his journal that "Christianity . . . takes off the film that had got on the human eye" but subsequently "neglected the improvement of the intellect." Emerson surmised that "the oculist did not wish the blind man to see the sun because he only removed the film & left him no directions what to do with his eyes" (*JMN* 3:101). Those directions Emerson himself attempted to provide in *Nature,* for as he argues in the first section of the book, "to speak truly, few adult persons can see nature. Most persons do not see the sun. At least they have a very superficial seeing" (*CW* 1:9).

I want to make one further point about the relationship of Emerson's vision in *Nature* to standard Christian doctrine which will continue to engage us as we move ahead through Emerson's career. As a beginning imaginative writer, Emerson was naturally not very far removed from the ministerial vocation in which he had been bred and which he continued fitfully to serve (for Emerson was not to abandon the pulpit definitively until early in 1839). Emerson's discourses would always, for many of his listeners and readers, carry the faint flavor of the sermon, as his manner would seem elevated and preacherly. But we can be more specific about the influence of the sermon on Emerson's literary method in at least one regard, namely, in his tendency to rely on a Bible text, or texts, to provide a point of departure (and sometimes return), though typically Emerson's use of his text would function to subvert its traditional meaning. Sometimes Bible text is quoted directly, as in the opening of "The Method of Nature" ("Where there is no vision, the people perish"; Proverbs 29:18); often it is "submerged" or embedded in the texture of his language. In either case, it can be an important guide to Emerson's meaning or intention. We ought at least to remind ourselves that Emerson's actual audience was normally quite familiar with the Bible, and therefore could be expected to respond even to an oblique biblical reference. Emerson, however, tends to avoid recondite allusions, staying for the most part with texts that would elicit easy recognition.[39]

Nature has at least three such texts, two in its exordium, the third in its peroration, which provide a valuable insight into the direction of Emerson's argument. The first is embedded in the second sentence of the book: "Our age is retrospective. It builds the sepulchres of the fathers." Surely there is an echo here of Christ's angry words to the lawyers in the eleventh chapter of Luke: "Woe unto you! for ye build the sepulchres of the prophets, and your fathers killed them. Truly ye bear witness that ye allow the deeds of your fathers: for they indeed killed them, and ye build their sepulchres." Emerson has, in a sense, collapsed his text by leaving out the prophets altogether, or at least insinuating that that is what his age does—building the sepulchres of the fathers and ignoring the prophets, those with direct knowledge of God. Though Emerson is not about to accuse "the fathers" of slaying prophets (he would come much closer to such a position as he himself assumed the prophetic role more explicitly at the time of the Divinity School Address), his assimilation of his own voice to that of Christ suggests that this opening paragraph of *Nature* is laced with more anger than we are normally willing to hear. In any case, we shall shortly notice that the voice of Christ, again from the gospel of Luke, explicitly surfaces at the end of Emerson's book.

The second and perhaps more significant text is not very deeply submerged in the fourth sentence of the opening: "The foregoing generations beheld God and nature face to face; we, through their eyes." Emerson's allusion is to a very familiar passage indeed from I Corinthians, chapter 13: "When I was a child, I spake as a child, I understood as a child, I thought as a child: but when I became a man, I put away childish things. For now we see through a glass, darkly: but then face to face. . . ." This text was so well known, at least in nineteenth-century America, that Mark Twain could easily expect to make humorous capital by fooling with it in his essay on Cooper ("Cooper's eye was splendidly inaccurate. Cooper seldom saw anything correctly. He saw nearly all things as through a glass eye, darkly").[40] And even Emerson at age sixteen was not above making his own joke at St. Paul's expense ("Been looking through a glass darkly this morning to see the Eclipse" [*L* 1:83]).

But Emerson's use of the text in *Nature* is serious indeed, and helps to advance his argument quite economically. For one thing, since he has been complaining strenuously about "the fathers," and particularly about being kept in what might be termed epistemological immaturity (seeing the world "through their eyes"), there is something wonderfully ironic about his depending on the authority of St. Paul to bolster his claim that he has a perfect right to put away such childish things. More importantly, however, Emerson is engaged in subverting the traditional Christian claim that full spiritual maturity, and the direct apprehension of the divine, will be attained only at the end of time, when the veil is finally removed. Notice that Emerson easily assumes that the foregoing generations have *already* beheld "God and nature face to face." Though he might be alluding to Moses, or the prophets, or to those who lived in the time of Christ, if it is the history of religion he has in mind, his lack of specificity is telling: *somebody* in the past has had an unmediated experience of God and nature. Why do we keep our heads so reverently turned to the past, he seems to be asking, if not because we believe that something has already taken place which is far more valuable than the "wool and flax" in our own fields? What has been done once, Emerson's logic clearly suggests, can surely be done again. He therefore insists on "an original relation to the universe" and demands his own "works and laws and worship." Emerson is convinced that his own eyes are adequate to any vision of the divine. As he would say in just two years, before the Divinity School at Harvard, "dare to love God without mediator or veil" (CW 1:90).

The text Emerson uses at the conclusion of *Nature* was a favorite of his and serves to culminate his quasi-religious vision in a way that picks up the Christian undertone of the essay and assimilates it to the naturalistic premise of his whole imaginative project. It is drawn from the seventeenth chapter of Luke: "And when he was demanded of the Pharisees, when the kingdom of God should come, he answered them and said, 'The kingdom of God cometh not with observation: Neither shall they say, "Lo here!" or "Lo there!" for, behold, the kingdom of God is within you.'" Emerson leans on these verses in a curious way: "The kingdom of man over nature, which cometh not with observation,

—a dominion such as now is beyond his dream of God,—he shall enter without more wonder than the blind man feels who is gradually restored to perfect sight" (CW 1:45). The obvious change Emerson has made is to substitute for the kingdom of God an even greater dominion—that of man's accommodation to and eventual control of all the things outside of his spirit from which he now feels alienated, including (as Emerson told us at the outset) his own body. This ultimate kingdom of integrated being is, accordingly, the place where Emerson's version of the holy marriage described in the twenty-first chapter of the book of Revelation will be celebrated—the marriage he has called for uniting perception and love, "science with the fire of the holiest affections." Though Emerson has insisted throughout his essay on the actual cleansing of vision as the agency of this redemption, he now surprises us by associating the gradual nature of this redemption with Christ's insistence that the kingdom does not come "with observation": the visionary perfection we seek has stolen upon us unawares and lies waiting within. Once again, we remember that journal entry of September 17, 1833. The "moral perfection" which Emerson has tirelessly sought, and which he thinks of as "the glory that shall be revealed," he realizes is not *future* at all; for "it is only the feebleness & dust of the observer that makes it future, the whole *is* now potentially in the bottom of his heart."

Though few contemporary readers of Emerson's first book seem to have had a clear sense of what he was about, Carlyle's response must have been heartening: "Your little azure-coloured *Nature* gave me true satisfaction. . . . It is the true Apocalypse this when the 'open secret' becomes revealed to a man"[41] Was Carlyle actually alluding to Emerson's apparent pretensions to rivaling, or replacing, the author of the book of Revelation? We know, at least, that Carlyle had his own view of the poet as apocalyptist, whose primary function is to help us unseal our eyes so that we might see the New Jerusalem.[42] Great Men, Teufelsdrockh tells us

> are the inspired (speaking and acting) Texts of that divine BOOK OF REVELATIONS, whereof a Chapter is completed from epoch

to epoch, and by some named HISTORY; to which inspired Texts your numerous talented men, and your innumerable untalented men, are the better or worse exegetic Commentaries, and wagon-load of too-stupid, heretical or orthodox, weekly Sermons. For my study the inspired Texts themselves![43]

Whether Emerson and his book indeed formed one of these inspired texts for Carlyle or just another solid heterodox sermon is not entirely clear.

But we can be more certain about Emerson's attitude toward his own work. At least by the time he came to publish his second series of *Essays* (1844), Emerson would think about "the total solitude of the critic," clearly with himself in mind, as being "the Patmos of thought" (W 3:106). And in the same book, he would argue that there was as much need for his own existence, and work, as for that of the inspired prophet of old: "If John was perfect, why are you and I alive?" (ibid., p. 240). But the most interesting hint about Emerson's view of his own high function may be found in a dream entered in his journal for October 1840:

I dreamed that I floated at will in the great Ether, and I saw this world floating also not far off, but diminished to the size of an apple. Then an angel took it in his hand & brought it to me and said "This must thou eat." And I ate the world. (*JMN* 7:525)

Though it might seem that Emerson was here simply symbolizing for himself his necessary recapitulation of Adam's primal sin—eating the fruit of worldly knowledge, but this time with divine sanction—other possiblities suggest themselves. His dream might also represent a figuration of the "Idealism" section of *Nature*, where man, "the immortal pupil," finds himself so dilated and deified that the whole world does indeed circulate through him, totally engulfed "in the apocalypse of the mind."[44] In this view, Emerson's dream might be seen as a kind of rehearsal of that tremendous sense of spiritual power which had inspired his first book (and which, to judge by this later journal entry, would largely evaporate by the mid-1850s: " 'Twere ridiculous for us to think of embracing the whole circle when we know we can live only while 50, 60, or 70 whirls are spun round the sun by this nimble apple we are perched upon. Can the gnat swallow the elephant?" [*JMN* 13:249]).

But the reader impressed by Emerson's prophetic and apocalyptist yearnings may hear another biblical echo behind Emerson's dream, this time from the tenth chapter of the book of Revelation:

> And the voice which I heard from heaven spake unto me again, and said, "Go and take the little book which is open in the hand of the angel which standeth upon the sea and upon the earth." And I went unto the angel, and said unto him, "Give me the little book." And he said unto me, "Take it, and eat it up; and it shall make thy belly bitter, but it shall be in thy mouth sweet as honey." And I took the little book out of the angel's hand, and ate it up; and it was in my mouth sweet as honey: and as soon as I had eaten it, my belly was bitter. And he said unto me, "Thou must prophesy again before many peoples, and nations, and tongues, and kings."

If Emerson's language and paratactic cadences really do betray the origin of his dream in this passage from the book of Revelation,[45] his allegory suggests how heavy was the burden for him of the sort of self-defined prophecy he had undertaken to produce. Forsaking the certainties of the Eucharistic meal in favor of a bittersweet experience of the world in its complex totality, Emerson had assumed the great, and difficult, aim as an artist of bringing forth scriptures of his own that might provide, as had the Hebrew and Greek ones, "bread of life to millions" (*CW* 1:92). "The beauty of nature reforms itself in the mind," he writes in *Nature,* "and not for barren contemplation, but for new creation" (*CW* 1:16). A work of art, he insists, must be "an abstract or epitome of the world . . . the result or expression of nature, in miniature" (ibid.). A true scripture must pierce the "rotten diction" of trivial literature and "fasten words again to visible things" so that it becomes a revelation of the actual underpinnings of experience (ibid., p. 20). Only thus can the writer/prophet help us to build a new heaven and earth of durable proportions.

The message of Saint John's parable of the little book, D. H. Lawrence tells us, is the universal one "of the destruction of the old world and creation of the new."[46] Emerson attempted to achieve both goals in *Nature*. As he wrote to Carlyle on September 17, 1836: "I send you a little book I have just now published, as an entering wedge, I hope, for something more worthy and significant." But Carlyle, in his reply, as we have noticed, magnanimously claimed that the "little book" was sufficiently worthy to be called a "true Apocalypse": "You say it is the first chapter of something greater. I call it rather the Foundation and Ground-plan on which you may build whatsoever of great and true has been given you to build."[47]

[III]

Throughout at least the first series of *Essays,* the idea of *revelation* continued to represent for Emerson the first flush and triumph of his Transcendental springtide. It was in fact *the* fundamental idea on which he was to build his new church: faith in the unlimited powers of the individual soul. That is the new "religion" which Emerson attempted to preach in his Divinity School Address. "Jesus Christ belonged to the true race of prophets," Emerson insists, because "he saw with open eye the mystery of the soul" (*CW* 1:81). And although he, like Emerson after him, "felt respect for Moses and the prophets," he did not scruple to postpone "their initial revelations, to the hour and the man that now is; to the eternal revelation in the heart" (ibid.). Emerson's understanding of Christ is that he preached the *apocalyptic* nature of the soul—its power to reveal truth and transfigure common experience. Men speak "of the revelation as somewhat long ago given and done, as if God were dead" (CW 1:84) because they have ceased to believe in this active power of the soul, which alone makes it redemptive. Under Emerson's "new revelation" each of us is enjoined to "dare to love God without mediator or veil" and thereby become "a newborn bard of the Holy Ghost" (ibid., p. 90). Make certain, Emerson says, that "fashion, custom, authority, pleasure, and money are nothing to you,—are not bandages over your eyes, that you cannot see." Abandoning such veils, we may find ourselves laid open to the "influx of the all-knowing Spirit, which annihilates before its broad noon the little shades and gradations of intelligence in the compositions we call wiser and wisest" (ibid., pp. 90–91).

Some of Emerson's most ecstatic expressions of this actual power of the soul, in its highest moments, to transcend the limitations of common experience and create a New Jerusalem in the heart, are to be found in "The Over-Soul." Whatever else Emerson intended in this difficult, and perhaps unfortunate, term, he surely meant to convey his belief in this self-actuating power of the human spirit. "Before the revelations of the soul," he writes in that essay, "Time, Space and Nature shrink away. In common speech we refer all things to time . . . and so we say that the Judgment is distant or near, that the Millennium approaches, that a day of certain political, moral, social reforms is at hand, and the like, when we mean that in the nature of things one of the facts we contemplate is external and fugitive, and the other is permanent and connate with the soul" (W 2:273–74). Emerson's sense of what "we mean" is, of course, his own; and this quietistic faith in a timeless personal beatitude that renders political activity or reform nugatory has never appealed to those with a more compelling belief in the need for social and political change. Here, if you like, we have Emerson in his most Transcendental and "moonshiny" mood. Though most characteristic of his early career, it is a mood he would never entirely lose and establishes his claim to being an unchurched religious teacher. Emerson has, however, a cannier side, as we have seen; and this dualism is characteristic of all the

Transcendentalists (except, perhaps, Bronson Alcott), since the movement displayed both political and social aspects, on the one hand, and "religious" ones, broadly speaking, on the other. Thoreau encompasses both the angry activist of "Civil Disobedience" and the self-styled "yogi" of Walden Pond.

Emerson thus concludes this passage with a high-Transcendental statement about the impermanence of everything for the soul save the fitful blessedness of its inner new heaven and earth:

> The things we now esteem fixed shall, one by one, detach themselves like ripe fruit from our experience, and fall. The wind shall blow them none knows whither. The landscape, the figures, Boston, London, are facts as fugitive as any institution past, or any whiff of mist or smoke, and so is society, and so is the world. The soul looketh steadily forwards, creating a world before her, leaving worlds behind her. She has no dates, nor rites, nor persons, nor specialties nor men. The soul knows only the soul; the web of events is the flowing robe in which she is clothed. (W 2:274).

We may notice here that we have another version of Emerson's apocalyptic dream about the apple of the world. It has fallen and been ingested, or otherwise internalized, by the individual soul, which has thereby freed itself to weave the web of events into the flowing robe of a New Jerusalem of the spirit.

Revelation, Emerson insists, is nothing more than "the disclosure of the soul"—"its manifestations of its own nature"; it is not "a telling of fortunes" (W 2:281–83). It is, in fact, in the very nature of human experience "that a veil shuts down on the facts of to-morrow," instructing us "to live in to-day" (ibid., p. 284). The present, when it is truly encountered, can burn for us like a holy fire—"vital, consecrating, celestial"—that is capable of dissolving "all things into the waves and surges of an ocean of light" in which, at last, "we see and know each other, and what spirit each is of" (ibid., p. 285). In such an intense moment, we may find that we have cast aside our "trappings" and are "dealing man to man in naked truth, plain confession and omniscient affirmation" (ibid., p. 291). Emerson seems to be talking about the possibility of a momentary union of self and other that shows us the world as a "perennial miracle" and sacramentalizes all things, teaching us "that there is no profane history; that all history is sacred; that the universe is represented in an atom, in a moment of time" (ibid., p. 297). Whoever is capable of experiencing such moments, Emerson insists in his conclusion,

> will weave no longer a spotted life of shreds and patches, but he will live with a divine unity. He will cease from what is base and frivolous in his life and be content with all places and with any service he can render. He will calmly front the morrow in the negligency of that trust which carries God with it and so hath already the whole future in the bottom of the heart.

Anyone is free to read that passage as an example of Emerson's complacent acceptance of the status quo, but that is not, I think, either what is intended or achieved in it. Emerson is interested, not in praising things as they are, but in opening up the possibility of an integration of the self that will serve as a modern correlative for the traditional idea of spiritual redemption. The garment we are invited to weave (the figure is persistent throughout the essay) is that of our own moral perfection—not a spotted one "of shreds and patches" such as Hamlet's unrepentant uncle Claudius wears, but the "garments of salvation" mentioned by Isaiah. This concluding paragraph of "The Over-Soul" carries us back, not only to Emerson's text at the end of *Nature* ("the Kingdom of God is within"), but also, and more explicitly, to his journal entry of September 17, 1833: "the whole *is* now potentially in the bottom of his heart." This message—that with each virtuous act of our unified being we are preparing our own holy city—is the one which St. Radulphus felt himself sent to reveal. As he insists in the Divinity School Address:

. . . in the soul of man there is a justice whose retributions are instant and entire. He who does a good deed, is instantly ennobled himself. He who does a mean deed, is by the action itself contracted. He who puts off impurity, thereby puts on purity. If a man is at heart just, then in so far is he God; the safety of God, the immortality of God, the majesty of God do enter into that man with justice. If a man dissemble, deceive, he deceives himself, and goes out of acquaintance with his own being. (CW 1:78)

While some might see nothing but heresy in such talk, others would discover in it a happy alignment of the old categories of Justification and Sanctification with the Romantic faith in the heart as "God's anointed."[48] But for Emerson himself, to use his felicitous phrase, he had simply found "Eden's balmier spring" (W 9:166) in the regeneration and renovation of his own moral being.

III

A Summer of Discontent: Emerson in 1838

1836–1839

Emerson had lost his brother Edward to tuberculosis in the fall of 1834, and his especially beloved youngest brother, Charles Chauncy, followed the same grim path in May 1836, leading Emerson to feel that a "gloomy epoch" was beginning in his own life (indeed, a year later, his lungs too brought the threat of severe ill-health). But there were in fact many compensations. Apart from the publication of Nature *and the birth of Waldo, 1836 brought Margaret Fuller, and probably Henry Thoreau, into Emerson's orbit. He was succeeding as a lecturer ("The Philosophy of History" series in the winter of 1836–37 was followed the next year by "Human Culture" and in 1838–39 by "Human Life"). Though the country fell into deep economic trouble in 1837, Emerson had the good fortune to receive the second installment of the Tucker estate in July of that year, bringing his investment capital to around $22,000. On August 31 he delivered "The American Scholar" address at Harvard (which Holmes called "our intellectual Declaration of Independence") and afterward had the pleasure of hearing himself toasted as "The Spirit of Concord" who "makes us all of One Mind." By the following summer, the genial agreement disappeared when Emerson read the Divinity School Address, his controversial thrust at the Unitarian establishment, on July 15. Reviled as a heretic, Emerson was probably relieved to get out of town about a week later, when he traveled to Dartmouth to deliver an oration later entitled "Literary Ethics." His own spirits were deeply affected by the storm he caused, and there followed a period of*

103

intense self-examination and reflection. But the die was cast. Emerson was no longer to be a sometime minister and amateur literatus but a professional lecturer and writer committed to the free expression and dissemination of new ideas. He reviewed his eventful revolutionary year in his lecture "The Protest" on January 16, 1839, and four days later preached his last sermon at Concord. Emerson's first daughter was born at this time. Named Ellen Tucker, after his first wife, she never married and served as Emerson's guide and support in old age.

THE PROTEST

[I]

It is difficult to choose among the various vintage years of the Emersonian harvest, but one can scarcely overlook 1838, culminating as it does with the delivery of the "Address ... Before The Senior Class in Divinity College, Cambridge," on Sunday evening, July 15. Emerson, it seems to me, was born for this act. It defines and distinguishes him now, as it did then, and constitutes a piece of sustained and passionate eloquence still capable of stirring the sympathetic and attentive reader. But, more than any other of Emerson's utterances, it lives and breathes in the situation and context that brought it forth. It is supremely, to use Wallace Stevens' phrase, "the cry of its occasion,"[1] and badly needs to be seen in historical perspective (and read with historical imagination). The sublime discontent that produced, in the summer of 1838, not only the Divinity School Address but also the (unfortunately) neglected Dartmouth Oration—"Literary Ethics"—had both a long seed-time and a substantial aftermath. There is more to be learned about Emerson in this period than at any other time in his long career. For 1838 was the year in which Emerson achieved his self-definition through defiance and dissent.

Perhaps the best frame for this tale is the lecture that Emerson delivered at the Masonic Temple in Boston on January 16, 1839 (and repeated in Concord on April 3). Entitled "The Protest," it amounts to a recasting of the events of Emerson's fateful year previous whereby, largely through a fascinating reworking and weaving together of 1838 journal entries, he attempted to universalize his personal struggles. It is, one might say, a startling mythology of the self that Emerson achieves here: the story of a youthful prophet who tries to redeem the world from the death-dealing grip of the elders and in the process either creates and affirms his own virile being or ceases to exist:

> God the Soul says one thing; the whole world says or seems to say another. Then arises War. The prophets call the word of the Lord that was given them a Burden. How shall it not be said? Yet how shall it be said to deaf and unwilling ears? . . . There is ill-concealed diversity of aim, of religion, of theory of life between every newly arrived soul and the existing population of the planet and it is always breaking out afresh. . . . The fact is very strange and the cause of it perhaps too deep in our constitution and too subtle to be explored, to know why we are such slaves of Custom; why it is so much easier to repeat an old, than to invent a new act; why we decline creation; why we dread to speak our own speech; and even to pray our own prayer. . . . always we crutch ourselves on other men's thinking . . . rather than obey those youthful impulses which prompt us to write our own law. . . . Society loves the past; society desponds; sneers; serves; sits. . . . It pillows itself in usages and forms until the man is killed with kindness. Its tediousness is torture to a masculine and advancing temper. . . . But somehow or other Life will live; soul does not die; God still is; still bright, still new, springs evermore the fresh ray of thought, the bounding pulse of virtue. The old, halt, numb, bedrid world must ever be plagued with this incessant soul. . . . By resistance to this strong custom . . . by obedience to the soul, is the world to be saved. The Redemption from this ruin is lodged in the heart of Youth. (EL 3:86–90)

Most men, however, Emerson laments, "accept how weary a load of tradition from their elders." Many a youthful dissenter "compromises" and "gets weary of struggling against the stream alone."

He postpones hostilities, "makes a feebler and feebler refusal and at last decides that his opposition was very youthful and unadvised and gives in his adhesion to Old Times and the wisdom of our ancestors, and goes down stream to darkness and to death" (ibid., pp. 91, 99). Such, of course, is not the posture of our Emersonian hero. Invoking Hamlet, who with "proud discontent" refuses "the opportunities of society," he screams his triumphant battle cry: "There must be a revolution. Let it come and let one come free into the earth to walk by truth alone" (ibid., pp. 95, 97).

Having arrived at the barricades with Emerson the lyceum lecturer in his talk of January 16, 1839, it is instructive to turn back to his journal for March 1838: "There must be a Revolution. Let the revolution come & let One come breathing free into the earth to walk by hope alone" (*JMN* 5:466). The lecture is retrospective and suggests an already existent creature and an achieved "truth." The journal entry, however, is prospective and evokes (looking toward the Divinity School Address) a new being breathing his first hopeful breath of life. "It were a new World," the journal continues (as "The Protest" does not), "& perhaps the Ideal would seem possible. But now it seems to me they are cheated out of themselves, & live on another's sleeve." This last phrase, reminiscent as it is of the opening of *Nature,* with its horror of putting "the living generation into masquerade out of [the] faded wardrobe" of the past (*CW* 1:7), suggests that the sleeve which harbors these diminished creatures belongs to the sepulchral fathers—the moribund elders of Emerson's "Protest." Here is the issue which had become sharpened for Emerson since he himself left the ministry in 1832. "The profession is antiquated," he wrote then. "In an altered age, we worship in the dead forms of our forefathers" (*JMN* 4:27). Five years later, in his Phi Beta Kappa Address, Emerson looked upon "the discontent of the literary class as a mere announcement of the fact that they find themselves not in the state of mind of their fathers" (*CW* 1:67). And about a month later, he complained in his journal of a young preacher whose "loud & hollow" preaching Emerson ascribed to his tacking "a solemn conclusion of a Calvinistic discourse" to "the end of a Unitarian sermon." Emerson likened this "ludicrous" performance to seeing "grandfather's hat & spectacles on a rogue of six years." He ended by lamenting "how few prophets are left," suggesting— whether wittingly or not—his own highest aspirations (*JMN* 5:380). He was preparing, as he would say later, to "shame the fathers"— and not "by brag," but rather "by the virtue of the sons" (*JMN* 9:27).

Eighteen thirty-eight was to be the year of sowing, but Emerson's clear intention to assert his manhood and supplant the elders reactivated his old uncertainties and stirred up deep ambivalence. On March 26 he recorded his sense of being in a transitional state: "I *Become* rather than *I am*. I am a *Becoming*. . . . I am now nothing but a prophecy of that I shall be." Emerson was insisting on "consciousness" over "authority," as he asserts in the same entry, but other men retort: "It is wrong. . . . We think you have no Father. We love to address the Father" (*JMN* 5:468). Here, in this bit of presumably invented dialogue, we have a measure of Emerson's inner division: warming to his own work, he nevertheless felt chilled by self-doubt and antagonism from without. "The weathers fit our moods," Emerson was to say later (*JMN* 9:236); and the climate in this spring of 1838 was not reassuring. On March 27, one of those chilly, overcast days, as he noted in the journal, "that deform my spring," he continued to debate the feasibility of letting "out all the length of all the reins" and making "a frank & hearty expression of himself." Riding from Concord to Acton, Emerson reproached himself for being mute and passive in his dealings with the world, and asserted: "I ought to go upright & vital & say the truth in all ways," even to the "stiff, hard, proud, clenched Calvinist" (*JMN* 5:468–70). And returning to his "meteorology of thought" (*JMN* 5:457), he made explicit the planting metaphor that expressed his own doubts in this seemingly unpropitious season:

> The effeminate rich man says in his shrug, in his gloves & surtout on the cold spring day, that he fears the earth will not yield

to man bread this year. The hard visaged farmer looks contented &
fearless. He has fronted the year cold & grim. He has embraced the
shovel & the ox yoke & ploughtail long ago & knows well that
the hardest year that ever blew afforded to such straining & sweat-
ing as his, milk, rye, potatoes . . . and he does not think of famine.
(*JMN* 5:470)

The weather persisted, and so did Emerson's uneasy rumina-
tions, though this entry for April 24 adds a distinctly new twist to
the argument:

This cold, dreary, desponding weather seems to threaten the farmer
who sourly follows his plough or drops pea seed in the garden. I
like to think that instinct, impulse would carry on the world, that
nature gives hints when to plant & when to stick poles & when to
gather. But the turning out of the farmers in this November sky
with coats & mittens to spring work, seems to show that calculation as well as instinct must be or that calculation must contravene
instinct. (*JMN* 5:478)

If Emerson's instinct was to cut and run, or stay indoors, postpon-
ing his inevitable work until a more genial and welcoming day, he
nevertheless seemed to see the folly of such an impulse. Revolutions
cannot wait upon the weather. It is probably worth noting that
just a week later, when the sun appropriately returned on May
Day, Emerson sat in the woods and "thought how wide are my
works & my plays from those of the great men I read of or think
of. And yet the solution of Napoleon whose life I have been reading, lies in my feelings & fancies" (*JMN* 5:487).

Two other issues deserve some consideration before we leave
these early months of 1838—two issues that give an interesting
indication of how tightly linked Emerson's impending storm in the
Boston washbowl was to other aspects of American history, both
past and present. To begin with actualities, the chilly April of this
year was further deformed for Emerson by a public event that not
only moved him deeply but also (and this has not generally been
noticed) intertwined itself with and exacerbated the complex emo-

tions that his projected defiance of ecclesiastical authority had already stirred up. I refer to the removal of the Cherokee nation from their homes in the east to lands beyond the Mississippi River. This tragic event, initiated by Jackson's administration, was to be carried out by President Van Buren, commencing on May 23, 1838 (two days before Emerson's thirty-fifth birthday). This issue caused much agitation in Concord and Emerson found himself, willy-nilly, in the thick of things. In his journal for April 19, he wrote of "this disaster of Cherokees" as something that would "blacken my days & nights." Feeling powerless, Emerson asked himself: "Why shriek? Why strike ineffectual blows?" (*JMN* 5:475). But the matter could not be disposed of and that very night, as Emerson noted the next day, he had "ill dreams"—"phantoms" that led him to "feel that every act, every thought, every cause, is bipolar & in the act is contained the counteract. If I strike, I am struck. If I chase, I am pursued. If I push, I am resisted.

If he hesitated to strike a blow, he did so, one might say, not so much because it was likely to be "ineffectual" as because it was likely to provoke a reaction that would make *him* feel ineffectual or threatened. Emerson, in other words, contemplating the general question of striking out at authority, finds himself facing the inevitability of violent response. His willingness to accept that response would be, in a very real sense, the precondition of his acting in the first place—whether that action was an impudent letter to Martin Van Buren or a bold oration flung in the face of Andrews Norton and the rest of the Harvard Divinity Faculty. Though he might wince in advance, he would be determined not to turn away from the blow when it was offered. And indeed, in his journal for October 1838, in the midst of the violent turmoil following his performance, Emerson would write: "It seems not unfit that the Scholar should deal plainly with society & tell them that he saw well enough before he spoke the consequence of his speaking, that up there in his silent study by his dim lamp he foreheard this Babel of outcries." He knew that the "bats & owls & nocturnal beasts ... would howl & shriek & fly at the torch bearer." Their "taunts & cries of hatred & anger" he foreknew and foresuffered. They had in fact fueled his fire and would continue to do so: "I have a great deal more to say that will shock you" (*JMN* 7:105).

What Emerson actually had to say to President Van Buren probably did not shock him very much, partly because the celebrated letter dated April 23 seems never to have reached him directly, and partly also because chief executives become understandably inured to such things. But it is interesting to note that the letter as sent was somewhat toned down from the fiery draft which we find in Emerson's journals. Strong language of the following sort was excised: "Sir we have no patience to argue this matter. . . . when houses burn or assassins strike men cry Fire & Murder without attempting logic. . . . We will not bear it. . . . Your chair is rottenness. . . ." (*JMN* 12:27–29). Though one might argue plausibly that Emerson rightly felt at the last that a degree of moderation would be more effective than vituperation, or that the President deserved more respect, it is probably worth speculating that Emerson's initial draft reflects the supercharged emotion which his own life situation was generating that spring. "This tragic Cherokee business," Emerson wrote in his journal on April 23, "is like dead cats around one's neck." His own letter, he added, was "merely a Scream but sometimes a scream is better than a thesis" (*JMN* 5:477). Normal politics might best be conducted with reasoned arguments, but an incipient revolution demands a battle cry.

The anger that percolates through Emerson's journal entries in this difficult period when he nerved himself for the dramatic utterances of his revolutionary summer is clearly directed at paternal, or patriarchal, figures. By February 1839, Emerson would be able to allegorize the generational conflict in a humorous anecdote (" 'A lovely child! I promise you he will be a great scholar.' A dear little child with soft hair. Tomorrow he will defy you" [*JMN* 7:168]); but the troubled prelude to Emerson's Thermidor cannot really be marked *giocoso*. In June, infuriated at those who insisted on strict decorum in their ministers and religious texts, Emerson called them "old grannies" who "squeak & gibber & do what they call sounding an alarm" (*JMN* 7:22); significantly, the phrase "squeak and gibber," drawn from *Hamlet,* would reappear in a crucial passage in the July oration at Dartmouth. Echoing Brutus, he pilloried "the foolishest preaching—which bayed at the moon" that he was subjected to in Concord and lashed out at his own step-grandfather, Dr. Ripley: "Go, hush, old man, whom years have taught no truth."[2] By the end of the month, Emerson was prepared to articulate his patricidal feelings in a ringing journal entry: "Do let the new generation speak the truth, & let our grandfathers die" (*JMN* 7:39).

But the most fascinating aspect by far of Emerson's revulsion of feeling toward his elders touches both his family relations and a crucial issue in American history. In view of Emerson's manifest interest in New England's past, especially as that past intertwined itself with the story of his own ancestors, it is hard not to notice (and feel that Emerson himself must at some level have been aware of) the fact that his fateful spring of 1838 marked precisely the two-hundredth anniversary of the excommunication of Mistress Anne Hutchinson from the First Church of Boston (March 22, 1638).[3] Allusions to this event surface in Emerson's journal at least by May 6: "The antagonism of goodies.—Sir, sir, did you speak of the S[unday]. S[chool].?—Pardon me, sir, I did.—Sir you are an antinomian" (*JMN* 5:492). Three days later, Emerson's defiance characteristically provoked its reaction internally, and he was moved to issue a warning to himself: "You have good philosophy & disdain the feeble routine & mere verbal learning & ritual virtue of the School & the Church. Well beware of Antinomianism. All men have a slight distrust of your novelties & think you do not esteem the old laws of true witness, just dealing, chaste conversing as much as they. They have some reason. For as they make a bad use of their old truths so we make a bad use of our new ones" (*JMN* 5:495). Writing to Carlyle on the very next day, Emerson called his wife Lidian "an incarnation of Christianity" and praised her for keeping his "philosophy from Antinomianism."[4]

There is little doubt that Emerson's conciliatory tone in this letter stemmed not only from his own inner doubts but also from an awareness that his testy friend (and future editor of *Oliver Cromwell's Letters and Speeches*) had deeply conservative instincts and could be expected to sniff at "Antinomianism." Indeed, when Bronson Alcott turned up at Carlyle's doorstep in 1842 with his decidedly unorthodox vegetarian gospel of salvation, Carlyle sniffed heartily to Emerson in a letter: "The disease of Puritanism was *Antinomianism;*—very strange, does that still affect the *ghost* of Puritanism?"[5] Emerson himself could express his hope to Margaret Fuller in 1840 that "our Dial [the new Transcendental journal] will get to be a little *bad,*" complaining that "this first number is not enough so to scare the tenderest bantling of Conformity" (*L* 2:316). But Carlyle, in the same letter quoted above, kept to true form in saying, "I cannot bid you quit the *Dial;* tho' it too, alas, is *Antinomian* somewhat!"

Though Emerson's interest in the Antinomian Crisis could have been rekindled by his reading of John Winthrop's *Journal* in 1835 as he prepared his "Historical Discourse" on the town of Concord,[6] there is another probable source that is literally much closer to home, namely, his father's *Historical Sketch of the First Church In Boston.* Here we have impressive evidence, I believe, for speculating that Emerson's self-consciously Antinomian posture in 1838 was profoundly involved with his attitude toward his father—an attitude which Emerson himself willfully, it might be said, wrapped in obscurity. It is difficult to say anything accurate about Waldo's relation to William Emerson, since his father died when he was eight years old and Emerson rarely spoke of him. Oliver Wendell Holmes reports the opinion of a friend of the family that "Waldo bore a strong resemblance to his father; the other children resembled their mother."[7] If Emerson himself knew of this supposed physical resemblance, it might have increased his determination to differentiate his own beliefs and opinions from those of his father as he boldly repudiated his father's ministerial profession.

In the most substantive reference he made to his father—a passage in a letter to his older brother William, written in 1850—

after remarking on the man's severity to the children, and in particular on the "mortal terror" which he inspired in the young Waldo by his autocratic insistence on the virtue of salt water bathing, Emerson notes: "his printed or written papers, as far as I know, only show candour & taste, or I should almost say, docility, the principal merit possible to that early ignorant & transitional *Month-of-March*, in our New England culture" (*L* 4:179). If this studiedly vague remark actually has reference to William Emerson's *Historical Sketch* (published in 1812 in a volume, also containing several sermons, which Emerson owned),[8] the world *docility* constitutes a reasonably accurate assessment, since this pastor of the First Church in Boston—twelfth in a line directly descending from the founders of the church—contented himself as a historian with justifying the official position of the religious establishment, particularly as regards the Antinomian Crisis.

The portion of his *Historical Sketch* that William Emerson completed before his death in 1811 covers about one hundred fifty years of history and occupies some two hundred printed pages, yet almost one-fifth of the whole is devoted to the two years (1636–38) that comprised the Antinomian Crisis. Governor Winthrop, predictably the hero of the story, is shown to be a supremely temperate man, "equally cautious of imbibing erroneous doctrine himself, and of rashly censuring the errours of others." Pastor Emerson patiently details the manner in which "one heretical opinion paved the way for another, and schism succeeded schism":

> It was maintained, that the Holy Ghost dwells in a believer as much, as he dwells in heaven; that a man is justified, before he believes; that faith is no cause of justification; that the letter of the scripture holds forth nothing, but a covenant of works; that the covenant of grace, which can be known only to believers, is the vital principle of the scriptures; that a man may attain to high eminence in sanctification, gifts, and graces, even so as to have special communion with Christ, and after all be damned. In short, with the persons holding these notions, nothing would answer, but an immediate revelation, assuring of divine acceptance.[9]

With appropriate allowance made for technical language and changing rhetorical fashions, it is as if the historian were preparing to describe his own son's apostasy two hundred years later. As Ralph Waldo would say in his Divinity School Address: "Yourself a newborn bard of the Holy Ghost,—cast behind you all conformity, and acquaint men at first hand with Deity" (*CW* 1:90). Or, in "The Transcendentalist": "He easily incurs the charge of antinomianism by his avowal that he, who has the Lawgiver, may with safety not only neglect, but even contravene every written commandment" (ibid., p. 204).

William Emerson also describes the famous Cambridge Synod held in the summer of 1637 to deal with these "erroneous opinions." The moderators were Thomas Hooker and "Rev. Peter Bulkley of Concord"—Waldo's ancestor in the seventh generation; and under the guidance of these two distinguished divines, the Synod resolved, among other things, that "an assemblage of females, consisting of sixty or more, as is now every week formed, in which one of them, in the character of principal and prophetess, undertakes to expound the scriptures, resolve casuistical cases, and establish doctrines, is determined to be irregular and disorderly." They also held that "though a private member may ask a question publickly after sermon for information, yet this ought to be very wisely and sparingly done, and never without leave obtained of the elders." [10] Here was to be the nub of the question for William's son: his divine right to "spiritual independence." As he would say at Dartmouth: "A false humility, a complaisance to reigning schools, or to the wisdom of antiquity, must not defraud me of supreme possession of this hour. If any person have less love of liberty, and less jealousy to guard his integrity, shall he therefore dictate to you and me? Say to such doctors . . . our day is come; we have been born out of the eternal silence; and now will we live,—live for ourselves,—and not as the pall-bearers of a funeral" (*CW* 1:102).

What needs to be stressed about William Emerson's *Historical Sketch* is that the question of "antinomianism" is not simply part of the story that he was bound to tell as chronicler of the First

Church. It is, in fact, the theme of his tale. And it culminates in his enthusiastic account of the pastorship of Charles Chauncy, the chief opponent of Jonathan Edwards and other apologists for the revivalistic Great Awakening of the eighteenth century. For William Emerson, Charles Chauncy was "a great man," and "it is therefore with a trembling hand" that he undertakes "to sketch the eminent and various merits of the late reverend and learned doctor."[11] (We ought at this point to remind ourselves that William Emerson's hero worship led him to name his youngest son Charles Chauncy.) Paying particular attention to Chauncy's work in the 1740s as an antagonist of Edwards, Whitefield, and other evangelicals, the historian first notices a sermon of 1742 "on the outpouring of the Holy Ghost":

> In this excellent discourse may be found the following sentiment, that the extraordinary effusions of the Holy Ghost did not make the subjects of them better men. This undoubtedly is a correct notion, and had been advanced by Whichcote and other english divines; but it was a novel sentiment among american theologians when Chauncy uttered it, and would by many be received with distrust, at the present day.[12]

What was still a source of distrust in 1810 or 1811 continued such until at least 1838, when William's troublesome offspring would step forth as a newborn bard of the Holy Ghost and directly challenge what, to his father, was an eminently "correct notion."

Chauncy's most celebrated treatise, *Seasonable Thoughts on the State of Religion in New-England,* is singled out for special praise by William Emerson, particularly for its historical preface which, in Chauncy's words, gives "an account of the antinomians, familists, and libertines, who infected these churches above an hundred years ago; very needful for these days; the like spirit and errours prevailing now, as did then." Bringing the issue up to date, William Emerson comments:

The story of the early spread of antinomianism in this country, with which he introduces the work, is interesting to every lover of american history as well, as to divines. He could hardly have better described, with the aid of inspiration, the temper and conduct of modern enthusiasts, than he has described them, in the practice of the antinomians of his own days.[13]

For Ralph Waldo's father, Chauncy's account of the "antinomian" Great Awakening and its roots in the Hutchinsonian antinomianism of the seventeenth century is thus seen as an uncanny prophecy of like tendencies in the nineteenth century. One feels in reading this (and could Waldo have avoided similar sentiments in perusing his father's *Sketch?*), that two hundred years of history have collapsed in on themselves and the famous performance in front of the Harvard Divinity Faculty somehow blends confusedly into a composite image of Anne Hutchinson before the church elders, the revivalists opposing Chauncy, and Ralph Waldo at once recalling his father's harshness and dismissing him blandly for docility and ignorance.

"All history becomes subjective," Emerson was to write; "in other words there is properly no history, only biography" (*W* 2:10). And Emerson must surely have read the following passage in his father's *Sketch* with a certain satisfaction, both for the constitutional levity that—for once, at least—seduced William Emerson into a drily witty laconicism and for his own awareness that various household anecdotes linked him with his great-grandfather, Joseph Emerson of Malden:

Some ministers indeed there were, who secretly and openly favoured these, what they called, revivals of religion, and zealously cooperated with Mr. Whitfield and his friends, invited them into their pulpits, and either published or wrote in their behalf. Among the clergy of this description were Messrs. Moodey of York, Emerson of Malden, and Bliss of Concord. The first was great-grandfather, the two last grandfathers of the writer of this tract.[14]

We have here, perhaps, a sufficient indication of the ambiguities—the mixture of antagonisms and continuities — which informed what we might call the Emersonian tradition, particularly as regards the history of religious controversy in America. In 1823, Ralph Waldo entered this significant anecdote in his journal: " 'Where are you going Mr. Whitfield?' said Dr. Chauncy. 'I'm going to Boston, sir.' — 'I'm very sorry for it,' said Dr. C. 'So is the Devil' replied the eloquent preacher" (*JMN* 2:369).

[II]

It is not easy to separate with absolute clarity the various springs of impulse and intent that finally issued in the summer of 1838 as the two streams labeled Divinity School Address and Dartmouth College Oration. And in fact, it is useful to conceive of the two addresses as flowing, initially at least, from a common if complex source. Emerson received the invitations to deliver both speeches in that chilly March–April to which we have already paid some attention, when he wrote his letter to Van Buren and meditated on his own role in relation to the necessity of protest, generational conflict, and revolution, as well as worrying about the inevitability of antagonizing — indeed, alienating — relatives, friends, and colleagues.

By May 9, obviously struggling deeply with conflicting feelings, Emerson vowed "never [to] scorn a man again" and attempted to force himself to a higher position, a kind of ultimate sublimation of Christianity, whence all differences would fall away and he would be enabled to say: "Henceforth I will call my enemy by my own name, for he is serving me with his might, exposing my errors, stigmatising my faults" (*JMN* 5:494). If it seems as if Emerson was trying improbably to combine the roles of revolutionary, social engineer, scholar, prophet, and martyr, corroboration is not far to seek. He would get more deeply into the issue of martyrdom in late May and early June. But on May 13, "walking under the pleasant

118

cloud-strown dim-starred sky" and searching "for topics for the young men at Dartmouth," one thing occurred to him, "namely, that the cure for bigotry & for all partiality is the recurrence to the experience, that we have been in our proper person Robinson Crusoe, & Saint John, Dr Pedant & Sardanapalus" (*JMN* 5:498). In view of the fact that this notion never found its way into the Dartmouth Oration at all, we may notice that Emerson is actually talking about his envisioned *postures* for the coming summer and not about his subjects. As in his dream on the night of April 19, when he felt that striking and being struck were necessarily the twin halves of a single act, Emerson seems quite simply to be predicting that he would be up in the pulpit dishing it out at one moment and down below taking it on the chin the next — or rather, doing both things at once. So he concludes his May 13 entry by saying:

> In the hour of spiritual pride when, unsuspecting, &, as it were, of course, we don the judgment robes, let it qualify the sentence that damns my brother, that I have been him & presently shall very naturally become him again.

It will be useful to keep this passage in mind when we notice later the extent to which the Dartmouth Oration constitutes a direct reaction to the Divinity School Address — except that the reaction is Emerson's own and was conceived before the event ("the Scholar . . . saw well enough before he spoke the consequence of his speaking . . .").

To put it another way, though Emerson was preparing quite seriously to don the prophet's robe, he was simultaneously forced to see the absurdity and arrogance of such a posture, and thus to view himself at the same time (as he would say at Dartmouth) as "a poor, ignorant man, in a white-seamed, rusty coat" talking to ordinary boys at a country college (*CW* 1:114). Here, one might say, is the slightly humorous, sharply realistic counterpoise that usually acts as ballast to Emerson's Transcendental flights and makes them credible. He always knows precisely where he is, and that ambience may seem mean enough ("a bare common, in snow puddles"), but the translations and transformations of the spirit are nevertheless still possible.

It is clear that the central impulse that underlay Emerson's twin utterances of July 1838 was his sense of himself as, alternately, an insignificant and fitfully rancorous scholar, on the one hand, and a true prophet, on the other (in June, he wrote in his journal: "Sometimes I am the organ of the Holy Ghost & sometimes of a vixen petulance" [*JMN* 7:9]). And it is possible to see the common genesis of both speeches taking place, in fact, as he was planning his Phi Beta Kappa address in the spring and summer of 1837. On May 7th of that year, under the heading of a sentence from Proverbs (29:18) that would serve as text for the opening of "The Method of Nature" — "Where there is no vision, the people perish" — Emerson complained about the empty sermonizing of Dr. Ripley's assistant, Barzillai Frost, in a passage that would be used in the middle of the Divinity School Address (*JMN* 5:324). The strain is picked up on July 29 in the midst of a passage used in "The American Scholar" ("Books are for the scholar's idle times"), though the sentence in question — "The poet, the prophet is caught up into the mount of vision, & thereafter is constrained to declare what he has seen" (*JMN* 5:347) — was excised from the passage. Most probably Emerson did so because he realized that it had less to do with his Phi Beta Kappa subject than with the more intense utterance, destined for the Divinity School, which was somehow already germinating. Four days later, he set down two sentences which seem again to belong with "The American Scholar," but are actually part of a new impulse: "Scholars; who being poor made many rich. Eyes were they to the blind, feet were they to the lame" (*JMN* 5:350). The latter sentence, drawn from the book of Job (29:15), would serve as text for the Dartmouth Oration. Along with the former, it records that sense of alternating dilation and deflation which would inform the two speeches of the following summer.

The Protest

It is not at all difficult to demonstrate that the Divinity School Address and the Dartmouth Oration developed throughout the spring and early summer of 1838 as Siamese twins that would be separated only shortly before their public appearances on July 15 and 24, respectively. On April 30, for example, Emerson complained again about Barzillai Frost, who was to be the central paradigm of the "formalist" preacher in the Divinity School Address: "[He] grinds & grinds in the mill of a truism & nothing comes out but what was put in. But the moment he or I desert the tradition & speak a spontaneous thought, instantly poetry, wit, hope, virtue, learning, anecdote, all flock to our aid" (*JMN* 5:481). As Emerson immediately notes, "this topic were no bad one for the Dartmouth College boys whom I am to address in July"; and, indeed, the passage is used in that oration. But precisely the same topic informs the passage in the Divinity School Address where Frost is actually alluded to.

On May 6, Emerson began an entry with thoughts of "the dead pond which our church is" and then sketched out a passage, used in the Divinity School Address, which likened the people to the "Imperial Guard of Napoleon," needing only a crisis and a leader to awaken their "latent virtue that slumbers in these lazy times in a church, in a college" (*JMN* 5:491–92). This quoted phrase, looking forward as it does to both of Emerson's speaking engagements at once, was naturally excised. But Napoleon appears in both speeches as a thinly veiled persona of the revolutionary speaker himself,[15] though Emerson removed a sentence from this passage when it went into the Divinity School Address which argued that "the masculine faculties of a quiet multitude" were only awaiting a revolution to demonstrate "their terror & their beauty." Such talk would have been wildly provocative for an audience of conservative theologians, most of whom were already convinced that atheistic Transcendentalism was simply a logical extension of the French disease that had commenced in 1789. But Emerson left in a sentence, obviously adumbrating his own stance in delivering his Address, which reported Napoleon's remark about Massena, "that he was not himself until the battle began to go against him; then awoke his powers of combination & he put on determination & Victory as a robe." As if to make up for having left out the sentence about revolutions, however, Emerson wickedly changed "determination" to "terror"; but adding, when he came to compose the Address: "So it is in rugged crises, in unweariable endurance, and in aims which put sympathy out of question, that the angel is shown" (*CW* 1:92). One wonders whether it was archness or honesty that persuaded Emerson to transform his Napoleonic avenging devil into a Concordian celestial creature with the mere turn of a sentence. But the truth is, he believed Napoleon combined both traits ("amidst all his fits of petulance or anger, a sentiment of justice still predominates" [*JMN* 5:483]), and on June 7, prior to filling two pages with quotations from Las Cases's *Journal of . . . Napoleon at Saint Helena,* Emerson cautioned himself to do likewise:

> . . . take care not to snap in petulance instead of jetting out in spouts of true flame. Reserve your fire. Keep your temper. Render soft answers. Bear & forbear. Do not dream of suffering for ten years yet. Do not let the word *martyrdom* ever scape out of the white fence of your teeth. Be sweet & courtly & merry these many long summers & autumns yet, & husband your strength so that when an authentic inevitable crisis comes, & you are fairly driven to the wall, cornered up in your Utica, you may then at last turn fairly round on the baying dogs, all steel — with all Heaven in your eye & die for love, with all heroes & angels to friend. (*JMN* 5:507)

Other journal passages throughout the month of June provide interesting glimpses of the various ways in which the two speeches are linked. On the 8th, Emerson set down a passage, filled with the spirit of Napoleon, which was taken up almost entirely into the Dartmouth Oration — except for the two opening sentences: "In this glorious summer day, I have taken a turn in my woods. How gaily the wind practises his graces there & every tree & all the woods bow with gentlest yet majestic elegance" (*JMN* 7:7). These sentences would provide partial inspiration for the magnificent opening of the Divinity School Address ("In this refulgent summer . . ."). Another single paragraph, entered on June 18, would be equally divided between the two speeches. More significant, perhaps, is this passage from the 27th:

> It is not much matter what you read, what you do. Be a scholar & you shall have the scholar's part of anything. As in the Counting Room, the merchant cares little whether the cargo be hides or barilla; the transaction a letter of credit or transfer of stocks; be it what it may, his commission comes gently out of it; so you shall get your commission out of the hour & the object whether it is a concentrated or a wasteful employment, even in reading a bad book, or working off the chare of a solicited criticism. (*JMN* 7:37)

The entry went directly into the Dartmouth Oration with various, mostly minor, changes. The most important one occurs in the last phrase, where the Oration reads: "even in reading a dull book, or working off a stint of mechanical day labor, which your necessities or the necessities of others impose" (*CW* 1:114). Emerson quite understandably substitutes "labor" for the rather archaic term "chare"; but that curious word suggests not simply *work* but also an *occasion* or *business*. In its original form, I believe the phrase carries a sharp personal reference which Emerson thought it best to diffuse when he delivered his Oration. The occasion which Emerson fully expected to solicit "criticism" — a criticism that he had great hopes of ultimately profiting by — was the Divinity School Address, which was doubtless already "growing under [his] eye" (*JMN* 7:42).

By far the most intriguing evidence, however, suggesting to what extent Emerson was preoccupied at this time with defining and distinguishing his two occasions and discourses, is contained in an extended letter that he wrote to Bronson Alcott on June 28 (*L* 2:138–40). Alcott had sent Emerson a long manuscript entitled

Psyche, and Emerson undertook the "irksome" task (as he called it in a letter of the same date to Margaret Fuller) of annotating and criticizing the work.[16] Emerson liked "the general design of the book," which he described "as an affirmation of the spiritual nature to an unbelieving age." He found "the topics good," "the form excellent," the ideas "commanding," and the book "holy." What perplexed him was the "want of unity of design in the book itself." And Emerson then put an interesting question to Alcott: "Is it a Gospel—a book of exhortation, & popular devotion? Or, is it a book of thought addressed to cultivated men? Which of these two?" As Emerson proceeded methodically to outline for Alcott the differing natures of these two sorts of scripture, he clearly— whether consciously or not—was in the process of clarifying his own intent with regard to the two discourses promised for delivery in July, and puzzling over problems of style and literary strategy which had direct relevance to his own practice:

> 1. Is it a Gospel? It evinces on every page great elevation of character, & often assumes, in the thought & expression, the tone of a prophet. Well; let it preach, then, to the chidden world. There is sin & sorrow enough to make a call; & the preacher believes in his heart. And, in this view, I certainly would not criticise this scroll any more than that of Habbakuk or Jeremy; but would sit & take with docility my portion of reproof.—But, as I read, it departs from that character. To the prophetic tone belongs simplicity, not variety, not taste, not criticism. As a book of practical holiness, this seems to me not effective. This is fanciful, playful, ambitious, has a periphrastic style & masquerades in the language of Scripture, *Thee & Thou, Hath & Doth.* The prophet should speak a clear discourse straight home to the conscience in the language of earnest conversation.

Emerson surely set himself an impossible task in attempting succinctly to define the "prophetic tone." If such was, as I believe, to be the essential character of the Divinity School Address, Emerson himself was to have problems eliminating, or at least integrating, "variety," "taste," and "criticism," not to mention "the language of Scripture." (He went on to advise Alcott to drop "the Scriptural termination, as in do*eth*, work*eth*," but would retain it himself in the Address erratically: "See how this rapid intrinsic energy worketh everywhere. . . . Man is the wonder-worker. . . . He saith yea and nay, only. . . . God is, not was . . . He speaketh, not spake. . . . None believeth in the soul of man . . . no man goeth alone.") His central prescription, at all events, was certainly sound and a fair version of the Emersonian aesthetic: "The prophet should speak a clear discourse straight home to the conscience in the language of earnest conversation." The achievement of the Divinity School Address would lie in uniting the clarity and naturalness of venacular discourse with the stance and tone of Jeremy.

Under his second heading Emerson placed "a book of thought addressed to literary men," which would certainly serve as a fair definition of "Literary Ethics." But in the description that follows —"the condition of which, is, that an observer quite passionless & detached—a mere eye & pen—sees & records, without praise without blame, without personal relation—like a god"—Emerson articulated, once again, his apparent aspiration and not his consistent practice. Since the Address and the Oration flowed from a single well of agitated energy, it would hardly be possible to keep them entirely separate as literary genres. "There runs throughout this book," he continued to Alcott, "as already intimated, a tone of scarcely less than prophetic pretension; which, however allowable in a gospel, is wholly out of place in philosophy, where truth, not duty, is the question." Emerson would find it as hard to maintain that distinction as Edgar Allan Poe did to separate Beauty and Truth.

One final aspect of Emerson's criticism deserves mention. Alcott would become well-known in Transcendental circles, and notorious outside them, for the vagueness, or—as it used to be called —the "ideality" of his prose; and Emerson himself, not entirely free of this tendency, would occasionally find himself faulted for the same reason. It is thus interesting to notice more than a touch of exasperation creeping into his letter when he reaches this issue. "I demand your propositions," he writes; "your definitions; your thoughts ... your facts observed in nature." Alcott's method Emerson found "the reverse of this. Your page is a series of touches. You play. You play with the thought: never strip off your coat, & dig, & strain, & drive into the root & heart of the matter." Lacking this radical relation to reality, *Psyche* was, for Emerson, "all stir & no go," and made him think "of the Indian jungles, vast & flowering, where the sky & stars are visible alway, but no house, no mountain, no man, no definite objects whatever, & no change, or progress." Curiously enough, within scarcely a year, Carlyle would criticize Emerson in almost precisely the same terms ("I long to see some concrete thing, some Event, Man's Life, American Forest, or piece of Creation, which this Emerson loves and wonders at, well *Emersonized:* depictured by Emerson, filled with the life of Emerson").[17] Clearly, Emerson himself was sharply aware of, and exercised by, the Transcendental propensity for moonshiny abstraction which bore little relation to the world of common experience. In the discourses he was preparing for the summer, he would both confront the problem and attempt to remedy it.

Despite his doubts, apprehensions, and occasionally flagging spirits, Emerson knew that he was as ready as he would ever be to assert himself fully and irrevocably. "I believe, I believe," he wrote in his journal on June 21. "I love the flush of hope" (*JMN* 7:27). Three days later, on Sunday, June 24, Emerson prepared himself to take the plunge by consciously donning the mantle of the prophet and consecrating himself to the service of the Lord:

> Thou Awful Father! who so slowly uncoverest my nature & hope to my curiosity & faith, I lowly strive to keep thy law, to bow no knee to the Baals fine with what jewels, mystic with what poetry soever, but to keep erect that head which thou gavest me erect against the solicitations, &, if it should so be, against the physical & metaphysical terrors of the Universe. This it is to have immortal youth. (*JMN* 7:32–33)[18]

BALM IN GILEAD

[1]

On the first of April preceding that momentous July evening when Emerson was to deliver his bombshell, he told a group of divinity students informally that "the preacher should be a poet" (*JMN* 5:471).[19] To a large extent, that is precisely the "doctrine" of his Address, which is both an exposition and an *enactment* of that belief. One of the key concepts, and words, in the Address is "beauty," for Emerson was determined to prove that "the institution of preaching,—the speech of man to men" (CW 1:92), is utterly nugatory if moral truth is separated from the delight of living, such as Emerson himself frequently found to be the case in his own experience of listening to sermons. Indeed, as he redefined his own role and vocation, Emerson could hardly help translating the "institution of preaching" into that of lecturing, or essay writing, or the literary vocation generally. It is worth noting here that Emerson's phrase in the Address quoted above—"the speech of man to men"—undoubtedly has its source in a letter that Carlyle wrote him in August 1834, in which Carlyle expounded his view

> that now at last we have lived to see all manner of Poetics and Rhetorics and Sermonics, and one may say generally all manner of *Pulpits* for addressing mankind from, as good as broken and abolished: alas, yes; if you have any earnest meaning, which demands to be not only listened to but *believed* and *done,* you cannot (at

least I cannot) utter it *there,* but the sound sticks in my throat, as when a Solemnity were *felt* to have become a Mummery; and so one leaves the pasteboard coulisses, and three unities, and Blairs lectures, quite behind; and feels only that there is *nothing sacred,* then, but the *Speech of Man* to believing Men! *This,* come what will, was, is and forever must be *sacred;* and will one day doubtless anew environ itself with fit modes, with Solemnities that are *not* Mummeries.[20]

In reading such a passage, one begins to understand just how crucial a role Carlyle played in helping Emerson to unchurch himself and to believe fully in the potentially sacramental nature and function of all writing.[21] In the last paragraph of his Address, Emerson would argue that though "the Hebrew and Greek Scriptures contain immortal sentences, that have been bread of life to millions," they lacked "epical integrity" (*CW* 1:92)—by which he clearly meant *literary* integrity, since in the notebook entry out of which this passage developed, Emerson writes: "The hope of mankind must rest in the sometime appearance of a true Messiah who shall complete the Epos of moral nature & write out those laws for the charmed world to read & to obey" (*JMN* 12:11). There is no doubt that Emerson identified himself with this true Messiah (in his essay "The Poet" he would describe that exalted figure as "the man of Beauty," whom he associates with "the Son" or "the Sayer" —the poet or orator whose thought is finally "ejaculated as Logos, or Word" [*W* 3:4, 6, 40]). The "new teacher" whom Emerson looks for in the last sentence of his Address is obviously a version of himself, the Christ/Preacher/Poet who is charged with showing "that the Ought, that Duty, is one thing with Science, with Beauty, and with Joy" (*CW* 1:93). Accordingly, those two final words— Beauty and Joy—govern Emerson's startlingly heretical portrait in the Address of the archetypal preacher, Christ, who is offered to us as a kind of first-century aesthete, replete with "locks of beauty," who was "ravished" by the "supreme Beauty" of the soul's mystery and went out in a "jubilee of sublime emotion" to tell us all "that

God incarnates himself in man, and evermore goes forth anew to take possession of his world." The man who is most enamored of the "beauty of the soul" and the world in which it is incarnated is called to serve as "its priest or poet," and Emerson urges such men to feel their call "in throbs of desire and hope" (ibid., pp. 81–84).

Since Emerson believed fervently that "a man's sermon should be rammed with life" (*JMN* 5:465), it is precisely the absence of any evidence of living emotions or experiences that impels Emerson to pillory the unnamed "formalist" preacher whom he invokes in a striking *exemplum* about halfway through the Address:

> I once heard a preacher who sorely tempted me to say, I would go to church no more. Men go, thought I, where they are wont to go, else had no soul entered the temple in the afternoon. A snowstorm was falling around us. The snowstorm was real; the preacher merely spectral; and the eye felt the sad contrast in looking at him, and then out of the window behind him, into the beautiful meteor of the snow. He had lived in vain. He had no one word intimating that he had laughed or wept, was married or in love, had been commended, or cheated, or chagrined. If he had ever lived and acted, we were none the wiser for it. The capital secret of his profession, namely, to convert life into truth, he had not learned. Not one fact in all his experience, had he yet imported into his doctrine. This man had ploughed, and planted, and talked, and bought, and sold; he had read books; he had eaten and drunken; his head aches; his heart throbs; he smiles and suffers; yet was there not a surmise, a hint, in all the discourse, that he had ever lived at all. Not a line did he draw out of real history. The true preacher can always be known by this, that he deals out to the people his life,—life passed through the fire of thought. But of the bad preacher, it could not be told from his sermon, what age of the world he fell in; whether he had a father or a child; whether he was a freeholder or a pauper; whether he was a citizen or a countryman; or any other fact of his biography. (*CW* 1:85–86)[22]

Emerson, now in the role of preacher himself, remembering how it felt to be sitting in front of this sincere but sham formalist, proceeds to move in thought down into the congregation and records a typical parishioner's experience: boredom.[23] If habit had not brought him to the church, there would be no other reason for going, for there is nothing to attract him, no promise of reality, no pleasure. The true preacher, the true poet, bases his verbal art on personal experience in the actual world that surrounds us all, thus transmuting "life into truth." Otherwise, words are mere counters that leave us untouched.

Emerson's real genius here, however, lies in the business of the snowstorm. Playing the role of listener, he allows his wandering attention to move outside the window and find its sole available pleasure in the "beautiful meteor of the snow." Perhaps only a New England consciousness could have invented such a phrase; but then, Emerson is writing of what he knows and loves (as in his poem "The Snow-Storm"). The fine irony of the passage lies in the fact that the preacher should seem *spectral* compared even to the frigid and ghostly reality of snow (reminding ourselves that Emerson is actually describing the Reverend Barzillai *Frost* should increase our sense of how intricate is his play of imagination here).[24] What Emerson has done is to insist on some sort of interpretation between that which goes on inside the church and the beautiful world outside. His example suggests that the skillful preacher will attempt to do the same.

Now, in our backward movement through the Address, let us confront the magnificent strategies of the opening passage. On what was apparently a splendid Sunday evening in July 1838, Emerson mounted the pulpit in Divinity Hall to speak, nominally, to the senior class in divinity; but they were a small group, and the room was packed with faculty members and friends. Emerson's intent, as I have noted, was to *demonstrate* that "the preacher should be a poet," that religious truth and human pleasure must coexist, and that the two worlds of chapel and physical universe are mutually enriching. Accordingly, in a prose that is consciously purple, Emerson began his Address by inviting this sternly theological audience to allow its attention to wander, as his own had wandered on that boring Sunday in winter, beyond the chapel window to the ripe world of nature outside:

> In this refulgent summer it has been a luxury to draw the breath of life. The grass grows, the buds burst, the meadow is spotted with fire and gold in the tint of flowers. The air is full of birds, and sweet with the breath of the pine, the balm-of-Gilead, and the new hay. Night brings no gloom to the heart with its welcome shade. Through the transparent darkness the stars pour their almost spiritual rays. Man under them seems a young child, and his huge globe a toy. The cool night bathes the world as with a river, and prepares his eyes again for the crimson dawn. The mystery of nature was never displayed more happily. The corn and the wine have been freely dealt to all creatures, and the never-broken silence with which the old bounty goes forward, has not yielded yet one word of explanation. One is constrained to respect the perfection of this world, in which our senses converse. (CW 1:76)

An example of how inattentive even some of the most devoted Emersonians have been to the master's art is provided by Stephen Whicher's comment: "the address itself was calculated to give no offense, on grounds of vocabulary at least, to a Unitarian audience."[25] It is *precisely* in its vocabulary that the barefaced effrontery of Emerson's gambit resides. There is probably not another place in all his writings where Emerson is so consciously arch. One of the few astute comments I have found on this passage belongs to Jonathan Bishop: "the immediate rhetorical motive, evidently enough, is shock: an address to a small group of graduating divinity students is not supposed to begin by an appeal to the sensual man."[26] Emerson's stance, as Bishop says, is that of a "voluptuary," and the word is well-chosen. Following what Bishop calls the "unusually aureate" *refulgent*—which suggests a kind of shining-forth, or epiphany, in the summer's beauty—Emerson explodes his real charge in the sentence: *luxury*. We must remind ourselves that Emerson's audience, trained in theology, was not likely to overlook the implications of that red flag, for *luxuria*, one of the seven deadly sins, means lust. Although that technical meaning, of course, is not Emerson's, a calculated air of aesthetic indulgence permeates this opening remark.[27]

In the sentences that follow, Emerson measures out his language with extreme care to one end: the creation in words of an unfallen world of the senses where formal, traditional religion is unnecessary because nature provides its own sacraments. It is hard to see how Emerson's frank appropriation of religious terms and concepts could have failed to offend much of his audience. The rays of the stars are *"almost* spiritual" (is not heaven then *really* above our heads? Conversely, can a natural phenomenon *almost* approach spiritual truth?). Man, returned to the innocence of childhood, is bathed by the cool night as in baptismal waters, whereby his eyes are *prepared* (a technical term)[28] for the dawn (a familiar type of the coming of Christ).[29] Another technical term, *mystery,* is applied to nature; but unlike theological mysteries, this one is openly and happily "displayed."[30] In the next sentence, Emerson announces that the central sacrament, the Eucharist (over which, of course, he had created a controversy when he left the Second Church of Boston six years earlier), is "freely dealt to all creatures" by nature—without condition or exclusion. Then, to a congregation still committed to the belief that the creation is fully expounded in the Bible, Emerson states that no "word of explanation" has been provided—and implies that none is needed.

Finally, this Christian audience, all children of the Puritans, are told that they are "constrained to respect" not (as we should expect) the dogmas and duties of their faith but rather the *perfection* of *this* world, a totally natural world, the one "in which our senses converse." Can we really doubt that to most of Emerson's listeners, all of this seemed the sheerest effrontery (although to many others since, it has seemed merely a flowery portal, the blandly poetic induction to a serious theological dissertation)? But it is clear that Emerson's aim was not fundamentally to offer an insult but to enact a meaning which would develop organically in the course of his Address and to which he would "come full circle" at the end: namely, as we have noted, that Ought and Beauty, Duty and Joy, Science and Ecstasy, Divinity and the World, must merge in the new hypostatic unity of a living religion of the soul.

There is "a sort of drollery," Henry James remarks, in the spectacle of a society in which the author of the Divinity School Address could be considered "profane." What they failed to see, James continues, is "that he only gave his plea for the spiritual life the advantage of a brilliant expression."[31] Perhaps we should add that Emerson was attempting to demonstrate, in fact, that the "spiritual life" could scarcely be said to exist at all without its adequate expression. Such was the extent of his developing faith in the responsibilities and potentialities of the literary vocation.

[11]

Having said all of the foregoing, I must, to use Gertrude Stein's phrase, "begin as if to begin"[32] and start over again. In this fashion, perhaps, we shall be taking a page from Emerson himself, whose works, it might be said, in imitation of his life, consist of a series of brave beginnings and renewals. In a letter to Bronson Alcott in April 1839, Emerson spoke of "writing a little and arranging old papers more" as he worked on the preparation of his first book of *Essays*. "By and by," he wrote, alluding to the projected volume, "I hope to get a shapely book of Genesis" (*L* 2:194). Thinking once more of Holmes' description of *Nature*, it is amusing to consider that Emerson had commenced by writing his Revelations and then was forced to go back and provide a foundation for his literary project by creating a Book of Genesis—stopping along the way, I might add, to set down at least one prophetic book also. Perhaps it was precisely through a perpetual reconceiving of his world that Emerson hoped to achieve the "immortal youth" which he prayed for as he consecrated himself to the prophetic task on June 24, 1838. At all events his mind was certainly running on this track the following spring, for two weeks after writing to Alcott about his Genesis, he said to Margaret Fuller (regarding her own "Experiment Chapter" for a projected book on Goethe): "On our beginnings seems somehow our self possession to depend a good deal, as happens so often in music" (*L* 2:197).

The superb self-possession that Emerson achieved in the Divinity School Address depends to a large extent, I believe, on its magisterial exordium. This is Emerson's music, his very self. And such a start could scarcely have been accomplished, as Emerson was to say of Whitman, without a long foreground. The opening of the Address draws upon an extraordinarily complex fund of experience in order to achieve its rich density of meaning and range of reference. It is well worth trying to account even more fully for the electrifying effect of Emerson's bravest beginning.

Once again, we may take our first hint from Oliver Wendell Holmes. Writing of the opening of the Address, Holmes not improbably compares it to the Song of Songs. But *this*, he continues,

> was the prelude of a discourse which, when it came to be printed, fared at the hands of many a theologian, who did not think himself a bigot, as the roll which Baruch wrote with ink from the words of Jeremiah fared at the hands of Jehoiakim, the King of Judah. He listened while Jehudi read the opening passages. But "when Jehudi had read three or four leaves he cut it with the penknife, and cast it into the fire that was on the hearth, until all the roll was consumed in the fire that was on the hearth." Such was probably the fate of many a copy of this famous discourse.

Holmes' analogy, drawn from the thirty-sixth chapter of Jeremiah, is intriguing and scarcely seems an offhand remark, since he goes on to characterize Emerson's discourse as at once "reverential" but "also revolutionary," an "alarming manifesto"; and yet he writes, "so changed is the whole aspect of the theological world since the time when that discourse was delivered that it is read as calmly today as a common 'Election Sermon,' if such are ever read at all."[33] Holmes' suggestion is startling, yet it was probably no more so to his readership in 1884 than was, as he claimed, Emerson's Address itself. For who would remember then, or now, that after about 1660, and continuing for well over a hundred years more, as Perry Miller tells us, the election sermons fell almost without exception into the category of the jeremiad: "The great jeremiads of the 1670's were the literary triumphs of the decade and deserve to rank among the achievements of the New England mind; some of them made so deep an impression that they were cited and quoted down to the eve of the Revolution. . . . Fifty years after the Great Migration, the literary form in which the New England mind found its most appropriate expression was a jeremiad. By 1680 forensic indictments of an apostatizing New England in the name of an idealized picture of its primitive sanctity had already become traditional and conventional." [34]

Miller's last sentence must surely ring some sort of a bell for the imaginative reader of Emerson's Address. But before we allow ourselves to be carried off irrevocably by the blast resistless, we ought to stop and ask ourselves patiently what in the world Holmes meant—if indeed he *did* mean it — by suggesting that the Divinity School Address might be seen as a species of jeremiad. Holmes, unfortunately, does not specify further. But one might, if one wished, formulate some general propositions to fit the case; as, for example, by pointing out that Emerson's discourse, like a jeremiad, seeks to respond to such questions as, "Where have we gone wrong?" or "What is our real duty?" or, perhaps better, "What must I do to be saved?" Such questions do seem to align themselves with the overall tendency and tone of Emerson's discourse. Perhaps that is all Holmes intended to suggest.

Let us remind ourselves, however, that we were examining the opening of Emerson's Address and trying to account more circumstantially for its peculiar eloquence and power:

> In this refulgent summer it has been a luxury to draw the breath of life. The grass grows, the buds burst, the meadow is spotted with fire and gold in the tint of flowers. The air is full of birds, and

sweet with the breath of the pine, the balm-of-Gilead, and the new hay.

The description is a curious mixture of the concrete and the abstract, one might argue; of real experience and of an idealized world. We have already noticed how Emerson drew on a particular journal entry for June 8, 1838 ("In this glorious summer day, I have taken a turn in my woods"). Another one occurs on June 22: "Splendid summer, abounding in South Wind whose fine haze makes the distant woods look twice as distant; & man & beast & bird & insect see their corn & wine grow in beauty" (*JMN* 7:29). This clearly adds one more piece to our mosaic ("The corn and the wine have been freely dealt to all creatures"), providing an example of how Emerson, as we have seen, could take his own experience in nature and give it a quasi-theological twist. Indeed, on March 28, 1835, Emerson made this entry in his journal:

> If life were long enough among my thousand & one works should be a book of Nature whereof "Howitt's Seasons" should be not so much the model as the parody. It should contain the Natural history of the woods around my shifting camp for every month in the year. It should tie their astronomy, botany, physiology, meteorology, picturesque, & poetry together. No bird, no bug, no bud should be forgotten on his day & hour. (*JMN* 5:25)

Emerson's reference is to William Howitt's extremely popular *Book of the Seasons,* which combined detailed natural description with sentimental and/or moralizing commentary. A chapter was provided for every month of the year, and each such chapter was adorned with a suitable scriptural epigraph. Despite Emerson's disparaging remark, he seems clearly to have been influenced by the book, both in his journal and subsequently in the Address. Under date of June 1835 we find: "It is luxury to live in this beautiful month. One never dares expect a happy day, but the hardest ascetic may inhale delighted this breath of June" (*JMN*

5:139). Turning to the "June" chapter of Howitt's book, we find the following passage (one, by the way, which Henry Thoreau quoted in a college essay in 1836):[35]

> It is the very carnival of nature, and she is prodigal of her luxuries. It is luxury to walk abroad, indulging every sense with sweetness, loveliness, and harmony. It is luxury to stand beneath the forest side. . . . It is luxury to haunt the gardens of old-fashioned houses in the morning . . . or at eve, when the honeysuckle and the sweet-briar mingle their spirit with the breeze. It is luxury to plunge into the cool river. . . .[36]

We may notice how Emerson reduces Howitt's cloyingly sweet repetitions of his key term to one tersely powerful use, leaning heavily on its theological implications.

Indeed, it is hardly possible, so it seems, to stray very far from theology when considering Emerson's exordium, since another clear source for it was his own sermon "Summer," which he preached for the last time on July 16, 1837, almost exactly one year before he delivered the Divinity School Address.[37] The sermon is provided with a text from Psalms ("The day is thine, the night also is thine: thou hast prepared the light, and the sun. Thou hast set all the borders of the earth, thou hast made summer") and begins this way:

> In this grateful season, the most careless eye is caught by the beauty of the external world. The most devoted of the sons of gain cannot help feeling that there is pleasure in the blowing of the southwest wind; that the green tree with its redundant foilage and its fragrant blossoms shows fairer than it did a few weeks since when its arms were naked and its trunk was sapless. The inhabitants of cities pay a high tax for their social advantages, their increased civilization, in their exclusion from the sight of the unlimited glory of the earth. Imprisoned in streets of brick and stone, in tainted air and hot and dusty corners, they only get glimpses of the glorious sun, of the ever changing glory of the clouds, of the firmament and of the face

of the green pastoral earth which the great Father of all is now adorning with matchless beauty as one wide garden. Still something of the mighty process of vegetation forces itself on every human eye. The grass springs up between the pavements at our feet and the poplar and the elm send out as vigorous and as graceful branches to shade and to fan the town as in their native forest.[38]

Though the parallels to the opening of the Address are obvious, the differences are far more striking: "In this grateful season"; "In this refulgent summer." The first, with its rather archaic use of "grateful" (meaning *pleasurable*) and the nonspecific "season," is flaccid and conventional; the second, with its gorgeously ornate "refulgent" and particularized "summer," is weighty and actual. The opening of the Address does not rely on vague references to "beauty" or use trite epithets like "the sons of gain," "the glorious sun," or "the great Father" (Emerson studiously avoids any allusion to God in the opening of the Address). In addition, the sermon depends on the timeworn Romantic opposition of city and country and moralizes flatly about the "great Father of all." It is loaded with conventional locutions and contains only one truly concrete reference ("the poplar and the elm"; we shall see shortly how that generic "poplar" is particularized both naturalistically and theologically in its passage into the Address). The Address, in contrast, makes its theological point by means of subtle allusion and terse irony. Indeed, as we have seen, it tends to make a mockery of the traditional theology which it subsumes.

The fact that Emerson, as it were, translated his sermon "Summer" into the Divinity School Address actually provides an interesting hint which the occasion, Emerson's own stance, and his subject and manner only tend to underline, namely that the discourse is itself a sermon—unconventionally but unmistakably so (on August 6 he wrote to Carlyle: "I have written & read a kind of Sermon to the senior class of our Cambridge Theological School a fortnight ago").[39] Perhaps it could be described as Emerson's swan song in that genre. In any case, consideration of the Address as a sermon brings us again to an issue that we have touched on in examining the opening (and indeed closing) of *Nature*—the issue, that is, of Emerson's tendency to rely on a text ("submerged" or explicit) in what seems a traditional fashion, though the normal effect of his practice is to subvert that text, as he does in *Nature*. Other examples are to be found in (but are not limited to) the opening of "The Method of Nature" ("Where there is no vision, the people perish") and the Dartmouth Oration (from Job: "Eyes is he to the blind; feet is he to the lame"). The question, then, quite simply is: what text, if any, is embedded in the opening of the Divinity School Address?

For one thing, as we listen to Emerson's rhetoric once again ("In this refulgent summer it has been a luxury to draw the breath of life. The grass grows, the buds burst. . . . The air is full of birds, and sweet with the breath of the pine"), with its unmistakable suggestion of a new world coming to birth, it is possible, I think, to hear a curious echo: "In the beginning God created the heaven and the earth . . . [and] formed man of the dust of the ground, and breathed into his nostrils the breath of life." What better way, one might argue, to begin a sermon that will insist on the possibility of "new love," "new faith," "new sight," "new hope and new revelation," and, above all, preach the "doctrine of *inspiration* [emphasis added]" (*CW* 1:92, 80), than by reenacting, so to speak, that original occasion when man drew "the breath of life"? That crucial phrase from Genesis used in the exordium returns, with a significant addition, as Emerson, commencing his peroration, comes full circle and urges us "to rekindle the smouldering, nigh quenched fire on the altar": "let the breath of new life be breathed by you through the forms already existing. For, if once you are alive, you shall find they shall become plastic and new" (ibid., p. 92). The startling suggestion is pure Emerson: arrogating to himself the primary function of the Deity, man can in one sweeping gesture reanimate both himself and his world and initiate a perpetual Genesis. Here, as he would do at Dartmouth nine days later, Emerson claims that for the individual soul, life can be an incessant process of self-recreation and the world forever "new, untried" (*CW* 1:105). He gives us "the universe a virgin to-day" and encourages us to feel like "the first man that ever stood on the shore, or entered a grove" (ibid., p. 106).

We have not, however, exhausted the wealth of allusion that informs the prelude of Emerson's great discourse. In fact, I believe that for the attentive reader (or listener), the best is yet to come. Once again, we return to the opening: "In this refulgent summer . . . The air is full of birds, and sweet with the breath of the pine, the balm-of-Gilead, and the new hay." Though I have conducted discussions of this passage many, many times with interested and alert students, I have never found one whose eye was sufficiently arrested by the phrase "balm-of-Gilead" to wish to dwell on it a moment—even for the purpose of simple elucidation. Nor have I ever come across any edition of the Address that provides at least an informational footnote on this rather uncommon bit of botanical nomenclature. My own queries invariably produce the same response: "Some kind of plant." Yet Emerson, in a manifestly economical passage, has taken the trouble to single out this "plant" for particular mention. (Perhaps we ought to invoke here a dictum about writing which he had arrived at by at least 1831: he was pleased to enter in his journal this sentence from Schlegel: "In good prose . . . every word should be underlined"; and he himself added, "in good writing every word means something" [*JMN* 3:271].)

The fact is that Emerson's reference would not have been lost on his audience in 1838, for the balm-of-Gilead, at least at that time and in Massachusetts, was a tree "more frequently planted for shade and ornament than any other tree of the genus." The quotation is from *A Report on the Trees and Shrubs Growing Naturally in the Forests of Massachusetts,* by George B. Emerson (Waldo's second cousin—a good friend and his erstwhile teacher), who informs us that the balm-of-Gilead is a poplar *(populus candicans)* with heart-shaped leaves that "is desirable near habitations, on account of its agreeable fragrance in spring."[40] Emerson's knowledge and experience of the tree was not merely literary,

however, for it was common in and around Concord (it is frequently mentioned by Thoreau in his journal), and, what is more
to the point, graced a part of the town that had special meaning
for Emerson. The Old Manse, the home of Emerson's step-grandfather, Dr. Ripley, and Emerson's temporary home when he wrote
Nature, was described by Hawthorne with a mixture of fancy and
fact as a "Paradise . . . [that] stands behind a noble avenue of Balm
of Gilead trees."[41]

The tree undoubtedly had special meaning for Emerson for at
least one other reason. In 1841, while rereading some of the letters
of his vexatiously orthodox but beloved Aunt Mary, Emerson
noted that every family has "its own little body of literature,
divinity, & personal biography,—a common stock which their
education & circumstance have furnished, & from which they all
draw allusion & illustration to their conversation whilst it would
be unintelligible (at least in the emphasis given to it) to a stranger."
He then went on to quote from a letter of hers, written to his
brother Charles, dated October 1831:

> O could you be here this afternoon—not a creature but the dog
> and me—we don't go to four-days-meeting. There's been one at
> the methodists', closing today, & such a rush from the other soci-
> ety. But such a day! Here's one balm of gilead tree—but a few
> leaves left, as though on purpose to catch the eye to see them play
> in the wind day after day,—& the deserted nest. Ah where are its
> anxious parents & their loved brood? Dead? Where the mysterious
> principle of life? (*JMN* 7:443)

Aunt Mary, who loved to remember the "earnest & religious spirit
of the puritans & especially the austere saints of Concord &
Malden," in this passage quite naturally moralizes on her single
autumnal balm-of-Gilead tree, turning it into a symbol of transience and death as easily as the heterodox Whitman would force his
sprig of lilac with its "heart-shaped leaves of rich green" to serve
as a symbolic tribute to the martyred Lincoln. Here then, perhaps,

is one reason why Emerson's use of the balm-of-Gilead tree as "allusion & illustration" would tend to be "unintelligible (at least in the emphasis given to it) to a stranger." It formed part of the body of "divinity" that he had inherited from his aunt.

Not, however, only from his aunt. We have already examined some of the ways in which Emerson deftly presses his natural descriptions in the exordium into the service of "theological" argument. His use of the balm-of-Gilead, far from being an exception, is unquestionably the most striking example of this device. For both him and his audience, it is a real tree which they know and cherish. But one can scarcely doubt that at that time, in that place, and for such a group of listeners, Emerson's invoking of the tree's name (followed, one might add, by the reference to "new hay") would immediately suggest a celebrated text from Jeremiah:

> The harvest is past, the summer is ended, and we are not saved. . . .
> Is there no balm in Gilead; is there no physician there?

We have returned, if by a rather circuitous route, to the prodigious Dr. Holmes and his pregnant analogy. But before we consider the (to me) startling implications of Emerson's allusion to Jeremiah, some further background may be useful.

In view of Emerson's ancestry and training, it does not seem necessary to seek explicit evidence for his knowledge of particular Bible texts, especially one so well-known as Jeremiah. Emerson regularly speaks (and with a certain irony) of the writings of such inspired Transcendentalists as Charles Newcomb and Bronson Alcott as needing only their "Baruch" for appropriate transcription.[42] More to the point, a letter to Margaret Fuller dated June 4, 1847, opens with a direct allusion to the very verse in the eighth chapter of Jeremiah which we have been considering ("The late spring has opened at last into honest summer, but our souls are not saved. . . ." [L 3:400]).[43] However, the student of Emerson's Divinity School Address will be much more interested in a series of journal entries, written in the fall of 1826, which show indeed how long a foreground that famous discourse required.

We are here dealing with Emerson in the period when he began his ministry (he preached his first sermon on October 15, 1826). His journal is therefore understandably given over, in the main, to discussions of large ethical, metaphysical, and theological questions. One such issue was that of "design" (i.e., the extent to which one's faith in the existence of God could be buttressed by precise knowledge of the order and purpose to be observed in natural phenomena).[44] In September, Emerson argued that individual details of design meant far less to him than did the "Whole . . . in its harmony," because "one instance of design how decisive soever in its character must always fail of proving the Deity from the known imperfection of the human understanding" (*JMN* 3:47). Ultimately, Emerson's interest in this question, and his own burgeoning organicism, would provide the extraordinary conclusion to a lecture delivered in 1834 ("I am not impressed by solitary marks of designing wisdom; I am thrilled with delight by the choral harmony of the whole. Design! It is all design. It is all beauty. It is all astonishment" [*EL* 1:49]). But in the fall of 1826, this was still an open question. One journal entry consists of a single-sentence paragraph that simply breaks off: "It is clearly the design of God that[.]" (*JMN* 3:49). That what? Emerson seems to have found one sort of answer a few pages later, on October 19, when he set down a paragraph which tended to argue that the human understanding *could* detect circular perfection and not eccentricity as the base of the design simply by paying attention to the endless round of the seasons:

> The changes of external nature are continually suggesting to us the changes in the condition of man. The leaves of the forest & the generations of men go down into the dust but the succession of seasons or of generations is not suspended. The Winter winds sound the dirge of the verdure, the life, the music that is departed, but the active principles are not checked which are preparing to

restore in equal profusion beauty & happiness to the face of the earth. (*JMN* 3:50–51)

The "old bounty," as Emerson was to write in the Divinity School Address, "goes forward," and in that ceaseless activity lies our only assurance of life everlasting. It is as if Emerson had completed his own sentence by writing: "It is clearly the design of God that we should place our faith in the refulgent summer and the perfection of this world in which our senses converse."

At the head of the page containing the paragraph quoted above, and directly preceding it, Emerson wrote: "The summer is past, the harvest is ended & we are not saved." Shall we fault him for misremembering his Jeremiah? Or simply note that his rearrangement of the verse brings it closer to the opening of the Address? In any case, the burden of Emerson's song—of his magnificent antijeremiad—should be clear: for true believers, men and women who depend on "first, soul, and second, soul, and evermore, soul," and whose faith blends "with the light of rising and of setting suns, with the flying cloud, the singing bird, and the breath of flowers" (*CW* 1:92, 85), summer will never be past and the balm-of-Gilead will continue to bloom. We can be saved, Emerson suggests, if only we learn where to look for our salvation. Emerson's crusty disciple, Henry Thoreau, would insist that "a town is saved, not more by the righteous men in it than by the woods and swamps that surround it."[45] Perhaps this is the place to recall Perry Miller's description of the jeremiads as "forensic indictments of an apostatizing New England in the name of an idealized picture of its primitive sanctity."[46]

And in line with this ironic application of Miller's sentence, one point, finally, ought to be stressed: namely, Emerson's clear intent to invert, or subvert, the very Bible texts that he frequently alludes to, or "submerges," in the openings to his discourses. In the case at hand, considering the nature of Emerson's audience, his appropriation of the voice and stance of Jeremiah can only be considered sheer impudence, though Emerson himself would not have described it that way. Undoubtedly, if he thought of it at all at the time, Emerson might have considered that in leaning on the language of the Bible, he was only speaking to the condition of his audience and, additionally perhaps, bringing the old Book up to date. By 1842, exasperated with biblical mumbo-jumbo, especially as he found it in Swedenborg, he would cry out: "I tell you, I love the peeping of a Hyla in a pond in April, or the evening cry of a whip-poor-will, better than all the bellowing of the Bulls of Bashan or all the turtles of whole Palestina." It was his own America that he wanted: "the County of Berkshire is worth all Moab, Gog, & Kadesh, put together" (*JMN* 8:233–34).

But Emerson had already referred to "this problem of a Vocabulary" in terms more suitable to the Divinity School Address, indeed in the aftermath of its delivery, in a journal entry for November 13, 1838, which suggests that he was preparing to change his literary habits—perhaps by exorcising this nervous tic of a Bible text. "Whenever . . . a soul is true, is simple, & expelling all wilfulness consents to God, & receives the Soul of the Soul into itself, then old things pass away, then means, teachers, texts, temples, fall." Determined, as always, "to see God face to face" (that text again!), he vowed *not* to imprison what he had to say

in the old Hebrew language, mimick David, Jeremiah, & Paul & disbelieve that God who maketh the stars & stones sing, can speak our English tongue in Massachusetts & give as deep & glad a melody to it as shall make the whole world & all coming ages ring with the sound.—Be assured we shall not always set so great a price on a few texts, on a few lives. When we were young, we repeated by rote the words of our grandames, of our tutors,—&, as we grew older, of the men of talents & character we met, & painfully recollected & recited the exact words they spake. (*JMN* 7:149–50)

Eager to take full possession of his manhood, he reconsecrated himself to yet another beginning, in which the tonality and music of his own voice would arise from and blend with the divine/ natural concord that nurtured him: "With new perception, we shall disburthen our Memory of all its trumpery when we can create. When a man lives with God, his voice shall be as sweet as is now the murmur of the brook & the rustle of the corn."

ESSAYING TO BE

[I]

"Talking," Gertrude Stein says, "can be a way of listening."[47] One feels that Emerson would have understood that remark very well. Always exquisitely attuned to his audience, Emerson habitually worried about the listener's or reader's probable reaction to his discourse and therefore built his anticipated sense of that reaction into his lectures or essays themselves. Emerson learned early on to listen to himself and thus became his own best audience. But one had to be careful not to be blinded, or deafened, by self-conceit. Speaking of the senior and junior pastors of the church in Concord, he would write: "Dr Ripley . . . preaches . . . to a congregation of Dr Ripleys; and Mr Frost to a supposed congregation of Barzillai Frosts. . . . Could this belief of theirs be verified in the audience, each would be esteemed the best of all speakers" (*JMN* 7:519). If Mr. Frost was *not* esteemed the best of all speakers (at least not by Ralph Waldo Emerson), it was because he presumably lacked the capacity to be bored, or the wit to perceive it in others, and assumed therefore that boredom did not exist. The Frost who listened was as dull as the Frost who spoke.[48]

Emerson's notion of paying attention to his own discourse was founded on a gift and propensity for self-criticism. The least effect of the oration might be its effect on the orator himself, he wrote in 1837, "yet it is something; a faint recoil; a kicking of the gun" (*JMN* 5:362). One had to have the capacity to feel kicked. In

147

February 1840, for example, he complained in his journal about how little pleasure he got from his own course of lectures: "Alas! alas! I have not the recollection of one strong moment. A cold mechanical preparation for a delivery as decorous,—fine things, pretty things, wise things,—but no arrows, no axes, no nectar, no growling, no transpiercing, no loving, no enchantment" (*JMN* 7:339). Undoubtedly Emerson was being too harsh with himself, but only by maintaining such an attitude could he spur himself on to those high achievements by which he is remembered, while the Barzillai Frosts of his generation were complacently preparing their own oblivion. "When I address a large assembly," he would write in 1844, "I am always apprised what an opportunity is there: not for reading to them as I do, lively miscellanies, but for painting in fire my thought, & being agitated to agitate. One must dedicate himself to it and think with his audience in his mind, so as to keep the perspective & symmetry of the oration" (*JMN* 9:70). For Emerson, listening to himself implied in a real sense making himself the very subject of his discourse. He could have his audience in his mind only by *taking* them into his mind. Somehow, that process would inform the actual point of view and shape of his speech.

On July 15, 1838, as we have seen, Emerson had argued passionately at the Harvard Divinity School that contemporary preaching—at least of the Unitarian variety—was bankrupt precisely because it was devoid of human content and thus the very negation of that exchange of hearts and minds which ought to constitute a literary transaction. The true preacher, Emerson insisted (and by "preacher" he meant to imply any and every speaker), must "convert life into truth"—deal "out to the people his life— life passed through the fire of thought." We may come to the meetinghouse or lyceum hall out of habit or for want of anything better to do, Emerson concedes. But we remain, or continue to devote our attention, only if a true word is spoken—a word that brings the life of the speaker into vital connection with our own. "We see it advertised," Emerson writes, "that Mr A. will deliver an oration on the Fourth of July & Mr B before the Mechanics

Association, but we know that these gentlemen will not communicate their own character & being to the audience & therefore we do not go. Every public oration is an escapade merely & not a communication: a non comittal, an apology, a self-gag, & not a speech, not a man" (*JMN* 7:166). What Emerson longs for is to see and hear some aspect of the speaker's life *enacted* before him, suggesting that Emerson's true intent is to make his oration or lecture a reflexive act—an exposition and demonstration of what he is becoming *through* his speech. "Ah," Emerson exclaimed in the summer of 1839, "could I hope to enact my thought!" (*JMN* 7:227).

It is abundantly clear from his journals and letters that in the difficult years immediately following the publication of his first book in 1836, Emerson had definite theories about lecturing and great expectations for his own ability to perform in that role. He looked upon the "Lecture room as the true church of today" (*JMN* 7:277) and told Carlyle that he was "always haunted with brave dreams of what might be accomplished" there. By 1845, he would claim extravagantly that the object of an oration was "to change the course of life in half an hour for many men" (*JMN* 9:210), and there can be little doubt that he wanted to be one of those thus affected. A year after delivering the Divinity School Address, in July 1839, Emerson wrote:

> A lecture is a new literature, which leaves aside all tradition, time, place, circumstance, & addresses an assembly as mere human beings,—no more—It has never yet been done well. It is an organ of sublime power, a panharmonicon for variety of note. But only then is the orator successful when he is himself agitated & is as much a hearer as any of the assembly. In that office you may & shall (please God!) yet see the electricity part from the cloud & shine from one part of heaven to the other. (*JMN* 7:224–25)

As Emerson's editors point out, "he accepts this new phenomenon not only as an expressive cultural fact but also as his own medium." Perhaps it would be more accurate to say that Emerson was determined to *make* it his own medium precisely in the way we have noticed and find verified in this entry: by taking his audience into his confidence, treating them as his counterparts, anticipating their own anxieties and desires, and conceiving of the experience as a joint experiment or voyage of discovery.[49] As Emerson avowed in another journal entry, "here is a pulpit that makes other pulpits tame & ineffectual." On such a platform he intended to "lay himself out utterly, large, enormous, prodigal, on the subject of the hour." Thereby he dared "to hope for ecstasy & eloquence" (*JMN* 7:265).

We know how Emerson's eloquent baring of his soul on that Sunday evening in July 1838 "agitated" his audience — ecstatically in the case of the young and the Transcendental, apoplectically in the case of the orthodox guardians of the faith. Unlike the formalist preacher whom he attacked in his Address, Emerson had certainly bored no one. But, especially in view of his own theory of the lecture as a form of self-culture, what had Emerson done to or for himself? If, as is generally believed, Emerson's poem "Uriel" represents a wry treatment of the event,[50] we may at least assume that he was somehow chastened by the stir he had caused, since he writes that

> A sad self-knowledge, withering, fell
> On the beauty of Uriel;
> In heaven once eminent, the god
> Withdrew, that hour, into his cloud. (*W* 9:14)

What sort of cloud did Emerson's heretical over-reaching (if, indeed, that is how he himself saw it) force him, or perhaps return him, to? Literally, at least, the statement seems inaccurate, since about a week after the performance in Cambridge, Emerson journeyed to Dartmouth to deliver his Oration (subsequently called "Literary Ethics").

Emerson scholars and critics have neglected this fascinating piece,[51] perhaps because it lies so directly in the shadow of "The American Scholar" and the Divinity School Address. Ralph Rusk, for example, in his still standard biography of Emerson, willingly disposes of the Oration in a few phrases, saying merely that it "was on the subject of literary ethics, was a poor relation of the Phi Beta Kappa oration of the year before, caused hardly a ripple of excitement, and was promptly forgotten by all but a few."[52] Among those who did not forget it, however, were some of Emerson's admirers in England. Harriet Martineau was to write a long notice of the address in the *Westminster Review,* Gladstone cited it in one of his own books, and—most importantly of all, perhaps, for Emerson himself—the Carlyles were (for them!) enthusiastic.[53] Jane Carlyle, and an unnamed friend, preferred it to "The American Scholar"; Carlyle himself thought it "not so good." But he nevertheless "read it over dinner in a chophouse in Bucklersbury, amid the clatter of some fifty stand of knives and forks; and a second time more leisurely at Chelsea," whereupon he pronounced it "a right brave Speech; announcing, in its own way, with emphasis of full conviction, to all whom it may concern, that great forgotten truth, *Man is still Man*. May it awaken a pulsation under the ribs of Death!"

One such pulsation was at least awakened, on this side of the Atlantic, in Emerson's friend and contemporary, the notably perspicacious Oliver Wendell Holmes, who in his own biography of Emerson devotes some fine pages to "Literary Ethics," reminding us importantly of the setting and audience for that oration:

> If any rumor of the former discourse [Divinity School Address] had reached Dartmouth, the audience must have been prepared for a much more startling performance than that to which they listened. The bold avowal which fluttered the dovecotes of Cambridge would have sounded like the crash of doom to the cautious old tenants of the Hanover aviary. If there were any drops of false or questionable doctrine in the silver shower of eloquence under which they had been sitting, the plumage of orthodoxy glistened with unctuous

repellants, and a shake or two on coming out of church left the study old dogmatists as dry as ever.[54]

Holmes' humorous metaphor amounts to this: since the old birds on the Dartmouth Faculty, and presumably the fledglings in the college as well, were all staunch Calvinists, they were effectively protected from Emerson's heresies by the imperviousness of their orthodoxy; whereas the Harvard Unitarians, by 1838 under attack from many quarters, had—to paraphrase Emerson—necks of unspeakable tenderness that winced at a hair. Emerson's own cut, from their point of view, was the unkindest of all and most resented because it effectively came from within the fold.

Unlike the Divinity School Address, of course, Emerson's lecture at Hanover on July 24 was not explicitly theological in character. But I believe it was less startling for another reason—one that relates to a fundamental split, or antinomy, in Emerson's character, about which it may be useful to generalize a bit. Erik Erikson notes that "men, especially in periods of change, are swayed by alternating world moods which . . . could not exist without the highly exploitable mood cycles inherent in man's psychological structure. The two most basic alternating moods are those of carnival and atonement: the first gives license and leeway to sensual enjoyment, to relief and release at all cost; the second surrenders to the negative conscience which constricts, depresses. . . ."[55] One might easily assimilate such a formulation to Marvin Meyers' paradoxical characterization of the Jacksonian spirit as being that of a "venturous conservative." And Meyers cites Tocqueville to good effect: " 'They love change,' Tocqueville's provocative formula for American democrats goes, 'but they dread revolutions.' "[56] That could stand as a pretty fair description of Emerson's general attitude. But whether one opts for Erikson's psychological explanations or Tocqueville's cultural ones, the fact is that Emerson's own writings provide the most representative and finest expression of this curious alternation or division in American character. The view of Emerson as a shallow optimist who approved of, or indeed helped inspire, the mindless boosterism or go-getting spirit so frequently associated with mid-nineteenth-century America is as false to Emerson as it is to our national character.[57]

It used to be said in Cambridge that when the new philosophy building—appropriately named Emerson Hall—was being completed in Harvard Yard early in this century, it was proposed to Harvard's redoubtable president, Charles William Eliot, that the frieze on the outside of the building be decorated with these optimistic lines of Protagoras: "Man is the measure of all things." But Eliot, sharply aware, it seems, both of the origins of the College and the darker side of the Emersonian spirit, is reported to have shaken his head and decided instead in favor of the line from the Psalms that is actually to be found on the building: "What is man, that thou art mindful of him?"[58] These alternative notions help to define the ebb and flow of the Emersonian tide. Man may be potentially divine and omnipotent, but as Emerson conceded in his first book, he "is a god in ruins" (*CW* 1:42). A more personal expression is to be found in the first series of *Essays* that he published five years later:

> Our moods do not believe in each other. To-day I am full of thoughts and can write what I please. I see no reason why I should not have the same thought, the same power of expression, to-morrow. What I write, whilst I write it, seems the most natural thing in the world; but yesterday I saw a dreary vacuity in this direction in which now I see so much; and a month hence, I doubt not, I shall wonder who he was that wrote so many continuous pages. Alas for this infirm faith, this will not strenuous, this vast ebb of a vast flow! I am God in nature; I am a weed by the wall. (*W* 2:306–7)

This lamentation over what we might call a manic-depressive mood swing is the furthest thing from being simply academic or merely perfunctory. To my ear, its tone is peculiarly intimate—as in the great essay "Experience," where Emerson avows that he has set his heart on "honesty" (W 3:69). But although the fiercely somber mood of that utterance is normally attributed to Emerson's despair over the death of his young son, the truth is that that tragic event only exacerbated a tendency discernible in Emerson's writings from the start—one which finds frequent expression in the six years or so between the publication of *Nature* and the death of little Waldo, and which may be said to culminate in, rather than to be initiated by, the essay "Experience." These years, stretching roughly between Emerson's thirty-third and fortieth birthdays, and interestingly coterminous with the very hard times that began at the end of Jackson's administration, were manifestly difficult ones for Emerson. His victories, such as they were, were clearly hard-won, for one finds in Emerson's journals and lectures of the period much evidence of low spirits, self-doubt, a nagging sense that time was swiftly passing and little had been accomplished. In "The Protest," delivered, let us recall, at the beginning of 1839, Emerson argued (strangely, it might certainly be felt, since Emerson at that time is supposed still to have been in the first ebullient flush of his Transcendental blossoming) that "the Fall of man is the first word of history and the last fact of experience." What, he asks, "is the account to be given of this persuasion that has taken such deep root in all minds? What but this that it is an universal fact that man is always in his actual life lapsing from the Commandments of the Soul":

> There is somewhat infirm and retreating in every action; a pause of self-praise; a second thought. He has done well and he says I have done well and lo! this is the beginning of ill. He is encumbered by his own past. His past hour mortgages the present hour. Yesterday is the enemy of Today. His deed hinders him from doing, his thought from thinking; his former virtue is apt to become an impediment to new virtue. (*EL* 3:87)

Emerson frequently quoted two lines from the fourth book of Wordsworth's "Excursion" which he considered to be "a sort of elegy" on his own times:

Essaying to Be

And the most difficult of tasks to keep
Heights which the soul is competent to gain.[59]

A paralyzing sense that the soul is *not* competent to sustain itself
on its own heights—a dreadful feeling of insecurity that both
drains one's pleasure in what has been done and renders one
incapable of further effort—was evidently Emerson's familiar
companion at this time. In his next lecture of this series on "Human Life," Emerson complained that life was dull, melancholy,
and grief-ridden. Generalizing, he said:

> It does seem too as if history gave no intimation of any society in
> which despondency came so readily to heart as we see and feel it in
> ours. As we see and know it, melancholy cleaves to the English
> mind in both hemispheres as closely as to the strings of an Aeolian
> harp. Young men, young women at thirty and even earlier have
> lost all spring and vivacity and if they fail in their first enterprizes
> there seems to be no remedial force in nature, no Roman recovery,
> but the rest of life is rock and shallow. (*E* 3:104)

Lest we are tempted to read such a passage too impersonally,
to take it as the detached observation of an objective historian
placidly surveying the mid-nineteenth-century *Zeitgeist,* we might
note that just a few years prior to this lecture, Emerson wrote in
his journal: "After thirty a man wakes up sad every morning
excepting perhaps five or six until the day of his death" (*JMN*
5:77). It is no wonder, then, that in his lecture Emerson described
existence as a "defensive war; a struggle against the encroaching
All, which threatens with certainty to engulf us soon, and seems
impatient of our little reprieve. How slender is the possession that
yet remains to us; how faint the animation! How the spirit seems
already to contract its domain, to retire within narrower walls by
the loss of memory, leaving what were its planted fields, to erasure
and annihilation. Already our own thoughts and words have an
alien sound" (*EL* 3:104). Notice here, as in the other passages we

have examined, that Emerson feels assaulted and weakened in two ways: his anxiety over the probable diminution of his powers in the future is deepened by his inability to believe in what he has already accomplished. In a sense, the bleakness of future prospects is allowed to cast a kind of retrospective pall over the past, as if in some perverse and self-punishing way, Emerson's perpetual feeling of unworthiness obliged him to poison the well of past achievement so that he would not be tempted to drink there in dry times to come. One might say, however, that there *is* a harsh nobility in such a habit of mind which, though it conceives of the future as a desert, or an empty room, is determined to live there, finding or making its opportunities out of the very barrenness of its premises. Emersonian self-reliance could hardly be put to a more stringent test.

To return to that refulgent summer of 1838, it seems clear that a cloud did settle over the brow of the presumably insolent and self-assured apostate who fluttered the dovecotes of Cambridge in his confident Divinity School Address. Characteristically, Emerson gave clear signs of suffering the kick of his own gun following his stunningly assertive performance. Responding, for example, to a critical letter from his old friend and colleague, Henry Ware, Jr., the distinguished minister and a member of the Harvard Divinity School Faculty, Emerson began by insisting that he was not "a stock or a stone . . . and could not but feel pain in saying some things in that place and presence," which he supposed, "might meet dissent . . . of [in a first draft he wrote "offend"] dear friends and benefactors." And though he stood firm in his convictions, he confessed himself sufficiently "admonished" by Ware's objections "to revise with greater care the address, before it is printed."[60] Since the manuscript of Emerson's Address as he delivered it has unfortunately never been located, it is impossible to know how much he may have toned it down for publication. The evidence, in fact, is contradictory. Rusk believes that Emerson yielded to Ware's strictures, as well as to the warnings of various friends and relatives that Emerson had gone too far and would be ruined by the Address

(Samuel Ripley, for example, a half uncle whom Rusk describes as "liberal-minded and loyal," fearing that his nephew would be classed with Tom Paine and the atheist Abner Kneeland, wrote: "you *must* make alterations, cut out exaggerations &c &c, which will cause it not to be the same that was heard").[61] Yet the prodigious Elizabeth Peabody, who not only "had the happiness of listening to this truly prophetic discourse," but also chanced to be visiting Emerson's home when he was correcting proof of the Address, gives us a different picture. Emerson read to her a paragraph, she says, omitted on the occasion itself because he thought he "was getting too long," which constituted "a *caveat* anticipating the development of a party, only half understanding him, which would fall into what he called the 'puppyism' of a criticism irreverent of the person of Jesus." She reports that she urged Emerson to include the omitted paragraph: " 'You will certainly print that passage, for it will convict Mr. Ware of misunderstanding and so misrepresenting you in his sermon.' (Mr. Henry Ware had just published a sermon controverting, as he thought, the doctrine of Mr. Emerson's Address.)" Her suggestion, she insists, was "unlucky," for after "a moment's silence, [Emerson] replied: 'No, it would be shabby to spring upon Mr. Ware this passage now. I must abide by what I delivered, whatever was its lack of full expression.' "[62]

In another letter to Ware, Emerson described himself as "cruelly" treated and insisted that in the role of "heretic," and therefore as a person "who is to make good his thesis against all comers," he felt himself to be "the most helpless of mortal men."[63] Though some have been tempted to argue that Emerson's tone in the letter is either coy or disingenuous—and, indeed, it wavers oddly between assertiveness and exaggerated humility—I believe he was simply being honest in calling himself helpless in the face of such sharp reactions.[64] The whole affair tapped a deep fund of self-doubt in Emerson. Throughout the rest of the summer and well into the fall of 1838, during this period of criticism and controversy, Emerson filled his journal with uneasy reflections on his *cause célèbre,* exposing his low spirits, acknowledging himself to be "sensitive as a leaf to impressions from abroad" (*JMN* 7:98), and owning that he was "often inclined to take part with those who say I am bad or foolish, for I fear I am both. . . . I know too well my own dark spots. . . . A few sour faces, a few biting paragraphs,—is but a cheap expiation for all these shortcomings of mine" (*JMN* 7:140). But although he could try to take refuge in a species of moral masochism that unfortunately came naturally to him ("I have no joy so deep as the stings of remorse" [*JMN* 7:116]), Emerson did not really feel that the "threatening paragraphs & odious nicknames" (*JMN* 7:98) were a spur to pleasure. He found it, on the contrary, "difficult not to be affected by sour faces." Sympathy actually provided the atmosphere in which he unfolded "easily & well." In the "thin iced difficult air" of controversy, where "sympathy leaves you & hatred comes," he discovered that "a man will, maugre all his resolutions, lose his sweetness & his flesh, he will pine & fret" (*JMN* 7:70).

Among other things, Emerson worried that the "heterodoxy" (as he named the Address for Carlyle's benefit), when it arrived in Chelsea, might destroy "us even in the Charity of our friend."[65] And although he assured Carlyle that his own position was "fortunately such as to put me quite out of the reach of any real inconvenience from the panic strikers or the panic struck,"[66] he spoke differently of the matter to his brother William. "I mean to lecture again in Boston the coming winter," he wrote in September, "& perhaps the people scared by the newspapers will not come & pay for my paper & pens. In that case, I should not be able to meet my expenses from October to April" (*L* 2:162). It is just possible that Emerson was trying here to find a way convincingly to avoid William's familiar request for a loan of money, but his own anxiety seems real enough. Writing at the same time to his Aunt Mary, and including a copy of the Address (which, according to Rusk, "she seems never to have ceased to regret"),[67] Emerson announced that young Waldo had "passed out of the little heaven of his daily health into the Purgatory of teething" (*L* 2:154). In view of the generally pert tone of this note, that remark reads as if it were a mini-allegory also of the father's situation. The elder Waldo too was cutting a set of new teeth and had consequently passed out of heaven into a small Purgatory of his own. This, perhaps, "was the lapse of Uriel, / Which in Paradise befell" (*W* 9:13).

Accordingly, when Oliver Wendell Holmes in his biography affirms that "Literary Ethics," like "The American Scholar," was "written and delivered in the freshness of [Emerson's] complete manhood . . . at a time when his mind had learned its powers and the work to which it was called,"[68] I think he glides far too easily over a significant rough spot in Emerson's development. The Dartmouth Oration is less startling, at least initially, than the one delivered at Harvard nine days before because Emerson seems to have completed it in a state of funk, his carnival mood at the Divinity School having given way to one of atonement. Some indication of his state may be gathered from a letter he wrote to Lidian a day or two before the occasion itself, in which he speaks of the "undone address" thus: "the oration prospers indifferent well I can't say I admire it much & since I have come hither and seen some of the young men, I think it unfit." Whatever the state of the manuscript, what was truly unfit, I believe Emerson felt, for a hopeful young audience was his own depressed spirit. Since we shall be paying particular attention, in accordance with Emerson's own dictum, to the "effect of the oration . . . on the orator," it is worth noting in advance that after his performance he would write, "Tell Elizabeth [Hoar] our speech is better than she thinks, and I have no doubt some of it found ears in the crowd" (*L* 2:145–46).

The opening of the Oration deserves close attention:

> The invitation to address you this day, with which you have honored me, was a call so welcome, that I made haste to obey it. A summons to celebrate with scholars a literary festival, is so alluring to me, as to overcome the doubts I might well entertain of my ability to bring you any thought worthy of your attention. I have reached the middle age of man; yet I believe I am not less glad or

sanguine at the meeting of scholars, than when, a boy, I first saw the graduates of my own College assembled at their anniversary. Neither years nor books have yet availed to extirpate a prejudice then rooted in me, that a scholar is the favorite of Heaven and earth, the excellency of his country, the happiest of men. His duties lead him directly into the holy ground where other men's aspirations only point. His successes are occasions of the purest joy to all men. Eyes is he to the blind; feet is he to the lame. His failures, if he is worthy, are inlets to higher advantages. (*CW* 1:99)

Even the most cursory comparison of this first page of Emerson's talk with the opening of either "The American Scholar" or the Divinity School Address reveals two things: that Emerson's mood here is much more personal, even confessional; and that he is beginning in a state of mind which is at least muted, if not explicitly despondent.

There is no reason for believing that Emerson was being merely conventionally self-deprecating in immediately sounding the note of *non sum dignus*. His phrase about doubts that he "might well entertain" of his ability seems curiously pointed and, reinforced as it is by his mention of "failures" shortly after, suggests that Emerson had a particular occasion in mind. Moreover, his pronouncement about having "reached the middle age of man" (he was just thirty-five), freighted as it is with all the Dantean associations of the *mezzo del cammin*, stands out with an odd kind of emphasis, drawing the hearer's attention to this moment in the speaker's life as to a time of spiritual crisis—a moment of disconsolateness or uncertainty that will either cripple or provide an occasion for regeneration. It is the *speaker* who seems to feel blind and lame. And here, we should remind ourselves that Emerson's "text" for his exordium is based upon two verses in the twenty-ninth chapter of Job ("I was eyes to the blind, / And feet was I to the lame"). Many years before, in the early 1820s, Emerson had in fact noted in his journal that "a reading selected from *29 & 30* chapters of Job, admits of great eloquence" (*JMN* 2:140); and on May 27, 1827, he had expressed a presumably temporary sense of tedium and worthlessness in a sentence ("my days run onward like the weaver's beam") which alludes to the seventh chapter of Job (*JMN* 3:78). The point of interest here is Emerson's transient identification in the past with the figure of Job. And we should notice that in the chapter Emerson chose for his allusion in the opening of the Dartmouth Oration, Job is eloquently bemoaning his decline from past glory and favor:

> Oh that I were as in months past,
> As in the days when God preserved me;
> When his candle shined upon my head,
> And when by his light I walked through darkness;
> As I was in the days of my youth,
> When the secret of God was upon my tabernacle;
> When the Almighty was yet with me . . .
> The young men saw me, and hid themselves:
> And the aged arose, and stood up.
> The princes refrained talking,
> And laid their hand on their mouth.
> The nobles held their peace,
> And their tongue cleaved to the roof of their mouth.
> When the ear heard me, then it blessed me;
> And when the eye saw me, it gave witness to me . . .
> I put on righteousness, and it clothed me:
> My judgment was as a robe and a diadem.
> I was eyes to the blind,
> And feet was I to the lame.

It would undoubtedly be foolish to lean too heavily on Emerson's use of the figure of Job as a kind of covert analogy for the rapid decline of his reputation and fortune. Indeed, the transition from Jeremiah to Job within the space of nine days might conjure up for some students the high comedy of Melville's agile confidence-man with his shape-shifting showmanship. But Emerson's voice and manner in the opening of the Oration are decidedly not comic; moreover, he is careful not to exaggerate. Emerson is neither Job nor Jeremiah, but rather a modern scholar who believes that the true function of history is to provide paradigms for our own self-understanding and self-realization. The figure of Job merely hovers behind, or beneath, the autobiographical texture of this opening paragraph. Though a distinct one, it is only a slight flavor. Meanwhile, we find Emerson once again engaged in undermining his own text as he uses it—at once identifying with the beleaguered Job and preparing to redeem him from his sorrow: "Eyes *is* he to the blind; feet *is* he to the lame." The shift in tense suggests an act in process; before our very eyes, failures are being transformed into "inlets to higher advantages"—opportunities for new self-creation.[69] Here, I believe, is the exciting strategy of Emerson's talk: we are invited to be present as this disheartened scholar demonstrates how hope, in Shelley's phrase, can create "from its own wreck the thing it contemplates."[70]

Pausing briefly to generalize from his own experience, Emerson laments the fact that America has failed to fulfill "what seemed the reasonable expectation of mankind"—namely to produce a race of literary Titans—and that "the diffidence of mankind in the soul has crept over the american mind" (CW 1:100). This diffidence, which he, at least fitfully, has shared Emerson attributes, as we should expect, to a lack of self-trust; so as he proceeds to outline the resources and the subject of a literary career, it is not surprising that it all comes down finally and inexorably to the simple facts of our own despised being. As if to stir himself from his own torpor, Emerson willfully becomes heated in tone as he thinks that he has allowed "a false humility" to defraud him "of supreme possession of this hour." In the passage that follows, it is not difficult to hear, in his flashes of anger, Emerson's own reaction (conceived in advance of the fact!) to the humiliating reception that his display of independent thinking was to find in Cambridge:

> If any person have less love of liberty, and less jealousy to guard his integrity, shall he therefore dictate to you and me? Say to such doctors, We are thankful to you, as we are to history, to the

pyramids, and the authors; but now our day is come; we have been
born out of the eternal silence; and now will we live,—live for
ourselves,—and not as the pall-bearers of a funeral, but as the
upholders and creators of our age. . . . Now that we are here, we
will put our own interpretation on things, and, moreover, our own
things for interpretation. Please himself with complaisance who
will,—for me, things must take my scale, not I theirs. I will say
with the warlike king, "God gave me this crown, and the whole
world shall not take it away." (Ibid., p. 102) [71]

That last sentence reminds us in a striking fashion that Emerson's
most persistent fantasy paradigm for himself was Napoleon, thun-
dering a fearful admonition to past and future detractors—especially the detested elder "doctors." Emerson's "crown," however,
is simply his own unique being. It is *that* which he will put "for
interpretation," building a literary career on the exposition of his
own growth.

   Though Emerson is fascinated, indeed obsessed, by great men
(and Napoleon, as we have seen, is notable among those he admired), he asserts characteristically that "the whole value of history, of biography, is to increase my self-trust, by demonstrating
what man can be and do." He is hungry to read the story of his
own potential in the record of their development; not to marvel at   ..
what they achieved, but to convince himself that such things may
be done by mere flesh and blood. [72] The greatest fortification of his
hope Emerson naturally finds in three great writers. And speaking
of this triumvirate whose work always lay so close to his heart,
Emerson set down a sentence which, in its fine—I might say,
stunning—verbal wit, establishes the terms of his whole literary
project here and in what is to come:

   If you would know the power of character, see how much you
   would impoverish the world, if you could take clean out of history
   the life of Milton, of Shakspeare, of Plato,—these three, and cause
   them not to be. See you not, instantly, how much less the power of
   man would be? I console myself in the poverty of my present

thoughts ... by falling back on these sublime recollections, and seeing what the prolific soul could beget on actual nature;—seeing that Plato was, and Shakspeare, and Milton,—three irrefragable facts. Then I dare; I also will essay to be. (Ibid., pp. 102–3)

Notice that Emerson does not say that he consoles himself in his dispirited moments by falling back on the *writings* of these three. What fortifies Emerson is the recollection that the prolific author begets on nature, creates out of his intercourse with the world, not simply what can be described as his works but rather *himself*—the being he has achieved through that work. (Emerson was fond of quoting Milton's remark that "he who would write heroic poems should make his whole life a heroic poem" [*JMN* 4:54].) His writings, so to speak, are the commentary upon that process. As Emerson said of Schiller, "his productions . . . were the fermentations by which his mind was working itself clear, they were the experiments by which he got his skill & the fruit, the bright pure gold of all was—Schiller himself" (*JMN* 4:55).

And so, Emerson utters his audacious sentence: "I also will essay to be." Anyone who doubts the intentionality of Emerson's vigorous and reverberating pun here should recall that this is the same writer who, in his first book two years earlier, described himself as a "transparent eye-ball" through which the "currents of the Universal Being circulate" and then called man "the immortal *pupil* [emphasis added]" (CW 1:10, 29).[73] But a direct and revealing adumbration of Emerson's sentence in the Oration may be found in his journal for May 1835, as he attempted apparently to define his life's work:

When will you mend Montaigne? When will you take the hint of nature? Where are your Essays? Can you not express your one conviction that moral laws hold? Have you not thoughts & illustrations that are your own; the parable of geometry & matter; the reason why the atmosphere is transparent; the power of Composition in nature & in man's thoughts; the Uses & uselessness of travelling; the law of Compensation; the transcendant excellence of truth in character, in rhetoric, in things; the sublimity of Self-reliance; and the rewards of perseverance in the best opinion? Have you not a testimony to give for Shakspear, for Milton? one sentence of real praise of Jesus, is worth a century of legendary Christianity. Can you not write as though you wrote to yourself & drop the token assured that a wise hand will pick it up? (*JMN* 5:40)

The linkages between this passage and both the Address and the Oration (not to mention the *Essays*) should be obvious. The point of particular interest, however, resides in the special weight Emerson gives the word "Essays" as his defining activity. Some four months after delivering the Oration and the Address, Emerson would write in his journal: "all that we say is the far off description merely, of the awful truth which in moments of life flashes on us, & bids us go months and years feeding on the remembrance of that light & essaying to tell what we saw" (*JMN* 7:150–51).

Essaying to be is the fundamental conceit of this greatest of American essayists. He too dares, endeavors, tries, attempts, essays (all these are the actual terms Emerson employs in the Oration) to create himself in the very process, in the very act, of setting words on paper or uttering them aloud. In order to exist, he must speak, for the speech validates itself—brings into being that which is envisioned or hoped for and gives Emerson a solid platform on which to stand ("Utterance," he wrote Carlyle in 1834, "is place enough").[74] As Emerson was to say in "The Poet": "The man is only half himself, the other half is his expression" (*W* 3:5). Not to speak, in this high Emersonian sense of speaking in the service of self-culture, is not to be; and despair might be defined as the settled belief that one is unworthy to utter oneself. Let us note the passage that follows Emerson's sentence about essaying to be:

The humblest, the most hopeless, in view of these radiant facts [i.e., Milton, Shakespeare, and Plato], may now theorize and hope. In spite of all the rueful abortions that squeak and gibber in the street, in spite of slumber and guilt, in spite of the army, the bar-room,

and the jail, *have been* these glorious manifestations of the mind;
and I will thank my great brothers so truly for the admonition of
their being, as to endeavor also to be just and brave, to aspire and
to speak. (*CW* 1:103)

The incomplete creatures who squeak and gibber in the street are
called "rueful abortions," not, I think, because of any fastidious
Emersonian disdain for ordinary people, but because their trivial
and degraded speech, issuing from a *rue*-ful spirit that is too ashamed
of its condition to aspire and speak more nobly, simply fails to
help them create themselves anew. They remain "abortions," because their utterances, and therefore their lives, are not *informed*
by a braver impulse.

I want to make one other observation about this key paragraph. Taking our cue from the mention of Shakespeare, and
noticing again that the phrase "squeak and gibber" is drawn from
Hamlet, we may pay particular attention to the insistency with
which Emerson rings changes on verbs and nouns of *being* ("cause
them not to be. See you not, instantly, how much less the powers
of man would be? . . . seeing that Plato was, and Shakespeare, and
Milton,—three irrefragable facts. Then I dare; I also will essay to
be . . . *have been* these glorious manifestations of the mind; and I
will thank my great brothers so truly for the admonition of their
being, as to endeavor also to be. . . . "). A passage from the
Divinity School Address is clearly related to this one in both intent
and language:

> The divine bards are the friends of my virtue, of my intellect, of my
> strength. They admonish me, that the gleams which flash across
> my mind, are not mine, but God's; that they had the like, and were
> not disobedient to the heavenly vision. So I love them. Noble
> provocations go out from them, inviting me also to emancipate
> myself; to resist evil; to subdue the world; and to Be. (*CW* 1:83)

Can there be any doubt that Shakespeare's conflicted poet-prince,
and his most famous speech, are Emerson's monitory paradigms

here and in the passage from the Oration? One could fill up a good deal of space evidencing Emerson's intense interest in *Hamlet,* which was clearly his favorite Shakespearean play.[75] In November 1838, he told Margaret Fuller that "Shakspeare has not done growing yet: and a great day it will be for any mind when it has come to put Shakespeare at a true focal distance"; whereupon he promised to show her Jones Very's essay on *Hamlet,* which he called "pretty great criticism" (*L* 2:173). Later on, Emerson would insist that "Hamlet was prophecy" (*JMN* 10:154) and "ask whether, if I sit at home & do not go to Hamlet, Hamlet will come to me; whether I shall find my tragedy written in his, and my wants & pains & disgraces described to the life" (*JMN* 9:438).[76]

Presumably, Emerson had already done so, since in "The American Scholar" he indeed invoked the noble Dane:

> Our age is bewailed as the age of Introversion. Must that needs be evil? We, it seems, are critical. We are embarrassed with second thoughts. We cannot enjoy any thing for hankering to know whereof the pleasure consists. We are lined with eyes. We see with our feet. The time is infected with Hamlet's unhappiness, —
>
> "Sicklied o'er with the pale cast of thought."
>
> Is it so bad then? Sight is the last thing to be pitied. Would we be blind? Do we fear lest we should outsee nature and God, and drink truth dry? I look upon the discontent of the literary class as a mere announcement of the fact that they find themselves not in the state of mind of their fathers, and regret the coming state as untried; as a boy dreads the water before he has learned that he can swim. (*CW* 1:66–67)

The prevalence of questions in this passage may be taken as the mark of its dominant mood—uncertainty; in particular, the uncertainty of the son as he considers his worthiness to supplant the father. In this connection, Emerson's allusion to learning to swim is of special interest. As a rather ominous figure of speech, it would resonate throughout his essays ("on the brink of the waters of life and truth, we are miserably dying" [W 3:33]; "an innavigable sea washes with silent waves between us and the things we aim at and converse with" [ibid., p. 48]). More to the point, however, is this journal entry in March 1837: "Every man has hydrophobia the first time in summer he goes into the salt water baths. Life" (JMN 5:289). And another from April 1834: "We are always on the brink of an ocean of thought into which we do not yet swim. We are poor lords—have immense powers which we are hindered from using. I am kept out of my heritage" (JMN 4:274). The linkage to Emerson's own father is provided by a story well-known in the lore of Emerson's family. The young Ralph was a sickly boy and a doctor prescribed curative baths in the sea, as a result of which, according to Rusk, Ralph's "fear of deep water, became a phobia." Rusk continues:

> William Emerson's [his father's] insistence on carrying out the doctor's advice stirred up long-lived resentment in the boy. Some forty years later Ralph could not forget the severity of a father "who twice or thrice put me in mortal terror by forcing me into the salt water off some wharf or bathing house, and . . . the fright with which, after some of this salt experience, I heard his voice one day, (as Adam that of the Lord God in the garden,) summoning us to a new bath, and I vainly endeavouring to hide myself." [77]

Fear, shame, and anger are thoroughly mixed in this account of Emerson's complex, and perdurable, reaction to his God-like father. The result seems to be, as with the paradigmatic Hamlet, a crippling habit of self-consciousness and self-questioning that threatens to paralyze the will. Emerson himself was manifestly *not* in the "state of mind" of his father—a firm pillar of the religious establishment, minister of the prestigious First Church of Boston —when he launched his attack against that establishment in the Divinity School Address. And let us recall that the stern old war-gods (such as Henry Ware, Senior, Professor of Theology) whom

Essaying to Be

Emerson was assailing and who reacted so badly were precisely of his father's generation. Closer to home Emerson had to deal with the wrath of his father's sister, the fiercely orthodox Mary Moody Emerson, whom he loved and revered in spite of, indeed in many ways because of, her firm faith.

It is thus easy to see why Emerson's first public trial of his new state, his bold attempt to launch himself into the deep seas of Transcendental theology, should have been fraught with so much anxiety and preceded, attended, and followed by a crushing onslaught of self-doubt. "Literary Ethics," as we have been noticing, represents both the record of that reaction *and* Emerson's determination to reconstitute his native hue of resolution. To return to our passage, Emerson's response to Hamlet's momentous question is a brave and hopeful Yes: "I also will essay to be." The world, as he insists in the Oration, "is his." But he must attempt to "possess it" (*CW* 1:109). Unlike the world-weary prince, who disgustedly consigns his sweetheart to a nunnery, Emerson insists on conceiving of *his* America, his new-found land, as an exciting invitation to exercise that manhood which he is in the process of rediscovering. As he says, "the perpetual admonition of nature to us, is, 'The world is new, untried. Do not believe the past. I give you the universe a virgin to-day' " (ibid., pp. 105–6).

Nature's exciting admonition, as tempting to Emerson as is Hester Prynne's to Arthur Dimmesdale, leads his thoughts, as with Hawthorne after him, away from the chilling, constricting elders and their opinions and toward the American wilderness, and the promise of both new life and new literature. In the fine passage that follows—one which epitomizes as well as anything else in Emerson's writings the thrilling expansions characteristic of his optative mood—Emerson at once exhorts the young in his audience and momentarily realizes his vision for himself:

> But go into the forest, you shall find all new and undescribed. The honking of the wild geese flying by night; the thin note of the companionable titmouse, in the winter day; the fall of swarms of

flies, in autumn, from combats high in the air, pattering down on the leaves like rain; the angry hiss of the wood-birds; the pine throwing out its pollen for the benefit of the next century; the turpentine exuding from the tree;—and, indeed, any vegetation; any animation; any and all, are alike unattempted. The man who stands on the seashore, or who rambles in the woods, seems to be the first man that ever stood on the shore, or entered a grove, his sensations and his world are so novel and strange. Whilst I read the poets, I think that nothing new can be said about morning and evening. But when I see the daybreak, I am not reminded of these Homeric, or Shaksperian, or Miltonic, or Chaucerian pictures. No; but I feel perhaps the pain of an alien world; a world not yet subdued by the thought; or, I am cheered by the moist, warm, glittering, budding, melodious hour, that takes down the narrow walls of my soul, and extends its life and pulsation to the very horizon. *That* is morning, to cease for a bright hour to be a prisoner of this sickly body, and to become as large as nature. (Ibid., p. 106)

What is remarkable about this passage, especially near its conclusion, is the delicate balance Emerson strikes between his hopes and his fears. Responsive to both by turns, Emerson tries to give accurate expression to that alternation of mood which inspired his talk even as he achieves a momentary victory over it. Meanwhile, we notice that by means of a kind of literary prestidigitation, Emerson has in fact managed to attempt the presumably unattempted—to describe that world which he claims to be undescribed. He has *essayed* in both senses of the word. Perhaps with a certain pleasant shock, we recognize in the "moist, warm, glittering, budding, melodious hour" which breaks down the defensive walls of his soul and swells his beating heart "to the very horizon" an evocation of precisely that "virgin" universe which Emerson was invited to try. As the passage ends, Emerson takes the measure of his world, ecstatically strains time and space to his enlarged soul, and thereby demonstrates that the American scholar, even at mid-life, can still be, as he is described in the last line of the address, the "beloved of earth and heaven" (ibid., p. 116).

[11]

We need only a brief coda to complete our survey of Emerson's momentous year. By early winter, he was greatly pleased to discover that his lecture series was thriving, and his attendant high spirits found expression in a letter: "The good city is more placable than it was represented & 'forgives,' like Burke, 'much to the spirit of liberty' " (*L* 2:177). Emerson's free quotation from Burke's speech on "Conciliation with the Colonies" humorously, but significantly, places him in the position of revolutionary America achieving some sort of recognition from the parent nation. And although "the old tyrant of the Cambridge Parnassus" (*JMN* 7:63), as Emerson dubbed Andrews Norton, might never forgive the "naughty heretic" (*JMN* 7:110), Emerson would live to see the son, Charles Eliot Norton, become his friend, admirer, and editor.

Slowly taking possession of his developing self-confidence and self-trust, Emerson could now evaluate his summer's work in terms that would both prophesy his future commanding role in American letters and hark back to his own high sense of spiritual rebirth during the first trip to Europe:

> There is no terror like that of being known. The world lies in night of sin. It hears not the cock crowing; it sees not the gray streak in the East. At the first entering ray of light, society is shaken with fear & anger from side to side. Who opened that shutter? they cry, Wo to him! They belie it, they call it darkness that comes in, affirming that they were in light before. Before the man who has spoken to them the dread word, they tremble & flee. They flee to new topics, to their learning, to the solid institutions about them, to their great men, to their windows, & look out on the road & passengers, to their very furniture, & meats, & drinks, anywhere, anyhow to escape the apparition. . . . They try to forget the memory of the speaker, to put him down into the same obscure place he occupied in their minds before he spake to them. It is all in vain. They even flatter themselves that they have killed & buried the enemy when they have magisterially denied & denounced him. But

> vain, vain, all vain. It was but the first mutter of the distant storm
> they heard,—it was the first cry of the Revolution,—it was the
> touch, the palpitation that goes before the Earthquake. (*JMN*
> 7:126)

The world of American literary culture, he seems to have believed,
would come to say "before Emerson" and "after Emerson" as
easily as they did B.C. and A.D.

By January 1839, when Emerson wrote out the history of 1838
in his lecture "The Protest," his summer of discontent could be
made (less gloriously, perhaps, but more believably) to yield two
concluding paragraphs which would have meaning for any young
American in Emerson's lyceum audience—not just for rural Ham-
lets and self-styled Jeremiahs:

> On the whole, then, we think that this crisis in the life of each
> earnest man, which comes in so forbidding and painful aspect, has
> nothing in it that need alarm or confound us. It is the inevitable
> result of the relation of the soul to the existing corruption of
> society. It puts to the man the question, Will you fulfil the demands
> of the soul or will you yield yourself to the conventions of the
> world? In some form the question comes to each. None can escape
> the challenge. But why need you sit cowering there pale and pout-
> ing or why with such a mock tragic air, affect such a discontent
> and superiority?
>
> There is nothing to fear. If you would obey the soul, obey it.
> Do your own work, and you shall have leave to do it. The bugbear
> of society is only such until you have accepted your own law. Then
> all omens are good; all stars auspicious; all men your allies; all
> parts of life take order and beauty. (*EL* 3:102)

Once again, as in the conclusion to *Nature,* Emerson had found a
way to rebuild his own world. This time, however, his language
was less elevated, his cadences closer to those of ordinary speech.
Emerson was learning, as Wallace Stevens would say, to find his
occasions and his accents "merely in living as and where we live."[78]
That would turn out to be his greatest lesson.

IV
THE FALL OF MAN

1839–1847

Emerson continued to lecture in the winter of 1839–40 ("The Present Age") and drew a good audience and financial return, notwithstanding the continuing hard times. He supported the Whigs against the incumbent Van Buren in the election of 1840, despite their weak candidate and foolish slogan ("Tippecanoe and Tyler too"), probably because he thought his investments would be more secure with the Democrats out of office. In July 1840, Emerson and Margaret Fuller brought out the first number of The Dial, *fervently hoping that it would "be one cheerful rational voice amidst the din of mourners and polemics." Fuller would bear the main editorial responsibility until 1842; Emerson would then continue until the demise of the journal two years later. His first book of* Essays *appeared early in 1841 and extended his reputation as a free-thinker (his Aunt Mary considered it a "strange medly of atheism and false independence"). In the summer, Emerson journeyed to Waterville College in Maine to deliver one of his most intense and orphic orations, "The Method of Nature," proclaiming ecstasy and metamorphosis as the ruling principles of the universe. Emerson's second daughter, Edith, was born in November, and one month later, on December 23, he expounded his "new views" to a Boston audience in "The Transcendentalist." Concord mourned the death of Henry Thoreau's brother John on January 11, 1842, but just over two weeks later, Emerson had a more severe and private grief to bear when his little Waldo was carried off by scarlet fever. It was a devastating blow from which he never quite re-*

covered, comprehending "nothing of this fact but its bitterness."
On his death bed forty years later, he would exclaim, "Oh that
beautiful boy." A second son, Edward, was born in July 1844, but
Emerson's vision seemed permanently darkened by Waldo's death.
In the second series of Essays, *published in October 1844, Emer-*
son exposed his benumbed state in "Experience" and expatiated
on the "Fall of Man." In the winter of 1845–46 he lectured on
"Representative Men" and identified closely with the disillusioned
and skeptical Montaigne. "Threnody," a moving elegy to the lost
boy, appeared in Poems, *published at the end of 1846.*

Descending

For so devoted a reader of Shakespeare as Emerson was, the tendency to view human life in terms of an "almanack of the soul" was an entirely natural one. Nothing could be more familiar to so eager a scholar of English literature than such lines as

> That time of year thou may'st in me behold
> When yellow leaves, or none, or few, do hang
> Upon those boughs which shake against the cold . . .

or, "my way of life/Is fall'n into the sear, the yellow leaf." But the Bible was as familiar to Emerson as the Bard, and it is not surprising that his symbols, or emblems, for the shape of an individual human life should also be drawn from that source. In the fall of 1840, Emerson noted in his journal that "every man has his Creation; Flood; Calling of Abraham; Exodus; Building of the Temple; Call of Cyrus; Advent of Christ, Death & Resurrection" (*JMN* 7:396). When that passage was incorporated into "History" in the first series of *Essays*, Emerson added "the Apples of Knowledge" (but deleted "Death & Resurrection"), suggesting that although he was uneasy with the notion of the "Fall," he felt obliged to give it at least oblique mention in his scheme of experience (*W* 2:39). That uneasiness is consistent with the general tendency of Emerson's first book of *Essays*. He argues in "Compensation" that "the soul refuses limits, and always affirms an Optimism, never a Pessimism" (*W* 2:122). Accordingly, he goes on to say that "the changes which break up at short intervals the prosperity of men are advertisements of a nature whose law is growth" (*W* 2:124). Man's outward biography "in time" *should* be "a putting off of dead circumstances day by day." And this growth will shock us, Emerson insists, only if we remain static, persisting "in our lapsed estate" (*W* 2:125).

An even more familiar passage frequently quoted as evidence of Emerson's ignorance of the Fall, and other dark moments in human experience, is this one from "Spiritual Laws":

> Our young people are diseased with the theological problems of original sin, origin of evil, predestination and the like. These never presented a practical difficulty to any man,—never darkened across any man's road who did not go out of his way to seek them. These are the soul's mumps and measles and whooping coughs, and those who have not caught them cannot describe their health or prescribe the cure. A simple mind will not know these enemies. (*W* 2:132)

It would be easy enough to be satiric about that last sentence, though the impulse to satire is quickly deflected by our knowledge that Emerson's beloved first-born son, Waldo, would be carried off by scarlatina scarcely a year after the publication of this essay. In a manner of speaking, one might say that Emerson would catch his childhood diseases then, in his maturity, when they are always more difficult to bear. But it should be noted that Emerson's aggressively polemical tone in this passage is purposeful—and understandable. He is still engaged in shucking off a crippling theological tradition that he knows only too well, and he can hardly be blamed for his overstatement when one views it in such a light. He is not saying that there is no suffering in the world; only that these "theological problems" are the diseases to which overly scrupulous youths are peculiarly liable.

If one feels (as there is ample justification for feeling) that Emerson himself had been just such a youth, it is possible to say that his protesting too much is another sign of his uneasiness with concepts of this nature. Emerson is attempting not, perhaps, to deny the existence of evil but rather to exorcise lingering traces of belief in it from his own soul. Another passage seems to have sharp personal reference:

> And why drag this dead weight of a Sunday-school over the whole Christendom? It is natural and beautiful that childhood should inquire and maturity should teach; but it is time enough to answer questions when they are asked. Do not shut up the young people against their will in a pew and force the children to ask them questions for an hour against their will. (W 2:136)

The effect of these obviously angry remarks is to amplify the passage originally quoted. If the young people are diseased with theological problems, it is because they were force-fed with the germs in their own childhood.

Further evidence suggesting that Emerson is engaged here in exorcising familiar demons may be found in another paragraph close by, where Emerson is presumably illustrating the happy notion that "we are begirt with laws which execute themselves":

> Let us draw a lesson from nature, which always works by short ways. When the fruit is ripe, it falls. When the fruit is despatched, the leaf falls. The circuit of the waters is mere falling. The walking of man and all animals is a falling forward. All our manual labor and works of strength, as prying, splitting, digging, rowing and so forth, are done by dint of continual falling, and the globe, earth, moon, comet, sun, star, fall for ever and ever. (W 2:137)

This is certainly a curious passage; for though it is ostensibly intended to assure us that all's right with the world, its effect is quite different.[1] It sounds as if Emerson were trying to exemplify the Second Law of Thermodynamics (Entropy). The law of nature seems to be the Fall; and an active imagination might be excused for hearing the echo of a Miltonic lapse in the final clause. Though

Emerson insists that his philosophy, being affirmative, "readily accepts the testimony of negative facts, as every shadow points to the sun" (W 2:155), it is his *positive* facts that sound ominous here in their ineluctably downward tendency.

Similar difficulties may be seen elsewhere in this presumably optimistic first series of *Essays*. Though "Love" might seem the ideal place for illustrating an "affirmative" philosophy, the opening of that essay is not entirely promising. Emerson naturally associates "the sentiment of love with the heyday of the blood" (W 2:169)—that is, with the health and optimism of youth. But his appropriation of a phrase from Hamlet's searing condemnation of his mother ("You cannot call it love, for at your age / The hey-day in the blood is tame") does not seem to bode well. And, indeed, Emerson goes on to say that he will "study the sentiment as it appeared in hope, and not in history. For each man sees his own life defaced and disfigured, as the life of man is not to his imagination":

> Every thing is beautiful seen from the point of the intellect, or as truth. But all is sour if seen as experience. Details are melancholy; the plan is seemly and noble. In the actual world—the painful kingdom of time and place—dwell care and canker and fear. With thought, with the ideal, is immortal hilarity, the rose of joy. Round it all the Muses sing. But grief cleaves to names and persons and the partial interests of to-day and yesterday. (W 2:171)

The world of experience, then, is a fallen one; for although love promises the stars and the heavens, it can only deliver trouble: "the lot of humanity is on these children. Danger, sorrow and pain arrive to them as to all" (W 2:185). All the wonderful things that drew them together, they will learn, were "deciduous, had a prospective end"—namely, "the purification of the intellect and the heart from year to year" (W 2:187). It is that grim sacrifice of the affections to a chastened heart to which love and friendship serve as a necessary apprenticeship in our lapsed estate. We do indeed "descend to meet" (W 2:199).

Descending

Although Emerson's acknowledgment of the Fall is usually dated from the death of Waldo (January 1842), there is ample evidence in his writings up to that time to show that his yea-saying was achieved in the face of a considerable tendency to say gloomier things.[2] Since he was trained as a minister, Emerson was of course familiar with all the "theological problems" which he was so eager to dismiss in "Spiritual Laws." But it is perhaps surprising to note the severity of the religious vocabulary which Emerson as a young *Unitarian* preacher found it natural to employ. In January 1827, for example, "anxious to sketch out the form of a sermon" which he had long had in mind upon the Crucifixion, he dwelt a good deal on sin and spoke of the "tremendous load of moral depravity by which the head of humanity has been so long borne down to the earth" (*JMN* 3:63). Some days later, he was still meditating on "mortal infirmity" and set down this passage:

> My friends we are sinful men. We can copy from our own memories the fatal history of the progress of sin. There is a tremendous sympathy to which we were born by which we do easily enter into the feelings of evil agents, of deep offenders in the hour of their temptation & their fall. We catch with intelligent ear the parley between the tempter & the tempted; we measure with sad alacrity the joys of guilt.
>
> This is a part of our condition, a part of our free agency & necessary to us as moral probationers. Let us then since it lies in our power observe these gradations by which he that stands in his purity suffers himself to decline to his fall. (*JMN* 3:67–68)

It might indeed be thought strange that a budding Unitarian minister raised on the enlightened anti-Calvinism of a William Ellery Channing should be seemingly so convinced of human depravity and so interested in the "gradations" that lead to the pit. As Emerson's modern editors note, "if the concern with sin is not obsessive either here or elsewhere, the young Emerson's intense conviction of sin still suggests more kinship between him and

Nathaniel Hawthorne than we have hitherto realized." [3] In this period, Emerson—like Young Goodman Brown or the Reverend Hooper—sometimes had a tendency to see sin everywhere ("in our cities, at our doors, in our chambers, in our bosoms. It is the custom of the time, it is the nature of man"), and to conclude that man "falls from innocence & like Adam in Eden is ashamed & seeks to hide himself" (*JMN* 3:69–70). He did not balk at composing a Fast Day Sermon in 1828, arguing that "when our fathers shook off the dust of the old world from their feet" they did not "shake off all its pollutions." Likening the early settlers to an unregenerate Christian in Bunyan's *Pilgrim's Progress*, Emerson avowed that this "dismal tradition appointing us with each returning /spring/equinox/ a day of Fasting, Humiliation, & Prayer" demonstrated that the "burden of vice" was still on their shoulders. Human nature does not "change with change of place," and man in America "stands the same being God made in the garden" (*JMN* 3:122).

One might argue, of course, that in these journal entries we find the young Emerson in his most conventionally ministerial posture, simply mouthing traditional phrases and doing the expected thing. But whose phrases? And by whom expected? This sort of expression is not truly characteristic of Unitarian Christianity in the Boston of the 1820s. [4] Perhaps one senses here the influence of Emerson's Aunt Mary Moody, who loved "the fiery depths of Calvinism," had "her bed made in the form of a coffin," and wore her shroud both in that bed by night and on horseback by day (*W* 10:403, 428). Emerson's respect for her doctrines and teaching cannot be ascribed to filiopietism alone, however, for something in his own character responded to her normally low estimate of human character and her disgust for the world and the flesh. His dour effusions on human depravity and the Fall may be accounted as much a part of Emerson as his "affirmative philosophy." Though he might come to conceive of evil as being merely privative—the absence of good—that absence, or emptiness, would always yawn somewhere at the bottom of Emerson's consciousness.

Descending

Though Emerson's quasi-orthodox adherence to notions of innate depravity and the Fall tended in the 1830s, as we should expect, to get translated into more purely symbolic, or existential, terms that could be subsumed in his constructive philosophy, it nevertheless continues to be heard as a bothersome undertone. In April 1837, Emerson noted that "the existence of a 'Paradise Lost,' a Dante's 'Inferno' argues a half disbelief of the immortality of the Soul" (*JMN* 5:308). Not quite willing to jettison his Milton and Dante, Emerson tried to absorb the inner meaning of their parables while rejecting their literal belief in lapsarian and salvific history. In August he asked himself:

> What means all the monitory tone of the world of life, of literature, of tradition? Man is fallen Man is banished; an exile; he is in earth whilst there is a heaven. What do these apologues mean? These seem to him traditions of memory. But they are the whispers of hope and Hope is the voice of the Supreme Being to the Individual.
>
> We say Paradise was; Adam fell; the Golden Age; & the like. We mean man is not as he ought to be; but our way of painting this is on Time, and we say *Was*. (*JMN* 5:371)

As "memory," the story of the Fall is dismal because it forms an ineluctable part of our history that casts a shadow wherever we turn. But taken as the symbolic discourse of the soul in its struggle for self-realization, it can be understood as a hopeful sign of our lively awareness that there are human limitations not yet transcended which may yet be. *Was* means that we have in fact done something wrong. Emerson's reading of the Fall as apologue suggests not a crime committed but a goal not yet reached—things still to be done right. "Let us hope infinitely," he wrote two years later, "& accustom ourselves to the reflection that the true Fall of man is the disesteem of man; the true Redemption selftrust" (*L* 2:213).

That is a fairly bloodless and comfortable version of the old fable, and we may be sure that Emerson himself was not contented with it. He was thinking a good deal about the Fall in 1839—

perhaps because of all the pain associated with his own "lapse" in the eyes of the Harvard Divinity Faculty; and his most interesting treatment of the idea occurs in the lecture of 1839 which we have already examined, "The Protest":

> What is the front the world always shows to the young spirit? Strange to say, The Fall of Man. The Fall of Man is the first word of history and the last fact of experience. In the written annals or in the older tradition of every nation this dark legend is told of the depravation of a once pure and happy society. And in the experience of every individual somewhat analogous is recognized.
>
> In all our reasonings respecting society this is assumed, that there has been violation and consequent penalty and loss, to bring things into the confessedly bad pass where they are. What is the account to be given of this persuasion that has taken such deep root in all minds? What but this that it is an universal fact that man is always in his actual life lapsing from the Commandments of the Soul? His enemy is indeed very near him as the cohort of angels in the Garden of Eden detected the Snake "squat close by the ear of Eve." (*EL* 3:86–87)

Although Emerson's point here is presumably the same one we have already noticed—namely, that the Fall represents nothing more than a lack of self-esteem or self-trust—he pays a good deal more attention to the Fall as a *fact* of history and tradition. He no longer treats it as mere apologue, since the individual human experience of the Fall is only "somewhat analogous" to the dark universal legends he finds everywhere. What we have, in effect, are two things: Emerson's application of the fable to man's condition as a moral being *and* his seemingly unshakable sense that something very like a historical event continues to reverberate in time. The Fall is thus given more weight as a hypostatization, helped along by the sinister presence of Milton's fallen angel.

Emerson immediately continues, to be sure, to draw out the moral implications of his fable ("there is somewhat infirm and retreating in every action; a pause of self-praise; a second thought"), but the certain sign of his inability to remain happy with this disposal of the issue is its return in other forms as the lecture progresses. Railing against the tendency he finds in writers to imitate old books (" 'The Classics,' 'the Classics'! forsooth; as if there were only twenty or fifty books to be called books to set the pitch for all thought"), Emerson bursts out in a fashion which his nominal subject hardly seems to justify: "Ah me! Is there any tragedy so dire as this deliquium, of this falling back, this epilepsy, this old age? that virtue should pause; and intellect pause, and decease out of the body, *it* remaining to drivel on for the pleasure of the senses" (ibid., pp. 88–89). Here Emerson's sense of the Fall as a *physiological* event in human experience is strong, and one feels his disgust at the physical limitations of human life, especially in the tendency of the body to decay.

On the next page, Emerson repeats his thought, this time as a separate paragraph: "This old age; this ossification of the heart; this fat in the brain; this degeneracy; is the Fall of Man." There can be little doubt, it seems to me, that Emerson has finally exposed a reaction to the idea of the Fall which is much more serious than his moralizing and is curiously persistent in his writing— namely, a generalized sense of horror at the entropic nature of the human condition. It is one thing to be "diseased" by "theological problems of original sin . . . and the like," which may be rooted out by right thinking. But when the disease, to paraphrase Alexander Pope, is the longer one of life itself, it is more difficult to know where to turn. Or perhaps not, at least for Emerson. Later in the lecture his motif returns, and we learn the final extent to which Emerson has descended in his exploration of the old legend. "Carlyle and others," he writes, "who complain of the sickly separation of the beauty of nature in this age from the thing to be done do not see that our hunting of the picturesque is inseparable from our protest against false society. Man is fallen but Nature is unfallen" (ibid., p. 98). Now the Fall seems final and ineluctable. Emerson's only solution is to flee the society of man and find refuge in his beloved nature. We shall see shortly how the passage quoted above finds its true resting place and fruition in the more thoroughly disillusioned context of the second series of *Essays*.

In other journal entries of this period, Emerson tended to associate the idea of the Fall, and sin generally, with the "sad riddle" of old age, and to treat it as the dark foil which helps to set off the dazzling power of his bright Transcendental vision. "It is a shade," he wrote in 1839, "which adds splendor to the lights" (*JMN* 7:250). In a passage that would be caught up in the essay "Circles," Emerson argued that if he allowed himself to "esteem it an entity" his hair would already begin to grizzle. He, on the contrary, would parry and annihilate age by wrapping himself "in God's eternal youth." "Every set sun rises," he insisted, "every loss has a gain":

> Nor shall even this hated phantom with its evil insignia of baldness, toothless gums, cracked voice, defaced face, & fumbling peevish trifling, stand in the wide beauty of the Universe hopeless. There is recovery from this lapse & awaking from this haggard dream.

The entry is important because it also feeds into Emerson's elegy on the death of Waldo, "Threnody," where—curiously—the "defaced face" of old age somehow comes to be associated with the boy's loss ("Ill day which made this beauty waste, / Plight broken, this high face defaced!" [*W* 9:153]). Emerson's sense, in the poem, of the possibility of "recovery from this lapse" is very different from what we find in "Circles," where all difficulties are obliterated in the dazzling sunlight of Emerson's frenziedly optimistic rhetoric:

> ... there is no sleep, no pause, no preservation, but all things renew, germinate and spring. Why should we import rags and relics into the new hour? Nature abhors the old, and old age seems the only disease; all others run into this one. We call it by many names —fever, intemperance, insanity, stupidity and crime; they are all forms of old age; they are rest, conservatism, appropriation, inertia; not newness, not the way onward. We grizzle every day. I see

no need of it. Whilst we converse with what is above us, we do not grow old, but grow young. Infancy, youth, receptive, aspiring, with religious eye looking upward, counts itself nothing and abandons itself to the instruction flowing from all sides. But the man and woman of seventy assume to know all, they have outlived their hope, they renounce aspiration, accept the actual for the necessary and talk down to the young. Let them then become organs of the Holy Ghost; let them be lovers; let them behold truth; and their eyes are uplifted, their wrinkles smoothed, they are perfumed again with hope and power. This old age ought not to creep on a human mind. In nature every moment is new; the past is always swallowed and forgotten; the coming only is sacred. Nothing is secure but life, transition, the energizing spirit. (W 2:319–20)

In a reversal of time involving a happy reinterpretation of myth, Emerson sees old age, or the Fall, as being equivalent to our past —to a resting in deeds, or misdeeds, already accomplished. In the perpetual future toward which this endless seeker without a past rushes, he sees eternal youth and the annihilation of historical time. Old age is viewed, in a sense, in postural terms: we fall when we begin to "talk down" instead of conversing "with what is above us." Emerson exhorts us to spring, aspire, look upward—lift up our eyes. The Fall is thus seen to be a question of *attitude:* moral supineness, the declension of the spirit, can be overcome by a radical repositioning of one's being. We must always be ready to "rise into another idea" and invent a better language of the spirit ("the Greek letters . . . are already . . . tumbling into the inevitable pit which the creation of new thought opens for all that is old" [W 2:302]). The heaven toward which we climb might be defined as simply the last stage of our individual self-realization: "Step by step we scale this mysterious ladder; the steps are actions, the new prospect is power" (W 2:305). Only if our faith becomes infirm and our will ceases to be strenuous do we run the risk of slipping —of being tossed out of heaven and finding ourselves nothing but a "weed by the wall" (W 2:307). The risk, however, is a very real one. We recall Emerson's fondness for those lines from Wordsworth's "Excursion" which he considered "a sort of elegy" for his age:

> And the most difficult of tasks to keep
> Heights which the soul is competent to gain.[5]

In general, however, Emerson seems to have intended his first collection of *Essays* to be largely controlled by figures of ascension.[6] In "Self-Reliance" we read that "the soul *becomes*," that power "resides in the moment of transition from a past to a new state, in the shooting of the gulf, in the darting to an aim" (*W* 2:69). The inchoate metaphor develops in "Compensation," where Emerson affirms that "the soul refuses limits," for man's "life is a progress, and not a station." The law of nature "is growth," and "the voice of the Almighty saith, 'Up and onward for evermore!' " (*W* 2:122, 124, 126). The method of man is "a progressive arrangement," we are told in "Spiritual Laws" (*W* 2:144); and this means, as regards the affections (in "Love"), that we must pass from lower attractions to higher ones: "the lover ascends to the highest beauty, to the love and knowledge of the Divinity, by steps on this ladder of created souls" (*W* 2:182–83). Since, in "Friendship," we "descend to meet," we must make room for one another's merits—"let them mount and expand"—parting, if need be, so that we may "meet again on a higher platform" (*W* 2:199, 209, 214). This is the "spiritual astronomy" of love (*W* 2:215), as it is the law of the soul's progress in "The Over-Soul" ("the soul's advances are not made by gradation, such as can be represented by motion in a straight line, but rather by ascension of state" [*W* 2:274]). Emerson's figure develops further, in the first series of *Essays,* with "Circles," which is essentially devoted to working out a set of variations on the notion of man as "a self-evolving circle," a rising spiral, who, as we have noticed, is exhorted to scale the "mysterious ladder" of upwardly mobile life (*W* 2:304–5). Emerson rushes eagerly "from the centre to the verge" of his orbit, warning us to think "how many times we shall fall back into pitiful

calculations before we . . . make the verge of to-day the new centre"
(*W* 2:315). In the last essay of the book, "Art," we are urged to
cast off the clogs of prudential consideration and believe that "the
soul is progressive." Like the biblical Jacob, Emerson shows man

> Retinues of airy kings,
> Skirts of angels, starry wings,
> His fathers shining in bright fables,
> His children fed at heavenly tables.

Catching up "both the days and firmament," Art can

> Teach him on these as stairs to climb
> And live on even terms with Time. (*W* 2:349–51)

Although "The Poet" stands at the head of the second series of
Essays, it actually serves as the culmination of the heady anti-
lapsarian vision which the first series works hard to achieve, and in
fact it was probably designed by Emerson, in a sort of literary
chiaroscuro, to offset the gathering darkness that follows ("Experience"). The Poet—the *true* Poet—is the Christ-like hero whose
logos breaks our chains and allows us to "mount above these
clouds and opaque airs" in which we normally dwell. The inferior
poet deceives and disappoints us, for "he does not know the way
into the heavens, and is merely bent that I should admire his skill
to rise like a fowl or a flying fish, a little way from the ground or
the water; but the all-piercing, all-feeding and ocular air of heaven
that man shall never inhabit." If we follow him, we "tumble down
again soon" into our old nooks (*W* 3:12–13). Great poets are
"liberating gods" who preach *"ascension,* or the passage of the
soul into higher forms . . . into free space" (*W* 3:32, 24, 28).
Released by this extraordinary savior into "celestial space," we live
the heavenly life of the redeemed imagination: "dream delivers us
to dream, and while the drunkenness lasts we will sell our bed, our
philosophy, our religion, in our opulence" (*W* 3:42, 33). Here

finally, perhaps, is Emerson's best attempt to recover from the lapse of sin and sorrow, as he shows us the sublime figure of the Poet delivering him from the "haggard dream" of decay to the wild opulence of Transcendental vision. "For the time of towns is tolled from the world by funereal chimes," but in the metamorphosed nature of the Poet, "the universal hours are counted by succeeding tribes of animals and plants, and by growth of joy on joy" (W 3:41). If we have allowed the magic of our own poetic guide, Emerson, fully to work on us, we do indeed find ourselves set up on a pinnacle far above the "weary kingdom of time" (W 3:23). But, alas, we have only to turn the last page of this essay in order to discover that we are the victims of a kind of deceit and to feel ourselves tumbling down to a considerably less joyful position. "Fled is that music:—Do I wake or sleep?"

Lordly Man's Down-Lying

Whether or not Emerson had Keats' "Ode to a Nightingale" in mind as he moved from "The Poet" to "Experience," the opening paragraph of the latter replicates strikingly Keats's initial mood in the poem of drug-induced confusion and uncertainty:

> My heart aches, and a drowsy numbness pains
>   My sense, as though of hemlock I had drunk,
> Or emptied some dull opiate to the drains
>   One minute past, and Lethe-wards had sunk . . .

Emerson begins his most moving essay in a similar state and with an ominous question, to which he provides a dubious response:

> Where do we find ourselves? In a series of which we do not know the extremes, and believe that it has none. We wake and find ourselves on a stair; there are stairs below us, which we seem to have ascended; there are stairs above us, many a one, which go upward and out of sight. But the Genius which according to the old belief stands at the door by which we enter, and gives us the lethe to drink, that we may tell no tales, mixed the cup too strongly, and we cannot shake off the lethargy now at noonday. Sleep lingers all our lifetime about our eyes, as night hovers all day in the boughs of the fir-tree. All things swim and glitter. Our life is not so much threatened as our perception. Ghostlike we glide through nature,

and should not know our place again. Did our birth fall in some fit of indigence and frugality in nature, that she was so sparing of her fire and so liberal of her earth that it appears to us that we lack the affirmative principle, and though we have health and reason, yet we have no superfluity of spirit for new creation? We have enough to live and bring the year about, but not an ounce to impart or to invest. Ah that our Genius were a little more of a genius! We are like the millers on the lower levels of a stream, when the factories above them have exhausted the water. We too fancy that the upper people must have raised their dams. (W 3:45–46)

I have quoted this fine paragraph in its entirety because not a word of it can be spared as an example of the complexity of Emerson's art in relation to his evolving career.

The mood of loss combined with numbness—the sense of being *out of touch*—which Emerson establishes here provides the keynote of the essay and is normally ascribed to the death of little Waldo in January 1842. That description of the genesis of the piece is certainly correct, in the main. Emerson was shattered by this most terrible of all losses, and the extremity of his reaction can be measured in the perdurability of the depressive state that he is exhibiting here. But the well from which Emerson drew his creations is an uncommonly deep one and difficult to fathom in any simple way. Thus, for example, we find in a letter to an intimate friend, Elizabeth Hoar, dated September 1840, one clear source for Emerson's striking opening: "We are very solitary—I am,—not only forsaken of companions but forsaken of thoughts—befriended only by the treacherous Sleep which hovers on all lids in these autumnal nights & *days*" (L 2:330). The associations that Emerson establishes here are of considerable interest. Feeling lonely, "forsaken," *emptied,* he finds that his only comfort—obviously a sinister one—is a pervasive sense of lethargy that offers the dubious gift of daytime sleep: which is to say, oblivion. Somehow, Emerson associates this mood with autumn, perhaps because the notion of being dragged off to hibernation unwillingly suggests the uneasy transition from fall to winter. The idea of sleeping before one's time, of course, also informs the opening of "Experience." In both cases, the fundamental threat is *blindness*, Emerson's old *bête noire* [*Nature:* "I feel that nothing can befall me in life—no disgrace, no calamity (leaving me my eyes), which nature cannot repair"]. One might say that Emerson's tragedy is a pastoral version of the one suffered more heroically by Milton's Samson ("Scarce half I seem to live, dead more than half. / O dark, dark, dark, amid the blaze of noon").[7]

Though immeasurably sharpened by the irremediable loss of his five-year-old son, Emerson's fear that he is pursuing a darkening way is thus not entirely a new one. Indeed, Emerson's indictment of nature here ("so sparing of her fire and so liberal of her earth"), suggesting that he has been endowed, unfortunately, with a "phlegmatic" humor, is directly linked to a passage in "The Poet" (also, incidentally, tinged with a Miltonic allusion):

> There is no man who does not anticipate a supersensual utility in the sun and stars, earth and water. These stand and wait to render him a peculiar service. But there is some obstruction or some excess of phlegm in our constitution, which does not suffer them to yield the due effect. Too feeble fall the impressions of nature on us to make us artists. Every touch should thrill. (W 3:5–6)[8]

Every touch *should* thrill; but Emerson feels numbed and blinded, threatened generally in his perceptions (he will shortly speak about his inability to feel *touched*). But a more important link between Emerson's mood at the opening of "Experience" and earlier problems may be found in the significant controlling figure here: that of *position*. Emerson's initial question—"Where do we find ourselves?"—though it is immediately answered ("in a series . . ."), implies a more fearful response: we do not know *where* we are.[9] His "series" is vague, without beginning or end, a staircase reminiscent of Piranesi's nightmarish engravings *(Carceri d'Invenzione)* of infinite ascent and descent.[10] In this case, there seem to be more stairs above than below ("above us, many a one, which go upward and out of sight"). Emerson has awakened *into* a ghastly dream in which he has miles to go before he is truly awake, but has neither the strength nor the clarity of vision needed to complete the job. In a sense, the objective correlative of his depression is the feeling of being *pushed down.*

Like Keats at the opening of his "Ode," Emerson has *sunk* Lethe-wards. His direction is down, toward the earth ("Did our birth fall in some fit of indigence and frugality in nature, that she was so sparing of her fire and so liberal of her earth . . . ?"). This sense of being *below* rather than *above* is confirmed at the conclusion of the paragraph, when Emerson speaks about feeling like a miller "on the lower levels of a stream" who is deprived of power because "the upper people . . . have raised their dams." We may notice also that this sensation of incapacity, and its attitudinal metaphor, directly revises the central figure used in the first series of *Essays.* As we have already seen, Emerson writes in "Circles": "Step by step we scale this mysterious ladder; the steps are actions, the new prospect is power." Now, the ladder is even more mysterious, the infinity of steps denies the possibility of action, and the prospect is powerlessness.

It is worth noting that in the journal entry which Emerson used almost verbatim for the opening sentences of "Experience," the only significant variation in the original version suggests a familiar biblical *topos:* "there are stairs above us many a one, they go up to heaven" (*JMN* 8:238). It seems, then, that Emerson initially had Jacob's ladder in mind ("and he dreamed, and behold a ladder set up on the earth, and the top of it reached to heaven: and behold the angels of God ascending and descending on it"). As always, Emerson's "text" is inverted, or subverted: his stairs go, not to any certain heaven, but "upward and out of sight"; there are no angels —he seems to be alone; and the presiding figure is not God, promising Jacob durable seed and the continuation of heaven's favor, but a sinister "Genius" who drugged Emerson in some indefinite past. Unlike Jacob, who knows where he is (Luz, Bethel), Emerson is in a "place" which is unnamed and phantasmagoric; trapped inside his own head in an endless dream ("dream delivers us to dream, and there is no end to illusion. . . . Temperament . . . shuts us in a prison of glass which we cannot see" [*W* 3:50, 51–52]). Indeed, Emerson explicates his "ladder" figure in this fashion later in the essay: "The consciousness in each man is a sliding scale, which identifies him now with the First Cause, and now with the flesh of his body; life above life, in infinite degrees" (*W* 3:72). As "Experience" begins, then, his higher consciousness is dimmed and he seems to be stuck at the bottom of the ladder.[11]

I have been arguing, in effect, that this opening paragraph of the essay provides a series of metaphoric correlatives for a version of the Fall, which Emerson continues to translate, in characteristically Romantic fashion, into psychological and epistemological terms. In a sense, the traditional story has been reversed: Emerson's lapse brings not knowledge but confusion and oblivion. The traditional punishment—death—as a finality and a clear border, would be, as Emerson says, "a grim satisfaction" and a deliverance: "There at least is reality that will not dodge us" (*W* 3:49). Instead, Uriel has fallen into a cloud of uncertainty that separates him from all objects and precludes the noble suffering of tragedy: "What opium is instilled into all disaster! It shows formidable as we approach it, but there is at last no rough rasping friction, but the most slippery sliding surfaces; we fall soft on a thought" (*W* 3:48). This softness is the ultimate horror, since we are made to feel confident that the world is really *there* by hitting against its "sharp peaks and edges." Emerson does not feel depraved but rather nonexistent—privative. Adam at least "fell" into the world of experience. But, as a modern refinement of torture, Emerson finds that he does not fall *into* anything definite; he continues to fall, feeling himself alone in space. The calamity of his son's death "falls" from him; "it was caducous." He cannot get a grip on anything. People no longer seem real; the world "has no inside" (*W* 3:64).[12] Reduced to that position of ultimate skepticism which he had only toyed with in *Nature*, unable to wander anywhere but in the ghastly labyrinth of his own perceptions, Emerson sees his internal blankness and emptiness everywhere: "Thus inevitably does the universe wear our color, and every object fall successively into the subject itself. The subject exists, the subject enlarges; all things sooner or later fall into place. As I am, so I see; use what language we will, we can never say anything but what we are" (W 3:79). The best measure of Emerson's *fallen* state lies in the language that he is inevitably driven to use.

At the heart of the essay, we find the celebrated passage in which Emerson tried explicitly to redefine the ancient fable in a way that appropriately expresses his nineteenth-century sense that "our life is not so much threatened as our perception":

> It is very unhappy, but too late to be helped, the discovery we have made that we exist. That discovery is called the Fall of Man. Ever afterwards we suspect our instruments. We have learned that we do not see directly, but mediately, and that we have no means of correcting these colored and distorting lenses which we are, or of computing the amount of their errors. Perhaps these subject-lenses have a creative power; perhaps there are no objects. Once we lived in what we saw; now, the rapaciousness of this new power, which threatens to absorb all things, engages us. Nature, art, persons, letters, religions, objects, successively tumble in, and God is but one of its ideas. (W 3:75–76)

The new power that engages Emerson is the power of his own mind to create the world of illusion in which he lives. It is the power, effectively and paradoxically, to make nothing out of some-thing—to absorb the world and turn it into uncertainties. Accord-ingly, self-consciousness—"the discovery we have made that we exist"—brings Emerson to call into question not only the existence of that very world in which alone our own existence can have any meaning but our being itself ("we suspect our instruments"). Flying without instruments, we are really in the dark. The rapacity of self-consciousness causes it to incorporate all things into its own null center, to force them to "tumble in," whereby we are left with a "world" which is totally fallen—within and without. Mephistophelean negativity reigns supreme—*der Geist der stets verneint* ("the Spirit that denies").[13] Perhaps Emerson's true reaction to his son's death is an anger directed at Being in general that he dares not express except in an oblique way. Anger, however, is not Emerson's strong suit. And one might say that his more characteristic way of exhibiting hostility toward the God who has offered him the ultimate insult of taking away his child is magisterially to deny Him reality.

In any case, the dominant mood of the essay is not anger but perplexity and a pervasive sense of incapacity in the face of experience. Most things are "very unhappy, but too late to be helped." If Emerson nourishes any Ahab-like impulse to strike out at the pasteboard mask, it is checked by his belief that it would be ineffectual: "Direct strokes [nature] never gave us power to make; all our blows glance, all our hits are accidents" (*W* 3:49–50). The only choice we have is "between soft and turbulent dreams" (*W* 3:84). A man dreaming is normally in a supine posture—the posture of powerlessness. Perhaps Emerson's most terrible definition of our fallen condition resides in this figure: we are not in a *position* to help ourselves.

But Emerson was always made acutely uncomfortable by the rhetoric of defeat and insists on snatching a small victory from his minor mood. To be sure, with the crushing weight that lies upon them, his affirmative sentences can only seem rather hollow reeds: "Why not realize your world? . . . Patience and patience, we shall win at the last" (*W* 3:85). Are they meant ironically? The very language seems to wobble (in the essay, nothing seems *real; patience* means suffering, and what is the use of winning *at the last?*). No, Emerson is serious, though apparently not very convinced by his own obligatory affirmations. The final effect, therefore, is that the despairing mood is further exacerbated by this weak attempt to recoup losses. Emerson is more successful, perhaps, at the beginning of his last sentence, where he manages to wed his positive impulse to the steadily accumulating pathos of the piece: "Never

mind the ridicule, never mind the defeat; up again, old heart!"
Emerson staggers to his feet, determined to continue up the ladder,
even though the darkness has not lifted. It may be that he was
encouraged by remembering his own sentence from the conclusion
to "Circles": " 'A man,' said Oliver Cromwell, 'never rises so high
as when he knows not whither he is going' " (W 2:322). As Emerson well knew, the stern old Puritan spirit had learned how to
make a virtue out of uncertainty.

[11]

"Threnody" (W 9:148–58), the Lamentation of our Concord Jeremiah over his "darling who shall not return,"[14] attempts to achieve
what "Experience" does not quite manage: a credible response to
the Fall. The poem begins in a mood close to despair, with the
return of "Life, sunshine and desire" in the fecundating breath of
the south-wind:

> But over the dead he has no power,
> The lost, the lost, he cannot restore . . .

Not only is the father powerless; not even the great generative
force of nature can restore the dead boy. And the very Fate that
took him is bound by its own decrees:

> Fate let him fall, Fate can't retake him;
> Nature, Fate, men, him seek in vain.

The Fall, then, appears absolute and irremediable. Little Waldo is
lost to the ground forever. Even in noticing the boy's playthings,
the father seems to suggest emblems of the inevitable descent:

> His gathered sticks to stanch the wall
> Of the snow-tower, when snow should fall;

The ominous hole he dug in the sand,
And childhood's castles built or planned . . .

Reenacting his suffering on the "shaded day" when his son
died, Emerson suggests that his personal agony expanded to include the feeling that a universal age of darkness was being ushered
in:

> . . . if I repine,
> And seeing rashly torn and moved
> Not what I made, but what I loved,
> Grow early old with grief that thou
> Must to the wastes of Nature go,—
> 'Tis because a general hope
> Was quenched, and all must doubt and grope.
> For flattering planets seemed to say
> This child should ills of ages stay . . .

Waldo, in his father's eyes, might have helped redeem the world
from its ancient evil; instead, he himself has fallen, and Emerson
feels drawn into a premature old age which represents his own
lapse:

> The eager fate which carried thee
> Took the largest part of me:
> For this losing is true dying;
> This is lordly man's down-lying,
> This his slow but sure reclining,
> Star by star his world resigning.

In these fine lines—perhaps the strongest in the poem—Emerson
articulates his belief that the true meaning of the Fall, and death, is
the *experience* of loss and of the inevitable declension of one's
private solar system. Entropy, in a sense, has been domesticated.
As we feel our world falling piece by piece, the actual process of
lapsing is brought directly home to us.

Emerson can get no lower, and so after ten more lines of

lament, the poem turns to its response as "the deep Heart" answers the inconsolable father:

> . . . Weepest thou?
> Worthier cause for passion wild
> If I had not taken the child.
> And deemest thou as those who pore,
> With aged eyes, short way before,—
> Think'st Beauty vanished from the coast
> Of matter, and thy darling lost?

Admittedly, those first lines are hard to take, with their flat assertion that the child is somehow better off dead. We may be excused for sympathizing with the presumably short-sighted father who takes the loss at face value *as* a loss—nothing less, or more. But what follows is more interesting, and (Emerson undoubtedly hopes) more convincing:

> Taught he not thee—the man of eld,
> Whose eyes within his eyes beheld
> Heaven's numerous hierarchy span
> The mystic gulf from God to man?
> To be alone wilt thou begin
> When worlds of lovers hem thee in?

Emerson's aim is to find a way of expressing believably the idea that those whom we truly love—those to whom we have consecrated out lives—can never be entirely lost to us. He accordingly begins by invoking the very figure whose presence we noted in the opening lines of "Experience": Jacob and his ladder.[15] Now, however, the vision of "the man of eld" has more positive connotations, suggesting to Emerson the possibility that the "mystic gulf" from earth to sky is not a terrifyingly empty abyss but a closed circuit filled with being.

It would be a mistake, I think, to assume that Emerson, in his grief, is simply falling back on a conventional notion of "Heaven" and all the appurtenances of traditional piety. That *might* be the case, though it need not be. Jacob's vision is presented as a totally inner one ("whose eyes within his eyes beheld . . .") and Emerson adopts it on what Santayana calls the "higher plane . . . of significant imagination, of relevant fiction, of idealism become the interpretation of the reality it leaves behind."[16] On this plane, "poetry raised to its highest power" becomes "identical with religion grasped in its inmost truth." For Emerson, Jacob's ladder is a true figuration of his belief in the subsistence of all those things which he has loved. Like Keats, Emerson seems "certain of nothing but of the holiness of the Heart's affections and the truth of Imagination."[17] He is therefore chided by the "deep Heart" of nature for appearing to falter in his belief in the power of his imagination to create a permanent place in his own heart for the lost boy:

> But thou, my votary, weepest thou?
> I gave thee sight—where is it now?
> I taught thy heart beyond the reach
> Of ritual, bible, or of speech;
> Wrote in thy mind's transparent table,
> As far as the incommunicable;
> Taught thee each private sign to raise
> Lit by the supersolar blaze.

Nature's injunction, *sursum corda,* echoes Jeremiah's ("Let us lift up our heart with our hands unto God in the heavens"). And that is what Emerson is struggling to do, as he had at the end of "Experience" ("up again, old heart!"), but in his own fashion and beyond the Bible's reach. He is attempting to translate "each private sign" of his own "past the blasphemy of grief" to the level of durable truth.

The section of the poem that immediately follows is perhaps less successful, arguing as it does in a more conventional way that the life-force by definition cannot be circumscribed or halted in its restless career:

Light is light which radiates
Blood is blood which circulates,
Life is life which generates,
And many-seeming life is one,—
Wilt thou transfix and make it none?

These are all truisms, of course (though the death of a child is especially poignant, childhood itself is transient, we are *all* in the midst of life moving toward death). And though we assent to them, they can hardly be expected to capture our faith or provide deep consolation. But Emerson now builds to better lines, italicized for emphasis, which return to the more personal theme of the holiness of the heart's affections and its power to consecrate:

. . . What is excellent,
As God lives, is permanent;
Hearts are dust, hearts' loves remain;
Heart's love will meet thee again.

Although the use of the second person singular gives the lines a somewhat old-fashioned air, they are still eloquent and memorable. Indeed, the high priest of literary Modernism, Ezra Pound, apparently could do no better than reach back and join hands with Emerson when he himself strove for an especially elevated rhetoric in a celebrated moment in the *Pisan Cantos*:

What thou lovest well remains, the rest is dross
What thou lov'st well shall not be reft from thee
What thou lov'st well is thy true heritage . . .[18]

But the best gloss on Emerson's lines, and on "Threnody" generally, is to be found in a letter of Santayana's, thoroughly permeated with the Emersonian spirit, which he wrote to the Marchesa Iris Origo after the death of her own little boy:

Lordly Man's Down-Lying

We have no claim to any of our possessions. We have no claim to exist; and as we have to die in the end, so we must resign ourselves to die piecemeal, which really happens when we lose somebody or something that was closely intertwined with our existence. It is like a physical wound; we may survive, but maimed and broken in that direction; dead there.

Not that we ever can, or ever do, at heart, renounce our affections. Never that. We cannot exercise our full nature all at once in every direction; but the parts that are relatively in abeyance, their centre lying perhaps in the past or in the future, belong to us inalienably. We should not be ourselves if we cancelled them. I don't know how literally you may believe in another world, or whether the idea means very much to you. As you know, I am not myself a believer in the ordinary sense, yet my *feeling* on this subject is like that of believers, and not at all like that of my fellow-materialists. The reason is that I disagree utterly with that modern philosophy which regards *experience* as fundamental. Experience is a mere whiff or rumble, produced by enormously complex and ill-deciphered causes of experience; and, in the other direction, experience is a mere peephole through which glimpses come down to us of eternal things. These are the only things that, in so far as we are spiritual beings, we can find or can love at all. All our affections, when clear and pure, and not claims to possession, transport us to another world; and the loss of contact, here or there, with those eternal beings is merely like closing a book which we keep at hand for another occasion. We know that book by heart. Its verses give life to life.[19]

Santayana's view of the incomprehensibility of experience—as it rumbles mysteriously up from the ground of being or peeps tantalizingly down from the eternal realms—might serve as a précis of Emerson's essay. Heaven can only be described as the book of "Being" which is inscribed by our affections. As Emerson writes in the poem:

Not of adamant and gold
Built he heaven stark and cold;

No, but a nest of bending reeds,
Flowering grass and scented weeds;
Or like a traveller's fleeing tent,
Or bow above the tempest bent;
Built of tears and sacred flames . . .

Heaven is the place in our heart where the transient objects of our love, themselves inevitably doomed to fall and cherished for that transience, find their only permanent shrine.

Emerson concludes by returning to, and revising, his old fable:

Silent rushes the swift Lord
Through ruined systems still restored,
Broadsowing, bleak and void to bless,
Plants with worlds the wilderness;
Waters with tears of ancient sorrow
Apples of Eden ripe tomorrow.
House and tenant go to ground,
Lost in God, in Godhead found.

Perhaps Santayana was not quite accurate when he said of Emerson in 1903 that "he retained no weakness for a sacred geography which is not exactly geography, or a sacred history which is not quite history."[20] Though his belief has evaporated, a certain "weakness" does indeed remain. What has been sacrificed in Emerson's books of geography and history is yet retained as a *topos* of the imagination. The Fall still reverberates for Emerson, though the traditional tones have now been made part of a new harmony. Those ancient tears continue to water apples of Eden which will be plucked and eaten tomorrow. They, and we, will naturally fall, as always. But are those prospective apples the fruit of sorrow alone? Emerson refuses to believe that. Casting his eyes down, Emerson sees that the ground on which he lies is also the ground of his being. The spirit that made Waldo will persist in its love and remembrance.

SONGS OF AUTUMN

"Life itself is a bubble and a scepticism, and a sleep within a sleep" (W 3:65). This sentence from "Experience" is a fair representation, from one point of view, of Emerson's autumnal music, for he seems to have associated that bittersweet season with the dubieties and disillusionments of the skeptical mood. That is the time of year when he found himself "counting and describing ... doubts or negations" and accordingly was moved to "celebrate the calendar-day of our Saint Michel de Montaigne" (W 4:173). If one felt spiritually sluggish and constipated, Emerson believed that "Montaigne & the skeptics help us as myrrh & fruit against costiveness" (*JMN* 9:278). This was a remedy that Emerson not infrequently had recourse to as he approached his fortieth year. In 1841 he wrote in his journal: "For me, what I may call the autumnal style of Montaigne keeps all its old attraction" (*JMN* 8:43).[21] When Emerson came to complete his chapter on "Montaigne; Or, the Skeptic" for *Representative Men,* he enlarged upon the notion, putting his own words in this favorite author's mouth:

> I like gray days, and autumn and winter weather. I am gray and autumnal myself, and think an undress and old shoes that do not pinch my feet, and old friends who do not contrain me, and plain topics where I do not need to strain myself and pump my brains, the most suitable. Our condition as men is risky and ticklish enough. One cannot be sure of himself and his fortune an hour, but he may be whisked off into some pitiable or ridiculous plight. Why should

I vapor and play the philosopher, instead of ballasting, the best I can, this dancing balloon? So, at least, I live within compass, keep myself ready for action, and can shoot the gulf at last with decency. If there be anything farcical in such a life, the blame is not mine: let it lie at fate's and nature's door. (W 4:167)

Emerson is in a mood to settle down, providing for himself the solidity he needs for blasting off, as it were, on the ultimate journey. This is the season for reconciling oneself to things as they are, as a sort of preparation and counterweight for the great unknown beyond. "Why be an angel before your time?" Emerson asks (W 4:156). Though there may be "no enthusiasms, no aspiration" in such a posture, it at least helps Emerson feel "contented, self-respecting," as he keeps "the middle of the road" (W 4:169).

The parallels between this Emerson and the Emerson of "Experience" are obvious enough. Life is "a tempest of fancies," he writes there, "and the only ballast I know is a respect to the present hour" (W 3:60). He tries to convince himself that "everything good is on the highway. The middle region of our being is the temperate zone" (W 3:62) and that "mid-world is best":

> Nature, as we know her, is no saint. The lights of the church, the ascetics, Gentoos and corn-eaters, she does not distinguish by any favor. She comes eating and drinking and sinning. Her darlings, the great, the strong, the beautiful, are not children of our law; do not come out of the Sunday School, nor weigh their food, nor punctually keep the commandments. (W 3:64)

Though the tone of Emerson's accommodationist philosophy seems as amiable and comfortable as the old shoes he is recommending, there is (as Emerson would say) "poor smell" here too—an undercurrent of bitterness at life's forcing him to sing *vive la bagatelle* so bravely. He is at heart disgusted, as he writes at the end of "Montaigne," that there should be such a chasm "between the largest promise of ideal power, and the shabby experience" (W 4:185).

The world he has been trying so hard to take to his bosom is one which is "eating us up"—one in which "things seem to tend downward, to justify despondency, to promote rogues, to defeat the just" (W 4:154, 185). Though Emerson seems to have set his heart in this chapter on singing Luther's jolly tune about wine, women, and song, he cannot help noticing "abyss open under abyss" as he concludes (W 4:153, 186).

Emerson, to be sure, is a compulsively dialectical thinker, and never likelier to remind himself of heaven than when he is treading the floor of the pit—whence the surprisingly optimistic endings one frequently finds tacked on to manifestly dour essays. Though his "Montaigne" leads us to the brink of a yawning abyss, we are to be assured that all is "at last contained in the Eternal Cause" and consoled by the flaccid line from Ellery Channing that improbably ends the piece ("If my bark sink, 'tis to another sea" [W 4:186]). Surely, Emerson's greatest weakness, especially in his later writings, appears when he is forced to rally himself with hollow rhetoric about the "great and beneficent tendency" that somehow streams through all the misery. Emerson's true autumnal music comes from a tougher mind—one that is capable of remaining clear-sighted and unflinching in the face of the gathering darkness. That aspect of the Emersonian spirit is exhibited in this journal entry of the mid-1840s: "When summer opens, I see how fast it matures, & fear it will be short; but after the heats of July & August, I am reconciled, like one who has had his swing, to the cool of autumn. So will it be with the coming of death" (*JMN* 9:393).

But there is, in fact, a much more convincing dialectic contained in the autumnal Emerson, the best model of which he himself sometimes found in his presumably unsaintly nature. I am speaking of the actuality and idea of Indian summer. Emerson was especially fond of this counter-current in which the declining year seems almost willfully to contradict its own general tendency. He called such days "the reconciling days which come to graduate the autumn into winter, & to comfort us after the first attacks of the cold. Soothsayers, prediction as well as memory, they look over December & January into the crepuscular lights of March & April" (*JMN* 8:292). Emerson appears to have associated Indian summer with the opportunity for self-recovery which inexplicably arises out of the autumnal season itself. On October 18, 1839, for example, Emerson set down in his journal an entry that seems naturally to expand in its implications beyond the business of planning a winter lecture series which provided the actual occasion for the passage:

> In these golden days it behoves me once more to make my annual inventory of the world. . . . Once more I must renew my work . . . What shall be the substance of my shrift? Adam in the garden, I am to new name all the beasts in the field & all the gods in the Sky. I am to invite men drenched in time to recover themselves & come out of time, & taste their native immortal air. (*JMN* 7:270–71)

Perhaps it is only a coincidence that Emerson's impulse toward self-renewal should be felt and articulated so strongly in the golden days of Indian summer, when nature pauses, as it were, to call attention to its inexorable time scheme and remember, and predict, other seasons. Emerson himself recalls the lost paradise and dreams, not of leading his audience back in time to recapture the ruined opportunity but rather of releasing them altogether from time into an eternal America of the spirit. Several years later, Emerson would note that the "American idea" is "Emancipation," which, "if followed, leads to heavenly places." Not, however, to any ordinary Republic which might be realized through political reform. Emerson was thinking of "a Columbia of thought & art which is the last & endless sequel of Columbus's adventure" (*JMN* 9:385).

Emerson, then, dreams of a "place," identified with an ideal "America," where he might find some "heavenly days," as he says in "Experience," which have been "intercalated" into his ordinary calendar (*W* 3:46). Thus, for Emerson himself, the most believable antithesis and corrective for the fallen mood of "Experience" is undoubtedly to be found not so much in the standard hortatory rhetoric which predictably brings up the rear of the essay as in this fine moment of exaltation that unexpectedly dispels the gloom about two-thirds of the way through:

> Underneath the inharmonious and trivial particulars, is a musical perfection; the Ideal journeying always with us, the heaven without rent or seam. Do but observe the mode of our illumination. When I converse with a profound mind, or if at any time being alone I have good thoughts, I do not at once arrive at satisfactions, as when, being thirsty, I drink water; or go to the fire, being cold; no! but I am at first apprised of my vicinity to a new and excellent region of life. By persisting to read or to think, this region gives further sign of itself, as it were in flashes of light, in sudden discoveries of its profound beauty and repose, as if the clouds that covered it parted at intervals and showed the approaching traveler the inland mountains, with the tranquil eternal meadows spread at their base, whereon flocks graze and shepherds pipe and dance. But every insight from this realm of thought is felt as initial, and promises a sequel. I do not make it; I arrive there, and behold what was there already. I make! O no! I clap my hands in infantine joy and amazement before the first opening to me of this august magnificence, old with the love and homage of innumerable ages, young with the life of life, the sunbright Mecca of the desert. And what a future it opens! I feel a new heart beating with the love of the new beauty. I am ready to die out of nature and be born again into this new yet unapproachable America I have found in the West. (W 3:71–72)[22]

Emerson's old love of "perfection" catches him up in the midst of his dreary autumnal pilgrimage and a very different music is heard. The reader who does not respond well to this passage will probably never be an Emersonian, because the excited shift of mood and the spontaneous exfoliation of joy out of literally nothing are among the best surprises Emerson has to offer. What occupies him is not only the "illumination" but the "mode" of it, which suggests that the possibility of ecstatic experience concerns not a simple question of yes or no but the more difficult one of *persistence*. One can help such experiences along—work one's way out of depression. Emerson's rhetoric is exploratory and constructively aposiopetic: "I do not make it; I arrive there, and behold what was there already. I make! O no! I clap my hands. . . ." Not sure whether he *makes* or *finds,* Emerson seems content to rest in celebration. For us, however, it is the explosive and whirling language that makes the experience—a verbal trick, if one likes. But that is the only sort of magic Emerson knows how to perform. He would undoubtedly have agreed with Wittgenstein when he says that "to imagine a language means to imagine a form of life,"[23] though Emerson might want to underline *imagine*. "People came, it seems, to my lectures," he wrote in 1843, "with expectation that I was to realize the Republic I described, & ceased to come when they found this reality no nearer. They mistook me. I am & always was a painter. I paint still with might & main, & choose the best subjects I can. Many have I seen come & go with false hopes & fears, and dubiously affected by my pictures. But I paint on" (*JMN* 9:49).

The visionary America that Emerson creates in "Experience" as a sort of compensation for the lost "beautiful estate" of his lamented Waldo is perhaps realized even more effectively in the essay "Nature" farther along in the book. This piece is especially interesting for us as we conclude our survey of Emerson's reactions to the idea of the Fall because it subsumes material from his writings of the 1820s and 1830s in a more comprehensive effort at reconciliation and renewal. Emerson's central theme in the essay is familiar: that the creative principle he finds in nature can be our only true guide and measure of perfection. Directly picking up his own language from the 1839 lecture "The Protest," Emerson states flatly that "man is fallen; nature is erect, and serves as a differential thermometer, detecting the presence or absence of the divine sentiment in man" (*W* 3:178). Emerson seems to detect so little of this divine presence in ordinary humankind that he is willing to assert that nature is "too bright almost for spotted man to enter without novitiate and probation" (W 3:173). And yet, he begins the essay by giving us a treasured glimpse of the immortal splendor of his own native land in a lush prose reminiscent of the opening of the Divinity School Address:

> There are days which occur in this climate, at almost any season of the year, wherein the world reaches its perfection; when the air, the heavenly bodies and the earth, make a harmony, as if nature would indulge her offspring; when, in these bleak upper sides of the planet, nothing is to desire that we have heard of the happiest latitudes, and we bask in the shining hours of Florida and Cuba; when everything that has life gives sign of satisfaction, and the cattle that lie on the ground seem to have great and tranquil thoughts. These halcyons may be looked for with a little more assurance in that pure October weather which we distinguish by the name of the Indian summer. The day, immeasurably long, sleeps over the broad hills and warm wide fields. To have lived through all its sunny hours, seems longevity enough. (W 3:169)

Once again, out of the heart, seemingly, of his bleak meditations on the Fall arise the perfect harmonies of Indian summer. Emerson holds out this redemptive vision even before he begins to lament over our low condition, as if to suggest that we may feel the workings of prevenient grace even though we have yet fully to examine the depths of our disgrace. We are saved even as we fall. Nature, somehow, is inclined to indulge us.

Though this descriptive opening is disarmingly naturalistic and seemingly gratuitous, presenting nothing more than a real Indian summer day in New England, it does in fact echo the opening of the more abstract passage we have just examined from "Experience" ("underneath the inharmonious and trivial particulars, is a musical perfection; the Ideal journeying always with us, the heaven without rent or seam"). But Emerson expands his range of reference very economically as he proceeds:

At the gates of the forest, the surprised man of the world is forced to leave his city estimates of great and small, wise and foolish. The knapsack of custom falls off his back with the first step he takes into these precincts. Here is sanctity which shames our religions, and reality which discredits our heroes. Here we find Nature to be the circumstance which dwarfs every other circumstance, and judges like a god all men that come to her. We have crept out of our close and crowded houses into the night and morning, and we see what majestic beauties daily wrap us in their bosom. How willingly we would escape the barriers which render them comparatively impotent, escape the sophistication and second thought, and suffer nature to intrance us. The tempered light of the woods is like a perpetual morning, and is stimulating and heroic. The anciently-reported spells of these places creep on us. The stems of pines, hemlocks and oaks almost gleam like iron on the excited eye. The incommunicable trees begin to persuade us to live with them, and quit our life of solemn trifles. Here no history, or church, or state is interpolated on the divine sky and the immortal year. How easily we might walk onward into the opening landscape, absorbed by new pictures and by thoughts fast succeeding each other, until by degrees the recollection of home was crowded out of the mind, all memory obliterated by the tyranny of the present, and we led in triumph by nature. (W 3:169–70)

It should not be difficult here for the reader to note an allusion to that famous book which Huckleberry Finn found "interesting but tough"—namely, Bunyan's *Pilgrim's Progress*—as Emerson describes the entrance of the "surprised man of the world" into nature's sacred precincts. Whosoever is permitted to enter this sanctified forest ceases to be fallen; rather, "the knapsack of custom falls off his back," as did Christian's bag of sins. We may now recall Emerson's notes for a Fast Day Sermon in 1828, in which he articulated his belief that the first settlers of New England, "when they came out of the roar of crowded cites into the desolate sea," did not leave behind them "that whisper of Temptation that is always heard in human ears." Unlike "the Pilgrim in the simple story of Bunyan," Emerson argued then, "as they went up the steep mountain of Difficulty . . . the burden of vice [did not] fall forever from their shoulders" (*JMN* 3:122). In 1844, as we have seen, Emerson is still bound to some version of the Fall. But he has counterbalanced his sense of loss with the faith that salvation is but a step away, so to speak, at the entrance to Walden woods. We may all make that pilgrimage into the divine and immortal splendor of Indian summer, and, if we walk far enough and seriously enough, find ourselves, like Christian, losing all "recollection of home" as we are "led in triumph" to nature's redemptive center. Nature, he will go on to say, "is loved by what is best in us. It is loved as the city of God" (*W* 3:178).[24]

We may also notice that in this opening paragraph of "Nature," Emerson provides a conscious antithesis to the first paragraph of "Experience," not only in the opposition of successful Pilgrim to failed Jacob but also in his manipulation of the epistemological analogues of the lapse. In "Experience" he finds himself lethargic and dim-sighted: "Sleep lingers all our lifetime about our eyes, as night hovers all day in the boughs of the fir-tree. All things swim and glitter." In "Nature," on the contrary, "the tempered light of the woods is like a perpetual morning, and is stimulating and heroic. . . . The stems of pines, hemlocks and oaks almost gleam like iron on the excited eye."

How are we to account for this change of state? Emerson would say there is no need. His alternation of mood represented not insincerity (as he was sometimes willing to concede) but honesty. If he had internalized a perpetual Fall, so had he an everlasting Indian summer. Meditating on the inexplicable death of his son "in the sixth year of his joy," Emerson could at once acknowledge his subjection to fate and yet also predict that he would one day feel full again and "see the disappearance of Fate." But perhaps it is wrong to state things in terms or time, for Emerson actually wrote, at the conclusion of these meditations, "I am *Defeated* all the time; yet to Victory I am born" (*JMN* 8:228). Both conditions exist simultaneously: the defeat is Emerson's despair, the victory his hope. The two songs sound together in the complex harmony of Emerson's autumnal season.

V

A WINTER'S TALE:
THE ELDER EMERSON

1847–1882

Restless and badly in need of stimulation, Emerson set sail for Europe a second time in October 1847, leaving his family in the able hands of Henry Thoreau. A substantial amount of fame (indeed, notoriety) preceded him, and his lectures in England and Scotland were well-attended and generally well-received. Both Emerson and Carlyle tried hard to transform their warm epistolary friendship into a new reality, but sharp differences of temperament and opinion stood ineluctably between them. Emerson met many notables and crossed the Channel to spend an eventful month in revolutionary Paris. He returned home, by way of Liverpool, on July 27, 1848. In English Traits *(1856) he would praise that great preserve of Anglo-Saxondom ambiguously, suggesting that the strength of the race might well be shifting to "the Alleghany ranges." Publication of* Representative Men *at the beginning of 1850 was overshadowed by the passage of the Fugitive Slave Law. Outraged, Emerson called it a "filthy enactment" and vowed not to "obey it, by God." In the summer of 1850, he dispatched Thoreau to Fire Island to search for effects of the drowned Margaret Fuller. Emerson lectured widely in the 1850s, traveling as far as St. Louis.* The Conduct of Life *was published in 1860. Emerson was much agitated by the coming of the Civil War, and eventually looked forward to it as a cleansing fire. Initially put off by Lincoln's apparent lack of refinement, Emerson mourned him after his death as the "father of his country." In 1866 Harvard honored the former heretic with the Doctor of Laws degree, and he was elected over-*

seer of the college the following year. In 1871 he traveled to San Francisco with his daughter Edith and her husband William Forbes, and visited an opium den, where he looked upon the "stupefied Mongolians" with "serene eye" (as Forbes' father reported). On July 24, 1872, Emerson's house burned, and the event precipitated a sharp downturn in his health. In the fall, he went abroad with his daughter Ellen, traveling to Europe and Egypt, and returned just after his seventieth birthday to a cheering crowd and a restored home. But his gentle decline into aphasia had begun. He died on April 27, 1882. Standing by his grave nine days later, Whitman noted: "A just man, poised on himself, all-loving, all-inclosing, and sane and clear as the sun."

Ebbing

In his most ebullient moments, Emerson would always claim that the man who is true to his "Genius" need not feel subject to "the weary kingdom of time" (W 3:22–23). Spiraling upward into the empyrean of his own enthusiasm in "Circles," Emerson could argue, as we have noticed, that age is unnecessary—that the tendency to "grizzle" is only evidence of our refusal to heed the interior Holy Ghost who bids us throw away the calendar:

> It is the highest power of divine moments that they abolish our contritions also. I accuse myself of sloth and unprofitableness day by day; but when these waves of God flow into me I no longer reckon lost time. I no longer poorly compute my possible achievement by what remains to me of the month or the year; for these moments confer a sort of omnipresence and omnipotence which asks nothing of duration, but sees that the energy of the mind is commensurate with the work to be done, without time. (W 2:317)

Of course, the waves of God may also flow out, even within the generally confident bounds of this essay. Emerson concedes that "a month hence, I doubt not, I shall wonder who he was that wrote so many continuous pages"; whereupon he is forced to lament "this infirm faith, this will not strenuous, this vast ebb of a vast flow!" (W 2:306–7). The reader of Emerson quickly gets used to this rapid alternation of thesis and antithesis, the flowing and ebbing of Emerson's dialectical tide, and is frequently hard pressed to decide just where the weight of Emerson's argument lies. "Our life is March weather," he writes, "savage and serene in one hour' (W 4:175).

The essay that Emerson wrote on "Old Age" is no exception to this general rule, although the fact that it was written as Emerson approached his mellow sixties clearly tipped the balance in the direction of serenity. Accordingly, Emerson begins by insisting that age, to some extent, is an illusion and does not always coincide with the leaves of the calendar. "Nature is full of freaks, and now puts an old head on young shoulders, and then a young heart beating under fourscore winters" (W 7:316). It is, of course, a familiar Emersonian belief that the mind is its own place and time; and he therefore goes on to say that

> That which does not decay is so central and controlling in us, that, as long as one is alone by himself, he is not sensible of the inroads of time, which always begin at the surface-edges. If, on a winter day, you should stand within a bell-glass, the face and color of the afternoon clouds would not indicate whether it were June or January; and if we did not find the reflection of ourselves in the eyes of the young people, we could not know that the century-clock had struck seventy instead of twenty. (W 7:318)

Life, however, does not only isolate the Transcendental spirit in its private bell-glass of belief; it also holds up a looking-glass that offers another view of things. And Emerson, stepping down from the higher platform, consents to look at age "under an aspect more conformed to the common-sense," whereby he comes to a less favorable conclusion: "From the point of sensuous experience, seen from the streets and markets and the haunts of pleasure and gain, the estimate of age is low, melancholy and skeptical." Emerson's own conclusion is reasonably grim: "Tobacco, coffee, alcohol, hashish, prussic acid, strychnine are weak dilutions: the surest poison is time" (W 7:318–19). That sentence actually derives from a journal entry set down when Emerson was about fifty, when he had already, on his own testimony, taken a stiff draught from the poisoned cup. And another sentence from "Old Age," closely following this one about "the surest poison," was drawn verbatim from his journal of 1850: "We postpone our literary work until we shall have more ripeness & skill to write, and we one day discover that our literary talent was a youthful effervescence which we have now lost!" (*JMN* 11:223).

The personal reference is clear, for there can be little doubt that the period around 1850 was a difficult one for Emerson in this regard. He could sometimes be comic about what he took to be the history of his attenuation: "The fate of my books is like the impression of my face. My acquaintances, as long back as I can remember, have always said, 'Seems to me you look a little thinner than when I saw you last' " (*JMN* 11:214–15). But the dominant tone is far from comic. And one obvious source for the grimness of Emerson's mood lay in the tragic death of Margaret Fuller in a shipwreck off Fire Island in July 1850. Emerson wrote in his journal: "I have lost in her my audience. I hurry now to my work admonished that I have few days left" (*JMN* 11:258). Shortly thereafter, he asserted that "a man of 45 does not want to open new accounts of friendship. He has said Kitty kitty long enough" (*JMN* 11:262).[1] And further along in the journals for 1850–51, one finds an even more ominous sentence: "In the streets I have certain darkenings which I call my nights" (*JMN* 11:327).

It would be inaccurate, however, to consider 1850, when Emerson was forty-seven, as *the* focal point of anxieties about the inception of old age. The refrain is far from being a new one in Emerson's writings. And indeed, so far as Emerson himself was concerned, it is easy to take as hyperbolic personal history his statement in the 1841 "Lecture on the Times" that, in America, "Old age begins in the nursery" (*CW* 1:180). Plagued with ill-health in his twenties, Emerson complained that "health, action, happiness" were ebbing from him, and identified with Sisyphus (*JMN* 3:45). He worried obsessively about the passage of time and stated repeatedly his belief that the age of thirty was a critical watershed for a man. "After thirty," he wrote when he was thirty-five, "a man is too sensible of the strait limitations which his physical constitution sets to his activity. The stream feels its banks, which it had forgotten in the run & overflow of the first meadows" (*JMN* 7:71). A more personal confession is to be found in 1837, the year previous to that entry, when Emerson stated: "I am already thirtyfour years old. Already my friends & fellow workers are dying from me. . . . I am too old to regard fashion; too old to expect patronage of any greater or more powerful" (*JMN* 5:322). It would not be far from the truth to say that Emerson celebrated each passing year as another millstone around the neck of his hopes and ambitions.

By at least as early as 1841, Emerson was much concerned with developing a strategy of survival for dealing with what he took to be his ever-diminishing capabilities, and debated with himself the question of whether he ought to seek new sources of stimulation or fall back on the notion of husbanding his strength. On the one hand, he exclaimed, "I die of ennui" and called for "one breath of fresh air, one creative word & action" (*JMN* 8:137); on the other, he praised the prudential virtue of continence. "It is better," he wrote in January 1841, "that joy should be spread over all the day in the form of strength than that it should be concentrated into extacies, full of danger, & followed by reactions" (*JMN* 7:411). Noticing his language here, one can scarcely doubt that Emerson's anxiety over encroaching age had some sort of physiological, or sexual, basis. In February he wrote:

> Lately it is a sort of general winter with me. I am not sick that I know, yet the names & projects of my friends sound far off & faint & unaffecting to my ear, as do, when I am sick, the voices of persons & the sounds of labor which I overhear in my solitary bed. A puny limitary creature am I, with only a small annuity of vital force to expend, which if I squander in a few feast days, I must feed on water & moss the rest of the time. (*JMN* 7:419)

Emerson's mixed metaphors are revealing. Though he believed in saving, he also longed to spend; though he loved to feast, he saw famine lurking behind it. Perhaps the most appropriate illustration of Emerson's problem and divided impulse in this period may be seen in the fact that as he prepared, the following summer, to deliver his passionate address—"The Method of Nature"— preaching ecstasy and abandonment to the students of Waterville College, he could also, writing to Carlyle, complain of his "puny body" and denominate himself a "cold, fastidious, ebbing person."[2] He dreamed of being otherwise. "Good vent or bad we must have for our nature," he wrote that fall; "somewhere we must let out all the length of all the reins. Make love a crime & we shall have lust. . . . We wish to take the gas which allows us to break through your wearisome proprieties, to plant the foot, to set the teeth, to fling abroad the arms, & dance & sing" (*JMN* 8:117).

These are the terms of Emerson's self-styled entrance into old age in the 1840s, and they draw into sharp focus an internal drama that evidently caused him much anguish throughout his life. Every student of Emerson becomes familiar very quickly with what this commanding figure of our literature considered to be his major failing: *"no animal spirits"* (*L* 4:101). That phrase comes from a letter written to his brother William in 1848, but the lament starts to sound early on in Emerson's writing. At the age of seventeen: "I need excitement" (*JMN* 1:39); and seven years later we read: "I am cold & solitary" (*JMN* 3:72). The lament returns predictably throughout the years, especially in the 1840s: "the capital defect of my nature for society (as it is of so many others) is the want of animal spirits. They seem to me a thing incredible, as if God should raise the dead" (*JMN* 9:18); "Life. A great lack of vital energy" (*JMN* 9:22); "Even for those whom I really love I have not animal spirits" (*JMN* 9:236).

But Emerson manifestly wished to be otherwise, and hoped that he might be. In February 1835, when he was courting Lydia Jackson, he wrote: "Do not think me a metaphysical lover. I am a man & hate and suspect the over refiners, & do sympathize with the homeliest pleasures and attractions by which our good foster mother Nature draws her children together" (*L* 1:434). It seems clear, however, that these promised pleasures and attractions were never adequately realized between them (or anywhere else, so far as Emerson was concerned). Writing with more perspective fifteen years later from Europe, Emerson acknowledged his failure as openly as he could:

> Ah you still ask me for that unwritten letter always due, it seems, always unwritten, from year to year, by me to you, dear Lidian,— I fear too more widely true than you mean,—always due and unwritten by me to every sister & brother of the human race. I have only to say that I also bemoan myself daily for the same cause —that I cannot write this letter, that I have not stamina & consti- tution enough to mind the two functions of seraph & cherub, oh no, let me not use such great words,—rather say that a photometer cannot be a stove. It must content you for the time, that I truly acknowledge a poverty of nature, & have really no proud defence at all to set up, but ill-health, puniness, and Stygian limitation. Is not the wife too always the complement of the man's imperfec- tions, and mainly of those half men the clerks? (L 4:33)

The student of Emerson's life will not want to violate Emerson's delicacy here, but neither should he overlook the issue that is being engaged. The letter that Emerson feels unable to write is a true love letter. He considers himself to be a measurer of light, not a source of heat. And he must take refuge behind his old fear—that the scholar, at base, is no better than half a man. Emerson's suggestion at the end that Lidian might somehow make up for his own "im- perfections" is interesting and curious. Did he call her "Queen of Sheba" because of the "hard questions" she put to him? Was he hoping that she would provide the excitement between them that he *could* not muster?

We do not know enough about Lidian to enable us to talk about her emotional and sexual nature. One Emerson scholar, at least, thinks that she was "more earthy and effusive" than Emerson himself.[3] That is surely the impression one gets from many of Emerson's journal entries in the early 1840s. "Queenie (who has a gift to curse & swear,)," he wrote in 1841, "will every now &

then in spite of all manners & christianity rip out on Saints, reformers, & Divine Providence with the most edifying zeal. In answer to the good Burrill Curtis who asks whether trade will not check the free course of love she insists 'it shall be said that there is no love to restrain the course of, & never was, that poor God did all he could, but selfishness fairly carried the day' " (*JMN* 8:88–89). One can scarcely read that as a satire on the lack of mutuality in her relationship with her husband (why would Emerson have put such a thing in his journal?); but it is a good indication of her spirit. A year later, however, Emerson copied down another sentence that surely seems to have a barb in it: "Queenie says, 'Save me from magnificent souls. I like a small common sized one' " (*JMN* 8:242). And it was she who was capable of saying (what it clearly pleased Emerson to set down) that for their little baby Edith, "the world goes round the sun only to bring titty-time" (*JMN* 8:289).

If Lidian felt let down by Emerson's own lack of earthiness, or by his capabilities as a lover, her experience at least was probably not very different from that of many another Victorian wife. And if such a thought did not console her, she would find other refuges in religion, sick headaches, and increasingly frequent periods of bed rest. Was this quip that Emerson copied into his journal in 1843 meant as a satire on his wife's attitude toward the resurrection or a sad joke about the decline of their sex life: "Queenie's epitaph: 'Do not wake me' "? (*JMN* 8:363).[4] What is one to make of this curious dream that Emerson recorded in his journal for 1840–41:

> A droll dream last night, whereat I ghastly laughed. A congregation assembled, like some of our late Conventions, to debate the Institution of Marriage; & grave & alarming objections stated on all hands to the usage; when one speaker at last rose & began to reply to the arguments, but suddenly extended his hand & turned on the audience the spout of an engine which was copiously supplied from within the wall with water & whisking it vigorously

about, up, down, right, & left, he drove all the company in crowds hither & thither & out of the house. Whilst I stood watching astonished & amused at the malice & vigor of the orator, I saw the spout lengthened by a supply of hose behind, & the man suddenly brought it round a corner & drenched me as I gazed. I woke up relieved to find myself quite dry, and well convinced that the Institution of Marriage was safe for tonight. (*JMN* 7:544)

Though analyzing someone else's dream is always a tricky and perhaps dubious business, Emerson himself seems to provide the terms of his own exegesis. Would it carry us beyond the bounds of simple description to call this a "wet" dream? People have gathered (as in Emerson's essay "New England Reformers") to discuss marriage, and the "usage" seems threatened; somehow it is conceived as a failure. The malicious and vigorous "orator," who seems to be a fantasy projection of Emerson himself, replies by releasing his prodigious "engine." Does one need "arguments" for marriage in the face of the overwhelming exigencies of sexuality? Emerson is "amused," but he too needs the drenching that his alter ego provides; the fluid will out. Whereupon Emerson awakes to find himself "quite dry, and well convinced that the Institution of Marriage was safe for tonight." Marriage is safe because Emerson has found an alternative way to express his drives and thereby reduce the pressure on the *Institution*. Oddly, and perhaps sadly, sexuality is seen as the thing that threatens the harmony of marriage rather than provides it.[5]

Another passage that offers a revealing glimpse of the crosscurrents that circulated beneath the calm surface of Emerson's nature occurs in a letter he wrote to Margaret Fuller from Manchester, England, in 1847:

In some senses I certainly do not grow old,—perhaps tis the worse for me—but, I believe, all the persons who have been important to my—imagination—shall I say? personal-imagination (is there no such thing in just psychology?) retain all their importance for me. I am their victim, & ready to be their victim, to the same extent as heretofore. When we die, my dear friend, will they not make us up better, with some more proportion between our tendencies & our skills; that life shall not be such a sweet fever, but a sweet health, sweet and beneficent, and solid as Andes? (*L* 3:447–48)

In that curious phrase "personal-imagination" Emerson seems to have been reaching for something like what we would call "sexual fantasy." He is saying that that aspect (unfortunately?) of his interior life is still very much alive. He continues to be victimized by his desires but incapacitated by his lack of "skills." His psycho-sexual life is therefore a kind of anguish—"a sweet fever"—rather than a solid satisfaction. Emerson's use of the phrase "ready . . . victim" to describe himself in this connection is thoroughly consistent with the attitudes expressed toward female sexuality in various journal entries of the period. Though he felt tempted, he feared what he termed the effeminating effects of sexual indulgence. "I have organs also," he wrote in the mid-1840s, "& delight in pleasure, but I have experience also that this pleasure is the bait of a trap" (*JMN* 9:115). It might seem facile to speak here of "castration fear," but how else should one respond to another journal entry of the same period?

> Eve softly with her womb
> Bit him to death
> Lightly was woman snared, herself a snare.
> (*JMN* 9:164)

A few years later, writing more sympathetically of female sexuality, Emerson would note that "nature itself seems to be in conspiracy against her dignity & welfare; for the cultivated, high thoughted, beauty-loving, saintly woman finds herself unconsciously desired for her sex, and even enhancing the appetite of her savage pursuers by these fine ornaments she has piously laid on herself. She finds with indignation that she is herself a snare, & was made such" (*JMN* 11:31). The victimization, when it occurs, is therefore mutual.

That Emerson should have written his confessional letter about the *croce e delizia* of sexual attraction to Margaret Fuller might seem odd, in view of her general reputation as a brilliant but ill-favored bluestocking. The evidence suggests, however, that the two were strongly attracted to one another, though Emerson's ambivalence made their relationship a perpetual frustration to Margaret.[6] Emerson, at least, carried on an epistolary flirtation with her, and after her death seems to have spent some time brooding over his lost opportunity.[7] Agreeing with Elizabeth Hoar, he avowed that "her heart, which few knew, was as great as her mind, which all knew," and that she was "the largest woman; & not a woman who wished to be a man" (*JMN* 11:257). Emerson clearly did not find her unattractive: "Her features," he writes, "were disagreeable to most persons so long as they were little acquainted with her, that is, until the features were dissolved in the power of the expression" (*JMN* 11:490). Emerson thought her full of "great tenderness & sympathy" (*JMN* 11:258–59) and, perhaps surprisingly, applied Shakespeare's lines describing Cleopatra to Margaret ("Nor custom stale / her infinite variety"). Setting down her birthdate (May 23), he undoubtedly noted its proximity to his own and must have thought of his familiar dictum asserting that one should marry a person born at the same time as oneself. Emerson seems to have been surprised, and perhaps chagrined, in reading through her papers, to notice the frank expressions of sexual need:

> The unlooked for trait in all these journals to me is the Woman, poor woman: they are all hysterical. She is bewailing her virginity and languishing for a husband.

> "I need help. No, I need a full, a godlike embrace from some sufficient love." &c. &c. (*JMN* 11:500)

Though Emerson could try to dismiss such comments as being merely "hysterical," his language suggests that he took them as a silent reproach. Noting her call, in the journal, for a "Hector,"

Ebbing

Emerson commented: "This I doubt not was all the more violent recoil from the exclusively literary & 'educational' connections in which she had lived. Mrs Spring told me that Margaret said to her, 'I am tired of these literary friendships, I long to be wife & mother' " (*JMN* 11:500). The possible application of these remarks to his own relationship with Margaret could scarcely have escaped Emerson. And he must have felt himself poignantly drawn to her in memory as he copied the following into his journal:

> Rome, March 10, 1849, "I have been . . . the object of great love from the noble & the humble. I have felt it towards both. Yet a kind of chartered libertine, I rove pensively always, in deep sadness often; 'O God help me,' is my cry." (*JMN* 11:503)

The phrase from *Henry V* ("chartered libertine") that Margaret used to describe herself was precisely the one Emerson had applied to *himself* in his celebrated letter to Henry Ware defending his Divinity School Address.

Emerson understood well enough that his inveterate tendency to intellectualize put "an interval between the subject & the object," whereas "affection would blend the two." As he noted in this 1842 journal entry: "For weal or for woe I clear myself from the thing I contemplate: I grieve, but am not a grief: I love, but am not a love" (*JMN* 7:466). He could see that this tendency was at least partly a defensive strategy, arising out of a fear of being hurt, though ultimately his emotional disabilities left him perplexed:

> I cold because I am hot,—cold at the surface only as a sort of guard & compensation for the fluid tenderness of the core,—have much more experience than I have written . . . more than I will, more than I can write. In silence we must wrap much of our life, because it is too fine for speech, because also we cannot explain it to others, and because somewhat we cannot yet understand. (*JMN* 7:368)

He felt, in 1840, that "the last chamber, the last closet," can perhaps never be opened, "there is always a residuum unknown, unanalysable" (*JMN* 7:347). Two years previous, however, reflecting similarly on this "incomplete" story of his life that he dared not tell and only imperfectly understood himself, Emerson did venture to say that his "strait & decorous way of living" which avoided anything "extravagant or flowing" and contented itself "with moderate, languid actions" was not only "strictly proper" to himself but "native to [his] family & . . . country" (*JMN* 7:131). His New England, after all, was the place, as Edwin Arlington Robinson would write

> . . . where the wind is always north-north-east
> And children learn to walk on frozen toes . . .
> Passion is here a soilure of the wits,
> We're told, and Love a cross for them to bear . . .

Though Emerson could still rouse himself against such a tradition (as in this entry from the spring of 1839: "My life is a May game, I will live as I like. I defy your strait laced, weary, social ways & modes. . . . I will play my game out" (*JMN* 7:208]), he unquestionably felt the chill deepen as he entered his forties. He avoided what he called the "Stygian anniversaries" of his Harvard class reunions, as he called them in 1845, because all "those hurrahs among the ghosts, those yellow, bald, toothless meetings in memory of red cheeks, black hair, and departed health" amounted only to "obituary eloquences" that clearly depressed him (*JMN* 9:221). The cadences of Edward Everett's Inaugural Discourse as President of the College Emerson found, the year following, "chilling & melancholy." The "coolness" of the formerly golden-tongued orator made Emerson think of the "corpse-cold Unitarianism & Immortality of Brattle street & Boston" (*JMN* 9:381). Though Bronson Alcott could avow, at about the same time, that "the happiness of old age consists in transforming the Furies into the Muses"

Ebbing

(*JMN* 9:361), Emerson was discovering that the former were not so easily placated and the latter sang lugubrious tunes:

> I grow old, I accept conditions;—thus far—no farther;—to learn that we are not the first born, but the latest born; that we have no wings; that the sins of our predecessors are on us like a mountain of obstruction. (*JMN* 9:363)

But he also, despite his admitted "want of ear," longed for a different kind of music—one that might serve "as a medicine" to stir him and make him soar: "We cannot spare any stimulant or any purgative, we lapse so quickly into flesh & sleep. We must use all the exalters that will bring us into an expansive & productive state, or to the top of our condition" (*JMN* 9:108–9). Changing his figure, Emerson claimed that what he needed most of all was "an electrical machine. Slumbering power we have, but not excited, collected, & discharged" (*JMN* 11:262).

It is precisely in the context of such anxieties and yearnings that one ought to consider Emerson's decision, in 1847, to unstop his ears and listen once again to the siren song of Europe. In many ways, his need was much greater now than it had been in 1832, when his prospects, though temporarily retarded, were in the natural process of unfolding. The spiritual uncertainties of Emerson's menopause, however, were tied to a physical process of aging which, though equally natural, yielded less easily to Emerson's affirmative philosophy. As he looked toward Europe in the early spring of 1847, he was no longer inspired by a single-minded belief in the Transcendental virtues of *easting* oneself, but rather searching instead, somewhat desperately, among the various alternatives, even old rejected ones, which might serve (and the term in his own) to flagellate "the drowsy muse" (*JMN* 10:137) and postpone the death that seemed already to threaten:

> We must have society, provocation, a whip for the top. A Scholar is a candle which the love & desire of men will light. Let it not lie

in a dark box. But here am I with so much all ready to be revealed to me as to others if only I could be set aglow. I have wished for a professorship. Much as I hate the church, I have wished the pulpit that I might have the stimulus of a stated task. N. P. Rogers spoke more truly than he knew, perchance, when he recommended an Abolition-Campaign to me. I doubt not, a course of mobs would do me much good. (*JMN* 10:28)

Did he think of the church mainly because he associated it with all the energy of his youthful protest? In language that vaguely recalls to mind the "Barzillai Frost" portion of the Divinity School Address, Emerson at once expressed his own fear of impotence and his lingering hope for rejuvenation: "A snowflake will go through a pine board, if projected with force enough" (ibid.). Dreaming of "a new companion," but not the "insular & pathetically solarity" types (as he would term them later [*JMN* 11:447]) who inhabited his own bare ambience, Emerson seized upon the Old World: "In this emergency, one advises Europe, & especially England" (*JMN* 10:29). One month later, accordingly, in April 1847, he wrote Carlyle: "This pleasing dream of going to England dances before me sometimes. It would be, I then fancy, that stimulation which my capricious, languid, & languescent study needs. At home, no man makes any proper demand on me." By the end of July, in his forty-fifth year, having determined to break loose from home and realize his dream, Emerson announced to Carlyle with muted triumph: "In my old age I am coming to see you."[8]

In terms of renewing his friendship with Carlyle, Emerson's second voyage abroad was a marked disappointment. But his work had won him a surprisingly large reputation in England, and he was sufficiently lionized. He arrived in Paris in time to observe the aftermath of the Revolution of 1848, heard Lamartine in the French Assembly, and met Tocqueville and Chopin. Still, as we have noticed in glancing at the letters he wrote while abroad to Lidian and Margaret Fuller, Emerson seems to have spent a fair amount of time brooding over the failure of his more familiar relations because of inadequacies that travel could hardly remedy. He achieved, not a renewal of life, but rather a happy respite from his sometimes deadening routine and the depression attendant on the ineluctable process of aging. Europe had indeed served as a whip for Emerson's top, but—as is usual in such cases—he stopped spinning not long after he returned to Concord.

Two journal entries made in the period just after Emerson's return give some indication of how grim was his mood as he consciously settled into what he conceived to be a permanent "sentence" of lonely decline. The first is a fierce little allegory which is patently autobiographical:

> Solitary Imprisonment is written on his coat & hat, on the lines of his face, & the limbs of his body, on his brow, & on the leaves of laurel on his brow. He wrestles hard with the judge, and does not believe he is in earnest. "Solitary Imprisonment," replies the Judge. Yet with some mitigation. Three times a day his keeper comes to the window, & puts bread & water on the shelf. The keeper's dog he may play with, if he will. Bow-wow-wow, says the dog. People may come from Asia to see him, if they like. He is only permitted to become his own friend. (*JMN* 11:165)

Despite his undeniable fame and past successes, our American Jacob feels himself somehow condemned and manifestly not blessed by the dark Angel with whom he wrestles.

The second passage exhibits less bitterness, more acceptance perhaps, and demonstrates that the spirit which would inform the book generally considered to be the finest expression of Emerson's mature wisdom descended upon him definitively at the age of forty-six:

> In the conduct of life, let us not parade our rags, let us not, moved by vanity, confess, & tear our hair, at the corners of streets, or in the sitting room; but, as age & infirmity steal on us, contentedly resign the front seat & the games to these bright children, our better representatives, nor expect compliments or inquiries,—much

less gifts, or love—any longer, (which to expect is ridiculous,) and, not at all wondering why our friends do not come to us, much more wondering when they do,—decently withdraw ourselves into modest & solitary resignation & rest. (*JMN* 11:166)

Emerson might indeed build altars to the "Beautiful Necessity," but on those very altars he was sacrificing hopes and desires which suffered cruelly under the knife. At about the same time, Emerson made a journal entry that most poignantly expresses the divided heart with which he greeted the early contraction of his personal firmament: "I meet in the street people full of life. I am, of course, at ebbtide; they at flood; they seem to have come from the south or from the west or from Europe. I see them pass with envy at this gift which includes all gifts" (*JMN* 11:86). All of the directions Emerson mentions here are ones through which—in actuality or in imagination—he had already passed. Now, as the tide receded, the wind seemed to blow more steadily from the north.[9]

Conducting Life

[1]

"Certainly," Emerson wrote in 1847, "if an age that is to come would know the history of this it will seek certainly to know what idea we attached to the word *Nature*" (*JMN* 10:169). Any respectable historian of ideas would not only agree with Emerson's remark but also want to extend it by saying that an understanding of the elusive term *nature*—i.e., that which is constitutive of reality —holds the main key to unlocking the thought of every age in the world's history.[10] Backing off from that awesome task, however, the student of Emerson will surely assent to his statement as it applies at least to his own career, since it is obvious that from the time he published his first book, Emerson was centrally concerned with defining "nature."[11] And, indeed, we find an explicit attempt at such a definition in 1836: "*Nature,* in the common sense, refers to essences unchanged by man; space, the air, the river, the leaf. *Art* is applied to the mixture of his will with the same things, as in a house, a canal, a statue, a picture" (*CW* 1:8). The distinction is simplistic and naïve, and Emerson himself sensed that such was the case. But his tendency in *Nature* is to establish a Cartesian dualistic struggle between World and Will (or Thought) whereby the latter might be seen, idealistically, to triumph. Emerson's later view is a more "holistic" or organic one, in which *nature* tends to be the more inclusive term, signifying that immense web of "tyrannous circumstance" which largely controls our existence. Though Emerson does establish a dialectic in "Fate" between the "negative power" of Nature and the "positive power" which is our own will, the balance clearly tilts in the direction of Nature (or Fate). The weight of Emerson's argument lies in the direction of saying that we are all Nature's, or Nature is all in us. Emerson would probably have felt considerable sympathy with the spirit that informs Molly Bloom's soliloquy in *Ulysses*.[12] And perhaps it is not surprising that Joyce thought Emerson one of the giants of his age, along with Rousseau and Carlyle.[13] Emerson's later definition of Nature, or "Natura," is "(to be born) Becoming or Transition" (*JMN* 10:89). It is the great generative principle that underlies and informs all creation and expression.

Another journal entry from 1847 provides us with a rich insight into the general direction of Emerson's thought in this period: "We wish to get the highest skill of finish, an engraver's educated finger, determination to an aim, — & then — to let in mania, ether, to take off the individual's interference & let him fly as with thunderbolt" (*JMN* 10:164). Emerson would begin by allowing art to do all it can, by encouraging the highest degree of conscious human activity; but the final touch must belong to nature, since the best that human talent, education, and will are capable of amounts only to an "interference" with the wild natural force that silently palpitates beneath all rational human endeavor. We may please ourselves with considering raw nature a brutal power that can, and must, be improved by the civilizing and (from a religious point of view) "higher" or divine moral nature of man, but our distinctions of "high" and "low" are mere child's play in the face of that all-encompassing primal energy. As Emerson was to write in "Fate": "We cannot trifle with this reality, this cropping-out in our planted gardens of the core of the world" (*W* 6:19).[14]

Emerson's metaphor in the sentence I have just quoted is sufficiently traditional to bring to mind the long debate in English writing—and particularly in the English Renaissance—over Nature versus Nurture, or Nature versus Grace.[15] But we need not stray, in this regard, from Emerson himself, because directly following the 1847 journal entry which I have glossed above, Emerson copied onto his page a great, and greatly illuminating, sentence: "Yet 'Nature is made better by no mean, but nature makes that mean.' " He is quoting, of course, from the central statement that lies at the heart of—and forms the crux of—Shakespeare's mature romance, *The Winter's Tale*.[16] Though the passage from which Emerson draws his sentence is familiar to Shakespeareans, we need to have the full context before us:

Perdita. Sir, the year growing ancient,
Nor yet on summer's death, nor on the birth
Of trembling winter, the fairest flowers of the season
Are our carnations and streak'd gillyvors,
Which some call nature's bastards: of that kind
Our rustic garden's barren, and I care not
To get slips of them.

Polixenes. Wherefore, gentle maiden,
Do you neglect them?

Perdita. For I have heard it said
There is an art which in their piedness shares
With great creating nature.

Polixenes. Say there be;
Yet nature is made better by no mean
But nature makes that mean: so, o'er that art
Which you say adds to nature, is an art
That nature makes. You see, sweet maid, we marry
A gentler scion to the wildest stock,
And make conceive a bark of baser kind
By bud of nobler race: this is an art
Which docs mend nature, change it rather, but
The art itself is nature.

Perdita. So it is.

Polixenes. Then make your garden rich in gillyvors,
And do not call them bastards.

Perdita.   I'll not put
The dibble in earth to set one slip of them;
No more than, were I painted, I would wish
The youth should say 't were well, and only therefore
Desire to breed by me. Here's flowers for you;
Hot lavender, mints, savory, marjoram;
The marigold, that goes to bed wi' the sun,
And with him rises weeping: these are flowers
Of middle summer, and I think they are given
To men of middle age. You're very welcome.

The full complexity of this rich Shakespearean moment can hardly detain us here, but we may at least speculate on Emerson's interest in the passage.[17] The debate between the innocent, and fastidious, Perdita and the more worldly-wise Polixenes has somewhat the complexion of a confrontation between youth and age, and images the distinction between the Emerson of *Nature* and the more mature thinker who was brooding on *The Conduct of Life.* The flowers of approaching winter seem to Perdita "bastards"— the unnatural offspring of a base carnal "art" which she finds offensive. But to Polixenes, Perdita's view of "art" is naïvely incomplete. For him, it is all *nature*—the "baser kind" as well as the "nobler race." Whatever is "made better"—either more elevated or more alluring—is made so by natural means and a natural impulse.[18] To put it most simply, Polixenes is more realistic sexually than Perdita. She may consider the desire provoked by a harlot's painting to be "unnatural," but it *is* desire nonetheless. "We must fetch the pump with dirty water, if clean cannot be had," Emerson writes in "Power" (W 6:60). Perdita seems to feel that the florid offspring of nature's declining year are no better than the flowers of evil. But Emerson, coming into sympathy with his own wintry mood, is approaching the view that "the torpid artist" quite *naturally* "seeks inspiration at any cost, by virtue or by vice, by friend or by fiend, by prayer or by wine" (W 6:60). If the core of the world contains mania and ether, the artist cannot avoid coming in contact with them, any more than he can avoid confronting and expressing the animal power that lies at the base of his own natural being. Thus, as Emerson brooded on what he conceived to be his own waning forces in the 1840s, he was inevitably brought to examine the *conduct* of life in physiological terms.

The manifest counter-current in the journals of the 1840s to Emerson's anxiety over his ebbing vitality is an obsession with *power,* viewed (not infrequently with ambivalence) in "natural" terms. Time and again, Emerson's thoughts on a wide variety of subjects tend to become a "physiology of" whatever is under consideration, and this general drift in his thinking was to provide a central structure for the lectures that became *The Conduct of Life.* For an alert reader of the journal, Emerson's obsessions in this period are to be seen not so much in individual journal passages as in clumps of entries that combine to form an unmistakable figure in the carpet. As an example, let us examine a run of entries which occur in the spring of 1847, around the time of Emerson's forty-fourth birthday. Emerson began a new journal notebook on May 23 with an entry, drawn from his reading, which seems apropos of nothing: "Boeckh estimates the Attic drachma of silver as nearly equal to 9¾ pence of English coinage; then, the mina, to £4, 1s. 3d.; and the talent to £243.15s" (*JMN* 10:59). Emerson seems to have been struck by the high value of Attic coinage, as if he immediately saw it as a fit symbol of the prodigal wealth of the Greek imagination (the word "talent," with its strikingly high equivalent in Sterling, provides one hint). The collocation of money and imagination is a natural one for a reader of Emerson to make, in view of this well-known journal entry from 1833: "This Book is my Savings Bank. I grow richer because I have somewhere to deposit my earnings; and fractions are worth more to me because corresponding fractions are waiting here that shall be made integers by their addition" (*JMN* 4:250–51). The issues raised here are the general ones of "saving" versus "spending"; and Emerson's figure naturally suggests an *economy* of the imagination. One might say, for example, that it was the investment of the Greek "talent" in the literary banks of the English Renaissance that produced the enormous intellectual wealth with which we are familiar.

All of this appears to be rather fanciful, but I am trying to trace the flow of Emerson's own thought. Some pages after the entry about Attic money, Emerson writes: "Great is the power of Compound Interest, which, in eleven years, doubles the principal. For not only is twice one cent two cents, but twice one planet is two planets" (*JMN* 10:67). The *idea,* then, of "Compound Interest" suggests to Emerson potentialities for enormous growth, and indeed, the creation of new worlds. Several pages later, he writes: "Scholar wishes that every book & chart & plate belonging to him should draw interest every moment by circulation" (*JMN* 10:78). Though Emerson's usual impulse is to save, he is also attracted by the notion of putting himself in "circulation" and thereby increasing, in a sense, his sphere of influence. But Emerson has a sharp awareness also of the dangers of being too prodigal. Turning and turning in this widening gyre of thought, Emerson is naturally brought to consider the potential of his own country as he gathers the terms of his personal debate into a larger cultural statement:

> Alas for America as I must so often say, the ungirt, the diffuse, the profuse, procumbent, one wide ground juniper, out of which no cedar, no oak will rear up a mast to the clouds! it all runs to leaves, to suckers, to tendrils, to miscellany. The air is loaded with poppy, with imbecility, with dispersion, & sloth. Eager, solicitous, hungry, rabid, busy-body America attempting many things, vain, ambitious to feel thy own existence, & convince others of thy talent, by attempting & hastily accomplishing much; yes, catch thy breath & correct thyself and failing here, prosper out there; speed & fever are never greatness; but reliance & serenity & waiting &, perseverance, heed of the work & negligence of the effect. (*JMN* 10:79)

It would be a mistake, I think, to attempt to reduce Emerson's rambling drift here to consecutive thought; its tendencies are clear enough, and clearly related to the journal material that precedes. America "the ungirt" ("that great sloven continent," as Emerson would say in *English Traits* [W 5:288]) wastes its "talent" now

seen in physiological terms, in a kind of lazy, imbecile, polymorphous pouring out of its vital energies. Instead of investing its force
in the erection of strong, large, durable trees, it allows itself to be
drained by "suckers" close to the ground. He wants America to
calm down, cool off, gather its forces, and invest temperately in
future growth.

And yet, the notion of being prodigal of one's natural or physiological talent still excites Emerson. Accordingly, two pages later,
he subsumes all these opposed tendencies in a personal fantasy
which culminates his ambivalent desire to spend freely by joining
it to nature in a durable and productive marriage:

> How attractive is land, orchard, hillside, garden, in this fine
> June! Man feels the blood of thousands in his body and his heart
> pumps the sap of all this forest of vegetation through his arteries.
> Here is work for him & a most willing workman. He displaces the
> birch & chestnut, larch & alder, & will set oak & beech to cover
> the land with leafy colonnades. Then it occurs what a fugitive
> summer flower papilionaceous is he, whisking about amidst these
> longevities. Gladly he could spread himself abroad among them;
> love the tall trees as if he were their father; borrow by his love the
> manners of his trees, and with nature's patience watch the giants
> from the youth to the age of golden fruit or gnarled timber, nor
> think it long. (*JMN* 10:80)

Emerson accomplishes here for himself and his own land what the
rest of the country seems incapable of: the rearing of tall trees that
express his desire for a joyful release of powerful energy which will
not threaten his life but extend it indefinitely into the future.
As he writes just a few pages later, he would be a "good husband" and waste "no globule of sap"; but he also insists that
that same good husband "waters his trees with wine" (*JMN*
10:82).

Other journal entries, interspersed between and surrounding
these which we have just examined, touch on the same issues in

related terms. Emerson cites Hafiz on loosing "the knot of the heart" and then exclaims: "Expression is all we want: Not knowledge, but vent: we know enough; but have not leaves & lungs enough for a healthy perspiration & growth" (*JMN* 10:68). Going on to survey his own circle of friends, Emerson then sets down a remarkably candid passage which eloquently exposes the mixed and warring impulses that he finds both in himself and in his New England ambience:

> An air of sterility, poor, thin, arid, reluctant vegetation belongs to the wise & the unwise whom I know. If they have fine traits, admirable properties, they have a palsied side. But an utterance whole, generous, sustained, equal, graduated-at-will, such as Montaigne, such as Beaumont & Fletcher so easily & habitually attain, I miss in myself most of all, but also in my contemporaries. A palace style of manners & conversation, to which every morrow is a new day, which exists extempore and is equal to the needs of life, at once tender & bold, & with great arteries like Cleopatra & Corinne, would be satisfying and we should be willing to die when our time came, having had our swing & gratification. But my fine souls are cautious & canny, & wish to unite Corinth with Connecticut. I see no easy help for it. Our virtues too are in conspiracy against grandeur, and are narrowing. . . . The true nobility has floodgates,—an equal inlet & outgo. (*JMN* 10:69)

As an indication of Emerson's vehemence here, he concluded this passage with the cancelled phrase "floodgates, floodgates." Emerson longs to release himself and says so in language that is sufficiently sexual; but the whole New England tradition is against him. That prodigious Greek "talent"—nourished on "savage . . . Pelasgic strength," as Emerson writes in another entry (*JMN* 10:82)—clearly languishes in the constricted New England air, while Emerson's neighbors worship the almighty Dollar—"a local deity," as he says a few pages further on, who seems satisfied when the people "bring it baked beans" (*JMN* 10:83).

Emerson's juxtapositions in this whole series of journal entries are curiously interesting. On one page, he sets down his belief that "literature should be the counterpart of nature & equally rich":

> I find her not in our books. I know nature, & figure her to myself as exuberant, tranquil, magnificent in her fertility,—coherent, so that every thing is an omen of every other. She is not proud of the sea or of the stars, of space or time; for ⟨every weed & grass shares the⟩ all her kinds share the attributes of the selectest extremes. But in literature her geniality is gone—her teats are cut off, as the Amazons of old. (*JMN* 10:83)

Emerson is here writing, so to speak, in the spirit of Polixenes. Nature—high and low—is all one, large, procreative, organically whole. Her "geniality" (Emerson, of course, means capacity to reproduce and give light and warmth) and lusty acceptance of all forms of life are missing from literature, in Emerson's view. Reading this passage, one unmistakably senses Whitman waiting in the wings. But Emerson goes on directly to another paragraph which discusses "the virtue of woman," and argues that it is not "lightly lost" because "unchastity with women is an acute disease, not a habit; the party soon gets through it." Men, Emerson concludes, "are always being instructed more & more in the chastity of women." The reader may well blink and wonder how he has gotten so quickly from a plea for all-embracing *alma natura* to the rather prudish assurances that follow. Whereupon we turn the page, to discover that Emerson believed "English scholars have been eaters & drinkers," and asserts for good measure that "the good & the true make us puke"! (*JMN* 10:84).

Such was Emerson's mood as he dreamed of rejuvenating himself in a second trip to Europe. He filled several pages with extracts from books of Arabian and Persian mythology which seem to exemplify, or provoke, fantasies of size, power, violence, debauchery and fertility ("If Kurroglou but so much as slap a groom, he knocks four teeth down his throat which the groom swallows"; "I am the true Azrail. I drag the corpses on the sand. I shall sow barley where you stand now"; "Rustem looked a year old when newborn, & required milk of ten nurses"; "Afrasiyab was as strong as an elephant, his shadow extended miles, his heart bounteous as the ocean, & his hands like the clouds when rain falls to gladden the thirsty Earth" [*JMN* 10:72–75]; "Sow, resow, sow again, sow perpetually, in short do nothing but sow"; "The peasant looked at him (Kurroglou) & saw a head like the cupola of a church, mustachios extending up beyond the ears, & a beard that reached down to the waist, & the height nearly equal to that of a minaret"; "Whenever he heard a woman's voice he used to lose his senses"; "in answer he shouted so loud that it seemed that a gun was fired from the well"; "His bill of fare. Prepare for me every day, for *breakfast,* 22½ lb of the best meat, lb 15 of the whitest bread, lb 15 of brandy, & lb 15 of wine" [*JMN* 10:85]). Interspersed with this material, we find comments about the power of "Genius" (it "magnetizes, inundates armies"), the nature of India, "with its colossal & profuse growth," and a remarkable paragraph detailing the privileges of heroic individuals:

> To a right aristocracy, to Hercules, Theseus, Odin, the Cid, and Napoleon; to Sir Robert Walpole, to Fox, Chatham, Webster, to the men, that is, who are incomparably superior to the populace in ways agreeable to the populace, showing them the way they should go, doing for them what they wish done, & cannot do;—of course, every thing will be permitted & pardoned, gaming, drinking, adultery, fighting—these are the heads of party who can do no wrong, —everything short of incest & beastliness will pass. (*JMN* 10:75)

Emerson's almost conscious fantasies seem nakedly exposed in the patterns formed by these groups of entries. The "American mind," he writes on the next page, is "a wilderness of capabilities." That is the dangerous labyrinth in which Emerson seemed almost willing to allow his soul to wander in these months, as he expanded his notion of the varieties of conduct available to the fullest expression of the life force.

Yet, as we have noticed repeatedly, Emerson's personal nemesis lurked always around the corner. His fantasy of being one with the land and its powerful trees is balanced by a fear of being possessed and destroyed by nature. "The devotion to these vines & trees & cornhills I find narrowing & poisonous ... these stoopings & scrapings & fingerings in a few square yards of garden are dispiriting, drivelling, and I seem to have eaten lotus, to be robbed of all energy, & I have a sort of catalepsy, or unwillingness to move." Reminding one of his lines about Eve with her womb-trap, Emerson thinks of his garden as being "like those machineries which we read of every month in the newspapers which catch a man's coatskirt or his hand & draw in his arm, his leg, & his whole body to irresistible death" (*JMN* 10:93). Though Emerson complains that the speeches of William Lloyd Garrison are weakened by their acceptance of "all the logic & routine of tradition," and Garrison loses thereby his "juice & animal spirits & elemental force," he confesses on the very next page that he himself can live "only by a most exact husbandry of my resources" (*JMN* 10:94). Though he admires some "beautiful Corinne" of his acquaintance for being a "spendthrift," [19] he draws back from such a perilous position himself. Emerson marvels at the "irresistibility of the American," with his lack of conscience and his "tall, restless Kentucky strength," and repeatedly praises this continent's ardency of race and Nature, "rushing up after a shower into a mass of vegetation" (*JMN* 10:95–96). But in the same pages, he laments that his own "trees send out a moderate shoot in the first summer heat and then stop. They look all summer as if they would presently burst the bud again, & grow, but they do not" (*JMN* 10:99). Such is the case with his own body: "We have experience, reading, relatedness enough, o yes, & every other weapon, if only we had constitution enough. But as the doctor said in my boyhood,—'You have no *stamina*' " (*JMN* 10:110).

Throughout this period, it seems, Emerson's restless spirit tossed back and forth in the painful crosscurrents of desire and uncertainly. One moment he would try forcefully to convince himself of the necessity of prudential retrenchment in the management of his impulses: "Shall a man . . . in his garden cut down the spindling shoots of his pear tree or pinch off the redundant buds of his grapevine to give robustness to the stock, & not learn the value of rejection in his own spiritual economy?" But the very next moment, he would copy down a passage in praise of freedom and expansion: "'The fountains of life must be stirred & sent bounding throughout our system, or else we ebb so soon into the Stygian pool of Necessity to drink of its infatuating bowl, & seal our doom" (*JMN* 10:112). Here was Emerson's fundamental question: how could life be *conducted* without the unimpeded circulation of vital energies? Which was more *natural,* control or release? What were the appropriate flowers for a man of late middle age? Emerson seemed to feel, at least part of the time, that by putting his dibble in European earth he might raise a crop of carnations and gillyvors which could help to enliven the approaching winter season.

[11]

Whatever were the expectations, doubtless not even clearly articulated to himself, which Emerson nourished for his second trip to Europe, they were bound to be defeated because of the patently divided attitude that he brought to the experience. He was a middle-aged man seeking renewal of his "animal spirits" who in fact considered himself to be a man early old, who never *had* sufficient spirits to begin with; and, furthermore, he was uneasy (one might say, guilty) about that whole side of human experience, in any case. Emerson agreed with Polixenes, but he seems to have *felt* like Perdita.

It is clear, at all events, that Emerson's determination to develop a healthy concern for the physiology of experience in 1847 hardened into something less pleasant after his return. His attitude toward the facts of life would tend to alternate between bitter, or at least testy, condemnation, on the one hand, and an almost prurient interest, on the other. Of course, he could sometimes simply sound sad about the whole business, as when he wrote in 1848: "An artist spends himself, like the crayon in his hand, till he is all gone" (*JMN* 10:320). By 1855, Emerson was manifestly not all gone as a writer, but his enthusiasm for the free expression of sexuality, as well as for traveling to Europe (always somehow linked in his mind), was all but spent, and the residue was a curious kind of ill-temper. He writes, for example: "At present, as we manage generation, 'tis with man as with the potato, bad seed, & every individual born with seminal cholera" (*JMN* 13:438). It is hard to know what Emerson meant by the last phrase. Probably he intended to suggest a peevish, or *choleric,* humor which he believed could be transmitted through the seed (an earlier entry in which he uses the term *cholera* equates it with "the decomposition of the potato" [*JMN* 11:173]). But the real interest comes in a slightly later entry which picks up the earlier language and sets it in a startling new context:

> All America seems on the point of embarking for Europe. Every post brings me a letter from some worthy person who has just arrived at the execution, as he tells me, of a long-cherished design of sailing for Europe. This rottenness is like the cholera in the potato.
> "She herself was not exempt" —
> *Lues Americana,* or the "European Complaint." (*JMN* 13:452)

Emerson's sentence about the unidentified lady seems obscure, though some light is shed by what follows. The editors gloss "*Lues Americana*" as "the American plague"; but Emerson surely knew that he was employing the medical term for syphilis, whence the surprising bitterness in the whole passage.[20] Emerson now associates the itch to go to Europe with venereal disease (perhaps we understand what he intended to imply in "seminal cholera"). And not even the best people seem exempt from this weakness. As in some of his earliest journal entries, Emerson sees Europe as the symbol of corruption and condemns his friends for feeling the need for such excitement.

Let us back away, however, from this last twist of the Emersonian knife and return to 1849 and the period just following his return from Europe. As with Emerson's journal for the spring of 1847, it is possible to discover, in a series of entries made around the same time, patterns that reveal much about his attitudes and state of mind. One such series, which is of particular interest, begins with this entry in the summer of 1849:

> 'Tis very certain that the man must yield who has omitted inevitable facts in his view of life. Has he left out marriage & the σπερματος ουσιης συντηρησιν, he has set a date to his fame. We are expecting another. (*JMN* 11:131)

As he himself was working on the lectures which were to become *The Conduct of Life,* Emerson insists that the author who would have a durable reputation must come to terms with the "inevitable facts" of life—namely, human sexual relations and sexuality. The Greek phrase employed here (undoubtedly as a kind of cipher against prying eyes) is construed by the editors of the *Journals* as "observation of one's own offspring." This not only makes little sense in Emerson's context; it also loses the sharp point of his concern. Emerson was actually remembering (or had looked up with the aid of his elaborate indexes) a sentence that he had copied many years before into his "Encyclopedia" from Plutarch's "Rules for the Preservation of Health." The annotations to the "Encyclopedia" give us the rather genteel traditional English version of the phrase with which Emerson was doubtless familiar: "observance of chastity" (*JMN* 6:153). But Emerson knew Greek fairly well, Plutarch (especially in his *Morals)* was one of his favorite authors, and it is likely that in the journal passage we have been considering, he thought of the phrase in more literal terms as meaning something like "keeping watch over one's sperm."[21]

Emerson wants to know where his authors stand on the question of sexual activity, for he seems himself not yet to have made up his mind whether sperm ought to be retained or released. Indeed, in a journal entry the following year on the "appetites," Emerson would say that "life must have continence & abandonment" (*JMN* 11:230).

Emerson regularly, at least in the early 1840s, thought of literary expression in explicitly sexual terms, and called for both "a spermatic book" (Plutarch was one example) and "initiative, spermatic, prophesying man-making words" (*JMN* 7:547; 8:148). He undoubtedly had such a concept in mind in an 1840 journal passage that praised Montaigne (and also Plutarch) for his strong "language of the street" (*JMN* 7:374). And the original version of what became a passage in "The Poet" treated utterance as almost a sexual necessity, since Emerson wrote of the "oestrum of speech" and of thought being "ejaculated as Logos or Word" (*JMN* 9:72).

Returning to the journal entry for the summer of 1849, we notice at least that Emerson is evincing a sharp interest in sexual habits and arguing that a literary account of life ought to deal with these matters. A few pages further on, we come upon a related entry: "I find what L. read me this morning from 'Conjugial Love' to be in a Goody-Two-Shoes taste, the description of gold houses, & Sinbad Sailor fruit trees,—all tinsel & gingerbread. . . . What to do with the stupendous old prig?" (*JMN* 11:133). As the editors tell us, Lidian seems to have been reading from Swedenborg's *The Delights of Wisdom concerning Conjugial Love: after which follow Pleasures of Insanity concerning Scortatory Love.* Clearly, in regard to the sexual matters which were manifestly engaging his thought, Emerson did not consider Swedenborg one of the authors he was expecting. Soon, in fact, he would condemn Swedenborg for treating "the warm many-weathered passionate peopled world" as little more than a "grammar of hieroglyphs" (*JMN* 11:179). Still, Swedenborg *did* become one of Emerson's *Representative Men;* and there seems to be a curious echo of the title of the book from which Lidian was reading, in Emerson's use of a rare word when he himself complained about "scortatory religions" in the "Worship" chapter of *The Conduct of Life* (W 6:207).

Turning the page of Emerson's journal, we find that Dante chimed in better with his mood, since he "knew how to throw the weight of his body into each act" and, like Montaigne and Plutarch, is "full of the *nobil volgare eloquenza.*" Emerson praises him for knowing "God damn" and being "rowdy if he please, & he does please." Emerson likes "an imagination that rivals in closeness & precision the senses," but feels, on the other hand, that he himself "can appropriate nothing" of Dante. There follows immediately another entry which is somewhat puzzling:

> M. was like a vigorous cock let into ⟨among a brood of hens⟩ the coop of a farm house. He trod the hundred hens of the barnyard, and the very partridges for a mile round, and for the next fortnight the whole country side was filled with cackle over the eggs which they laid. (*JMN* 11:134)

"M" is not further identified, but since Emerson has been thinking about authors and their relative sexual vigor, it is likely he is talking about Montaigne, whom he elsewhere calls an "unbuttoned sloven" (*JMN* 5:415). Such is the kind of literary energy Emerson seems disposed to admire. And it is perhaps not surprising that, on the following page, in a list of "good names" which pleased Emerson, we find "dandy" and "cocktail"—as well as "catamite" (*JMN* 11:135).

It is perfectly clear that Emerson's interest in all these matters formed part, indeed a large part, of the impulse that was helping to germinate *The Conduct of Life,* since several pages further on, we find the first version of what became the penultimate paragraph of the chapter "Wealth," with its patently sexual language ("Will you spend your income, or will you invest it? 'Tis worth seeing how far this question holds good. All your bodies & organs are jars in which the liquor of life is stored. Will you spend it for pleasure? You are a sot. Will you husband it?" [*JMN* 11:142]).

Sandwiched in between this and a sentence which became part of the last paragraph of "Wealth," we find what is undoubtedly the most curious and revealing of all the entries in this series. Emerson heads his page with the names of two famous physicians ("Eustachius Boerhaave") and then writes:

> Mr P died of too much perspiration.
>
> Buna was engaged in writing a book on the conduct of life, & today in the chapter on Crickets. It could not be said of Buna, that she lived entirely for her dinner, though she was tenderly patiently absorbed in that capital event of the day, no, for she was not less dedicated to her supper, nor less to her breakfast. He had studied her character imperfectly who thought she lived in these. . . . No, she wished to keep her feet warm, & she was addicted to a soft seat & expended a skill & generalship on securing the red chair & a corner out of the draft & in the air worthy of a higher seat in heaven.
>
> Neither on these was she exhausted her ample genius insisted on he
>
> In a frivolous age Buna was earnest. She screamed, she groaned, she watched at night, she waited by day for her omelet & her lamp with smooth handle & when she went out of the house it was a perfect *row* for half an hour.
>
> Buna had catarrh, pleurisy, rush of blood to the head, apoplexy, diabetes, diarrhea, sunstroke, atrophy, worms, palsy, erisypelas, consumption & dropsy. (*JMN* 11:142–43)

The name "Buna" is a puzzle,[22] but there can be little doubt that Emerson here set down one of his autobiographical allegories (such as we have already looked at), though this one is unique for the Swiftian savagery of its self-satire. As we have seen, Emerson would shortly caution himself, "in the conduct of life," not to "parade our rags . . . confess, & tear our hair," but here is the darker side of the project. We are offered a glimpse of Emerson, on the threshold of old age (as he conceives it), actually writing the book which arises out of his meditations on the physiological basis of human conduct. The cost to his own consciousness, Emerson seems to be saying, is tremendous, because his preoccupation with bodily functions has driven him to think of human creatures as insects or animals in decay (a few pages ahead, he says that "the houses in Acton seemed to be filled with fat old people who looked like old tomatoes, their faces crumpled into red collops, fatting & rotting at their ease" [*JMN* 11:147]).

Buna is an autobiographical persona who bodies forth an old Emersonian nightmare about the "puniness" of the literary man, adumbrated as far back as "The American Scholar" ("there goes in the world a notion that the scholar should be a recluse, a valetudinarian. . . ." [*CW* 1:59]). In his garden, two years earlier, Emerson felt dispirited, "drivelling . . . robbed of all energy," afflicted with "a sort of catalepsy," and "grown peevish & poorspirited" (*JMN* 10:93). Now, in his study, and writing *this* book, he views himself in fantasy as threatened with almost every disease known to old age, his vital fluids drying up or running out. Like Mr P, Emerson seems to be dying of "too much perspiration." Or, as he would write in "Fate," the first chapter of *The Conduct of Life:* "In youth we clothe ourselves with rainbows and go as brave as the zodiac. In age we put out another sort of perspiration,— gout, fever, rheumatism, caprice, doubt, fretting and avarice" (*W* 6:41). That last word tolls us back to the series of journal entries we have been considering, where a few pages beyond the "Buna" fragment we find the sentence which, in a slightly different version, would become the penultimate sentence of "Wealth": "The true Economy of man, then, is always to prefer spending on the higher plane; always to invest & invest, with holy avarice, that he may spend in spiritual creation & not in begetting animals" (*JMN* 11:154). In the book, Emerson would print "not in augmenting animal existence" (*W* 6:126).

It is fair to say that Emerson's attitude toward the physiological conduct of life became more or less negative after the period of ferment which we have just examined. Apart from a brief flurry of more positive interest caused, it would seem, by a visit from Horatio Greenough in 1852, Emerson was not disposed to be pleased by evidence that the sexual instinct is widely diffused throughout human experience. As he writes in 1851:

> ... it does not seem to me much better, when the gross instincts are a little disguised, and the oestrum, gadfly ... of sex takes sentimental forms. I like the engendering of snails better than the same ⟨rut⟩ masquerading in Watts's psalms to the Church, the bride of Christ, or an old girl forming sentimental friendships with every male thing that comes by, under the pretence of *"developing a new side."* (*JMN* 11:376)

Emerson wants to have sexuality unmasked and seen for the brutal force that it is, rather than to allow it shyly to pervade other aspects of the conduct of life. He must have winced at his own 1844 journal entry about "the oestrum of speech." And if Emerson had read *The Scarlet Letter* when it appeared in 1850, it would have been interesting to get his reaction to such a sentence as the following: "The virgins of [Dimmesdale's] church grew pale around him, victims of a passion so imbued with religious sentiment that they imagined it to be all religion, and brought it openly, in their white bosoms, as their most acceptable sacrifice before the altar." Such, undoubtedly, was not what Emerson intended when he advised the Harvard Divinity graduates to feel their call "in throbs of desire and hope" (*CW* 1:84).

At this time, as Emerson worked over his chapter on "Fate," he explicitly equated it not only with "Nature" but with sexual passion: "In feeble individuals, the sex & the digestion are all, absorb the entire vitality," and render such people the "children of fate" (*JMN* 11:376; cf. 12:585). Emerson wished that "these drones" might perish and improve the hive. He thought "most men ... mere bulls & most women cows." That sentence would get toned down in the printed book ("most men and most women are merely one couple more" [*W* 6:11]) but Emerson's attitude was obviously no less severe: by couple, he clearly intends to suggest *copulating*.

Another journal entry—which found its way, again in a milder version, into the "Behavior" chapter of *The Conduct of Life*—appears in harsher form when it was first set down in 1853:

> The meaning of the famous saying of Jacobi (and of Mr Dean) is the fact, that the poet sprains or strains himself by attempting too much; he tries to reach the people, instead of contenting himself with the temperate expression of what he knows. Sing he must & should, but not ballads; sing, but for gods or demi-gods. He need not transform himself into Punch & Judy. A man must not be a proletary or breeder, but only by mere superfluity of his strength, he begets Messias. He relieves himself, & makes a world. (*JMN* 13:258–59)

Behind the Olympian view of creation here being expounded, one also senses a certain fear of being depleted sexually by any strong effort at engaging the teeming democratic masses. Whitman, of course, would argue otherwise.

One final episode, which I have already alluded to, deserves mention as an indication of the great complexity of Emerson's imagination, especially when it touched on the sexual conduct of life. The death of Horatio Greenough in 1853, just a short time after he paid a visit to Concord that evidently excited Emerson very much, was clearly a blow that drove another nail into Emerson's coffin. Emerson was much impressed by Greenough's lustiness, masculine vigor, great force of mind, and belief that "everything is generative" (*JMN* 13:85).[23] It is quite surprising, and revealing, to see Emerson not only accepting but copying into his journal Greenough's definition of Emerson's "contemplations" as "the masturbation of the brain" (*JMN* 13:84), especially as we recall that 1833 journal entry about the "Savings Bank." Once more, and perhaps for the last time, Emerson was disposed to let himself go in Greenough's company. When he died, Emerson wrote to Carlyle:

Our few fine persons are apt to die. Horatio Greenough, a sculptor, whose tongue was far cunninger in talk, than his chisel to carve, & who inspired great hopes, died two months ago at 47 years. Nature has only so much vital force, & must dilute it, if it is to be multiplied into millions. "The beautiful is never plentiful."[24]

The last sentence is Emerson's own, and his drift is hardly clear here unless one turns to the 1853 journal entry where the sentence first appears:

The beautiful is never plentiful.

"A young ass of a good size in the space of one month readily emitted as much seed as would fill a hat." *Leeuwenhoek.* (*JMN* 13:267)

Why does Emerson follow his own sentence by the observation of the great Dutch physiologist? Presumably, the copious production of seed by the young ass is an example of how plentiful is the *un*-beautiful. As Emerson applies his sentence to Greenough in the letter to Carlyle, he seems to imply that the "vital force" of Greenough's fine seed had to be diluted by death in order for it to be made available to inseminate "millions." Nature herself, somehow seen to be on the wane, has only a limited amount of such stuff. She is diminished, and she has let Emerson down.

But the student of Emerson's writing must surely find his mind boggled when he notices that this whole crux, inspired by Greenough's visit and death, curiously informs a larger cultural statement which Emerson was to make in "The Fortune of the Republic":

The flowering of civilization is the finished man, the man of sense, of grace, of accomplishment, of social power,—the gentleman. What hinders that he be born here? The new times need a new man, the complemental man, whom plainly this country must furnish. Freer swing his arms; farther pierce his eyes; more forward and forthright his whole build and rig than the Englishman's who, we see, is much imprisoned in his backbone.

'Tis certain that our civilization is yet incomplete, it has not ended nor given sign of ending in a hero. 'Tis a wild democracy; the riot of mediocrities and dishonesties and fudges. Ours is the age of the omnibus, of the third person plural, of Tammany Hall. Is it that Nature has only so much vital force, and must dilute it if it is to be multiplied into millions? The beautiful is never plentiful. Then Illinois and Indiana, with their spawning loins, must needs be ordinary. (W 11:537–38)

Emerson seems to see Greenough's death as a commentary on his own hopes for sexual and spiritual renewal. The sexual— indeed, the political—future does not belong to such as he (or Greenough), but to the common seed and "spawning loins" of Illinois and Indiana. Abraham Lincoln, and not Emerson, would be the Father of his country.

Economizing

[I]

As we have noticed, one important conclusion which Emerson seems to have arrived at by 1849 was that the characteristic expression of youth—love—gives way in age to the "perspiration" of avarice (*JMN* 11:168). Whether or not it is fair to say in general that an intense concern for money and property frequently replaces sexual interest in older people, it is clear that some such notion steadily took hold of Emerson's imagination as he contemplated the conduct of life. Emerson wrote out his physiology of money in "Wealth," a lecture which he delivered in various places in 1851–52, and both the subject and the treatment seemed to appeal to Emerson's audiences, which were large and enthusiastic. "Those who went to hear Transcendentalism," reported the *Schenectady Reflector* in December 1852, "came away astonished to find that they had understood, admired, and most heartily approved" (*L* 4:324).

Money and banking were tremendously important issues in Emerson's time and constitute a dominant sub-theme in Emerson's own career. Though he could lament in 1840, "Ah, my poor countrymen! Yankees & Dollars have such inextricable association that the words ought to rhyme" (*JMN* 7:341), he knew perfectly well that that same music informed his own cultural vocabulary. Emerson did not need a James Russell Lowell to tell him, as he noted in 1847, that a "remarkable trait in the American character is the union not very infrequent of Yankee cleverness with spiritualism" (*JMN* 10:171). Emerson believed, in fact, that "a young person of superior intellectual powers," such as he early knew himself to be, who frequently failed to make best use of those powers because of a lack of self-confidence, could be transformed into "an adroit fluent masterful gentleman" by spending some time learning to deal with large sums of money. When he made these observations in 1834, Emerson added: "My manners & history would have been very different, if my parents had been rich, when I was a boy at school" (*JMN* 4:262–63). Perhaps it is no coincidence that this journal entry was made only a few months before Emerson received the first half of his inheritance from Ellen Tucker's estate. His dead angel was about to compensate him for this failing in his parents and help give his spirit the impetus it needed to take possession of its Transcendental springtime.

Though Emerson considered himself "no very good economist," he also knew that he was shrewd about money and believed that "economy is a science [which] must be devoutly studied, if you would know it" (*L* 2:64). On the evidence of his letters, at least, especially those to his brother William and to Carlyle, he did not neglect this area of his studies. Emerson might dream occasionally of turning away from "Jacksonism & Bankism" and refreshing himself instead with "the phenomena of the Polar Regions" and "the geographical problem of the Niger" (*L* 1:404); or he could long to "pay no tax, own no City Bank stock," and become instead one with "the blowing of the sleet over the pond & the fields" which carried him "to Canada, to Labrador, or to the Atlantic Main" (*JMN* 8:100). But, in actuality, he managed surprisingly well to divide his attention between natural history and the world of finance. Although Emerson scholars have generally given short shrift to such matters as the Tucker inheritance and other pecuniary dealings, Emerson himself was careful not to make that mistake. His journal was not the only "savings bank" in which he took pains to deposit his earnings. Indeed, had he done otherwise, he would not have had the leisure to keep his journal.

Economizing

It can be highly instructive to set Emerson's writing career, and the careers of his contemporaries, in the context of America's economic history.[25] We ought to remind ourselves, for example, that the year of Emerson's great address on "The American Scholar"—he delivered it in Cambridge on August 31, 1837, one day after Harvard's commencement—is also memorable as the year of the great financial panic which ushered in half a decade of economic depression and distress. Emerson could hardly be expected to overlook such a momentous event and indeed grieved over the "calamitous times" (*L* 2:64) in his letters and journal entries, making notes on the "loud cracks in the social edifice" (*JMN* 5:304) and concluding grimly on May 14, 1837: "The land stinks with suicide" (*JMN* 5:334). Interestingly, he reported on June 29 that he himself had lost "almost one month . . . to study by bodily weakness & disease" (*JMN* 5:339).

Other members of Emerson's circle were equally concerned. Henry Thoreau, in fact, graduated from Harvard College on August 30, 1837, after a Cambridge experience marred by his own ill health and relative poverty. Years later, he recalled with some bitterness that a small scholarship awarded him, which was based on the income from a Chelsea estate, required that he himself collect the rents—a distasteful and difficult job.[26] The Thoreau family always lived in genteel poverty, and, because of a lack of job opportunities, Henry unwillingly undertook after graduation to teach in the Concord public school—a career that came abruptly to an end not long after it started when the School Committee discovered that the new master did not believe in whipping children. Perhaps when we think about the doctrine of Transcendental detachment and inaction that Thoreau and other Concordians were preaching or about to preach, or when we read the chapter on economy in *Walden,* we should keep in mind that, for Thoreau at least, such notions were well nigh unavoidable; there just weren't any good jobs around for Harvard graduates—not to mention ordinary mortals.

One such, an eighteen-year-old living in Albany, New York,

who was later to boast that a whaling ship was his Yale and Harvard College, also became a reluctant schoolteacher in the fall of 1837 for want of other opportunity. Financial disaster was a hallmark of the Melville family, and after his abortive attempt at teaching, and a few other things, Herman Melville shipped aboard the brig *St. Lawrence* on May 31, 1839, bound for Liverpool and the career we are familiar with. The sea represented an opportunity not only to escape from the gloomy, indeed doomed, atmosphere of the Melville home but also to make and save some money at a time when money was difficult to come by.

It might seem disrespectfully un-Transcendental to cast a cold eye on Emerson's own financial situation in 1837, but we may be able to learn something thereby. Through what can only be considered an incredible stroke of good fortune, Emerson finally got his hands on the remaining portion of the Tucker inheritance— $11,674.49—in July 1837. Since Emerson's second wife, Lidian, whom he married in 1835, brought a small but not insubstantial dowry with her, Emerson's financial condition in that gloomy summer was unquestionably secure. Though he could not call himself a wealthy man, he had, apart from Lidian's money, a house and land in Concord, as well as some $23,000 of Tucker money invested at 6 percent or better; and was earning between $400 and $800 per year on the lecture circuit.[27] His bank stock, to be sure, sometimes failed to pay dividends, and Emerson had to work hard for his lecture fees, but in general one might say that, in personal terms at least, he was justified in optimistically declaring the independence of the American scholar on August 31, 1837. Though the detestable iron horse would disturb Thoreau's peace as he sojourned on Emerson's Walden woodlot in the mid-1840s, that same Fitchburg Railroad was putting dividends in Emerson's bank account.[28] By 1844, when he published his second series of *Essays,* Emerson could serenely announce to a nation just beginning to emerge from hard times that "money . . . in its effects and laws" is "as beautiful as roses": "Property keeps the accounts of the world, and is always moral. The property will be found where the labor, the wisdom and the virtue have been in nations, in classes, and . . . in the individual also" (*W* 3:231). Such sentiments, admittedly, are very far from representing the best of Emerson, but they *are* his sentiments and suggest how his own relative financial ease could affect his notions.[29]

Emerson, to be sure, with his intensely scrupulous New England conscience, never ceased to fret over the implications of his situation. In September 1838, for example, in the aftermath of the Divinity School affair, he noted: "I please myself with the thought that my accidental freedom by means of a permanent income is nowise essential to my habits, that my tastes, my direction of thought is so strong that I should do the same things,—should contrive to spend the best of my time in the same way as now, rich or poor. If I did not think so, I should never dare to urge the doctrines of human Culture on young men" (*JMN* 7:71). Still, he continued to feel obliged to justify himself. Two years later, he wrote: "I have been writing with some pains Essays on various matters as a sort of apology to my country for my apparent idleness." He went on to insist that what some people (and his own conscience, we might add) tended to call indolence did not make nature love him less, and there he was resolved to stay despite criticism:

> You think it is because I have an income which exempts me from your day-labor, that I waste, (as you call it,) my time in sungazing & stargazing. You do not know me. If my debts, as they threaten, should consume what money I have, I should live just as I do now: I should eat worse food & wear a coarser coat and should wonder in a potato patch instead of in the wood—but it is I & not my Twelve Hundred dollars a year, that love God. (*JMN* 7:404–5)

Emerson's imaginary interlocutor might have responded that it is easier to love God *with* twelve hundred a year than without, whence Emerson's presumed cosmic optimism. Indeed, when Emerson touched back on the subject a few years later, he seemed in fact to hint at some special relationship with the divine which caused him, by a happy paradox, to suffer more in his wealth than other men did in their poverty, thereby expiating his nagging sense of guilt:

> My Genius loudly calls me to stay where I am, even with the degradation of owning bankstock and seeing poor men suffer whilst the Universal Genius apprises me of this disgrace & beckons me to the martyr's & redeemer's office. (*JMN* 9:62).

Another sometime Concordian and friend of Emerson's, Nathaniel Hawthorne, found himself beckoned to a very different office by financial need and the politics of the time. Emerson said that Andrew Jackson (who, he told Carlyle, was "a most unfit person" to be President)[30] made him feel "dirty," and in his journal he roundly damned what he called "Van Burenism," but Hawthorne—a loyal Democrat—was fortunate that his party was in power. Through the influence of a good friend, the historian and fellow party member George Bancroft, Hawthorne obtained a job in the Boston Customhouse in 1839, the year he became engaged to Sophia Peabody. There he remained until the Democrats were turned out of office in March 1841, whereupon Hawthorne, still worried about his finances and eager to marry Sophia, invested $1,500 in Brook Farm (we should recall that that utopian experiment was actually a joint stock company and its members hoped to see a good return on their investments). The West Roxbury Community proved to be a fiasco for Hawthorne, both intellectually and financially, and that failure would strongly color his attitudes when he came to write *The Blithedale Romance.* Money continued to be a problem for him. Shortly after the Democrats were returned to office in the election of 1845, Hawthorne was appointed Surveyor of Customs in Salem, with what results we know, since that experience germinated *The Scarlet Letter,* as he tells us in "The Custom-House" essay which precedes the narrative proper. Though the torpor induced by his government job numbed his imagination and he would curse "Uncle Sam's gold" as "the Devil's wages," Hawthorne could not live without the job and, after all, he did find the Scarlet Letter on Satan's golden premises. It is doubtful that the secure rentier's life in rustic Concord would have brought forth such a brooding and disquieting book.

The same is true of Melville. Financial distress, not just wanderlust, sent him to sea in the first place, and it was a weird combination of maritime experience, metaphysics, and a desperate need for commercial success that shaped Melville's career at its height. That Melville was hard-pressed all readers of *Moby-Dick* can attest, for Chapter 32 concludes with a clear expression of the author's woes: "O Time, Strength, Cash, and Patience!" In fact, on May 1, 1851, when Melville was deep into the writing of the book, money problems forced him to borrow $2,050 at 9 percent interest. One month later, he sent a long—now famous—letter to Hawthorne which suggested that his strange mixing of adventure and philosophical speculation owed at least something to the exigencies of the market: "Dollars damn me . . . What I feel most moved to write, that is banned,—it will not pay. Yet, altogether, write the *other* way I cannot. So the product is a final hash, and all my books are botches." We may wish to protest, with *Moby-Dick* in mind, that Melville's "botches" are worth far more than most authors' successes. But we also must acknowledge the sense of desperation enforced on Melville by economic pressures. In that same letter to Hawthorne, Melville exclaimed with great bitterness: "Tho I wrote the Gospels in this century, I should die in the gutter."[31]

As it turned out, that fate had been reserved for another great contemporary of Melville's. He himself would publish his last prose work in 1857 and then, so far as the literary world was concerned, fall silent until his death in 1891 after a long posthumous existence which included nineteen years in limbo at the New York Customhouse. His wages there, we are told, were four dollars a day,[32] which was apparently sufficient to dispel the terrible anxiety over money that had plagued Melville for so long. But, though he would write and publish poetry and leave the manuscript of *Billy Budd* in his desk, Melville's life as a minor government functionary would engender no more *Moby-Dicks*. He had, however, avoided ending up in the street.

Poe was not so lucky. Two years before Melville made his remark to Hawthorne, on October 3, 1849, to be exact, Edgar Allan Poe was picked up from a Baltimore street and taken to the hospital, where he died four days later without recovering consciousness. Uncannily anticipating Melville's complaint that even a true nineteenth-century prophet would end up in the gutter, Poe had brought forth, a year before his death, his apocalyptic prose-poem-romance *Eureka*. Filled with excitement in the belief that he had laid bare the secrets of the universe, Poe predicted that a first edition of 50,000 copies would be required. His hard-headed publisher, however, agreed to advance him $14 on the book, which eventually sold—slowly—750 copies.[33] On April 28, 1849, one of Poe's last poems, "For Annie," was published in the *Home Journal* with an introduction by the popular and successful magazine writer N.P. Willis. Mindful of the wretched penury in which Poe had always existed, Willis magnanimously suggested that "money . . . could not be better laid out for the honor of this period of American literature—neither by the government, by a society, nor by an individual—than in giving Edgar Poe a competent annuity."[34] No such patronage, of course, was forthcoming, and in any case it would have been too late; the disappointed author, worn down to the nub by his constant struggle, consciously prepared himself for the grave. Writing in July 1849 to Maria Clemm, the mother of his child-bride Virginia—then two years dead—Poe said: "It is no use to reason with me *now*. I must die. I have no desire to live since I have done 'Eureka.' I could accomplish nothing more."[35] Clearly, Poe "could accomplish nothing more" not only because he had finally written his sacred book but also because he was sick, destitute, and discouraged beyond the point of recovery. Three months later he was gone, leaving behind a body of writing filled with death and disaster—the fitting emblem and embodiment of his own tough life.

Economizing

In view of Melville's accurate remark, it is appropriate that he should have found the means to use Poe's career as a symbol of the plight of impoverished genius in mid-nineteenth-century America, suggesting archly, as he did so, that the cash nexus obtained as much in the literary world as elsewhere. The incredible confrontation that Melville dreamed up is, fittingly enough, between Edgar Allan Poe and Ralph Waldo Emerson.[36] It occurs in Melville's last published prose work, *The Confidence-Man,* a book whose action takes place on April Fool's Day and which, as its title suggests, has a good deal to do with money. It was brought out on April 1, 1857 —a year when America would experience another major financial panic. In Chapter XXXVI of the book, the Confidence-Man appears as the Cosmopolitan—a sort of amiable and cultured swindler who acts as master of ceremonies—and he is speaking to a "mystic," Mark Winsome, who is obviously a satiric portrait of Ralph Waldo Emerson. Winsome is described as "a kind of cross between a Yankee peddler and a Tartar priest, though it seemed as if, at a pinch, the first would not in all probability play second fiddle to the last." (It should be recalled that this way of describing Emerson—as a mystic who yet kept a shrewd eye open for the main chance—had been popularized by Lowell in 1848 in his *Fable for Critics,* where he had spoken of Emerson as "A Greek head on right Yankee shoulders, whose range/ Has Olympus for one pole, for t'other the Exchange.") Interrupting the conversation between the Cosmopolitan and the canny Transcendentalist, a strange figure stumbles on the scene—the specter of Edgar Allan Poe:

> . . . a haggard, inspired-looking man now approached—a crazy beggar, asking alms under the form of peddlng a rhapsodical tract, composed by himself, and setting forth his claims to some rhapsodical apostleship. Though ragged and dirty, there was about him no touch of vulgarity, for, by nature, his manner was not unrefined, his frame slender, and appeared the more so from the broad, untanned frontlet of his brow, tangled over with a disheveled mass of raven curls, throwing a still deeper tinge upon a complexion like

that of a shriveled berry. Nothing could exceed his look of picturesque Italian ruin and dethronement, heightened by what seemed
just one glimmering peep of reason, insufficient to do him any
lasting good, but enough, perhaps, to suggest a torment of latent
doubts at times, whether his addled dream of glory were true.

Accepting the tract offered him, the cosmopolitan glanced over
it, and, seeming to see just what it was, closed it, put it in his
pocket, eyed the man a moment, then, leaning over and presenting
him with a shilling, said to him, in tones kind and considerate: "I
am sorry, my friend, that I happened to be engaged just now; but,
having purchased your work, I promise myself much satisfaction in
its perusal at my earliest leisure."

In his tattered, single-breasted frock-coat, buttoned meagerly
up to his chin, the shatter-brain made him a bow, which, for
courtesy, would not have misbecome a viscount, then turned with
silent appeal to the stranger. But the stranger sat more like a cold
prism than ever, while an expression of keen Yankee cuteness, now
replacing his former mystical one, lent added icicles to his aspect.
His whole air said: "Nothing from me." The repulsed petitioner
threw a look full of resentful pride and cracked disdain upon him,
and went his way.

"Come now," said the cosmopolitan, a little reproachfully,
"you ought to have sympathized with that man; tell me, did you
feel no fellow-feeling? Look at his tract here, quite in the transcendental vein."

"Excuse me," said the stranger, declining the tract, "I never
patronize scoundrels."

"Scoundrels?"

"I detected in him, sir, a damning peep of sense—damning, I
say; for sense in a seeming madman is scoundrelism. I take him for
a cunning vagabond, who picks up a vagabond living by adroitly
playing the madman."

Though Melville's ironies here are many, I want to stress one
in particular: since Melville, echoing Lowell, has already presented
Emerson as a seeming mystic with a good head for business, he
manages in this confrontation to have Emerson project onto Poe

precisely his *own* duplicity, since Winsome condemns the beggar for feigning madness in order to pick up the odd shilling. Thus Melville is suggesting that Emerson is Transcendental only north-north-west; when the wind blows from State Street, he knows how to hang on to his coins. Of course, Melville's interview is imaginary; and he is hardly being fair to Emerson by insinuating that the latter was a pennypinching hypocrite. But by 1857 Melville's bitterness over his own failed career was sufficiently strong so that he felt compelled to let his audience know, however cryptically, that in the literary world there decidedly were haves and have-nots. Genius was going a-begging, and he and Poe were brothers in dispossession.

[11]

When Wordsworth wrote, in 1806, that "getting and spending, we lay waste our powers," he could hardly have known that he was providing one of the best introductions to nineteenth-century America. He must have known, however, that his anxiety about a draining involvement in worldly affairs was clothed in language that was all but explicitly sexual. Shakespeare, in fact, in a familiar sonnet that seems clearly to lie behind Wordsworth's lines, had agonized over "th' expense of spirit in a waste of shame" which is "lust in action." Elsewhere, in *All's Well That Ends Well,* for example, Shakespeare uses the word "spending" ("spending his manly marrow in her arms") with that sexual meaning which was to become so important to Victorian writers of pornography. Though I do not place Whitman in this category (some of his contemporaries would have), just about fifty years after Wordsworth wrote his sonnet, the American barbarian would shock readers of the second edition of *Leaves of Grass* by speaking openly of his "love-spendings."[37]

Whitman, and his exact contemporary, Herman Melville, might waggishly be characterized as the last of the big-time spenders in nineteenth-century American literature. The first, with his "semitic muscle" ever at the ready, would always insist, as he puts it in "Song of Myself," on "spending for vast returns," scattering himself freely in the service of cultural fecundation.[38] Melville, proponent of that form of polymorphous perversity known in the whaling industry as sperm-squeezing, joined hands with Whitman, metaphorically at least, in opposing their New York extravagance and prodigality to the calculating parsimony which they associated with the New England tradition. In the same book in which Melville portrayed Emerson as an ice-water-consuming skinflint, he set himself to the devilish task of convincing readers to exchange their cash for nature's own remedy. The savvy among Melville's audience were expected to understand that the confidence-man's Omni-Balsamic Reinvigorator promised renewed potency to those willing to spend a few shillings. Melville's point seems to be that emotional expansiveness, in the case of Emerson, and sexuality, in the case of the sick man suffering from a "long apathy of impotence," are incompatible with parsimony.

That the general, or abstract, issues being engaged here — prodigality versus economizing — should have been expressed equally by Whitman, Melville, *and* Emerson in explicitly sexual terms might seem merely odd or idiosyncratic, but the fact is that students of this period have come increasingly to see that debates over some of the key questions of the time were conducted in terms that clearly suggest an underlying psycho-physiological anxiety, particularly among American males.[39] It is not difficult to demonstrate, I believe, that two of the hottest issues which preoccupied Jacksonian America — religious revivalism and the banking question — were suffused with what one scholar has called the "spermatic economy";[40] and that Emerson, the "venturous conservative" (to use the term which I have already appropriated from Marvin Meyers' *Jacksonian Persuasion*), gives representative expression to this pervasive motif.

In recent years, various students of nineteenth-century America have shown that masturbation was a primary focus of anxious attention for medical men and moralists.[41] The "spermatorrhoeic quacks," as they have been called,[42] were strongly in possession of the field, and one scholar, Ben Barker-Benfield, has provided impressive documentation for this American obsession. As Barker-Benfield points out, "concentration of energies"[43] was a central social concern in the period; and though he does not cite Emerson on this point, he might have, as when Emerson says, in "Power," that "the one prudence in life is concentration; the one evil is dissipation. . . . Everything is good which takes away one plaything and delusion more and drives us home to add one stroke of faithful work. . . . Only so can that amount of vital force accumulate which can make the step from knowing to doing" (*W* 6:74).

Barker-Benfield notes that the deepest anxiety concerned "spermatic *loss.*" He cites an article in the *Boston Medical and Surgical Journal* for 1835 which warns that "this drain upon the system [i.e., ejaculation of sperm in copulation] should be reserved to mature age and even then . . . it should be made but sparingly. . . . Sturdy manhood . . . loses its energy and bends under the too frequent expenditure of this important secretion." Barker-Benfield continues:

> The discharge of sperm, it was generally believed, "obliterated," "prostrated," and "blotted out" all of "the energies of the system." Instead of "concentrating" onto the nonsexual end of success, the masturbator concentrated what was left of them onto his penis and testicles. "All the remaining energies of animal life [the *Boston Medical and Surgical Journal* argues] seem to be concentrated in these organs, and all the remaining power to gratification left is in the exercise of this . . . loathsome and beastly habit." That the ejaculation of sperm then diminished and exhausted all of the rest of the body's energy suggests that, somehow, in its focussing on the genital organs the previously undefined energy was transformed into sperm. . . . The American sex expert, Dr. Gardner, said in 1872 that sperm was "the concentrated powers of man's perfected being. . . . Sperm is the purest extract of the blood and according to the expression of Feruel, *totus homo semen est.*"[44]

As Barker-Benfield argues, "the underlying model for the operation of the whole man, psychological and physiological, was economic."[45] One could scarcely ask for a better illustration of the attitudes expressed in the material quoted above than this characteristic entry from Emerson's journal of 1850:

> Talent sucks the substance of the man . . . the accumulation of one point has drained the trunk. Blessed are those who have no talent! The expressors are the gods of the world,—Shakspeare & the rest, but the sane men whom these expressors [secretly] revere, are the ⟨sound⟩ solid balanced undemonstrative citizens who make the reserved guard, the central sense of the world. (*JMN* 11:226)

Reminding ourselves of Emerson's 1847 entry about Greek coinage, we might say that three years later he seemed willing to exchange his Attic salt for the solid, conservative sense of State Street. Art, he went on to suggest, is the "fine or expiation" that the literary man pays for his self-indulgence. And he concludes, leaning, it seems, toward a sterner economy for himself: "I have never met a person superior to his talent; one who had money in his pocket, & did not use it."

With Emerson's physiologico-economic figure, we may conveniently turn to a consideration of the banking issue in the Jacksonian period. Our principal guides in this connection will be William M. Gouge and Theophilus Fisk—perfectly real characters, although their names suggest an apposite Dickensian invention. Gouge's main work, *The Curse of Paper-Money and Banking*, was well-known in its time and had the dubious distinction of being reprinted in London in 1833 with an introduction by William Cobbett. Though Cobbett improved the occasion to suggest that an "r" should be added to Gouge's name because of the over-inflated contents and price of the American edition, he applauded Gouge's position, which amounted to an exposure of the evils of "factitious money." Gouge quoted Alexander Hamilton on "paper emissions," which Hamilton called "so seducing and dangerous an expedient." Paper money, in Gouge's view, is essentially false money ("paper is paper, and money is money") which invariably leads to extravagant speculation followed by collapse: "In one respect the comparison of paper Banking with steam power is an apt one. The danger of an explosion is very great, and the effects of an explosion would be tremendous." Gouge insists that paper money leads to a kind of orgy of credit which is always followed by moral and economic ruin.[46]

The moral issues are more fully engaged in a work published in 1837 by Gouge's colorful disciple, Theophilus Fisk. The book, entitled *The Banking Bubble Burst; or The Mammoth Corruptions of the Paper Money System Relieved by Bleeding* . . . , speaks in part of its long subtitle of "the deleterious effects upon public morals and private happiness" produced by the American banking system. Fisk's book, among other things, is a veritable anthology of contemporary opinion on the banking issue, and the quotations tend to show that Fisk's own excited rhetoric is characteristic of the genre. One writer, cited early in the book on the evils of excessive paper money, argues that "temporary excess is succeeded by a temporary deficiency, one extreme invariably tends to another." The country, we are told, in the physiological metaphor which is everywhere in the book, moves from "undue excitement" to "undue depression"; "these vibrations," Fisk's source insists, "introduce at one moment a spirit of wild and daring speculation, and at another, a prostration of confidence, and stagnation of business." Banking fluctuations "intoxicate enterprise, only to enfeeble it." Banking establishments are "like the syren of the fable, they entice to destroy."[47]

Fisk's key point, illustrated by many pages of quotations, is not so much that banking and paper money produce an ineffective economic system as that they inevitably lead to moral corruption, to a wild expenditure of individual wealth on "luxuries to pamper the appetite" which are a "positive injury to . . . health and morals." As an emblem of the disgusting sexual excess induced by speculation, Fisk describes one New Yorker "who by means of

Bank bubbles had inflated himself into a mushroom, overbearing, supercilious aristocrat" and thereupon "imported a bedstead which alone cost twenty-five hundred dollars, with the hangings and fringes. Had the man *earned his money* by honest labor," Fisk insists, "he would have employed it in a different manner from this." Clearly, the way to employ money is not to spend it freely and publicly but to conserve it at home. "If every man kept his own money in his own pocket," Fisk argues, "how could a panic, a pressure, a scarcity be produced?"[48] This seems to have been a commonplace of anti-bank rhetoric, for we may remember Ezra Pound's Canto 37:

> "No where so well deposited as in the pants of the people, Wealth
> ain't," said President Jackson.[49]

Perhaps this is the place not only to recall Emerson's remark about pocketing his "talent" but also to note that in 1834, lamenting the fact that "the life seems dying out of all literature & this enormous paper currency of Words is accepted instead," Emerson conceded that "the evil may be cured by this rank rabble party, the Jacksonism of the country, heedless of English & of all literature—a stone cut out of the ground without hands—they may root out the hollow dilettantism of our cultivation in the coarsest way & the new-born may begin again to frame their own world with greater advantage" (*JMN* 4:297).

Jackson himself is cited by Fisk to the effect that the paper system weakens "public virtue" and will "inevitably lead to corruption" and the destruction of "purity . . . of government." More pointed are the remarks of the celebrated LocoFoco Democrat, William Leggett, who says that paper money "is capable of being prostituted to subserve the interests, and even the fraudulent purposes, of a set of harpies, who are marring or devouring all the blessings which heaven with a prodigal hand has been lavishing upon us." Leggett goes on to argue that the "spirit of hazardous but enticing speculation" will conduct America to the "baneful contamination . . . of the pristine purity of stern republican virtue." Are we prepared, he asks, "to sink into the vices and corruptions which have debased the most enslaved and degraded nations of ancient or modern times . . . shall the general pollution extend to all the private relations of social and domestic life?"[50]

Leggett's fears are amplified in the overheated remarks of a northern editor cited by Fisk. "This unnatural and artificial increase of money," he insists, "created all kinds of extravagance, licentiousness, splendor and show." Echoing Gouge's figure, which suggested the spasmodic release of tremendous energy, the editor claims that enormously expensive parties followed one upon the other "with the rapidity of steam power." Like Fisk, he focuses on the bedroom: "manufacturers filled their habitations with splendid bedsteads, $2500 each. . . . Beneath a gay and smiling exterior the grossest licentiousness prevailed. Some of the great men, like eastern pachas, kept their harems filled up with costly furniture, and gorgeous paintings. The marriage tie was broken as easily as you would break a pipestem." Such, he concludes, "is only a feeble picture of the terrible dissoluteness of manners—the subversion of moral principle—the destruction of truth—and the general corruption of mind and heart, which have followed the fearful augmentation of speculation and overtrading, *stimulated by overbanking.*"[51] Excessive stimulation, here conceived in manifestly sexual terms, is viewed as the great evil of the paper money system. Perhaps Emerson had something similar in mind when he wrote this cryptic and undated remark in one of his notebooks: "⟨Paper⟩ inflated currency instantly increases population" (*JMN* 12:337).

Though I want to leave Emerson's treatment of these issues to the end of this discussion, I might simply mention here that in his chapter on "Wealth" in *English Traits,* Emerson clearly displaced his anxieties about the banking question, as he did so much else, to our old home, adopting a stance not unlike that which we have been reviewing. The machine of English industry, Emerson argues, "unmans the user. What he gains in making cloth, he loses in general power. There should be temperance in making cloth, as well as in eating" (W 5:167). But worse even than steam power, which "was dreadful with its explosion," is the financial monster. "Harder still it has proved to resist and rule the dragon Money, with his paper wings." Inveighing against "the mischief of paper-money," Emerson claimed that the "aims of a manly life" had given way to "an erudition of sensation" (W 5:168–71). Perhaps Emerson felt that he could afford to assume a superior position on this problem (which was, after all, as salient in America as in England) simply because he was from Massachusetts. Some, at least, of his neighbors would have agreed.

On July 15, 1841, a meeting was held in Boston by a group called "Friends of a National Bank," as a result of which an interesting pamphlet was issued that argued the case for locating the proposed bank in Boston. Pointing out that Boston is known for "integrity and thrift" and that her "watchword shall be 'Steady!'," the group cited a local newspaper, the *Boston Atlas*, to bolster their argument:

> New York is the city of impulse. The Mother Bank should be as free from impulse as possible, and should act, to the whole country, as the balance-wheel of the money-market. Boston and Salem are remarkable places for keeping comparatively cool, when New York is excited.[52]

New York, it seems, was as excitable in finance as it was in religion. Emerson might express his disgust with the "corpse-cold Unitarianism of Brattle Street and Harvard College," but when it came to coupon-clipping he knew that the New England chill could be a positive advantage. The *Boston Atlas,* in fact, went on to compare the Boston climate to New York's in language that is unmistakably moralistic:

> In summer, our pure, cool atmosphere, bracing sea-breeze, and comfortable nights will attract pleasure and business travellers, from all parts of the Union, in preference to New York, which is

remarkably hot in the warm season, and which, having but few common-sewers, is at that time, neither so salubrious nor so free from impurities as Boston is.[53]

Would it be an exaggeration to say that that sounds like the spirit of New England's Augustinian piety inveighing against the flesh-pots of the south? "Why is it," Thoreau asks in *Walden,* "that a bucket of water soon becomes putrid, but frozen remains sweet forever? It is commonly said that this is the difference between the affections and the intellect."[54] Everyone knew which faculty Boston represented. "It is true, is it not?" Emerson would note in 1855, "that the intellectual man is stronger than the robust animal man; for he husbands his strength, & endures." (*JMN* 13:455).

[III]

It is either one of the strangest coincidences in American history, or a fact of the greatest significance, that the Jacksonian years witnessed not only a terrific economic boom but also a religious one. As Whitney R. Cross has written, "the series of crests in religious zeal begun by the Great Revival formed the crescendo phase of a greater cycle. Strenuous evangelism mounted irregularly from the 1790s to reach a grand climax between 1825 and 1837."[55] Cross, who wrote the standard history of enthusiastic religion in New York's Burned-over District, was himself uncertain about the relationship between religious and economic boom, for at the out-set he offers the traditional view that "then, as now, many people sought God more earnestly in adversity than in prosperity."[56] The rest of his study, however, perfectly contradicts this received opinion. Later in the book, Cross states that "religious ultraism reached its peak about 1836. Then it quite suddenly collapsed. For six years more, roughly coinciding with the economic depression following the 1837 panic, its personnel floundered about in a period of readjustment." He goes on to explain that, during the time of prosperity, "reformer-capitalists had the more money to spend; and all the zealots could look the more eagerly toward millennial conditions within the framework of general optimism over economic affairs." When economic depression came, it "reacted upon religious enterprises by pinching their purses. . . . Stringency of money during a considerable interval was perhaps the most decisive single factor causing the disintegration of ultraism." Cross concludes that "the optimistic mood had overextended itself in politics, economics, and religion alike when the panic of 1837 pricked the bubble. Retrenchment and confusion followed in all fields while people regained their bearings."[57]

One link, at least verbally, between the paper-money boom and evangelical religion in the period may be found in the term, and concept, of "excitement." In his *Lectures on Revivals of Religion,* delivered in New York in 1834 and published the following year, the great evangelist Charles Grandison Finney made clear in his opening pages that the main impetus to religious renewal had to be emotional fervor:

> God has found it necessary to take advantage of the excitability there is in mankind, to produce powerful excitements among them, before he can lead them to obey. Men are so sluggish . . . that it is necessary to raise an excitement among them, till the tide rises so high as to sweep away the opposing obstacles. They must be so excited that they will break over these counteracting influences, before they will obey God.[58]

The word rings like a bell throughout this first lecture, suggesting a notion as central to revivalism as it was to the rhetoric of the anti-bank people. Sinners, Finney insists, "never will give up their false shame . . . till they are so excited that they cannot contain themselves any longer." Though his book is not without warnings about overdoing the "spasmodic" and "feverish" aspects of revivalism, Finney nevertheless argues for "an ingenuous breaking down" and "a pouring out of the heart" till "the flood-gates will soon

276

burst open, and salvation will flow over the place." It is literally, and not simply metaphorically, the release of bodily fluid that Finney is advocating:

> I have never known a person sweat blood; but I have known a person pray till the blood started from the nose. And I have known persons pray till they were all wet with perspiration, in the coldest weather in winter. I have known persons pray for hours, till their strength was all exhausted with the agony of their minds. Such prayers prevailed with God.

"Sinners," Finney insisted, had to be "melted down."[59]

Ten years after he had exhorted his congregation to a kind of emotional incontinence in the service of religious revival, Finney's doubts would seem to have gotten the best of him, and he would write: "The more I have seen of revivals, the more I am impressed with the importance of keeping excitement down."[60] What had he seen? The religious history of New England, to be sure, beginning at least with the Antinomian crisis, contained monitory examples of how religious "excitement" could lead to emotional, indeed sexual, extravagance.[61] A century earlier, Charles Chauncy, the eminently rationalistic pastor of Boston's First Church, had warned that enthusiastic religion had more to do with physiology than theology: "The cause of this *enthusiasm* is a bad temperament of the blood and spirits; 'tis properly a disease, a sort of madness."[62] Finney himself knew, from his experience in the Burned-over District, that excitement in religion could easily get out of hand. When women, for example, were allowed to pray together with men in what were called "promiscuous assemblies," "the freer reign for exuberant emotionalism," as Cross puts it, "could permit some of the more amazing expressions of ardor to rise out of the temptation to confuse heavenly and earthly love."[63]

In his *Lectures* Finney had lamented the fact that so many evangelists, faced with cold congregations, had literally to wear themselves out in the service of religious excitement. As Cross

277

remarks, "scarcely one escaped some moment when either his lungs let blood or in some other fashion he approached collapse." It seems, however, that blood was not the only fluid that was let. Having left wife and family behind, many an evangelical preacher found himself thrown

> constantly with a majority of feminine associates: zealous, excited women who looked to him for spiritual guidance and hovered about him as the immediate representative of that heavenly piety they so thirsted to attain. On occasion such distraught and fawning females attempted to prove their sanctification by intimacies which showered upon the preacher tokens of a love supposedly, but not always completely, cleansed of earthly attributes. John Humphrey Noyes found a rational, scriptural solution for this problem, but at least thirty settled clergymen became its victims within four years.[64]

More than one New York State community apparently harbored its Arthur Dimmesdale and Hester Prynne. Among others, any number of Millerite millennialists were carried by their zeal down the primrose path to "remarkable extravagances." Believing fervently in their perfected natures, they were heard to say "they are immortal, cannot die, and have got to raise up spiritual children." There were reports of "foot washing," "indiscriminate kissing," and "licentious advances." As Cross notes, "extreme fervor, whatever its exact nature, had periodically run over into experiments in sex relations."[65] This sort of thing was surely not what Emerson intended, as I have noted, in his own spirited attack on cold preaching in 1838, when he exhorted Harvard's senior class in divinity to "feel" their "call in throbs of desire and hope" (*CW* 1:84). Perhaps Finney, when he recanted in 1845, had seen the recently published *Adventures of Simon Suggs,* in which humorist J. J. Hooper offered his own version of "excitement" at a camp-meeting:

> "Keep the thing warm!" roared a sensual seeming man, of stout mould and florid countenance, who was exhorting among a bevy

278

of young women, upon whom he was lavishing caresses. "Keep the thing warm, breethring!—come to the Lord, honey!" he added, as he vigorously hugged one of the damsels he sought to save.[66]

It is not known whether or not Emerson had any interest in Simon Suggs, but there is amusing—and, in the context of this discussion, rather telling—evidence of his reaction to Finney. In February 1855, Emerson wrote Lidian from Rome, New York, where he had himself gone to lecture, that he "heard Mr Phinney, the noted revivalist preach." Emerson "thought the preacher had extolled God's heart at the expense of his head" and reported that he did not like Finney much better than when he had heard him in Boston twenty-five years earlier (*L* 4:493). But Emerson set down a more circumstantial, and pointed, version of his encounters with Finney in a letter to Edward Everett Hale, probably written in 1870:

> . . . the sermon I heard from Mr Finney was in Park Street Church after Furness had described to me in Philadelphia the wonderful effect of his sermon there from the text "The wages of sin is death," & with particular enumeration of the great points & charged me to hear him if I could. He came to Boston & I took courage & went. His text was, "The wages of sin is death," and I recognized in succession all the topics & treatments the assembled universe of souls & whithersoever they looked on the arch of Heaven they read Wages Wages Wages—
>
> I recognized all but the effect which my friend had reported. I think this must have been preached in Park Street about 1829 or 1830; but cannot without more research than I have time for certify the date. It was twenty five years later, as I remember to have counted at the time, when I next saw Mr Finney, soon after his return from London, that I found myself on a Sunday in Rome, New York, & learned that he was to preach there. I went, & his text was "The Wages of sin is death" & the sermon in the main & I suppose in all particulars the same. Wages Wages was written as before on the arch of the Universe. It was plain that he was as bad as a hack lecturer like myself. (*L* 6:123)

In view of the amusing connection Emerson makes between his own itinerant peddling of lectures and Finney's sermonizing, it would be funny to think that Emerson had in fact brought along his popular talk on "Wealth" (we do not know what his subject was at Rome, though he had delivered "Wealth" at Schenectady a little over two years before).[67] It is sufficient, however, to note Emerson's jaundiced awareness that Finney was still working the same side of the street, earning his own living by harping away at another sort of economy.

But a more reliable indication of Emerson's probable reaction to the extravagances of revivalism as he grew older may be found in his enthusiastic reception of an important book of this period, Horace Bushnell's *Christian Nurture,* first published in 1847. To an extraordinary degree, and in a way which has not, I think, been noticed, Bushnell's treatise exposes the emotional—indeed, sexual—assumptions implicit in revivalism and provides what might be called an exemplary New England response—an economy of the religious affections. Though Bushnell was chary of condemning all manifestations of revivalism outright, his fundamental opposition to them forms the basis of his argument. Bushnell's primary allegiance is to the family, which he liked to characterize as "the church that is in the house," whereas he conceives of revivals as adventures in spiritual libertinism which drain one's vital force. "We have been expecting to thrive too much by conquest," he writes, "and too little by growth." Evangelical "scenes," as he calls them, are "scenes of victory" rather "than of piety." In them, he argues, "we strain every nerve of motion, exhaust every capacity of endurance, and push on till nature sinks in exhaustion. . . . We do many things, which, in a cooler mood, are seen to hurt the dignity of religion, and which somewhat shame and sicken ourselves." In place of "conquest" Bushnell offers "internal growth" and asks "whether there is not a fund of increase in the very bosom of the church itself"—which, of course, implies the family.[68]

Reviewing the history of "ecstatic" religion in the eighteenth century, Bushnell laments the fact that "the inferior characters of the day, from Whitefield down to Davenport, were all for impulses and divine concussions":

> They encouraged outcries, and visions, and trances, and faintings; they counted nothing a conversion which did not explode like a rocket in mid heaven, and the number of these explosions was accepted as the gauge of all progress. But finally, when confusion had run itself to a limit in disgrace, and the fuel of passion was quite burned away, then suddenly the New Light power gave out as a motion that is spent, and religion subsided, falling into a long and dreary decline.[69]

The "New Light" revivalism of his own day Bushnell views in the same way, as an orgiastic "religion that begins explosively, raises high frames, carries little or no expansion, and after the day is spent, subsides into a torpor." The trouble with such "religious individualism" is that "it makes nothing of the family" and depends entirely upon "some sudden and explosive experience, in adult years," a kind of *"ictus"* or "epiphany," "a miraculous epidemic, a fireball shot from the moon." Revivalism, then, is seen as a series of orgasmic episodes that periodically raise one up and drop one down, leaving one spent and empty. Instead, Bushnell proposes "sound health in the place of spasmodic exaltations." Otherwise, he says, "nothing stands in a natural attitude, there is no regular pulse of life left, and we only know that we live by the spasms we suffer."[70]

The central chapter of Bushnell's book is significantly entitled "Spiritual Economy of Revivals of Religion" and his subject, he announces, is "Divine Husbandry." Decrying revivalistic scenes as desperate experiences that leave the participants "secretly sickened," Bushnell finally allows himself to allude directly to the sexual excess associated with evangelical religion which seems to have formed the basis of his own disgust:

> Many have made so heavy a draft on their religious vitality or capacity, that something seems to be expended out of the sensibility

even of their conscience—they sink into neglects, or crimes close upon the verge of apostasy; or they betake themselves to the cheap and possible perfectionism of antinomian irresponsibility.[71]

For him, this is a dissolute economy of waste. "Effort spent in this way, produces additional exhaustion and discouragement." Instead, Bushnell proposes a husbanding of one's forces whereby both the peaks and the lows are reduced and one's natural vigor is invested for future return: "The pendulum swings in smaller vibrations. There is no wide chasm of dishonor, no strained pitch of extravagance, but only a sacred ebb and flow of various but healthful zeal." In the following chapter, entitled "Growth, Not Conquest," Bushnell at last exposes the truly organic nature of his own argument in a series of passages that link all of those concerns of the Jacksonian period which we have been examining—economic theory, religion, and sexuality:

> True piety is itself a principle of industry and application to business. It subordinates, according to its measure, the love of show and all the tendencies to extravagance. It rules out those licentious passions that war with order and economy, and hurry so many thousands into profligacy. It excludes those vices which prey upon the health and substance of their victims. It moderates that exceeding haste to be rich, by which so many overreach themselves, and even make shipwreck of their characters. Piety is itself a basis of credit, and credit is capital.[72]

Like his fellow Yale man, Theodore Sedgwick, whose *Public and Private Economy* (published between 1836 and 1838) has been characterized by Marvin Meyers as "a moral treatise on household economy, a puritanical Jacksonian's home companion," and whose commandments were "do not squander, do not waste, hold on,"[73] Bushnell in the end wraps himself in the mantle of New England's self-righteous frugality. Whence comes, he asks, the "high prosperity and substantial wealth" of his beloved part of the country? Not so much from "sharpness and parsimony" as from the favor of the Lord, who "has cast the habits of our people, made them patient in their industry, given them character and credit, cut off profligacy and profusion." It will be observed, Bushnell continues, "that a large proportion of the world without are continually perishing by vice and extravagance; and when they do not perish themselves, are entailing the effects of their profligacy on the diseased and half-endowed constitution of their families." Not so America, if it will only follow the example of New England. Warming to the scope of his argument, Bushnell attacks the annexation of Texas as another example of his country's failure to conserve its vital force and then concludes:

> The habit of conquest runs to dissipation and irregularity. It is as if a nation, forgetting its own internal resources, were scouring the seas, and trooping up and down the world, in pursuit of prize-money and plunder, forsaking the loom and the plow, and all the regular growths of industry. Whereas, if the church were unfolding the riches of the covenant at her firesides and tables—if the children were identified with religion from the first, and grew up in a Christian love of man, the missionary spirit would not throw itself up in irregular jets, but would flow as a river.[74]

Rejecting spasmodic adventures outside the home, Bushnell concludes by saying: "Life is no mere camp-meeting scene." Rhapsodic and paroxysmal preaching may be all very well for those detached from all sacred ties and wandering "a thousand miles from home . . . but a regular established Christian congregation, who expect to live and grow on the same spot, from age to age, must be required to gird up the loins of their mind." Bushnell urges intellectual sobriety and containment within the safety of domestic precincts. "It is not wisdom," he says, "to overwork the harvest, so that we have no strength left for the bread."[75]

Emerson greatly admired Bushnell's book, calling it in 1848 the first pamphlet he had "saved to bind" in ten years (*JMN* 11:20).

To a certain extent, Bushnell returned the compliment, but he had serious reservations about Emerson's effect on the reader. Granting that Emerson was a true master of English, Bushnell nevertheless, and characteristically, worried about being sapped of his intellectual vigor by the Concord wizard's pyrotechnics:

> Intoxicated by his brilliant creations, the reader thinks, for the time that he is getting inspired. And yet, when he has closed the essay or the volume, he is surprised to find—who has ever failed to notice it?—that he is disabled instead, disempowered, reduced in tone. He has no great thought or purpose in him; and the force or capacity for it seems to be gone. Surely, it is a wonderfully clear atmosphere that he is in, and yet it is somehow mephitic.[76]

Considering that Bushnell found Emerson's ordinary published works noxious, one wonders what he might have thought of the following fantasy which the nineteen-year-old Emerson set down in his journal for 1822. Indeed, Bushnell could even have read it, for, surprising as it may seem, this astonishing exercise in unconscious self-revelation was actually published in *The Offering* for 1829, edited by none other than the redoubtable Unitarian Pope who was to be Emerson's great adversary, Andrews Norton.[77] Here is Emerson's story:

> When I was a lad—said the bearded islander—we had commonly a kind of vast musical apparatus in the Pacific islands which must appear as fabulous to you as it proved fatal to us. On the banks of the rivers there were abundance of Siphar Trees which consist of vast trunks perforated by a multitude of natural tubes without having any external verdure. When the roots of these were connected with the waters of the river the water was instantly sucked up by some of the tubes and discharged again by others and when properly echoed the operation attended by the most beautiful musical sounds in the world. My countrymen built their churches to the Great Zoa upon the margin of the water and enclosed a suitable number of these trees, hoping to entertain the ears of the god with

this sweet harmony. Finding however by experience that the more water the pipes drew the more rich and various were the sounds of the Organ, they constructed a very large temple with high walls of clay and stone to make the echoes very complete, and enclosed a hundred Siphars. When the edifice was complete six thousand people assembled to hear the long expected song. After they had waited a long time and the waters of the river were beginning to rise, the Instrument suddenly began to emit the finest notes imaginable. Through some of the broader pipes the water rushed with the voice of thunder, and through others with the sweetness of one of your lutes. In a short time the effect of the music was such that it seemed to have made all the hearers mad. They laughed and wept alternately and began to dance and such was their delight that they did not perceive the disaster which had befallen their Organ. Owing to the unusual swell of the River and to some unaccountable iregularity in the ducts the pipes began to discharge their contents within the chapel. In a short time the evil became but too apparent, for the water rose in spouts from the top of the larger ducts and fell upon the multitudes within. Meantime the Music swelled louder and louder, and every note was more ravishing than the last. The inconvenience of the falling water which drenched them, was entirely forgotten until finally the whole host of pipes discharged every one a volume of water upon the charmed congregation. The faster poured the water the sweeter grew the music and the floor being covered with the torrent the people began to float upon it with intolerable extacies. Finally the whole Multitude swam about in this deluge holding up their heads with open mouths and ears as if to swallow the melody whereby they swallowed much water. Many hundreds were immediately drowned and the enormous pipes as they emptied the river swelled their harmony to such perfection that the ear could no longer bear it and they who escaped the drowning died of the exquisite music. Thenceforward there was no more use of the Siphar trees in the Pacific islands. (*JMN* 2:29–31)

As an astute Emerson scholar, Evelyn Greenberger, has noted, "the sexual nature of this imagery can hardly be ignored."[78] Here, when Herman Melville was about three years old, Emerson was dreaming up his own peep at Polynesian life which certainly rivals

Typee in its manifest eroticism. It would seem fair to say, moreover, that the youthful Emerson's position on the spermatic economy would probably have appeared extraordinarily mephitic in Bushnell's Hartford. This incredible production can hardly be read as other than a masturbatory fantasy of orgasmic ecstasy and release. The "disaster which had befallen their Organ" was that it discharged its "contents within the chapel," providing the basis for a religion of pleasure beside which the prescriptions of the Divinity School Address seem pale indeed. "And now," Emerson would say in 1838, "let us do what we can to rekindle the smouldering, nigh quenched fire on the altar" (*CW* 1:92). Whatever he might suggest, it would not involve the use of Siphar trees, though he would insist that Ought and Duty should not be separate from Beauty and Joy.

The fact is that up until about the mid-1840s Emerson's writings would evince an attitude toward the spermatic economy which seems to ally him more with Melville and Whitman than with Horace Bushnell. Though strongly conservative in his instincts and by training, he nevertheless ventured forth in the direction of expansiveness. He lamented in his first book that "man is the dwarf of himself. Once he was permeated and dissolved by the spirit. He filled nature with his overflowing currents. Out from him sprang the sun and moon. . . ." Then, "his waters retired; he no longer fills the veins and veinlets; he is shrunk to a drop" (*CW* 1:42). Emerson claimed otherwise for himself: "I dilate and conspire with the morning wind" (ibid., p. 13). He would suffer, to be sure, from the periodic nature of his fillings and emptyings—"Alas for this infirm faith, this will not strenuous, this vast ebb of a vast flow! I am God in nature; I am a weed by the wall" (*W* 2:307). Nevertheless, in language often markedly androgynous, Emerson would celebrate what he called in "The Method of Nature" "that redundancy or excess of life which in conscious beings we call *ecstasy*" (*CW* 1:127). Echoing his own fantasy of the Siphar trees, he claimed in this same address that to whoever listened "with insatiable ears, richer and greater wisdom is taught him, the sound swells to a ravishing music, he is borne away as with a flood. . . . His health and greatness consist in his being the channel through which heaven flows to earth, in short, in the fulness in which an ecstatical state takes place in him. It is pitiful to be an artist when by forbearing to be artists we might be vessels filled with the divine overflowings" (*CW* 1:130).

Still, the vessels do fill up and Emerson, ceasing to be content with forbearance, calls for what might be termed masculine expression. We have already noticed Emerson's call for "initiative, spermatic, prophesying, man-making words" that go to the production of books he calls "vital and spermatic, not leaving the reader what he was" (*JMN* 8:148; *W* 7:197). In another journal entry, Emerson expatiates on the sorts of authors he truly admires:

> Now and then, rarely, comes a stout man like Luther, Montaigne, Pascal, Herbert, who utters a thought or feeling in a virile manner, and it is unforgettable. Then follow any number of spiritual eunuchs and women, who talk about that thought, imply it, in pages and volumes. . . . Great bands of female souls who only receive the spermatic *aura*, and brood on the same but add nothing. (*J* 9:197–98).

With such a background, I think it is possible to turn to Emerson's seminal essay on "The Poet"—that rhapsodic description of the ideal artist which unquestionably brought Whitman to the boil —and see that Emerson means precisely what he says when he states that "the religions of the world are the ejaculations of a few imaginative men" (*W* 3:34). Emerson is insisting, at his most impassioned, that all great expression is spermatic and involves the orgasmic release of energy; otherwise we are thwarted and stilled. "Hence," as we have seen, "the necessity of speech and song; hence these throbs and heart-beatings in the orator, at the door of the assembly, to the end namely that thought may be ejaculated as Logos, or Word" (*W* 3:40). The true artist, Emerson argues, desires to express himself "abundantly, not dwarfishly and fragmentarily." He therefore says, "By God it is in me and must go forth of me." Emerson accordingly urges his disciple to release himself:

> Doubt not, O poet, but persist. Say "It is in me, and shall out."
> Stand there , balked and dumb, stuttering and stammering, hissed
> and hooted, stand and strive, until at last rage draw out of thee
> that *dream*-power which every night shows thee is thine own; a
> power transcending all limit and privacy, and by virtue of which a
> man is the conductor of the whole river of electricity. (W 3:40).

The true poet, like the Siphar tree, draws forth the pent-up rivers
of the soul and pours them out freely in ecstatic melodies which, as
Emerson says, "ascend and leap and pierce into the deeps of infinite time" (W 3:24).[79]

Our main focus here, however, is not the more youthful author
in his spasmodic mood but rather the elder, wintry Emerson, whose
most characteristic mature expression is to be found in *The Conduct of Life* (1860), where he retreated to a position more suitable
for the man who would become an overseer of Harvard College in
seven years. *The Conduct of Life* presents a remarkably coherent
case for conservation and continence. Emerson's obsession in the
book is "power," and the principal mode of attaining power in
personal terms is expressed over and over again by the term "self-
possession" (W 6:171). Self-reliance, he tells us, "is the basis of
behavior, as it is the guaranty that the powers are not squandered
in too much demonstration" (W 6:190). Though Emerson does
attempt robustly to argue "that all kinds of power usually emerge
at the same time; good energy and bad . . . the ecstasies of devotion
with the exasperations of debauchery" (W 6:64), it is clearly not
the latter that he favors. In the essay "Worship" he decries the
"divorce between religion and morality" (W 6:207) and pro-
nounces contemporary religions "either childish and insignificant
or unmanly and effeminating." He singles out for particular attack
what he calls "scortatory"—that is to say, fornicatory—religions
(both he and Bushnell probably had John Humphrey Noyes in
mind), and finds "even in the decent populations, idolatries wherein
the whiteness of the ritual covers scarlet indulgence." The popula-
tion of large cities he calls "not men, but hungers, thirsts, fevers

and appetites walking" (W 6:208). Everywhere Emerson sees what he calls "the quadruped interest" or "beast-force" in possession of contemporary life (W 6:252). Surrounded by foolishness, or worse, Emerson can only recommend "phlegm"—an olympian aloofness and indifference. "How to live with unfit companions?" he asks; for with such, life is for the most part spent; and experience teaches little better than our earliest instinct of self-defence, namely not to engage, not to mix yourself in any manner with them, but let their madness spend itself unopposed" (W 6:270). Even his beloved impulse to speech seems to Emerson now a violation and waste of vital force, and he quotes Jacobi approvingly to the effect that "when a man has fully expressed his thought, he has somewhat less possession of it" (W 6:191). Reverting frequently to an economic metaphor, Emerson voices the desire to keep a tight hold on himself: "I prefer to be owned as sound and solvent, and my word as good as my bond, and to be what cannot be skipped, or dissipated, or undermined, to all the *éclat* in the universe" (W 6:323).

Emerson's retrenchment here to what we may consider the stringent economies of his old age does not represent, of course, a totally unexpected impulse in his life and writings. He always knew what it meant to be an American, especially one raised in New England. In 1835, while preparing his "Historic Discourse at Concord," he set down a sentence in his notebook which was never used in the address. "Economy," he wrote, "is at once the virtue & the vice of our republic." And he added: "It is in Concord very very rigid" (*JMN* 12:32). Emerson's economies are those of his place and time and, from this point of view, simply offer us the clearest expression of the cultural milieu that nurtured him. Our final example, at which we have already taken a preliminary glance, the closing paragraphs of "Wealth," constitutes documentation both for Emerson's later tendencies and for the obsessive presence of the spermatic economy in nineteenth-century American culture and writing generally.

Calling money "another kind of blood," Emerson insists that

"the estate of man is only a larger kind of body, and admits of regimen analogous to his bodily circulations." He then concludes:

> The merchant's economy is a coarse symbol of the soul's economy. It is to spend for power and not for pleasure. It is to invest income; that is to say, to take up particulars into generals; days into integral eras—literary, emotive, practical—of its life, and still to ascend in its investment. The merchant has but one rule, *absorb and invest;* he is to be capitalist; the scraps and filings must be gathered back into the crucible; the gas and smoke must be burned, and earnings must not go to increase expense, but to capital again. Well, the man must be capitalist. Will he spend his income, or will he invest? His body and every organ is under the same law. His body is a jar in which the liquor of life is stored. Will he spend for pleasure? The way to ruin is short and facile. Will he not spend but hoard for power? It passes through the sacred fermentations, by that law of Nature whereby everything climbs to higher platforms, and bodily vigor becomes mental and moral vigor. The bread he eats is first strength and animal spirits; it becomes, in higher laboratories, imagery and thought; and in still higher results, courage and endurance. This is the right compound interest; this is capital doubled, quadrupled, centupled; man raised to his highest power.
>
> The true thrift is always to spend on the higher plane; to invest and invest, with keener avarice, that he may spend in spiritual creation and not in augmenting animal existence. Nor is the man enriched, in repeating the old experiments of animal sensation; nor unless through new powers and ascending pleasures he knows himself by the actual experience of higher good to be already on the way to the highest. (W 6:125–27)

We may consider that a brutal passage, if we imagine that Emerson's notion of transforming sexuality into economic power expresses and encourages the excesses of America's imperial mission. But we should note that Emerson himself ends, characteristically, "on the way to the highest." One is free to read that as an example of the pathological Victorian insistence on sublimation, but the fact is that Emerson's life's work consisted of turning transient experience into permanent literature. Emerson's "Savings Bank," as he called his journal, capitalized the small change of daily existence into poems, essays, and books that contain not only the strictures of the New England conscience but also dithyrambic ejaculations and rivers of electricity.[80] Though he himself might have difficulty spending for pleasure, Emerson could conceive of doing so and inspire disciples—notably Whitman, of course—capable of investing themselves in that way. "We are tendencies," Emerson writes, "or rather, symptoms, and none of us complete" (W 4:19). His peculiar gift or mission was that he could give eloquent expression to more tendencies than he could himself complete; his symptoms have accurately pointed both to American diseases and American strengths. One might say, with the advantage of historical hindsight, that Emerson's economies have made most of our literary extravagances possible.

EPILOGUE:
REPRESENTATIVES

LUTHER

On July 11, 1822, Emerson began his seventh "Wideworld" journal with a significant inscription: "I dedicate my book to the Spirit
of America" (*JMN* 2:3). Providing an adequate description of that
spirit would occupy Emerson throughout his literary career, but
here, at the age of nineteen, he seemed content simply to follow the
lead of Cotton Mather and sing the wonders of his native land
"flying from the Depravations of *Europe*," [1] though Emerson would
extend his criticism to other continents ("Asia, Africa, Europe, old,
leprous & wicked, have run round the goal of centuries. . . . But
now a strong man has entered the race & is outstripping them all"
[*JMN* 2:218]). Emerson refused to "believe that it is ignorance to
esteem my birthright in America as a preferable gift to the honours
of any other nation that breathes upon Earth" (*JMN* 1:127); and
two years later, in 1824, he headily insisted that "this nation is
now honourably distinguished above all others for greater moral
purity" (*JMN* 2:226).[2]
   Such sentiments would appear to bestow little literary distinction on the young Emerson's journals, since this sort of rhetoric
was the staple of American public discourse on patriotic occasions.
Perhaps Emerson's own teacher, the golden-tongued Edward Everett, had encouraged this kind of thing in his lectures at Harvard,
for he himself retailed similar commonplaces in his Phi Beta Kappa
address at Cambridge in 1824: "When the old world afforded no
longer any hope, it pleased Heaven to open this last refuge of
humanity. The attempt has begun and is going on, far from foreign

corruption, on the broadest scale, and under the most benignant auspices. . . ."[3] Should we, then, pass over the dedication of Emerson's journal as being of no special interest or importance in a consideration of what is most peculiarly or characteristically Emersonian in these early writings? The answer may lie in the rest of the dedication:

> With a spark of prophetic devotion, I hasten to hail the Genius, who yet counts the tardy years of childhood, but who is increasing unawares in the twilight, and swelling into strength, until the hour, when he shall break the cloud, to shew his colossal youth, and cover the firmament with the shadow of his wings. (*JMN* 2:4)

Even if one discounts the inflated and self-conscious manner in which the nineteen-year-old Emerson assumed the prophetic mantle, it is difficult not to feel the seriousness of intent here; the tremendous self-reference that palpitates within the young American's seemingly conventional invocation to the nascent genius of this land of infinite promise. What appears, that is, to be a rhetorical gesture issuing from simple—even simplistic—patriotic piety may in fact be seen as the early indication of a bad (good?) case of spiritual megalomania. Emerson's book is dedicated to himself, or rather, to the possibility of a self-realization which he identifies with a collective national ambition.[4]

The reader of Emerson's early journals must be struck by the frequency with which meditations on individual greatness that clearly imply Emerson's personal aspirations are also linked to the enormous promise of his own young nation. In March 1823, for example, describing himself as merely "one youth among the multitudes of mankind, one grain of sand on the seashore, unknown in the midst of my contemporaries," Emerson insisted that he was "hastening to put on the manly robe" and distinguish himself:

> From childhood the names of the great have ever resounded in my ear. And it is impossible that I should be indifferent to the rank

which I must take in the innumerable assembly of men, or that I should shut my eyes upon the huge interval which separates me from the minds which I am wont to venerate. Every young man is prone to be misled by the suggestions of his own ill founded ambition which he mistakes for the promptings of a secret Genius, and thence dreams of an unrivalled greatness. (*JMN* 2:111–12)

Though he despaired of realizing his own "majestic dream," Emerson exhorted himself to gather his powers and *"Make Haste"* (*JMN* 2:113). Resuming the argument in April, he remarked that "powerful & concentrated motive . . . is necessary to a man, who would be great" and attempted to counter the objection of "young men . . . whose hearts burn with the desire of distinction . . . that they have fallen in too late an age to be benefactors of mankind" by insisting that they avert their gaze from the corrupt Old World and contract and concentrate their motives in the ample bosom of their youthful native land: "Let the young American withdraw his eyes from all but his own country, and try if he can find employment there, considerable enough to task the vigorous intellect he brings. I am of opinion that the most extraordinary powers that ever were given to a human being would lose themselves in this vast sphere" (*JMN* 2:114–15). The Emersonian injunction to "trust thyself" is thus tacitly equated here with faith in America's potential. "To America . . . monarchs look with apprehension & the people with hope." Though Emerson was anxious about the possibility that the "raw multitudes" who were rushing westward—the "ignorant & licentious people"—would pay no attention to "the Oracles of Moral law and Intellectual wisdom," he nevertheless had high hopes: "if the senates that shall meet hereafter in those wilds shall be made to speak a voice of wisdom & virtue, the reformation of the world would be to be expected from America" (*JMN* 2:116).[5] What the young Emerson expected from himself was equally momentous: if he could purify his intention and conduct, marshal his forces, and assume spiritually the *toga virilis,* he might hope to spread the wings of genius over the American firmament and make it pregnant with new thought.

But Emerson fretted continually over what he conceived to be his own tendency to linger in "the tardy years of childhood" and feared that he might be the "dupe of hope," fated to die before completing his task (*JMN* 2:241–42). With a scrupulosity which may seem to us ridiculous in one so young, but which serves to highlight his agonized sense of being singled out for a special destiny that his own fears and failings might keep him from achieving, Emerson meditated just before his nineteenth birthday on his delayed maturity:

In twelve days I shall be nineteen years old; which I count a miserable thing. Has any other educated person lived so many years and lost so many days? I do not say acquired so little for by an ease of thought & certain looseness of mind I have perhaps been the subject of as many ideas as many of my age. But mine approaching maturity is attended with a goading sense of emptiness & wasted capacity; with the conviction that vanity has been content to admire the little circle of natural accomplishments, and has travelled again & again the narrow round, instead of adding sedulously the gems of knowledge to their number. Too tired and too indolent to travel up the mountain path which leads to good learning, to wisdom & to fame, I must be satisfied with beholding with an envious eye the laborious journey & final success of my fellows, remaining stationary myself, until my inferiors & juniors have reached & outgone me. And how long is this to last? How long shall I hold the little acclivity which four or six years ago I flattered myself was enviable, but which has become contemptible now? It is a child's place & if I hold it longer I may quite as well resume the bauble & rattle, grow old with a baby's red jockey on my grey head & a picturebook in my hand, instead of Plato and Newton. Well, and I am he who nourished brilliant visions of future grandeur which may well appear presumptuous & foolish now. My infant imagination was idolatrous of glory, & thought itself no mean pretender to the honours of those who stood highest in the community, and dared even to contend for fame with those who are hallowed by time & the approbation of ages. (*JMN* 1:133)

It is hard not to sense a psychological or psychosexual element here in Emerson's guilt-ridden "true picture of a barren & desolate soul" (as he himself calls it), especially in all its references to childish habits. In fact, the single journal entry for the previous day, heavily cancelled, speaks of "a nasty appetite which I will not gratify." But Emerson's anxiety over what he seems to feel are regressive tendencies in himself suggest also almost a wish that he might be spared the heavy cup of manhood—heavy, because of the extravagance of his own expectations in the face of a strong sense of ineptitude. Two years later, on the eve of becoming *"legally* a man"* (Emerson's own emphasis; *JMN* 2:237), he would complain of his weakness, shame, and want of confidence, saying, "in my frequent humiliation, even before women & children I am compelled to remember the poor boy who cried out, 'I told you, Father, they would find me out'" (*JMN* 2:240–41). Emerson's fear/desire about lingering in childhood, as well as his concern for aging, may be taken as a measure of his own high, and burdensome, sense of purpose.

Writing of the young Martin Luther, Erik Erikson has speculated analogously about the feeling of time running out that haunts the youthful genius:

> I could not conceive of a young great man in the years before he becomes a great young man without assuming that inwardly he harbors a quite inarticulate stubbornness, a secret furious inviolacy, a gathering of impressions for eventual use within some as yet dormant new configuration of thought—that he is tenaciously waiting it out for a day of vengeance when the semideliberate straggler will suddenly be found at the helm, and he who took so much will reveal the whole extent of his potential mastery. The counterpart of this waiting, however, is often a fear of an early death which would keep the vengeance from ripening into leadership; yet the young man often shows signs of precocious aging, of a melancholy wish for an early end, as if the anticipation of prospective deeds tired him. Premonitions of death occur throughout Luther's career, but I think it would be too simple to ascribe them

to a mere fear of death. A young genius has an implicit life plan to complete; caught by death before his time, he would be only a pathetic human fragment.[6]

I introduce Luther, or rather Erikson's Luther, here not simply because the parallels between his own vocational, and psychic, crises in early manhood and Emerson's are striking, but also because Emerson himself exhibits, especially in the 1830s, what might be called a minor obsession with Luther, culminating in his 1835 lecture on the great dissenter.

For Emerson, "Martin Luther the Reformer is one of the most extraordinary persons in history and has left a deeper impression of his presence in the modern world than any other except Columbus" (*EL* 1:119). Luther was the archetypal Protestant—a "representative" of "objective religion" (*JMN* 4:360; 12: 41); a "great man" who "acted poems" (*JMN* 4:340); a "standard Man" (like Newton or Bonaparte) whose life accuses or approves "our own ways of thinking & living by comparison" (*JMN* 4:256). Emerson felt closest to Luther's mind not so much through his works as through his "historical position," as Emerson meditated on it in relation to his "own mind" (*JMN* 4:348). He was less interested in comparing his religious beliefs to Luther's than in perceiving the fundamental congruities that attracted him to this sixteenth-century alter ego: "Do you imagine that because I do not say Luther's creed all his works are an offence to me? Far otherwise. I can animate them all that they shall live to me. I can worship in that temple as well as in any other. I have only to translate a few of the leading phrases into their equivalent verities, to adjust his almanack to my meridian & all the conclusions, all the predictions shall be strictly true" (*JMN* 4:352).

Emerson attempted one such translation as he was in the middle of the controversy that led to his abandoning the Unitarian ministry in 1832. Although Emerson scholars have noted that the young minister's crucial and painful decision to step down from the pulpit of the Second Church of Boston brought to his own mind Luther's Wittenberg theses and his momentous words at the Diet of Worms, the possible significance of this parallelism has not really been drawn out.[7] With Erikson as our guide, however, we man be able to gain some insight into the latent implications of Emerson's conscious identification with Luther.

For one thing, both men experienced a major crisis in belief centering in their intense desire for an unmediated union with the divine. This crisis is initially focused on the issue of the Eucharist, and comes at a time of great psychic stress relating to the full assumption of manhood and a true vocation. More specifically, to cite Erikson, it occurs "about the age of thirty—an important age for gifted people with a delayed identity crisis."[8] Though in darker moments of horological uncertainty Emerson could try to elevate his flagging spirits to the level of chronometrical trust ("a great man escapes out of the kingdom of time; he puts time under his feet. He does not look at his performance & say I am 20, I am 30, I am 40 years old, & must therefore accomplish somewhat conspicuous" [*JMN* 5:493]), there is no question that he considered the age of thirty an ambiguous watershed in his own life. "I have heard," he told his lecture audience in 1837, "that after thirty a man wakes up sad every morning" (*EL* 2:169).

Emerson's difficulty—and it is here that his identification with Luther becomes most interestingly problematic—was that he too had made a personally momentous *volte-face* at about the age of thirty and embarked upon a new career filled with uncertainty and conflict, but that he lacked the firm self-assurance which he attributed to Luther, Rather, Emerson seems to have feared that he had bartered his early ecclesiastical promise for a mess of controversial pottage and was too old to achieve greatness. He told his audience in 1839, when he was not quite thirty-six: "It is said the great geniuses have done their best things before thirty. . . . After thirty a man begins to feel the walls of his condition which before the soul did overflow—asks himself if he have not done something that he may sit down and enjoy. He would enjoy his fame" (*EL* 3:88–89). Though Emerson immediately goes on to combat this view ("genius has no retrospect . . . if you rest on your oars, if you stop, you fall"), the shakiness of his logic is a measure of his own submerged disappointment. In his very next lecture, the refrain returns, suggesting once again how large a shadow that thirtieth birthday had cast on Emerson's hopes: "Young men, young women at thirty and even earlier have lost all spring and vivacity and if they fail in their first enterprizes there seems to be no remedial force in nature, no Roman recovery, but the rest of life is rock and shallow" (*EL* 3:104).

Apart from its personal reference, such a remark seems altogether appropriate—scarcely two years after the great panic of 1837, when the country was still in deep economic trouble; and indeed, Emerson would use a version of the same sentence to conclude a paragraph in his essay "The Fortune of the Republic," a paragraph in which, significantly, the central financial problem of the Jacksonian period, the alternation of wild speculation and bankruptcy, is seen as simply an aspect of that primary failing in American character—inconstancy, capriciousness, irresoluteness—which the young Emerson manifestly found in himself: "That repose which is the ornament and ripeness of man is not American. That repose which indicates a faith in the laws of the universe,—a faith that they will fulfill themselves, and are not to be impeded, transgressed or accelerated. Our people are too slight and vain. They are easily elated and easily depressed" (*W* 11:531–32). Levity alternating with despondency, elation followed by depression —these polarities of Emerson himself, exacerbated in his thirties, he saw writ large in the American soul, and Emerson's internal debate spilled over into public utterance (for example, though in "Self-Reliance" he would himself insist that "our system of education fosters restlessness" [*W* 2:82], he could also, at the same time, testily fault Tocqueville's parallel speculations in his chapter on "why the Americans are so restless in the midst of their prosperity" [*EL* 3:367]).[9]

Emerson fundamentally believed, however, and would say, that "the hero is he who is immovably centered" (*W* 6:277); and herein lies the reason for Emerson's fascination and wavering identification with Luther. The great man who could say, "I cannot and will not recant. It is neither safe nor prudent to do aught against conscience. Here stand I; I cannot otherwise," was for Emerson without crack or schism in his nature—a unified soul who was an inexhaustible source of power, the George Washington of German history (*EL* 1:138). It is surely significant that in "The Fortune of the Republic," while describing his notion of a national hero, a man "who can live in the moment and take a step forward" ("the Genius or Destiny of America is no log or sluggard, but a man incessantly advancing" [*W* 11:537]). Emerson included Luther along with Columbus, John Adams, Patrick Henry, and Thomas Jefferson. Luther was Emerson's resolute ideal self, a true American *democratic* paradigm. As an 1835 journal entry argues (and the emphasis is Emerson's own), Luther presents the "spectacle of an individual contending victoriously *by such means only as are within the reach of all* against all the gifts of fortune & all the terrors of power" (*JMN* 5:110).

The chief means Emerson had in mind, and the subject on which finally any discussion which conjoins these two figures must come to rest, is eloquence. Here, too, in fact, lies the center of Erikson's presentation of Luther—a badly divided soul who (like Emerson, we should note) eventually was "forced to speak his mind in public" and thereby "realized the rich spectrum of his verbal expression, and gained the courage of his conflicted personality." [10] But we must begin with Emerson himself. His tenth "Wideworld" journal was dedicated on March 18, 1823, to Eloquence: "who that has witnessed its strength, and opened every chamber of his soul to the matchless enchanter, does not venerate it as the noblest agent that God works with, in human hearts? My Muse, it is the idol of thy homage and deserves the dedication of thine outpourings" (*JMN* 5:105).

About a year later, just before his twenty-first birthday, Emerson made a long and extraordinarily candid journal entry in which passages of painful self-criticism alternate with a hopeful accounting of possible virtues. Emerson accused himself of a "levity of the understanding" that led to "a sore uneasiness in the company of most men & women, a frigid fear of offending & jealousy of disrespect, an inability to lead & an unwillingness to follow the current conversation, which contrive to make me second with all those among whom I chiefly wish to be first." He found himself radically lacking "that good humoured independence & self esteem" which in fact he was to remark on later in Luther (*JMN* 2:238–39). Without "an impregnable confidence in one's own powers," Emerson concluded, law and medicine were unthinkable career choices. But the Church was another matter. There, his reverence for the power of the word, which Emerson seemed to see as a national gift, would serve him well: "in Divinity I hope to thrive. I inherit from my sire a formality of manner & speech, but I derive from him or his patriotic parent a passionate love for the strains of eloquence." Though he still found himself, for lack of confidence, daily uttering "a score of words . . . of which I am not the master," he nevertheless "hoped to put on eloquence as a robe" and go forth to convert his countrymen to virtue and truth (*JMN* 2:240–242). By 1834, convinced that the existing ecclesiastical forms were an irremediable clog on his ambitions, Emerson would launch himself into literary greatness by resolving "not to utter any speech, poem, or book that is not entirely & peculiarly my work" (*JMN* 4:335). Thenceforth, he would make an imperishable name for himself by speaking and writing only those things, to use Oliver Wendell Holmes' phrase, which were "Emersonially Emersonian."[11]

What should be stressed here, however, is that Emerson's struggle in the 1830s to find his own voice and gather the courage to use it was closely tied to his central personal and philosophical problem: namely, that of rooting his idealism, his sense of himself as a spiritual force, firmly in the real circumstances of his emotional and physical existence. That nervous alternation between immersion in raw experience and the desire for higher truth which Emerson saw as the basis of national character (and which such critics as Santayana and Van Wyck Brooks would later point to as the source of America's divided spirit) was reflected in his own dilemma. Emerson's wavering sense of what is real, his early tendency to split his mental or spiritual life off from the mere epiphenomena of concrete existence and to exalt that interior life over the scoriae of material experience, projected him at once both to the megalomaniac heights of self-trust and to the abysses of shame and self-reproach. As we have noticed before, he would write in "Circles": "alas for this infirm faith, this will not strenuous, this vast ebb of a vast flow! I am God in nature; I am a weed by the wall" (W 2:307). To believe in himself securely as God *in* nature, Emerson would have to learn to identify less ambiguously with his natural body and accept the modalities of its experience as potential sources of transcendence; otherwise, the withdrawal of the divine afflatus would leave him nothing but a wilted vegetable—a dying animal ashamed of its irrepressible urges and inexplicable needs.

Furthermore, the spirit was not *efficient* without the body. Elevation, he found, was simply not possible unless it was rooted in "sufficient *bottom*" (*JMN* 2:240). Philosophically considered, as he tried so to consider it in 1836 in the opening pages of *Nature,* the creation maybe divided into Me (soul) and Not-Me (my body, other bodies, nature), but such a division would leave Emerson solipsistically alienated from both his own feelings and that external world in which thoughts are effective. The *inner,* Emerson realized, must be *outered*—spirit made manifest; and the best paradigm of that union is true utterance, the pressing out of spirit with physical force and emotional conviction so as to imprint it on the world. Surely, the celebrated equations offered by Emerson in the "Language" section of *Nature* ("1. Words are signs of natural facts. 2. Particular natural facts are symbols of particular spiritual facts. 3. Nature is the symbol of spirit" [CW 1:17]) are significant, not as linguistic theory, but as a way of saying that speech, the creation of man's spirit, serves mainly to mediate between soul and flesh—to unify heart and head. "For all men," Emerson would say in a few years, "live by truth and stand in need of expression" (and

that *and* really has the force of a *but*): "In love, in art, in avarice, in politics, in labor, in games, we study to utter our painful
secret.

The man is only half himself, the other half is his expression" (*W*
3:5). Dumb spirit is but demi-selfhood; we must learn not to be
ashamed of ourselves as physical presences and complete the circle
of our existence in public utterance. Emerson was pleased to copy
into his quotation book an important sentence by his chief exem-
plar of this great truth: " 'Whoso can speak well,' said Luther, 'the
same is a man' " (*JMN* 6:134).[12]

Emerson's difficult transition from self-divided minister to self-
affirming lecturer and author bears a striking analogy to Erik
Erikson's portrayal of the difference between Martin the monk and
Luther the preacher. As an Augustinian, he was anxiety-ridden and
conflicted; as a Lutheran, he was his own man: "His posture was
manly and erect, his speech slow and distinct."[13] Erikson argues
that the young Luther's mind was crucially shaped by his learning
from Occam that the "vertical" and the "horizontal," the transcendent and the experiential, were sharply discontinuous. Here was
the fundamental problem, as with Emerson's divided and distinguished worlds of Reason and Understanding.[14] What Luther discovered as an answer to Occam, according to Erikson, is that "the
intersection of all the paradoxes of the vertical and the horizontal
is . . . to be found in man's own divided nature. The two *regna,* the
realist sphere of divine grace and the naturalist sphere of animality,
exist in man's inner conflicts and in his existential paradoxes."[15]

What Luther provided was a "new emphasis on man in *inner*
conflict and his salvation through introspective perfection."[16] The
resolution of the spirit/body conflict must be looked for precisely
in its articulation—in that expression which transforms spiritual
division into an authentic affirmation of the self in relation to
others. "To Luther, the inspired voice, the voice that means it, the
voice that really communicates in person, became a new kind of
sacrament, the partner and even the rival of the mystical presence
of the Eucharist."[17] One could scarcely find a better description of

what happened to Emerson between the controversy over the Lord's Supper in 1832 and the Divinity School Address six years later. He would tell the Harvard divinity students in 1838 that the great advantage of Christianity was "the institution of preaching,—the speech of man to men" (*CW* 1:92). That was the true communion which could transform the bread and wine of common life into the mystical body and blood of truth.

The great thing about Luther, as Emerson insisted in "The Protest," was that he growled his "mighty No" only as preparation for "his own Yes," namely, the unlocking of "the Bible into the vernacular tongue" (*EL* 3:100–1). It is not hard to feel that Emerson, in 1835, was articulating his expectations for himself as he approvingly noted Luther's "singular position in history" as "that of a scholar or spiritual man leading a great revolution, and from first to last faithful to his position. He achieved a spiritual revolution by spiritual arms alone." Luther's words were "half battles" and their thunder "was the arsenal of his power which made men's ears to tingle, and stimulated their imaginations as the accents of a superior being." All agree, Emerson insisted, with Melanchthon's view that Luther was "a very miracle among men; whatever he writes, penetrates their minds, and leaves astonishing stings in their hearts." Here was a paradigm, for Emerson, of what a poet *could* be: a great leader of men who shakes empires to their center simply "by the force of private thoughts" uttered with vernacular elegance (*EL* 1:127, 123–24, 143). The fact that words could have such a tremendous effect clearly sustained Emerson substantially as he tried to conduct his own precarious literary career in the midst of a society which, though nurtured in the language of the spirit, increasingly came to disdain that language in the name of action and material advantage. Such a divorce was the negation, not only of the meaning and purpose of America, but also of that very union of body and soul that Emerson himself had worked so painfully to achieve in his own life.

For all his interest in and identification with Luther, Emerson would finally come to feel that his own emotional and physical fastidiousness, which he fretted over but never quite overcame, marked the crucial difference between the great German leader and himself. In his journal in 1847, Emerson joined Luther with Webster (and others) under the heading, *"A national man,"* which he defined as "a large well-built brain with a great trunk below to supply it, as if a fine alembic were fed with liquor for its distillations from broad full vats in the vaults of the laboratory" (*JMN* 10:40–41). If that were the sort of robustness required in the great leader of a nation, Emerson could only admire that role from afar. His own dedication to the spirit of America, though no less ardent, was stamped with a lower proof, and he would more and more have to content himself with being alternately the bemused or angry observer of a nation that seemed willing to exchange true eloquence and probity for the hollow rhetoric and moral compromises of the later Webster.

If Emerson had had the advantage of an Eriksonian view of Luther, he might have continued to believe that a scrupulous and even anguished poet could somehow serve in the role of "national man." As a fearfully uncertain nation approached its own political and spiritual Reformation in 1861, however, it did in fact choose as its leader and defender of its fragile union just such a brooding figure, whose most enduring legacy, as Emerson himself seemed to feel, was his eloquence. Emerson linked John Brown's speech at Charlestown with Lincoln's at Gettysburg as "the two best specimens of eloquence we have had in this country" (W 8:125), and he also praised Lincoln for speaking "his own thought in his own style" in the Emancipation Proclamation (W 11:310). After Lincoln's death, Emerson would say:

> He is the true history of the American people in his time. Step by step he walked before them; slow with their slowness, quickening his march by theirs, the true representative of this continent; an entirely public man; father of his country, the pulse of twenty millions throbbing in his heart, the thought of their minds articulated by his tongue. (W 11:335)

Luther

At what personal cost that public resoluteness was purchased could not have been known to Emerson, for the tragic inner divisions that marked Lincoln, as with Luther before him, were scarcely understood (except, perhaps, by the preternaturally perceptive Whitman). And there is little question that Emerson himself would have been extremely diffident about seeing in his own hard-won affirmations the truest epitome of American national character. Yet it may be that the America that has survived all the turmoil and agony of its adventure in Southeast Asia is finally prepared to hear itself speaking in that most characteristically complex utterance of the Emersonian spirit. "I am *Defeated* all the time; yet to Victory I am born" (*JMN* 8:228).

THOREAU

In 1836, the year of Emerson's *Nature,* the popular American writer Nathaniel P. Willis published a rather Irvingesque book of sketches, *Inklings of Adventure,* narrated by an urbane and sophisticated figure—a kind of Geoffrey Crayon *redivivus*—named Philip Slingsby, who clearly is meant to embody one aspect of Willis' character. Anticipating a literary device that would be considerably developed by Mark Twain, Willis also created a more homespun alter ego for his mature Tom Sawyer, a seven-foot "gentle monster" dubbed Forbearance Smith, whose nickname is "Job." Slingsby's "shadow," as he terms him, is a "Vermontese, a descendant of one of the Puritan pilgrims," who "had a general resemblance to one of Thorwaldsen's unfinished Apostles—larger than life, and just hewn into outline." These two representative Americans, the Prospero and Caliban of Willis' brave new land, spend four years together at Yale and establish a friendship which, Slingsby tells us, "was proverbial." [18]

Introducing his admirable but ludicrous friend, Slingsby/Willis formulated some general remarks which would be considerably refined by a subtler student of the subject:

> I have observed that of all the friends one has in the course of his life, the truest and most attached is exactly the one who, from his dissimilarity to yourself, the world finds it very odd you should fancy. We hear sometimes of lovers who "are made for each other," but rarely of the same natural match in friendship. It is no great

marvel. In a world like this, where we pluck so desperately at the fruit of pleasure, we prefer for company those who are not formed with precisely the same palate as ourselves.

Such a gourmandizing view of friendship might suffice for a New York literatus, but Concord would naturally reach for a more serious and complex theory of dissonance. "Friendship," Emerson writes in his first series of *Essays,*

> requires that rare mean betwixt likeness and unlikeness that piques each with the presence of power and of consent in the other party. Let me be alone to the end of the world, rather than that my friend should overstep, by a word or a look, his real sympathy. I am equally balked by antagonism and by compliance. Let him not cease an instant to be himself. The only joy I have in his being mine, is that the *not mine* is *mine.* I hate, where I looked for a manly furtherance or at least a manly resistance, to find a mush of concession. Better be a nettle in the side of your friend than his echo. (W 2:208)

One's friend, Emerson goes on to say, should be "for ever a sort of beautiful enemy" (W 2:210). Real sympathy, by means of a perfectly Transcendental paradox, comes to one in the guise of what might appear to be a lack of sympathy; and the true friend helps us to further the development of our best selves by resisting the easy impulse to make any concessions to our lesser—or less honest—selves.

Despite their differences, as it turns out, beautiful enemies Slingsby and Smith are not, since the latter tends more toward sentiment than conscience. But a graduate of Harvard College, at least in the nineteenth century, presumably was made of sterner stuff than his counterpart at New Haven and knew how to turn Willis' parable to more serious account. Thus Henry Thoreau, in his journal for 1851, bravely toed Emerson's narrow line as he set down some Transcendentally friendly observations about his celebrated mentor:

> One of the best men I know often offends me by uttering made
> words—the very best words, of course, or dinner speeches, most
> smooth and gracious and fluent repartees, a sort of talking to
> Buncombe, a dash of polite conversation, a graceful bending, as if
> I were Master Slingsby of promising parts, from the University. O
> would you but be simple and downright! Would you but cease
> your palaver! It is the misfortune of being a gentleman and fa-
> mous.[19]

In what he took to be Emerson's patronizing urbanity, Thoreau
obviously felt that Emerson, in the process of becoming a successful Philip Slingsby, had cast off his Job Smith homespun and was
treating his young disciple as a mere pint-size version of his own
worldly self. But Thoreau is determined to remain a back-country
nettle, a refractory Job Smith who feels it is his duty to goad his
master into returning to the simple and natural ways that distinguish the true Transcendental religion. "The manners and talk of
highly cultivated people were all thrown away on him," Emerson
was to write in his funeral oration on Thoreau, inadvertently con-
firming Thoreau's satiric view of their relations. "He much preferred a good Indian, and considered these refinements as impedi-
ments to conversation, wishing to meet his companion on the
simplest terms" (W 10:454–55).

Willis' expectations notwithstanding, his pair of friends never,
of course, achieved the proverbial status of a Tom Sawyer and
Huck Finn, but it is probably fair to say that Emerson and Thoreau, among all the linked figures in America's literary history,
have come closest to filling the bill. Although later nineteenth-
century critics, such as James and Arnold, tended to juxtapose
Emerson's name with that of Carlyle for purposes of cultural comparison and contrast, that friendship has been all but totally eclipsed
in our own time, with the enormous growth of Thoreau's reputation, by the pairing of Emerson with Thoreau. Moreover, and
interestingly, Emerson himself seems to have been tempted to exercise his Plutarchan tendency to draw parallel lives by conjoining,

or opposing, his own character not to Carlyle's but to Thoreau's.[20] Carlyle was Emerson's best epistolary friend, but Emerson's bond with Thoreau was far more personal, and their friendship touched his thought and feelings in more vital ways.

One possible indication of Emerson's willingness, at least when he was in a sportive mood, to divide the nineteenth-century scene between himself and his disciple may be found in an 1849 journal entry which provided an alternative title page for the forthcoming *Representative Men*. Opposite the *"Bigendians"* Goethe and Napoleon, Emerson set down "RWE" and "Thoreau" as their counterpart *"Littleendians."* Although Emerson's linking of Thoreau with the Little Corporal might seem a purely whimsical gesture worthy of Gertrude Stein (who would describe Henry James as a general, Washington as a novelist, and Picasso as Napoleon), it is not really difficult—and indeed, may be rather illuminating—to attempt to figure out what he had in mind.

Thinking initially, perhaps, of Thoreau's French blood, Emerson presumably associates him with Napoleon also in terms of physical stature, since both might be described as bantams—small but powerful and feisty. Moreover, Emerson thought of Thoreau as having a revolutionary temperament, considering him, in social terms at least, "a born protestant" *(à outrance)* who was always spoiling for a fight (W 10:452–56).[21] "There was somewhat military in his nature," Emerson writes in the eulogy, "not to be subdued, always manly and able, but rarely tender, as if he did not feel himself except in opposition. He wanted a fallacy to expose, a blunder to pillory, I may say required a little sense of victory, a roll of the drum, to call his powers into full exercise." It is clear that Emerson was not simply and carelessly spinning out a figure of speech here, since the best-known paragraph in his eulogy picks up and completes his thought:

> Had his genius been only contemplative, he had been fitted to his life, but with his energy and practical ability he seemed born for great enterprise and for command; and I so much regret the

loss of his rare powers of action, that I cannot help counting it a fault in him that he had no ambition. Wanting this, instead of engineering for all America, he was the captain of a huckleberry-party. Pounding beans is good to the end of pounding empires one of these days; but if, at the end of years, it is still only beans! (*W* 10:480)

Effectively, Emerson is suggesting that Thoreau might have been an emperor instead of merely the captain of a huckleberry-party. In the journal entry from which Emerson drew for this paragraph, he also wrote: "He is a boy, & will be an old boy" (*JMN* 11:404). Thus, in a manner of speaking, Emerson regrets that Thoreau would remain a perpetual Huck Finn instead of growing into a shrewd engineer like Twain's Connecticut Yankee, Hank Morgan, who could singlehandedly change the face of an ossified society. In another journal entry on Thoreau, Emerson wrote: "though we pine for great men, we do not use them when they come. Here is a Damascus blade of a man such as you may search through nature in vain to parallel, laid up on the shelf in our village to rust & ruin. It seems as if they were never quite available for that very idea which they represent" (*JMN* 8:118).

From one point of view, then, what Thoreau "represented" seems to have been the furtherance and completion of Emerson's own Napoleonic fantasies. In February 1839, as he was meditating on his revolutionary year and expressing the resultant complexity of his feelings in "The Protest," Emerson called Thoreau in a letter "my protester," as if he had already decided to pass that mantle on to his young alter ego (*L* 2:182). But it would be misleading to suggest that in gravitating toward the role of Goethe, and therefore standing for "truth" (as he put it in another journal entry [*JMN* 9:145–46]), while arrogating to Thoreau the role of Napoleon, who stands mainly for "power," Emerson had relinquished all claim to being a revolutionary. Though the two figures may be separated for purposes of analysis, like Emerson and Thoreau themselves, they are continuous in Emerson's own mind and have a tendency to blend. Thus he writes in the "Goethe" chapter of *Representative Men*, "I join Napoleon with him, as being both representatives of the impatience and reaction of nature against the *morgue* of conventions,—two stern realists, who, with their scholars, have severally set the axe at the root of the tree of cant and seeming, for this time and for all time" (W 4:289). That, one might say, is a much better description of Waldo and his brave Henry than it is of its nominal subjects.

But such a procedure should hardly surprise us, since it was always a fixed article of belief with Emerson that the prime function of history, and historical characters, was simply to provide us with representative fables, or models, for our evolving selves. Emerson did not want to worship great men but rather to *use* them—even to use them up—in measuring his own stature and preparing for future growth. If Emerson had a tendency to see himself and his friends writ large in the biographies of the famous dead, it was precisely because their fame and their pastness, by distancing them from the reality of his own experience, had diminished their actual force, and such a diminution could be remedied only through the translation of their lives into his own "village" terms. As he writes in "Uses of Great Men," "it is hard for departed men to touch the quick like our own companions, whose names may not last as long" (W 4:14). He could therefore say "Damn George Washington!" (ibid., p. 27) and dress up Henry Thoreau in Napoleon's robe and himself in Goethe's gown, believing—perhaps not very secretly—that as the wheel of fame turned, Concord's Littleendians might one day supplant the great world's Bigendians.

For the student who is willing to read *Representative Men* with a truly Emersonian latitude, the most amusing set of translations may be seen in his "parallel" portraits of Plato and Socrates. Though it is impossible for us to be precise about the degree of conscious manipulation that is taking place, it is hard not to feel that Emerson was somehow aware of the striking congruences that joined him to Plato and Thoreau to Socrates, and mirrored the complexities of their master/disciple relationship in the curious conjunction of their Greek antecedents. The fact that Emerson sketched a Plato who strongly resembles himself has frequently been noted by commentators and ought to be obvious to any reader who knows his Emerson.[22] The same "balanced soul" that joined the "unity of Asia" with the "defining, result-loving, machine-making, surface-seeking, opera-going Europe," that both "made transcendental distinctions" and drew its illustrations "from mares and puppies; from pitchers and soup-ladles" (W 4:53–55), informed not only the Academy at Athens but also the Concord School of Philosophy more than 2,000 years later. It should be equally clear, if one compares Emerson's description of Socrates with his portrait of Thoreau, that another reincarnation took place in Emerson's imagination:

> ... a man of humble stem, but honest enough; of the commonest history; of a personal homeliness so remarkable as to be a cause of wit in others ... a cool fellow, adding to his humor a perfect temper and a knowledge of his man, be he who he might whom he talked with, which laid the companion open to certain defeat in any debate,—and in debate he immoderately delighted. ... He affected a good many citizen-like tastes, was monstrously fond of Athens ... thought everything in Athens a little better than anything in any other place. He was plain as a Quaker in habit and speech, affected low phrases, and illustrations from cocks and quails, soup-pans and sycamore-spoons, grooms and farriers, and unnamable offices,—especially if he talked with any superfine person. He had a Franklin-like wisdom. ... Plain old uncle as he was, with his great ears, an immense talker. ... He is very poor; but then he is hardy as a soldier, and can live on a few olives; usually, in the strictest sense, on bread and water, except when entertained by his friends. His necessary expenses were exceedingly small, and no one could live as he did. ... A pitiless disputant, who knows nothing, but the bounds of whose conquering intelligence no man had ever reached. ... The tyrannous realist! ... This hard-headed humorist, whose strange conceits, drollery and *bonhommie* diverted the young patricians, whilst the rumor of his sayings and quibbles gets abroad every day,—turns out, in the sequel, to have

a probity as invincible as his logic, and to be either insane, or at least, under cover of this play, enthusiastic in his religion. (*W* 4:70–74)

... he had a perfect probity, was exact in securing his own independence, and in holding every man to the like duty. ... He had no talent for wealth, and knew how to be poor without the least hint of squalor or inelegance. ... There was somewhat military in his nature. ... He wanted a fallacy to expose. ... It seemed as if his first instinct on hearing a proposition was to controvert it, so impatient was he of the limitations of our daily thought. ... No one who knew him would tax him with affectation. He was more unlike his neighbors in his thought than in his action. ... He had a strong common sense ... always ready for any excursion that promised well, or for conversation prolonged into late hours ... a searching judge of men. At first glance he measured his companion, and, though insensible to some fine traits of culture, could very well report his weight and calibre. And this made the impression of genius which his conversation sometimes gave. He understood the matter in hand at a glance, and saw the limitations and poverty of those he talked with, so that nothing seemed concealed from such terrible eyes. I have repeatedly known young men of sensibility converted in a moment to the belief that this was the man they were in search of, the man of men, who could tell them all they should do ... what searching and irresistible speeches, battering down all defenses. ... [He] dedicated his genius with such entire love to the fields, hills and waters of his native town, that he made them known and interesting to all ... not a particle of respect had he to the opinions of any man or body of men, but homage solely to the truth itself. ... He grew to be revered and admired by his townsmen, who had at first known him only as an oddity. ... Whilst he used in his writings a certain petulance of remark in reference to churches or churchmen, he was a person of a rare, tender and absolute religion, a person incapable of any profanation, by act or by thought. (*W* 10:452–77)

Though Emerson could hardly have been expected to speak of Thoreau's homeliness, we can accept Hawthorne's verdict that he was "as ugly as sin";[23] and, of course, a few additional minor changes must be made (Concord for Athens, Thoreau's nose for Socrates' ears). Otherwise, the similarities are so remarkable as to suggest that Emerson really meant it when he said, again in "Uses of Great Men," that "the student of history is like a man going into a warehouse to buy cloths or carpets. He fancies he has a new article. If he go to the factory, he shall find that his new stuff still repeats the scrolls and rosettes which are found on the interior walls of the pyramids of Thebes" (*W* 4:4–5).

Emerson's identification of the friendly nettle in his own side with Plato's gadfly should surely be a sufficient indication of the extent to which he came to think of Thoreau's character and achievement as being inseparable from his own. Nor was it a question of his considering Thoreau as his "disciple." Indeed, Emerson prided himself on not having any disciples because his intent had been not to bring men to himself "but to themselves" (*J* 9:188–89). With such a view of his own function, he could honestly believe that his scholars might serve him in a reciprocal way, proving that they had truly learned Emerson's best lesson by helping *him*, in turn, to realize some of his own latent or inchoate tendencies. Seen in this light, the importance of distinguishing between himself and his young friend might have appeared to Emerson almost as futile and insignificant, say, as the insistence on delineating the difference between Raphael's hand and that of his most gifted pupil. In this regard, Emerson's comments on the relationship between Socrates and Plato are instructive:

> Socrates and Plato are the double star which the most powerful instruments will not entirely separate. Socrates again, in his traits and genius, is the best example of that synthesis which constitutes Plato's extraordinary power. . . . The rare coincidence, in one ugly body, of the droll and the martyr, the keen street and market debater with the sweetest saint known to any history at that time, had forcibly struck the mind of Plato, so capacious of these contrasts; and the figure of Socrates by a necessity placed itself in the

foreground of the scene, as the fittest dispenser of the intellectual treasures he had to communicate. It was a rare fortune that this Aesop of the mob and this robed scholar should meet, to make each other immortal in their mutual faculty. The strange synthesis in the character of Socrates capped the synthesis in the mind of Plato. Moreover by this means he was able, in the direct way and without envy to avail himself of the wit and weight of Socrates, to which unquestionably his own debt was great; and these derived again their principal advantage from the perfect art of Plato. (W 4:70, 75)

Though Socrates was older, and therefore presumably the teacher, the younger man may be said to have *perfected*, or completed, the work of his master. One can say that there would have been no Plato without Socrates or no Socrates without Plato, but the truth is that they created each other, exemplified each other, and synthesized each other. That seems to have been how Emerson thought of the relationship between himself and Thoreau. Though Emerson's identification of Thoreau with Socrates and himself with the disciple might be ascribed to the former's earthiness or to his own inveterate love for Plato, it is also clear that Emerson often felt *himself* to be the pupil in his relationship with Thoreau. In a journal entry on Thoreau in the 1840s, Emerson noted that in America "the very boys are . . . soon ripe" and went on to say: "Spinosa pronounced that there was but one substance;—yea, verily; but that boy yonder told me yesterday he thought the pinelog was God, & that God was in the jakes. What can Spinoza tell the boy?" (*JMN* 9:104). Or he himself, for that matter, Emerson must have thought occasionally.

Especially in the early years of their friendship, Emerson seems frequently to have looked upon Thoreau almost as a physical extension of his own being, or as a potential source of new physical vitality. "He is thus far a great benefactor & physician to me," Emerson said of Thoreau in June 1841, "for he is an indefatigable & a very skillful laborer & I work with him as I should not without him. and expect now to be suddenly well & strong though

I have been a skeleton all the spring until I am ashamed" (*L* 2:402). In literature too, Emerson expected his promising young scholar and poet to put new flesh on his own bones and both extend and surpass the reach of his own genius. "As private secretary to the President of the Dial," Emerson wrote a year later, "his works & fame may go out into all lands, and, as happens to great Premiers, quite extinguish the titular Master" (*L* 3:47). Of course Emerson, exercising a bit of conscience hyperbole, is both being too modest about himself and claiming too much for the barely fledged Thoreau; but it seems equally true that his close identification with the potentialities and aspirations of the younger man enabled him to feel thoroughly *represented* by Thoreau, in the sense of being reproduced in a new shape which would be both an enlargement and a transformation of his own nature. It is not a question of rivalry, because the Emerson represented by Thoreau, one might say, is an Emerson whom the Master acknowledged himself incapable of realizing alone. Perhaps this journal entry of 1852 makes the point best:

> Observe, that the whole history of the intellect is expansions & concentrations. The expansions are the claims or inspirations from heaven to try a larger sweep, a higher pitch than we have yet tried, and to leave all our past, for this enlarged scope. Present power, performance of any kind, on the other hand, requires concentration on the moment, & the thing doable. But all this old song I have trolled a hundred times already, in better ways, only, last night, Henry Thoreau insisted much on "expansions," & it sounded new. But of the congelation I was to add one word, that, by experience, having learned that this old inertia or quality of oak & granite inheres in us, & punishes, as it were, any fit of geniality, we learn with surprise that our fellow man or one of our fellowmen or fellow-women is a doctor or enchanter, who snaps the staunch iron hoops that bind us, thaws the fatal frost, & sets all the particles dancing each round each. He must be inestimable to us to whom we can say what we cannot say to ourselves. (*JMN* 13:27–28)

Thoreau releases an expanded Emerson (Thoreau's own word would be "extravagant")—an Emerson who longs to become heated, kick over the traces, and dance in a frenzy. It is the Emerson of "Bacchus" who calls for

> Wine of wine,
> Blood of the world . . .
> That I intoxicated,
> And by the draught assimilated,
> May float at pleasure through all natures . . .
> (W 9:125)

But Emerson's momentary indulgence in what we might call a Thoreauvian or Whitmanesque fantasy of ecstatic enlargement or levitation of the self seems always to activate his old ambivalence about letting himself go. His excitement carries him to the brink of fear (of ego-loss? of expressing something he will later regret? or of not being able to regather his diffused energies?); and when his mood changes and the old inertia repossesses his soul, Emerson draws away from this corrupting Socrates, this Napoleonic egotist, this Spinoza of the jakes, this "enchanter" who sings the siren-song of the "NOT ME":

> Henry Thoreau is like the woodgod who solicits the wandering poet & draws him into antres vast & desarts idle, & bereaves him of his ⟨wits⟩ memory, & leaves him naked, plaiting vines & with twigs in his hand. Very seductive are the first steps from the town to the woods, but the End is ⟨indigence⟩ ↑ want ↓ & madness.—
> (*JMN* 10:344)

It is as if Emerson saw himself in the role of Euripides' King Pentheus, seduced and destroyed by a Thoreau whose country manners thinly mask the terrible face of Dionysus. If such a comment seems too extreme a way of figuring the manifestly dual attitude with which Emerson regarded this exponent of the Wild whom he had himself inspired, we might note this hitherto unpublished entry from a series of jottings Emerson set down in 1864 as he was reading through Thoreau's journal:

In Journal, 1852, August 6, he writes, "Hearing that one with whom I was acquainted had committed suicide, I said, 'I did not know when I planted the seed of that fact, that I should hear of it.' "

I see the Thoreau poison working today in many valuable lives, in some for good, in some for harm.[24]

Such a remark should not, of course, be taken as Emerson's final judgment on Thoreau but rather as a clear indication of how ambivalently he loved this alter ego whom he reacted to as a father does to a recalcitrant son. In 1843 Emerson copied into his journal Elizabeth Hoar's comment, "I love Henry, but do not like him," and then added, with striking prescience: "Young men like Henry Thoreau owe us a new world & they have not acquitted the debt: for the most part, such die young, & so dodge the fulfilment" (*JMN* 8:375). Coming only a year after the death of little Waldo, this observation suggests that Emerson expected to be bereaved of yet another star in his private firmament and looked forward almost with anger to the fresh insult he could himself foresee. There certainly seems to be a strong personal note in these sentences from the conclusion to Emerson's funeral oration on Thoreau: "The country knows not yet, or in the least part, how great a son it has lost. It seems an injury that he should leave in the midst his broken task which none else can finish, a kind of indignity to so noble a soul that he should depart out of Nature before yet he has been really shown to his peers for what he is" (*W* 10:484–85). Emerson felt himself, one might say, to be the injured party, for he believed that Thoreau had departed before completing the task of adequately expressing and perfecting the Emersonian philosophy.

We know otherwise, of course. The presumably unfinished apostle did finally come forth, in the language of *Walden*, to enjoy his perfect summer life at last, and, in the process of bragging for himself and humanity, to help represent the capacious spirit of his teacher.

EMERSON

Nothing engaged Emerson more throughout his whole life than the search for a truly representative man.[25] He ransacked the history of the world and America's past, the contemporary scene abroad and at home, his nation, state, village, family, and household, for a figure sufficiently comprehensive to satisfy his craving imagination. We ought to keep this notion in mind when we marvel at the extravagance of Emerson's reaction to the appearance of Walt Whitman in the summer of 1855, at a time in his own life when, in general, his capacity for new enthusiasms had diminished considerably. Whitman reanimated, electrically, this old longing which might become dormant but could never quite die out in Emerson. It is interesting to consider in this context a note Emerson made in his journal while lecturing in Rome, New York, in February 1855: "What occurred this morning touching the imagination? In meeting a new student, I incline to ask him, Do you know any deep man? Has any one furnished you with a new image? for to see the world representatively, implies high gifts" (*JMN* 13:386). Emerson was looking for a new symbol-maker—poet or prophet—capable of stringing "worlds like beads" on his own thought (ibid., p. 392), and the entry suggests that he never tired of asking if such a creature had been sighted. When Whitman providentially surfaced about five months later, Emerson, as we know, became so excited that he pronounced himself ready to strike his tasks and head straight for New York to pay his respects.

One aspect of that first edition of *Leaves of Grass* (and of

Whitman's writing generally) that deserves to be stressed is the extent to which Whitman had absorbed not only *Nature*, "Self-Reliance," and "The Poet" but also Emerson's crucial idea of the "representative man." Take, for example, this passage from the 1855 Preface:

> The direct trial of him who would be the greatest poet is to-day. If he does not flood himself with the immediate age as with vast oceanic tides . . . and if he does not attract his own land body and soul to himself and hang on its neck with incomparable love and plunge his semitic muscle into its merits and demerits . . . and if he be not himself the age transfigured . . . and if to him is not opened the eternity which gives similitude to all periods and locations and processes and animate and inanimate forms, and which is the bond of time, and rises up from its inconceivable vagueness and infiniteness in the swimming shape of to-day, and is held by the ductile anchors of life, and makes the present spot the passage from what was to what shall be, and commits itself to the representation of this wave of an hour and this one of the sixty beautiful children of the wave—let him merge in the general run and wait his development.[26]

Though the prose is incomparably Whitman's, the central notion that informs it is Emerson's idea of *representation*, which Whitman had intuitively grasped and assimilated as well as anyone. Indeed, it is uncannily as if Whitman had not only read *Representative Men* but also been given the opportunity to leaf through Emerson's journals. "Homer," he wrote there in 1835, "is to us nothing personal, merely the representative of his time. I believe that to be his sincerest use & worth" (*JMN* 5:50). But Emerson also believed that this supra-personal supreme poet would be not only "the age transfigured" but also the vital link between past and future. In a very early journal entry which foreshadows Whitman's own persistent image of himself as the archetypal American pioneer, Emerson claimed that the original explorer "who invades the coast of an unknown continent and first breaks the silence which hath reigned there since the creation" by setting his axe "to the root of the forest" performs an act which echoes down through the ages and "ceases to be an ordinary adventurer, providing for himself and his son, or his friend,—but becomes the representative of human nature, the father of the Country, and, in a great measure, the Arbiter of its future destinies" (*JMN* 1:146–47). The *ideal* pioneer creates his nation's future by providing the representative paradigms capable of generating a race truly worthy of being called Americans. If the poet is not prepared to accept that responsibility, Whitman argues, he had better hold his tongue until he has grown large enough for the role. Naturally, Whitman felt that he himself was more than equal to the task. And when Thoreau visited him in 1856, Whitman readily and shamelessly introduced himself "as representing America." Thoreau's acerbic reply—he claims to have said that he "did not think much of America"—is so manifestly alien to the spirit of his own writings that one can only assume he was outraged at being denied *his* clear title to the post![27]

Both Thoreau and Whitman were at least sufficient representatives of the devouring egotism of great genius, and this fact may account for Emerson's backing away from these quasi-disciples after his initial enthusiasm, as if he feared the abridging of his own reputation. Indeed, Emerson could be quite witty on this subject, as in the following journal entry from 1853:

'Tis said that the age ends with the poet or successful man, who knots up into himself the genius or idea of his nation; and that, when the Jews have at last flowered perfectly into Jesus, there is the end of the nation. When Greece is complete in Plato, Phidias, Pericles, the race is spent & rapidly takes itself away. When Rome has arrived at Caesar & Cicero, it has no more that it can do & retreats. When Italy has got out Dante, all the rest will be rubbish. So that we ought rather to be thankful that our hero or poet does not hasten to be born in America, but still allows us others to live a little, & warm ourselves at the fire of the sun, for, when he

comes, we others must pack our petty trunks, & begone. (*JMN*
13:120)

Walden was only a year away, of course, and when it came,
Emerson would have to "account Henry the undoubted King of all
American lions" (*L* 4:460)—until at least the New York giant
began to make noises that suggested to Emerson "buffalo strength." [28]
The truth is, however, that Emerson thought the English-speaking
mind large enough to contain multitudes of geniuses and so concluded his journal entry by arguing that "Saxondom is tough &
manyheaded, & does not so readily admit of absorption & being
sucked & vampyrized by a Representative as fluider races." But
such a remark, reminding us as it inevitably must of Emerson's
physiological anxieties, suggests that he was not entirely satisfied
with his jocular disposing of the problem. Even so apparently mild
a contender for the crown as Bronson Alcott could sometimes seem
to pose a threat, as in this journal entry for 1842:

> This noble genius discredits genius to me. I do not want any more
> such persons to exist. Part of this egotism in him is a certain
> comparing eye which seems to sour his view of persons prosper-
> ously placed, & to make his conversation often accusing & mina-
> tory. He is not selfsufficing & serene. (*JMN* 8:215)

Alcott, to be sure, would never publish a book, as Whitman
did, with Emerson's praise stamped in gold on the back cover; or
poke fun at the Master, publicly, as Thoreau did in *A Week on the
Concord and Merrimack Rivers*. He might make Emerson uncomfortable in conversation occasionally, but it was Whitman and
Thoreau, as Emerson undoubtedly knew, who were the real com-
petitors. Which is not to suggest that Emerson was fundamentally
mean-spirited or invidious in his attitude toward these two most
promising of his pupils. Quite the contrary. Emerson's sincere
desire to discover and nourish new genius led him to acts of
generosity that often threatened to devour his time, substance, and

reputation (witness his relations with Carlyle). And he would need to remind himself, to use the language of "Self-Reliance," that he had his own stern claims and perfect circle.

Indeed, it is probably fair to say that only Emerson's inveterate scrupulousness and humility—as well as his nagging lack of self-trust—kept him searching outside his own study for the best representative of the American mind when his own heart so often whispered that he was himself the man he sought. Was this why he hesitated to include an American in the select portrait gallery he called *Representative Men?* He might, of course, have chosen Webster, whom he long admired inordinately as the representative of both the American people and this continent's titanic nature.[29] But Webster's infamous support of the Fugitive Slave Act in 1850, the year when Emerson's book was published, would have been sufficient reason for Emerson to cross his name out, as Beethoven did that of Napoleon from the manuscript of the *Eroica* symphony. By the summer of 1852, Emerson had a head of Washington hanging in his dining room which, he insisted, he could not take his eyes off. "It has a certain Apalachian strength, as if it were truly the first-fruits of America, & expressed the country. The heavy leaden eyes turn on you, as the eyes of an ox in a pasture. And the mouth has a gravity & depth of quiet, as if this man had absorbed all the serenity of America, & left none for . . . his restless, rickety, hysterical countrymen" (*JMN* 13:63). Emerson imagined such a "noble aristocratic head" listening with majestical irony to "the effronteries of Mr Webster" as would a "god."

And there, in fact, was the problem. Though Washington expressed the aspirations of the country in some high, magisterial, perhaps timeless, way, Emerson's notion of what it meant to be *representative* seems to have had a different emphasis. Once he had seen phoenixes, he noted in the mid-1840s, now he saw such no longer:

> . . . but the world is not therefore disenchanted. The vessels on which you read sacred emblems have turned out to be common

pottery, but the sacred pictures are transferred to the walls of the world. You no longer see phoenixes; men are not divine individuals; but you learn to revere their social & representative character. They are not gods, but the spirit of God sparkles on & about them. (*JMN* 9:171–72)

What Emerson wanted was not a god, or an American demi-god (in F. O. Matthiessen's phrase),[30] but examples of common clay touched fitfully with the divine afflatus. To be representative, as he puts it elsewhere, is to be "alive"; not "accurately & thoroughly great" (*JMN* 12:521), but *acutely* human and available, therefore, to provide succor and inspire emulation. An indication, perhaps, of what Emerson was working toward may be found in this 1846 journal entry:

> A man who can speak well to a public assembly, I must respect, and he is *ipso facto* ennobled. Like a great general or a great poet, or a millionaire, he may wear his coat out at elbows, and his shoes & his hat as he will. He has established relation, representativeness, that he is a good apple of his kind, proved by the homage of the apples, and not merely like your lonely man of genius, that he is an apple shaped like a cucumber. He is not a curiosity but capable of yielding aid & comfort to men. (*JMN* 9:85)

Now Luther, one might say, has been thoroughly domesticated, and Whitman prepared for ("I wear my hat as I please indoors or out").[31] But principally, of course, Emerson wants to see himself in this extraordinary-ordinary orator who has the same shape as his fellows, only more so, and helps them to realize their best selves. In this regard, Emerson felt that Thoreau failed. "He speaks at Lyceum or other meeting," Emerson wrote in 1851, "but somebody else speaks & his speech falls dead & is forgotten. He rails at the town doings & ought to correct & inspire them" (*JMN* 11:404).

An almost perfect model for what Emerson had in mind is undoubtedly to be found in this sketch of his great-grandfather, Joseph Emerson of Malden, with whom Emerson so often identified himself. Reading his diary in 1847, Emerson was struck with what he finely calls the "useful egotism of our old puritan clergy":

> The minister *experienced* life for his flock. He gave prominence to all his economy & history for the benefit of the parish. All his haps are providences. If he keeps school, marries, begets children, if his house burns, if his children have the measles, if he is thrown from his horse, if he buys a negro, & Dinah misbehaves, if he buys or sells his chaise, all his adventures are fumigated with prayer & praise, he/preaches/improves it/ next Sunday on the new circumstance and the willing flock are contented with this consecration of one man's adventures for the benefit of them all, inasmuch as that one is on the right level & therefore a fair representative. (*JMN* 10:177)

One may compare this with the portrait of Barzillai Frost, the "formalist preacher," in the Divinity School Address (*CW* 1:85–86). Joseph Emerson, in contrast to that frigidly correct and self-concealing figure, lives his life in public *with* and *for* his flock. His experience is not different from theirs, only more thoroughly aired and improved. The "right level" at which he conducts his adventures lies somewhere between the mundane and the sacramental; and his personality is *used up*, one might say, for the sake of others, so that finally he is seen as the least of egotists. Alcott, on the other hand, is an example for Emerson of the pure egotist who represents nothing but himself. "Unhappily, his conversation never loses sight of his own personality. He never quotes; he never refers; his only illustration is his own biography. His topic yesterday is Alcott on the 17 October; today, Alcott on the 18 October; tomorrow, on the 19th. So will it be always." But the poet, Emerson continues— and he might be speaking of his great-grandfather in a more secular context—"rapt into future times or into deeps of nature admired for themselves, lost in their law, cheers us with a lively charm" (*JMN* 8:215).

Undoubtedly, Emerson had little desire to emulate Alcott. More to the point, however, Alcott—the "tedious archangel"—was not *usable;* he bore no vital relation to the past, or to those around him, and was not a consumer of culture in the best sense. Emerson's own unflagging interest in biography, local and foreign, past and present, was inspired by a need to make "always a silent comparison between the intellectual & moral endowments portrayed & those of which we are conscious" (*JMN* 4:256). The purpose of such comparison was the never-ending creation of his own character. "The reason why the Luther, the Newton, the Bonaparte concerning whom we read, was made the subject of panegyric, is, that in the writer's opinion, in some one respect this particular man represented the idea of Man" (ibid). Emerson accordingly had to find out what portion of that idea, in each case, fitted his own evolving human sketch—*human,* we should note, and not the "rough deific" sketch (however comic) of the self-apotheosizing Whitman.[32] Perhaps what really drove Emerson out of the church was his ineluctable feeling that traditional ideas of divinity lacked actuality (that is, in the French sense, *presentness*)[33] and were not useful to him in his process of representative self-projection. "The nature of God may be different from what he is represented," Emerson wrote as early as 1827. "I never beheld him. I do not know that he exists. This good which invites me now is visible & specific. I will at least embrace it this time by way of experiment" (*JMN* 3:69). Emerson's experiment concerned the creation of a tangible human personality in which he could himself believe and which he could render credible to others. He had to find ways of representing himself fully and truly.

Emerson was therefore driven, either by introjection or conscious assimilation, to incorporate the best aspects of his intellectual and material universe. Plato and Jesus and Shakespeare thus became for him no more than "the gracious marks of our own growth," because "slowly like light of morning it steals on us the new fact that we who were pupils or aspirants are now society: do compose a portion of that head & heart we are wont to think worthy of all reverence & heed: we are the representatives of religion & intellect, & stand in the light of Ideas whose rays stream through us to those younger & more in the dark" (*JMN* 8:127). Emerson literally ingested his authors. Reading the *Life* of the distinguished Italian poet, dramatist, and autobiographer Vittorio Alfieri in 1847, Emerson noted first that this "dear lover of Plutarch & Montaigne, a passionate lover of beauty & of study," died the year he himself was born, as if to suggest some mysterious transmigration of souls. "His rare opportunities & the determination to use them, make him a valuable representative," Emerson continued, drawing Alfieri into his Concord granary; "One has many thoughts, in reading this book, of the uses of Aristocracy & Europe to the native scholar" (*JMN* 9:464–65).

Apart from books—and this insatiable scholar insisted much on his life apart from reading—Emerson was determined to invest every action and event, no matter how small, with total intention "so that in doing that, it was all one as if I had builded a world." The world comes into being, he seems to be saying, when we take each part of it seriously. "I was thereby taught, that everything in nature should represent total nature" (*JMN* 8:224). *Should* represent total nature. That auxiliary verb suggests that the miraculous transformations Emerson is recommending are dependent on a human act—the performative process which is Emerson's own. He *makes* things representative by relating parts to a whole which is in fact his own life. A journal entry of 1851 clarifies the point: "In some sort, the end of life, is, that the man should take up the universe into himself, or, out of that quarry leave nothing unrepresented, and he is to create himself" (*JMN* 11:440–41). Although such remarks have tempted many to call Emerson the most sublime egotist or most unregenerate Transcendentalist who ever lived, his egotism consists simply in taking a frankly and totally *human* point of view. How can there be a world for us apart from the world we create by living our own human life in it? We measure the greatness of an author by the extent to which the verbal universe he spins out of himself adequately represents the world in which we all live.

In 1846, under the title *"Walking one day in the fields I met a man,"* Emerson set down his own mini-Vision of Piers Plowman for an age that believed in the supreme value of self-culture and self-expression. "We shall one day talk with the central man," he begins, "and see again in the varying play of his features all the features which have characterised our darlings, & stamped themselves in fire on the heart." The personal tone here suggests that among the representative "darlings" whom Emerson goes on to enumerate (Socrates, Shakespeare, Raphael, Michelangelo, Dante, Jesus) walks also the spirit of his beloved lost son, upon whose death he wrote to Carlyle: "How often I have pleased myself that one day I should send to you, this Morningstar of mine, & stay at home gladly behind such a representative!"[34] That, of course, was not to be; the elder Waldo could not dodge the responsibility of having to represent himself. As the vision ends, "it appears that these great secular [i.e., enduring] personalities were only expressions of his face chasing each other like the rack of clouds." By "his face" Emerson means the face of the "central man," but of course, it is also his own. He finds himself "alone": "I dreamed & did not know my dreams" (*JMN* 9:395). This great inclusive figure, chasing his own incarnations down through the years, whom Emerson one day expects to meet and talk to, is in fact the very self he has always been talking to, though the future tense suggests that full centrality, or representativeness, can only be said to have been achieved when the total experiment of self-creation has come to an end at death.

"I am here to represent humanity," Emerson wrote in 1854, and although that sounds like arrogance, it was not intended to be so, since he goes on to explain, "it is by no means necessary that I should live, but it is by all means necessary that I should act rightly" (*JMN* 13:327). Having been given the gift of life, Emerson felt a strong responsibility to acquit himself honorably as an example of humankind. Whether or not he can be said to "represent humanity" in a larger sense each reader must decide for himself. The aging Whitman believed his own book to be "a candidate for the future" mainly because it was "an attempt, from first to last, to put a *Person,* a human being (myself, in the latter half of the Nineteenth Century, in America,) freely, fully and truly on record." And he added: "I could not find any similar personal record in current literature that satisfied me."[35] Arguably, Emerson did a better—which is to say, more comprehensive—job. But as Doctor Holmes notes, "comparisons between men of genius for the sake of aggrandizing the one at the expense of the other are the staple of the meaner kinds of criticism."[36]

Santayana, writing of William James, argues that he was "too spontaneous and rare a person to be a good mirror of any broad general movement; his Americanism, like that of Emerson, was his own and within him, and perhaps more representative of America in the past than in the future."[37] One might respond by saying that "Americanism," at least in cultural terms, can hardly be said to exist without the achievement of such cranky geniuses. And it is hard to conceive of any future America that can afford to discard such a past. To be sure, Santayana also said of Whitman (in the same book that contains his famous essay on Emerson) that "he is surely not the spokesman of the tendencies of his country, although he describes some aspects of its past and present condition; nor does he appeal to those whom he describes, but rather to the *dilettanti* he despises. He is regarded as representative chiefly by foreigners, who look for some grotesque expression of the genius of so young and prodigious a people."[38] Fortunately, what seemed plausible to Santayana in 1900 has proven dead wrong, though we did need the help of quite a few "foreigners" to recover, in time, the unique value of our best classic American authors.

More interesting, perhaps, is Santayana's point about whether an Emerson or a Whitman or a William James or a John Dewey can be considered a "spokesman of the tendencies of his country." At issue is the meaning of "tendencies." If we have in mind some vague notion of the way things are going, or are likely to go, in general, we shall probably not find very compelling reasons to view any of these four—or analogous figures—as accurate commentators or prophets. Serious writers and thinkers are not normally very successful themselves in defining broad movements or helping to inspire popular trends, though others may discover ways of transforming their complex literary particulars into universally acceptable slogans.

But we may apply a different meaning to "tendencies." These figures can be regarded as culturally representative if we conceive of them as exemplifying in their lives and works central tendencies or *potentialities* of our national spirit. Santayana remarks of John Dewey that "his philosophy is calculated to justify all the assumptions of American society";[39] and we may take this observation to apply more generally if we understand "justify" to mean *test* or *prove*. If our country can be defined as one that remains committed to examining its own assumptions, it surely will continue to find spokesmen in such names as Santayana mentions, even though each may be seen to be limited in definable ways (gender, class, race) and bound to a particular historical moment.

Perhaps a final quotation from Emerson may help to clarify the question:

> He who shall represent the genius of this day, he who shall, standing in this great cleft of Past & Future, understand the dignity & power of his position so well as to write the laws of Criticism, of Ethics, of History will be found an age hence neither false nor unfortunate but will rank immediately & equally with all the masters whom we now acknowledge. (*JMN* 7:274).

Drawing out the implications of Emerson's remark, we might say that the American writer who succeeds at the task of representing the spirit of his age will be a candidate for the future only in the sense that he can expect to be prized by an audience that has not lost the ability to acknowledge and identify with such an achievement. He will be found true by those Americans who know where and how to look for their truth-speakers. The fortunes of the author will thus keep pace with the fortunes of the republic. In this sense, Emerson's reputation as a representative man is, and will remain, a measure of our own stature.

NOTES

Introduction: Emerson and His Circle

1. See Irving Howe, *The American Newness: Culture and Politics in the Age of Emerson* (Cambridge: Harvard University Press, 1986).

2. *Margaret Fuller: American Romantic*, ed. Perry Miller (New York: Anchor Books, 1963), pp. xvi–xvii.

3. Useful discussions of Emerson's rhetoric and stance in "Circles" are: Jack Null, "Strategies of Imagery in 'Circles,' " *Emerson Society Quarterly* (4th Quarter, 1972), 18(4):265–70; Albert H. Tricomi, "The Rhetoric of Aspiring Circularity in Emerson's 'Circles,' " *ibid.*, pp. 271–83; David M. Wyatt, "Spelling Time: The Reader in Emerson's 'Circles,' " *American Literature* (1976), 48(2):140–51.

4. See *L*, vol. 1, frontispiece.

5. Cf. "The Method of Nature": "Nature can only be conceived as existing to a universal and not to a particular end, to a universe of ends, and not to one,—a work of *ecstasy*, to be represented by a circular movement, as intention might be signified by a straight line of definite length. . . . We can point nowhere to anything final; but tendency appears on all hands: planet, system, constellation, total nature is growing like a field of maize in July; is becoming somewhat else; is in rapid metamorphosis. The embryo does not more strive to be man than yonder burr of light we call a nebula tends to be a ring, a comet, a globe, and parent of new stars" (CW 1:125–26).

6. *Preparatory Meditations*, Second Series, 1.

7. "A Valediction: Forbidding Mourning."

8. Henry James, "Emerson," in *The Art of Fiction and Other Essays* (New York: Oxford University Press, 1948), p. 235.

9. See Ralph C. LaRosa, "Bacon and the 'Organic Method' of Emerson's Early Lectures," *English Language Notes* (1970), 8(2):107–14.

10. *Alphabet of the Imagination: Literary Essays of Harold Clarke Goddard,* ed. Eleanor Goddard Worthen and Margaret Goddard Holt (Atlantic Highlands, N.J.: Humanities Press, 1974), p. 209.

11. Susanne K. Langer, *Philosophy in a New Key* (New York: New American Library, 1948), p. 16. See also Charles Feidelson, Jr., *Symbolism and American Literature* (Chicago: University of Chicago Press, 1953).

12. *Complete Poems of Robert Frost* (New York: Holt, 1949), p. 318.

13. Cf. *JMN* 3:72–73: "We are the changing inhabitants of a changing world. The night & the day, the ebbing & flowing of the tide, the round of the seasons . . . these are the monitors among which we live."

14. See Maurice Gonnaud, *Individu et société dans l'oeuvre de Ralph Waldo Emerson: Essai de biographie spirituelle* (Paris: Didier, 1964).

15. Letter to George and Georgianna Keats, February 19, 1819.

16. See F. O. Matthiessen, *American Renaissance: Art and Expression in the Age of Emerson and Whitman* (New York: Oxford University Press, 1941), pp. 635 ff.; Constance Rourke, *American Humor* (New York: Anchor Books, 1953), passim.

17. See Gonnaud, *Individu et société,* p. 367; cf. Gonnaud's "The Humane Seer: Humor and Its Avatars in Emerson," in *Ralph Waldo Emerson: New Appraisals,* ed. Leonard Nick Neufeldt (Hartford: Transcendental Books, 1973), p. 84. See also V. L. O. Chittick, "Emerson's 'Frolic Health,' " *New England Quarterly* (1957), 30(2):209–34.

18. Sacvan Bercovitch, in *The Puritan Origins of the American Self* (New Haven: Yale University Press, 1975), p. 148, cites a later example (1899) of this sort of apocalyptic comedy: "the United States of America, —bounded on the north by the North Pole; on the South by the Antarctic Region; on the east by the first chapter of the Book of Genesis and on the west by the Day of Judgment."

19. See Richard Poirier, *The Renewal of Literature: Emersonian Reflections* (New York: Random House, 1987).

I: LEGENDS OF AN AMERICAN SAINT

Hagiography

1. *The Correspondence of Emerson and Carlyle,* ed. Joseph Slater (New York: Columbia University Press, 1964), pp. 201, 14 (this edition

I: Legends of an American Saint

will be cited hereafter as CEC); Ralph L. Rusk, *The Life of Ralph Waldo Emerson* (New York: Scribner's 1949), p. 195.

2. Moncure Daniel Conway, *Emerson at Home and Abroad* (Boston, 1882), p. 1.

3. Ibid., pp. 6–7.

4. Oliver Wendell Holmes, *Ralph Waldo Emerson* (Boston, 1885), p. 103.

5. John Jay Chapman, "Emerson," in *The Shock of Recognition*, ed. Edmund Wilson (New York: Modern Library, 1955), p. 645.

6. George Edward Woodberry, *Ralph Waldo Emerson* (New York, 1907), p. 1; W. C. Brownell, *American Prose Masters*, ed. Howard Mumford Jones (Cambridge: Harvard University Press, 1967), p. 94.

7. Cited by F. O. Matthiessen in *The Achievement of T. S. Eliot* (New York: Oxford University Press, 1959), p. 24.

8. T. S. Eliot, *Complete Poems* (New York: Harcourt, 1952), p. 18.

9. Malcolm Cowley, *Exile's Return* (New York: Viking, 1956), p. 227.

10. *A Dial Miscellany*, ed. William Wasserstrom (Syracuse, N.Y.: Syracuse University Press, 1963), p. 151.

11. Cited by James Elliot Cabot, *A Memoir of Ralph Waldo Emerson* (Boston, 1888), 1:37.

12. Holmes, *Emerson*, p. 357.

13. *Selected Writings of Gertrude Stein*, ed. Carl Van Vechten (New York: Modern Library, 1962), p. vii.

14. Ibid., p. 585.

15. Gertrude Stein, *Four in America* (New Haven: Yale University Press, 1947), p. 1.

16. Gertrude Stein, *The Autobiography of Alice B. Toklas* (New York: Harcourt, 1933), p. 187.

17. Stein, *Four in America*, p. 53.

Henry James' "Fine Adumbration"

18. James, *The Art of Fiction*, p. 238.

19. "The Correspondence of Carlyle and Emerson," *The Century* (1883), 26(4):265.

20. Ibid., p. 270.

21. Henry James, *Hawthorne*, in *The Shock of Recognition*, p. 491.

22. Ibid., p. 491.

23. *The Writings of Henry David Thoreau,* Walden Edition (Boston, 1906), 1:193.

24. *The Shock of Recognition,* pp. 479–80.

25. *The Complete Writings of Nathaniel Hawthorne,* Old Manse Edition (Boston, 1900), 1:liv–lv.

26. Cited in Leon Edel, *Literary Biography* (Bloomington: Indiana University Press, 1973), p. 146. Edel has some valuable pages here on the James-Emerson relationship.

27. Henry James, *Autobiography,* ed. F. W. Dupee (New York: Criterion Books, 1956), p. 358.

28. James, *The Art of Fiction,* pp. 220 ff.

29. Ibid., pp. 223–24.

30. See F. W. Dupee, *Henry James* (New York: Anchor Books, 1956), p. 192.

31. James, *The Art of Fiction,* p. 224.

32. Ibid., pp. 229–30.

33. Ibid., pp. 230, 233, 235.

34. Stephen E. Whicher, "Emerson's Tragic Sense," in *Emerson: A Collection of Critical Essays,* ed. Milton Konvitz and Stephen E. Whicher (Englewood Cliffs, N.J.: Prentice-Hall, 1962), p. 39.

Santayana's Emerson: Ultimate Puritanism

35. See *The Works of George Santayana,* Triton Edition (New York: Scribner's, 1937), 11:vii ff.

36. Many illuminating comments about the Harvard background of Santayana's novel are scattered throughout his *Letters* and autobiographical volumes, especially *Persons and Places.* See also Maurice F. Brown, "Santayana's American Roots," *New England Quarterly* (1960), 33(2):147–63, and my article, "Santayana at the 'Gas House,' " *New England Quarterly,* (1962), 35(3):337–46.

37. Joe Lee Davis, "Santayana as a Critic of Transcendentalism," in *Transcendentalism and Its Legacy,* ed. Myron Simon and Thornton H. Parsons (Ann Arbor: University of Michigan Press, 1966), p. 166. Davis provides useful bibliographical references in his notes.

38. George Santayana, *My Host the World* (New York: Scribner's, 1953), p. 13.

39. Ibid., p. 13. The lines are slightly misquoted. See W 9:153. Santayana had already cited the same lines, correctly, in his *Three Philosophical Poets* (1910).

40. George Santayana, *The Last Puritan: A Memoir in the Form of a Novel* (New York: Scribner's, 1936), pp. 579–80.

41. Ibid., p. 580. Cf. Emerson, *EL* 3:262; *CW* 1:39, 57; *W* 2:309; *W* 3:81.

42. George Santayana, *Interpretations of Poetry and Religion* (New York: Scribner's, 1900), p. 217.

43. Holly Stevens, *Souvenirs and Prophecies: The Young Wallace Stevens* (New York: Knopf, 1977), p. 68.

44. *The Philosophy of George Santayana*, ed. Paul Arthur Schilpp (New York: Tudor, 1951), p. 35.

45. Santayana, *The Last Puritan*, pp. 200–1.

46. Santayana, *Interpretations of Poetry and Religion*, p. 231.

47. Ibid., pp. 220, 228.

48. Ibid., pp. 220–21.

49. "The Optimism of Ralph Waldo Emerson," in *George Santayana's America*, ed. James Ballowe (Urbana: University of Illinois Press, 1967), pp. 73–74.

50. Ibid., p. 72.

51. Ibid., p. 83.

52. "Emerson the Poet," in *Santayana on America*, ed. Richard Colton Lyon (New York: Harcourt, 1968), p. 270.

53. Ibid., pp. 271, 273.

54. Santayana, *Interpretations of Poetry and Religion*, p. 218.

55. Lyon, *Santayana on America*, pp. 273–74.

56. Ibid., pp. 270–74.

57. Ibid., p. 278.

58. Ibid., p. 282.

59. *The Shock of Recognition*, p. 428.

60. Santayana, *The Last Puritan*, pp. 92, 171, 552, 404, 416, 518.

61. Ibid., pp. 507, 126, 509.

62. Ibid., pp. 313–14.

63. Ibid., p. 315.

64. Ibid., p. 316.

65. Wallace Stevens, *The Necessary Angel* (New York: Vintage Books, 1951), p. 130.

66. Daniel B. Shea, "Emerson and the American Metamorphosis," in *Emerson: Prophecy, Metamorphosis, and Influence,* ed. David Levin (New York: Columbia University Press, 1975), p. 46. Santayana's abiding interest in the figure of Jacob's ladder is attested by its presence in *Platonism and the Spiritual Life* (1927) and *Dominations and Powers* (1951).

67. Apart from the obvious Platonic source of the ladder of transcendence (Oliver Alden's essay on Plato in *The Last Puritan,* written for Santayana's philosophy course, deals with love in the *Phaedrus* and the *Symposium),* it is likely that both Santayana and Emerson were recollecting Dante in general and, in particular, his use of Jacob's ladder in *Paradiso* XXII. Santayana had discussed Dante at length in his *Three Philosophical Poets,* and Emerson was manifestly interested in Dante throughout his life. Kenneth Walter Cameron has given evidence of the presence of the *Paradiso* in Emerson's sermons (*Emerson Society Quarterly* [3rd Quarter, 1958], 12:8), and Emerson himself quotes from *Paradiso* in one of his early lectures (*EL* 2:351). A very careful survey of Emerson's experience of Dante is Joseph Chesley Mathews, "Emerson's Knowledge of Dante," *University of Texas Studies in English,* July 8, 1942, pp. 171–98.

68. Santayana, *The Last Puritan,* pp. 400–1.

69. Ibid., pp. 561, 580.

70. Ibid., p. 10.

71. Ibid., p. 602.

II: RITES OF SPRING

Eastering

1. Cf. Alfred R. Ferguson's "Foreword" to *JMN* 4:xii.

2. See *JMN* 4:53–54.

3. James Elliot Cabot, *A Memoir of Ralph Waldo Emerson* (Boston, 1888), 1:173.

4. Horace, *Epistles,* Book One, XI:27: "They change the sky but not their souls who run across the sea."

5. "The great series of revolving ages begins anew" is the fifth line of Virgil's Fourth *Eclogue.* Emerson himself quotes part of the following line

II: Rites of Spring

in Latin *(" . . . Redeunt Saturnia regna")* in *JMN* 7:220, and translates it in *EL* 3:264.

6. *The Writings of Henry David Thoreau,* Walden Edition (Boston, 1906), 1:157.

7. Cf. *JMN* 4:159, and L1:375. At the age of twenty-six, Henry James would write home to his brother William, in 1869: *"Que vous en dirai-je?* At last—for the first time—I live!" For this and other enthusiastic responses of American travelers to Italy in the period, see Paul R. Baker, *The Fortunate Pilgrims: Americans in Italy, 1800–1860* (Cambridge: Harvard University Press, 1964), esp. pp. 198–212, "The Meaning of Italy."

8. As Baker notes (p. 155), "Religion was the component of Italian life that the visiting American viewed with greatest disfavor, and the practices and beliefs of the Roman Catholic Church antagonized him more than anything else he found in Italy." It is against such a pertinent generalization as this that one measures, with surprise, Emerson's reaction to Easter Sunday at St. Peter's.

9. *The Complete Writings of Nathaniel Hawthorne,* Old Manse Edition (Boston, 1900) (*Notes of Travel,* 3), 21:310.

10. Or perhaps, as Maurice Gonnaud remarks, it is Proust's predecessor, Huysmans, who comes to mind in connection with Emerson's rich descriptions of Easter Sunday. See *Individu et société dans l'oeuvre de Ralph Waldo Emerson: Essai de biographie spirituelle* (Paris: Didier, 1964), p. 140.

11. The source of the sentence, as Edward W. Emerson informs us in his note to the passage, is Plato's *Phaedrus* (W 3:309).

12. For discussions of the influence of Coleridge on Emerson, see Kenneth Walter Cameron, *Emerson the Essayist* (Raleigh, N.C.: Thistle Press, 1945), 1:78–223, and Sherman Paul, *Emerson's Angle of Vision* (Cambridge: Harvard University Press, 1952), passim.

13. See *JMN* 5:337. For a general treatment of Emerson's reaction to Böhme, see Lionel Braham, "Emerson and Boehme: A Comparative Study in Mystical Ideas," *Modern Language Quarterly* (1959), 20:31–35.

14. *CEC*, p. 296.

15. *CEC*, p. 353.

16. *CEC*, p. 220.

17. *CEC*, p. 242.

18. Thoreau, *Writings,* 1:103; see my article, "Transcendental Antics,"

in *Veins of Humor*, ed. Harry Levin, *Harvard English Studies 3* (Cambridge: Harvard University Press, 1972), pp. 181–82.

19. Ralph L. Rusk, *The Life of Ralph Waldo Emerson* (New York: Scribner's, 1949), p. 469.

A Living Leaping Logos

20. In *The Shock of Recognition*, ed. Edmund Wilson (New York: Modern Library, 1955), p. 44.

21. Perry Miller, *The Transcendentalists* (Cambridge: Harvard University Press, 1950), p. 12.

22. *The Christian Examiner* (March 1833), 14(1):108–29.

23. Miller, *The Transcendentalists*, provides extensive documentation of the unfolding epistemological controversy between the Unitarians and the Transcendentalists. See, too, George Hochfield, *Selected Writings of the American Transcendentalists* (New York: New American Library, 1966), esp. "Introduction."

24. The fullest treatment of Emerson's relations with Ellen Tucker, remarkably tactful on the question of Ellen's fortune, is Henry F. Pommer, *Emerson's First Marriage* (Carbondale, Ill.: Southern Illinois University Press, 1967).

25. Pommer notes (p. 62) that "the proportion of one to ten may not have held in Ellen's case, but lawyers did what they could to reach it."

26. See Pommer, p. 67.

27. In *Nature* Emerson would write, in a passage suggesting sharp personal reference, of "Debt, grinding debt, whose iron face the widow, the orphan, and the sons of genius fear and hate;—debt, which consumes so much time, which so cripples and disheartens a great spirit with cares that seem so base" (CW 1:24).

The Book of Revelation of St. Radulphus

28. Henry James, *Hawthorne*, in *The Shock of Recognition*, p. 449.

29. Cf. *JMN* 7:401.

30. Rusk, *Life*, p. 199.

31. Oliver Wendell Holmes, *Ralph Waldo Emerson* (Boston, 1885), p. 103.

32. There are many discussions of the centrality of vision in Emerson's writing. See, for example, Sherman Paul, *Emerson's Angle of Vision*,

II: Rites of Spring

passim; Kenneth Burke, "I, Eye, Ay—Emerson's Early Essay 'Nature': Thoughts on the Machinery of Transcendence," in *Transcendentalism and Its Legacy,* ed. Myron Simon and Thornton H. Parsons (Ann Arbor: University of Michigan Press, 1966), pp. 3–24; Tony Tanner, *The Reign of Wonder* (New York: Harper, 1967), chapter 2, "Emerson: The Unconquered Eye and the Enchanted Circle"; Richard Poirier, *A World Elsewhere* (New York: Oxford University Press, 1966), chapter 2, "Is There an I for an Eye?: The Visionary Possession of America"; Warner Berthoff, *Fictions and Events* (New York: Dutton, 1971), " 'Building Discourse': The Genesis of Emerson's Nature," esp. pp. 209–13; and my own article, "The Problem of Emerson," in *Uses of Literature,* ed. Monroe Engel, *Harvard English Studies 4* (Cambridge: Harvard University Press, 1973), pp. 101–5.

33. Sampson Reed, *Observations on the Growth of the Mind,* 4th ed. (New York: 1841), pp. 49, 51. For discussions of Reed and Emerson, see Kenneth Walter Cameron, *Emerson the Essayist* (Raleigh, N.C.: Thistle Press, 1945), 1:253–94; Clarence Paul Hotson, "Sampson Reed, a Teacher of Emerson," *New England Quarterly* (1929), 2(2):249–77; and Carl F. Strauch, "Emerson Rejects Reed and Hails Thoreau," *Harvard Library Bulletin* (1968), 16(3):257–73.

34. M. H. Abrams, *Natural Supernaturalism: Tradition and Revolution in Romantic Literature* (New York: Norton, 1971), pp. 47, 344.

35. Ibid., p. 28.

36. See Holmes, *Emerson,* p. 93.

37. For a full discussion of this issue, see Cameron, *Emerson The Essayist* 1:361–99.

38. Holmes, *Emerson,* p. 101.

39. See Harriet Rodgers Zink, "Emerson's Use of the Bible," *University of Nebraska Studies in Language, Literature, and Criticism* (1935), no. 14.

40. Mark Twain, "Fenimore Cooper's Literary Offenses," in *The Shock of Recognition,* pp. 586–87.

41. *CEC,* p. 157. It is interesting to note that the mystic and poet Jones Very, who was to come into close relation with Emerson in 1838–39, was reminded of the Book of Revelation as he read *Nature* in 1836 and scribbled references to it in the margins of Emerson's book. See Edwin Gittleman, *Jones Very: The Effective Years, 1833–1840* (New York: Columbia University Press, 1967), pp. 122–30.

II: Rites of Spring

42. See Abrams, *Natural Supernaturalism,* pp. 307–11.

43. Thomas Carlyle, *Sartor Resartus* (London: Chapman & Hall, n.d.), pp. 122–23.

44. Cf. CW 1:29.

45. Ralph C. LaRosa has noticed that a passage in Emerson's 1835 lecture, "On the Best Mode of Inspiring a Correct Taste in English Literature," plays against this text in Revelation: "The teacher may well reflect that no man can teach more than he knows, or inspire a taste which he has not himself. Therefore let him acquaint himself with these treasures; let him mark, learn, eat, and digest these books as Scriptures approved by the voice of Human Nature in several ages. They shall be sweet in the mouth and sweet in the belly" (*EL* 1:212). Wittily building on John's parable, Emerson thus suggests that a "correct taste" in literature can best be acquired through devouring the world's secular scriptures! See LaRosa's "Invention and Imitation in Emerson's Early Lectures," *American Literature* (1972), 44(1):29. See also his article "Necessary Truths: The Poetics of Emerson's Proverbs," in *Literary Monographs 8,* ed. Eric Rothstein and Joseph A. Wittreich (Madison: University of Wisconsin Press, 1976), p. 154. Clarence Paul Hotson, in the article cited above, points out that in his journal for 1829, Emerson commented approvingly on an interpretation of Revelation 10 that he found in the *New Jerusalem Magazine,* insisting that although the interpretation was "doubtless wholly false," the exegete's use of the Bible passage as a medium for his own true sentiment was legitimate: "The wider that sentiment can be spread & the more effect it can have on men's lives, the better. And if the fool-part of man must have the lie, if truth is a pill that can't go down till 'tis sugared with superstition, why then I will forgive the last in the belief that the truth will enter into the soul so natively & so assimilantly that it will become part of the soul & so remain, when the falsehood grows dry & lifeless & peels off" (*JMN* 3:165–66).

46. D. H. Lawrence, *Apocalypse* (New York: Viking, 1966), p. 124.

47. *CEC,* pp. 149, 157.

48. Cf. Herman Melville, *Pierre: Or, the Ambiguities,* ed. Henry A. Murray (New York: Hendricks House, 1949), p. 107.

III: A Summer of Discontent

III: A SUMMER OF DISCONTENT

The Protest

1. Wallace Stevens, *Collected Poems* (New York: Knopf, 1957), p. 473.

2. The editors of *JMN* 7 inexplicably refer in their note to Barzillai Frost, Dr. Ripley's assistant. But Frost was not an "old man" (indeed, he was about Emerson's own age). Conrad Wright identifies the object of Emerson's wrath as Dr. Ripley himself. See "Emerson, Barzillai Frost, and The Divinity School Address," *Harvard Theological Review* (1956), 49(1):33.

3. Moncure Conway long ago claimed Anne Hutchinson as a "prophetess" of Transcendentalism. See *Emerson at Home and Abroad* (Boston, 1882), pp. 64–65. On Emerson's "antinomianism" see Eleanor Tilton, "Mr. Emerson—of Boston," in *The Chief Glory of Every People*, ed. Matthew J. Bruccoli (Carbondale, Ill.: Southern Illinois University Press, 1973), pp. 82 and 266, n. 9.

4. *CEC*, p. 184.

5. *CEC*, pp. 326–27.

6. See *L* 1:455, and *JMN* 12:4.

7. Oliver Wendell Holmes, *Ralph Waldo Emerson* (Boston, 1885), p. 14.

8. See Walter Harding, *Emerson's Library* (Charlottesville: University Press of Virginia, 1967), pp. 94–95.

9. William Emerson, *Historical Sketch of the First Church in Boston* (Boston, 1812), pp. 30, 33.

10. Ibid., pp. 44, 47.

11. Ibid., p. 181.

12. Ibid., pp. 186.

13. Ibid., pp. 188 ff.

14. Ibid., p. 190.

15. "Was Emerson, in his heart of hearts, a Napoleon?" asks Perry Miller. See "Emersonian Genius and the American Democracy," in *Nature's Nation* (Cambridge: Harvard University Press, 1967).

16. The text has been printed by Cameron in *Emerson the Essayist* (Raleigh, N.C.: Thistle Press, 1945), 2:101–25.

17. *CEC*, p. 215.

III: A Summer of Discontent

18. Cf. "The Protest," *EL* 3:100, where the sentiments are ascribed to some generic "youth" and deprived of their prophetic intensity. Nevertheless, as Maurice Gonnaud notes, "The Protest" is "indissolublement autobiographique." *Individu et société dans l'oeuvre de Ralph Waldo Emerson: Essai de biographie spirituelle* (Paris: Didier, 1964), p. 269.

Balm in Gilead

19. A valuable treatment of the evolution of Emerson's notion of the preacher-poet, especially in relation to the Unitarian background, is Lawrence I. Buell, "Unitarian Aesthetics and Emerson's Poet-Priest," *American Quarterly* (Spring 1968), 20:3–20. See also Frederick May Eliot, "Emerson and the preacher," *Journal of Liberal Religion* (Summer 1939), 1:5–18.

20. *CEC*, p. 104. Joseph Slater notes that Carlyle's remarks also found their way into "Self-Reliance."

21. See also Randolph J. Bufano, "Emerson's Apprenticeship to Carlyle, 1827–1848," *American Transcendental Quarterly,* Part One (Winter 1972), no. 13, pp. 17–25.

22. The hapless preacher referred to here was actually Barzillai Frost, and Emerson's experience is recorded in *JMN,* 5:463. In his article cited above ("The Protest," n. 2), Conrad Wright reviews the event trenchantly. Noticing that Frost was only one year younger than Emerson, Professor Wright suggests that Emerson viewed Frost as the lifeless and benighted preacher he himself might have become had he not left the Unitarian ministry in 1832. "Part of the extraordinary vehemence of his reaction to Frost's theology," Wright notes, "may well have stemmed from the fact that he was condemning a part of his earlier self. In religion it sometimes happens that the intensest reaction occurs when the convert is confronted by those whom he has left behind."

23. See Robert Spiller's introduction to the Address, *CW* 1:71.

24. It is worth noting that the journal passage that Emerson worked up here for the Address, though it parallels the finished paragraph rather closely, does not mention "the beautiful meteor of the snow." That represents the touch of the poet, shaping remarks into literature. By a stroke of metaphysical wit, Emerson suggests that Frost's "cold" preaching makes the snow seem positively hot. O. W. Firkins, in his *Ralph Waldo Emerson* (Boston: Houghton Mifflin, 1915), p. 163, mordantly observes: "Emerson's discourse drew its matter and coloring largely from private

III: A Summer of Discontent

experience, and the bitter hours which he had passed under the ministrations of Mr. Frost of Concord—a preacher who seems to have justified his name in the congealing effect he produced upon the most distinguished of auditors—and other clergymen of the glacial type spoke out in these biting and restive paragraphs."

25. Stephen E. Whicher, *Freedom and Fate: An Inner Life of Ralph Waldo Emerson* (Philadelphia: University of Pennsylvania Press, 1953), p. 74. In "The Rhetoric of Apostasy," *Texas Studies in Literature and Language* (Winter 1967), 8:547–60, Mary Worden Edrich argues persuasively that Emerson's language throughout the Address was carefully calculated to shock.

26. Jonathan Bishop, *Emerson on the Soul* (Cambridge: Harvard University Press, 1964), p. 88.

27. It is interesting to survey definitions of *luxury* in American dictionaries that Emerson might have consulted. Webster's first edition (1806) gives simply "excess in eating, dress, or pleasure." By 1830 this entry has been expanded, and the first meaning is "a free or extravagant indulgence in the pleasures of the table; voluptuousness in the gratification of appetite; the free indulgence in costly dress and equipage." The Latin sense of *luxuria*, "lust; lewd desire," is offered as definition no. 4 and marked obsolete. However, the 1832 American edition of Johnson's dictionary gives as its first meaning "voluptuousness; addictedness to pleasure," and cites Milton ("lust; lewdness"). As late as 1846, Worcester's dictionary gives "voluptuousness" as the first meaning. Emerson's own use of the word in the 1820s and 1830s tends to lean, not surprisingly, in Milton's direction. Thus, in 1821–22, "wealth induces luxury, and luxury disease" (*JMN* 1:300); in 1831, "I am extremely scrupulous as to indulging my appetite. No ⟨splendour⟩ luxury, no company, no solicitation can tempt me to ⟨luxury⟩ excess . . . because . . . I count my body a temple of God, & will not displease him by gratifying my carnal lust?" (*JMN* 3:225). In a letter to Carlyle in 1834 Emerson says, "to write luxuriously is not the same thing as to live so, but a new & worse offence. It implies an intellectual defect also, the not perceiving that the present corrupt condition of human nature (which condition this harlot muse helps to perpetuate) is a temporary or superficial state. The good word lasts forever; the impure word can only buoy itself in the gross gas that now envelopes us, & will sink altogether to the ground as that works itself clear in the everlasting effort of God" (*CEC*, p. 108).

III: A Summer of Discontent

28. Emerson was surely familiar with the long and stormy history of the term in Calvinist theological disputation. Perry Miller cites Samuel Willard's definition of *preparation* in his *Compleat Body of Divinity* (1726): "that time in which the soul is not yet redeemed but is merely in *'a posture and readiness for the exerting of the act of Faith, which follows thereupon.'* " See " 'Preparation for Salvation' in Seventeenth-Century New England," in Miller, *Nature's Nation,* pp. 50–77.

29. See, for example, Jonathan Edwards' *Images or Shadows of Divine Things,* ed. Perry Miller (New Haven: Yale University Press, 1948), entry nos. 40, 50, 54, 80, 85, 110, 111. Emerson himself used the figure in a sermon preached before the Second Church upon his return from Europe in 1833. See Cameron, *Emerson the Essayist,* 1:182. The Swedenborgian *Dictionary of Correspondences, Representatives, and Significatives,* first published in Boston in 1841, informs us that *dawn* signifies the time "when conjunction is at hand." Under *Aurora* ("day dawn") we find: "Dawn or redness denotes when conjunction begins." *Conjunction* (the union of God and man) is achieved through Christ, the "divine human."

30. Webster (1828) defines *mystery* as follows: "In *religion,* any thing in the character or attributes of God, or in the economy of divine providence, which is not revealed to man." In medieval drama, *mystery* plays generally dealt with episodes from the life of Christ.

31. Henry James, "Emerson," in *The Art of Fiction and Other Essays* (New York: Oxford University Press, 1948), p. 223.

32. *Selected Writings of Gertrude Stein,* ed. Carl Van Vechten (New York: Modern Library, 1962), p. 517.

33. Holmes, *Emerson,* pp. 117–18.

34. Perry Miller, "Declension in a Bible Commonwealth," in *Nature's Nation,* p. 24. On this very large subject, see also Miller's *The New England Mind: From Colony to Province* (Boston: Beacon Press, 1961), pp. 27–39 and passim; Alan Heimert, *Religion and the American Mind* (Cambridge: Harvard University Press, 1966); Sacvan Bercovitch, "Horologicals to Chronometricals: The Rhetoric of the Jeremiad," in *Literary Monographs 3,* ed. Eric Rothstein (Madison: University of Wisconsin Press, 1970), pp. 3–124; David Minter, "The Puritan jeremiad as a literary form," in *The Puritan Imagination,* ed. Sacvan Bercovitch (Cambridge: Cambridge University Press, 1974), pp. 45–55. It is worth noting here that Emerson's father, despite his liberal propensities, also tried his hand at the genre. His "Sermon on the death of Mr. Charles Austin" (1806)

was not only a funeral oration for a promising senior at Harvard College but also, in William Emerson's own words, a "lamentation and testimony against the evil principles and manners of the times." Its text is from Jeremiah 6:26. See *American Transcendental Quarterly,* Part One (Winter 1972), no. 13, pp. 91–97.

35. See Henry D. Thoreau, *Early Essays and Miscellanies,* ed. Joseph J. Moldenhauer, Edwin Moser, and Alexander C. Kern (Princeton, N.J.: Princeton University Press, 1975), p. 32.

36. William Howitt, *The Book of the Seasons* (London, 1831), pp. 176–77.

37. See Conrad Wright, "Emerson, Barzillai Frost. . . ," p. 35.

38. Arthur C. McGiffert, *Young Emerson Speaks* (Boston: Houghton Mifflin, 1938), p. 39.

39. *CEC,* p. 191.

40. *Report on the Trees and Shrubs Growing Naturally in the Forests of Massachusetts* (Boston, 1850), pp. 245–46. Emerson owned a copy of the 1875 edition of this book. See Harding, *Emerson's Library,* p. 89.

41. Nathaniel Hawthorne, *The American Notebooks,* ed. Claude M. Simpson (Columbus: Ohio State University Press, 1972), pp. 315–16.

42. See *L* 3:51 and *L* 4:56. Emerson's interest in both Jeremiah and his scribe was very likely intensified by Washington Allston's painting of the prophet dictating to Baruch, which was included in an exhibition of Allston's paintings in the summer of 1839. Emerson, who was always manifestly intrigued by Allston, went to the exhibition several times and afterward repeated his old complaint (see *JMN* 5:195, 210) that Allston's genius was not masculine enough. For this reason, Emerson praised the treatment of the scribe: "in the Jeremiah, the receiving Baruch is the successful figure. [Allston's] best figures read & hear: and always his genius seems feminine & not masculine" (*JMN* 7:211). Although Margaret Fuller, in her review of the exhibition in *The Dial* (1:73–83), agreed with Emerson's judgment about Baruch, it was not because she found the prophet insufficiently masculine but rather because she preferred the marks of sensibility in the scribe: "Allston's Jeremiah is not the mournfully indignant bard, but the robust and stately Jew, angry that men will not mark his word and go his way. But Baruch is admirable! His overwhelmed yet willing submission, the docile faith which turns him pale, and trembles almost tearful in his eye, are given with infinite force and beauty." One might conjecture that Emerson's uneasiness over the issue of masculinity/

femininity in Allston's picture was more a measure of his own inner uncertainty, and of his need to convince himself that he could fulfill the role of a forceful and vigorous prophet, than it was of Allston's actual achievement in his Jeremiah. Indeed, a few years later, well out of the Divinity School crisis, he seems to have taken a different view of Allston's painting. Writing to Lidian from the Capitol in January 1843, he described his positive reaction to Horatio Greenough's titanic sculpture of George Washington this way: "The statue itself greatly contents me [.] I was afraid it would be feeble but it is not but reminds one of Allston's Jeremiah & of the Jupiter of Phidias about equally, in the attitude & draping" (*L* 3:120–21).

43. It is probably worth noting also that the "October" chapter of Howitt's *Book of the Seasons* has the following epigraph: " 'The harvest is past, the summer is ended, Jeremiah, viii, 20.' " Consistent with the generally sentimental bearing of his book, Howitt leaves off the dour conclusion.

44. See Gay Wilson Allen, "A New Look at Emerson and Science," in *Literature and Ideas in America: Essays in Memory of Harry Hayden Clark*, ed. Robert Falk (Athens: Ohio University Press, 1975), esp. pp. 64–65; also, Eleanor Tilton, *The Chief Glory*, pp. 86–87.

45. Thoreau, *Excursions* (Boston, 1863), p. 190. Stanley Cavell has noticed that Thoreau himself appropriates the voice and language of Jeremiah 8:18–20, in "The Bean-Field." See *The Senses of Walden* (New York: Viking, 1972), pp. 24–25.

46. One further point about Emerson's relation to the jeremiad tradition might be made here. As Bercovitch notes ("Horologicals to Chronometricals," p. 41), "the ministers' diatribe against the unconverted, expressed through the image of 'the God of . . . *Godly Parents*' rebuking a 'degenerating Generation,' actually proposes the latter's redemption through its ancestry. In part, this takes the form of a plea, repeated almost with formulaic persistency, that the children recall their origins . . . the jeremiads use the plea to elevate the founders to heroic stature. Their intent here is obviously pragmatic: to shame the youth into conformity." As Emory Elliott points out, though an occasional jeremiad, such as Thomas Walley's *Balm in Gilead . . . or a treatise wherein There is a Clear Discovery of the Most Prevailing sickness of New England* (1669), might urge "moderation by both the young and the old" ("for the young people he prescribed patience and greater obedience and respect toward the elders;

for the older generation he urged a deeper awareness of the problems and needs of the young"), it nevertheless "focussed upon the conflict between the generations." See *Power and the Pulpit in Puritan New England* (Princeton, N.J.: Princeton University Press, 1975), pp. 93–95. Emerson's attack upon the "Fathers" of the Unitarian establishment may thus be seen as a calculated and conscious inversion of the traditional jeremiad. Perhaps the best evidence I can offer as a demonstration that Emerson's Address was so taken by that establishment is the response of Henry Ware, Jr., in his sermon "The Personality of the Deity," preached on Sunday, September 23, 1838. As a clear rebuke to Emerson, Ware deliverd a *real* jeremiad (his text is from Jeremiah 10:10—"He is the living God and an everlasting King"), arguing that "it is for every man's interest to conform [to God as in] affectionate subjection to a Parent." Ware stresses throughout his sermon man's weakness and need for a strong parent, and warns of the terrible danger of "the disapprobation of a Living Father." See Kenneth Walter Cameron, "Henry Ware's *Divinity School Address*—A Reply to Emerson's," *American Transcendental Quarterly*, Part One (Winter 1972), no. 13, pp. 84–91.

Essaying To Be

47. Gertrude Stein, *Selected Writings,* p. 241.

48. A letter of James Russell Lowell, written eight days after Emerson delivered his Divinity School Address, provides an amusing glimpse of Frost (who was tutoring the rusticated Lowell in Concord): "Yesterday afternoon during Bar[zillai Frost]'s sermon, I saw a man stand up to avoid going to sleep, so at tea I provokingly asked that respectable and reverend individual, what he supposed was the cause of this erection—B. was puzzled—he didn't like to say that the man was afraid of being thrown into a sounder than magnetic sleep by his homily—so he hemmed—but Mrs. F[rost]. very ingenuously said that she supposed he felt drowsy—B. then considered it necessary to explain, that it was *not* the sermon, 'but he was tired from having worked hard all the week; besides, his mind not being accustomed to intellectual exertion, was unable to follow a train of ideas'. What a capital expression that is for such a railroadlike mind as Bar's! which has the same train travelling over & over it agai[n &] again. . . . I believe I told you how B. likes to contradict Locke? Well the other day L. (i.e. his book) made the remark that it was impossible for the mind

ever to be without an idea of some sort. B. immediately attacked it & said 'Why, I myself frequently have no idea in my mind!' 'Yes Sir, very likely' remarked I with a very lamblike aspect. Alas! B. was happy in his dulness [:] he didn't perceive the wit." We should undoubtedly take Lowell's description with a grain of salt, since, as Joel Myerson points out in his introduction, Lowell was angry at having been sent down from Harvard and unloaded his resentment on his tutor (I should add that Emerson also gets a going over in the letter). See "Lowell on Emerson: A New Letter from Concord in 1838," *New England Quarterly* (1971), 44(4):649–52.

49. Roland F. Lee, "Emerson Through Kierkegaard: Toward a Definition of Emerson's Theory of Communication," *English Literary History* (1957), 24(3):229–48, argues persuasively that Emerson's essays demonstrate a theory of communication suggesting the possibility of a vital relationship between writer and reader that fosters an authentic sense of inwardness and existential truth: "His works are meant to *do* something to people, not merely to *tell* them something."

50. See Edward W. Emerson's note on the poem, W 9:408 ff.; cf. Whicher, *Freedom and Fate,* and his *Selections from Ralph Waldo Emerson* (Boston: Houghton Mifflin, 1957), pp. 502–3.

51. Two exceptions are B. R. McElderry, Jr., "Emerson's Second Address on the American Scholar," *The Personalist* (October 1958), 39:361–72, and Merton M. Sealts, Jr., "Emerson on the Scholar, 1838: A Study of 'Literary Ethics,' " in *Literature and Ideas in America: Essays in Memory of Harry Hayden Clark,* ed. Robert Falk (Athens: Ohio University Press, 1975), pp. 40–57.

52. Ralph L. Rusk, *The Life of Ralph Waldo Emerson* (New York: Scribner's, 1949), p. 273.

53. CEC, pp. 215, 223, 209, 199–200.

54. Holmes, *Emerson,* pp. 131–32.

55. Erik Erikson, *Young Man Luther* (New York: Norton, 1962), p. 75.

56. Marvin Meyers, *The Jacksonian Persuasion* (Stanford: Stanford University Press, 1967), pp. 42–43.

57. See Daniel Aaron, "Emerson and the Progressive Tradition," in *Emerson: A Collection of Critical Essays* ed. Milton Konvitz and Stephen E. Whicher (Englewood Cliffs, N.J.: Prentice-Hall, 1962), pp. 85–99, esp. pp. 93–94.

58. Henry James, *Charles W. Eliot* (Boston: Houghton Mifflin, 1930),

2:198, tells us that "Eliot kept a complete set of Emerson in the house at Northeast Harbor as well as in his library in Cambridge. He knew Emerson's essays almost as well as he knew the Bible." See also Hazen C. Carpenter, "Emerson, Eliot and the Elective System," *New England Quarterly* (1951), 24(1):13–34.

59. *JMN* 8:242–43; cf. *JMN* 4:87, 274; 9:123; 10:480.

60. See *L* 2:146 ff. and James Elliot Cabot, *A Memoir of Ralph Waldo Emerson* (Boston, 1888), 2:690–91.

61. See *L* 1:xxv and 2:147–49; see Rusk, *Life,* pp. 269–70.

62. E. P. Peabody, "Emerson as Preacher," in *The Genius and Character of Emerson,* ed. F. B. Sanborn (Boston, 1885), pp. 159–60.

63. *L* 2:166–67 and Cabot, *Memoir* 2:693–94. Emerson was acknowledging receipt of Ware's sermon on "The Personality of the Deity" (see above, "Balm in Gilead," n. 46).

64. Gonnaud, for example, speaks of Emerson's "innocence calculée" in the letter (*Individu et société,* p. 266); and Firkins notes that the " 'babe-like Jupiter' that Emerson was could not coo more innocently after the launching of his thunderbolt" (*Emerson,* p. 79; cf. p. 300).

65. *CEC,* p. 211.

66. *CEC,* p. 197.

67. *L.* 2:149.

68. Holmes, *Emerson,* p. 133.

69. It is worth noting that the paraphrase from the verse of Job which Emerson entered in his journal for August 2, 1837, and upon which he obviously drew for this passage in the Oration, is in the past tense. See *JMN* 5:350.

70. See Demogorgon's final speech in *Prometheus Unbound,* Act IV.

71. Cf. *JMN* 7:8 and note. In *JMN* 9:156, Emerson set down a French version of Napoleon's line ("*Dieu me l'a donnée gare à qui la touche!*"). Readers of Tolstoy's *War and Peace* will recall that the line appears in both French and Italian in the opening scene of the book.

72. In his essay on Milton in the *Christian Examiner* (1826), William Ellery Channing had written: "We believe that the sublime intelligence of Milton was imparted, not for his own sake only, but to awaken kindred virtues and greatness in other souls. Far from regarding him as standing alone and unapproachable, we believe that he is an illustration of what all, who are true to their nature, will become in the progress of their being; and we have held him forth, not to excite an ineffectual admiration, but

to stir up our own and others' breasts to an exhilarating pursuit of high and evergrowing attainments in intellect and virtue." Cited in R. E. Spiller, "A Case for W. E. Channing," *New England Quarterly* (1930), 3(1):79. Spiller notes that Emerson himself acknowledged the importance to him of Channing's essays on Napoleon and Milton. See also William M. Wynkoop, *Three Children of the Universe: Emerson's View of Shakespeare, Bacon, and Milton* (The Hague: Mouton, 1966); cf. Harry Hayden Clark, "Conservative and Mediatory Emphases in Emerson's Thought," in *Transcendentalism and Its Legacy,* ed. Myron Simon and Thornton H. Parsons (Ann Arbor: University of Michigan Press, 1966), p. 42.

73. Cf. what Emerson writes in "History": "Thus in all ways does the soul concentrate and reproduce its treasures for each pupil. He too shall pass through the whole cycle of experience. He too shall collect into a focus the rays of nature" (W 2:38).

74. *CEC,* p. 109.

75. See Rusk in *L* 1:xxxiii.

76. Emerson echoed Hamlet's momentous question while meditating on whether or not to leave the church on July 15, 1832 (see *JMN* 4:29). In *Representative Men* he would claim that "it was not until the nineteenth century, whose speculative genius is a sort of living Hamlet, that the tragedy of Hamlet could find such wondering readers" (W 4:204). When Jones Very arrived at the Emerson household for a five-day visit in October 1838, he brought his essay on *Hamlet* with him, but it is likely that he and Emerson had already discussed the subject when Very was in Concord lecturing the previous April. Surely this wild visionary, who had visited Kronberg Castle at the age of ten with his beloved sea-captain father (who was fated to die the next year), came as close as any of Emerson's young friends to being a "living Hamlet" (see Gittleman's *Jones Very,* passim). Emerson himself suggests in a journal entry for September 5, 1838 (*JMN* 7:64), that he thought of those friends who felt ambivalent about his Divinity School Address as playing the role of Polonius to his Hamlet ("George [Bradford] says his intellect approves the doctrine of the Cambridge Address, but his affections do not. I tell him I would write for his epitaph 'Pity 'tis, 'tis true' "). For a rather extreme treatment of Emerson's Hamlet "complex" see Erik Ingvar Thurin, *The Universal Autobiography of Ralph Waldo Emerson* (Lund: Gleerup, 1974), pp. 66 ff.

77. Rusk, *Life,* p. 23; cf. *L* 4:179.

78. Wallace Stevens, *Collected Poems,* p. 326

Descending

1. See Jeffrey L. Duncan, "The Curse and Blessing of Emerson's Art," *American Transcendental Quarterly*, Supp. 1 (Summer 1976), no. 31, p. 12.

2. On Emerson's darker side, see Stephen E. Whicher, "Emerson's Tragic Sense," in *Emerson: A Collection of Critical Essays*, ed. Milton Konvitz and Stephen E. Whicher (Englewood Cliffs, N.J.: Prentice-Hall, 1962), pp. 39–45. See Harry Hayden Clark in *Transcendentalism and Its Legacy*, ed. Myron Simon and Thornton H. Parsons (Ann Arbor: University of Michigan Press, 1966), pp. 32–5.

3. *JMN* 1:xxvii.

4. See William R. Hutchison, *The Transcendentalist Ministers: Church Reform in the New England Renaissance* (New Haven: Yale University Press, 1959), pp. 3 ff. See also Joseph Haroutunian, *Piety Versus Moralism: The Passing of the New England Theology* (New York: Holt, 1932), and Conrad Wright, *The Beginnings of Unitarianism in America* (Boston: Beacon, 1955). Although Emerson's father died too soon to call himself a Unitarian, he was considered decidedly liberal in his opinions. James Russell Lowell's father, Dr. Charles Lowell, is quoted by Holmes as saying that "in his theological opinions [William Emerson] was, to say the least, far from having any sympathy with Calvinism" (Oliver Wendell Holmes, *Ralph Waldo Emerson* [Boston, 1885], p. 11). But in his 1803 "sermon at the ordination of Thomas Beede" (which Waldo owned), William Emerson defended the "doctrine of human depravity . . . whose truth is sanctioned by universal observation and experience," as a "doctrine of the Christian revelation." See Kenneth Walter Cameron, "Emerson on his Father and Step-Grandfather," *Emerson Society Quarterly* (1st Quarter, 1957), 6:16–19. On Emerson and his father's generation, see also Lewis P. Simpson, "Emerson and the Myth of New England's Intellectual Lapse," *Emerson Society Quarterly* (1st Quarter, 1958), 10:28–31.

5. See "Essaying To Be," n. 59.

6. See Vivian C. Hopkins, *Spires of Form: A Study of Emerson's Aesthetic Theory* (Cambridge: Harvard University Press, 1951), p. 3.

IV: The Fall of Man

Lordly Man's Down-Lying

7. *Samson Agonistes*, ll. 79–80.

8. Cf. *EL* 3:355.

9. See Jonathan Bishop, *Emerson on the Soul* (Cambridge: Harvard University Press, 1964), p. 193. The reader who is alert to the complicated turnings of Emerson's wit may suspect that this opening question ("Where do we find ourselves? In a series . . .") at least obliquely suggests that Emerson feels lost in his own work (we recall that both books of *Essays* are subtitled First and Second *Series*)—in that seemingly endless progression of essays to which he has committed himself and which he now seems to lack the energy to complete. Reemphasizing his sleepy and dreamy mood, Emerson might be describing himself a few pages further on when he says: "Who cares what sensibility or discrimination a man has at some time shown, if he falls asleep in his chair?"

10. Emerson's mention of "lethe" and "opium" brings to mind De Quincey's descriptions of his "fallen" state in *Confessions of an English Opium Eater*, where Piranesi's engravings are described and the artist himself is seen lost in the maze of his own phantasmagoric staircases. See my article, "In the Hands of an Angry God: Religious Terror in Gothic Fiction," in *The Gothic Imagination: Essays in Dark Romanticism*, ed. G. R. Thompson (Pullman: Washington State University Press, 1974), pp. 47 ff. Emerson tells us in *English Traits* (*W*, 5:4) that prior to setting out for Europe in 1832, he had already thought of De Quincey has being one of the "three or four writers" whom he wished to see in Great Britain.

11. See Northrop Frye, *The Anatomy of Criticism* (Princeton, N.J.: Princeton University Press, 1957), pp. 203–4. In Frye's terms, Emerson's vision would be seen as anti-apocalyptic and associated with the Fall. Emerson's use of this *topos,* and the opening of "Experience" generally, might well be compared with Robert Frost's "After Apple-Picking" ("My long two-pointed ladder's sticking through a tree / Toward heaven still . . .").

12. In "Circles," we recall, both God and man were described as infinite centers without bounding circumferences. Now everything seems to be merely superficies with no pith at the core.

13. *Faust* 1:1338.

14. It is interesting to observe that William Emerson's "jeremiad" of 1806 "on the death of Mr. Charles Austin" (see "Balm in Gilead," n. 34)

contains very moving passages on the death of children, some of which seem to find echoes in Emerson's elegy for the "deep-eyed boy" ("Where now," writes Emerson's father, "is that eye, which was as bright as the diamond, and rapid as lightning? . . . And of all that motion, colour, vital heat, nothing can be found but an heap of lovely ruins!").

15. See Stephen E. Whicher, *Selections from Ralph Waldo Emerson* (Boston: Houghton Mifflin, 1957), p. 503, note to line 183.

16. George Santayana, *Interpretations of Poetry and Religion* (New York: Scribner's, 1900), p. 290.

17. Keats, letter to Benjamin Bailey, November 22, 1817.

18. *The Cantos of Ezra Pound* (New York: New Directions, 1972), pp. 520–21.

19. *The Letters of George Santayana,* ed. Daniel Cory (New York: Scribner's, 1955), p. 281.

20. *Santayana on America,* ed. Richard Colton Lyon (New York: Harcourt, 1968), p. 271.

Songs of Autumn

21. See Charles Lowell Young, *Emerson's Montaigne* (New York: Macmillan, 1941), pp. 71–78.

22. See on this passage Michael H. Cowan, *City of the West: Emerson, America, and Urban Metaphor* (New Haven: Yale University Press, 1967), pp. 119–20.

23. Ludwig Wittgenstein, *Philosophical Investigations* (New York: Macmillan, 1968). p. 8e.

24. On Emerson and Bunyan, see Cowan, *City of the West,* pp. 76–77, 84–85. See also *American Transcendental Quarterly,* Supp. Part One (Winter 1972), no. 13.

V: A WINTER'S TALE

Ebbing

1. Emerson's reference is to an earlier journal entry: "When I saw the sylvan youth I said, 'very good promise but I cannot now watch any

more buds: Like the good Grandfather when they brought him the twentieth babe he declined the dandling, he had said "Kitty, Kitty," long enough' " (*JMN* 8:242).

2. *CEC*, p. 303.

3. Evelyn Barish Greenberger, "The Phoenix On the Wall: Consciousness in Emerson's Early and Late Journals," *American Transcendental Quarterly*, Part One (Winter 1974), no. 21, p. 52.

4. Whicher remarks on "a certain estrangement between Emerson and his wife" which left its mark on the journals of the early 1840s (*Selections from Ralph Waldo Emerson* [Boston: Houghton Mifflin, 1957], p. 480, note to p. 142). And Edward Wagenknecht cites "an undated letter fragment in which Fanny [Longfellow] speaks of a report she had heard that 'Emerson does not live happily with his wife; how many alas! wear a bleeding side under their cloak' " (*Longfellow* [New York: Longman's, Green, 1955], p. 237). I would conjecture that whatever sexual tensions and difficulties existed between Emerson and Lidian were probably exacerbated by the death of Waldo.

5. A somewhat different, but cognate, interpretation of this dream is offered by Vivian Hopkins in "Emerson and the World of Dream," in *Emerson's Relevance Today: A Symposium,* ed. Eric W. Carlson and J. Lasley Dameron (Hartford, Conn.: Transcendental Books, 1971), p. 62.

6. See especially Carl F. Strauch, "Hatred's Swift Repulsions," *Studies in Romanticism* (Winter 1968), 7(2):65–103.

7. Strauch (p. 72) argues convincingly that Emerson's poem "Days" expresses his "regrets over lost opportunities."

8. *CEC*, pp. 420, 426.

9. Cf. "Terminus," ll. 23–30:
> Curse, if thou wilt, thy sires,
> Bad husbands of their fires,
> Who, when they gave thee breath,
> Failed to bequeath
> The needful sinew stark as once,
> The Baresark marrow to thy bones,
> But left a legacy of ebbing veins,
> Inconstant heat and nerveless reins,—(W 9:252)

V: A Winter's Tale

Conducting Life

10. See, for example, Arthur O. Lovejoy, " 'Nature' As Aesthetic Norm," in *Essays in the History of Ideas* (New York: Capricorn Books, 1960), pp. 69–77.

11. On Emerson's equivocal use of the term "nature" as indicating his attempt to achieve a sufficiently comprehensive concept, see Paul Lauter, "Truth and Nature: Emerson's Use of Two Complex Words," *English Literary History* (1960), 27(1):66–85, esp. 79 ff.

12. See Josephine Miles, *Ralph Waldo Emerson* (Minneapolis: University of Minnesota Press, 1964), p. 33.

13. *CEC*, p. 72, note.

14. Cf. "The Problem," ll. 13–17:

> Out from the heart of nature rolled
> The burdens of the Bible old;
> The litanies of nations came,
> Like the volcano's tongue of flame,
> Up from the burning core below,—(W 9:6–7)

15. The issues are nicely summarized in Frank Kermode's Introduction to *The Tempest* in the Arden Shakespeare (Cambridge: Harvard University Press, 1958).

16. *The Winter's Tale* IV.iv.88–90.

17. In two of his early lectures, Emerson applied the lines both to the idea of "cultivation" (*EL* 1:44) and to his belief that the "vegetable principle" pervades the whole of creation (*EL* 2:35). See too Gay Wilson Allen, "A New Look At Emerson and Science," in *Literature and Ideas in America: Essays in Memory of Harry Hayden Clark*, ed. Robert Falk (Athens: Ohio University Press, 1975), pp. 65–66; cf. Leo Marx, *The Machine in the Garden* (New York: Oxford University Press, 1964), pp. 241–42.

18. See G. Wilson Knight, " 'Great Creating Nature': An Essay on *The Winter's Tale*," in *Crown of Life* (London: Methuen, 1961), p. 105; Derek Traversi, *An Approach to Shakespeare* (New York: Anchor Books, 1956), pp. 273–76.

19. Most likely Margaret Fuller. See *JMN* 8:524. On Fuller as "Corinne," see *Margaret Fuller: American Romantic*, ed. Perry Miller (New York: Anchor Books, 1963), "Foreword."

20. The form of Emerson's mock-title—*Lues Americana,* or the "European Complaint"—unquestionably alludes to the presumed source for the familiar name of the disease in the poem of Fracastorius, *Syphilis, sive Morbus Gallicus (Syphilis, or the French Disease).* Traditionally, of course, each nation blames the disease on its neighbor (e.g., in Italy it was called the "French Pox").

21. Goodwin's *Plutarch's Morals* (Boston, 1870), for which Emerson wrote a historical and critical introduction, is so chary of the passage that it manages to disguise completely its reference to sex, saying only that Plutarch counsels us "to keep in nature." Yet Emerson himself says in his introduction that "the plain-speaking of Plutarch as of the ancient writers generally, coming from the habit of writing for one sex only, has a great gain for brevity, and, in our new tendencies of civilization, may tend to correct a false delicacy." For Emerson's knowledge of Plutarch generally, see Edmund G. Berry, *Emerson's Plutarch* (Cambridge: Harvard University Press, 1961). As Berry points out, Emerson normally preferred to read his classical authors in translation. "We should remember, however, that he was able to read at least ordinary Greek and Latin fairly easily when it was necessary" (p. 297, n. 6). Emerson's Greek remained good enough to allow him, even "in his old age, to compare Goodwin's translation with the original" (p. 37). Emerson seems to have been familiar with the "Rules for the Preservation of Health" as early as 1828, perhaps with the help of a French translation.

22. It may refer to his poem "Fable" (dating from 1845, according to E. W. Emerson), in which a patently Emersonian squirrel named "Bun" puts down the posturings of an overbearing "mountain." See W 9:75.

23. On the relations between these two "organicists," see Nathalia Wright, "Emerson and Greenough," *Harvard Library Bulletin* (1958), 12(1):91–116.

24. *CEC,* p. 486.

Economizing

25. In the following discussion, I am much indebted to the work of William Charvat, particularly those papers collected in *The Profession of Authorship in America,* 1800–1870, ed. Matthew Bruccoli (Columbus: Ohio State University Press, 1968).

26. See Walter Harding, *The Days of Henry Thoreau* (New York: Knopf, 1965), p. 47.

V: A Winter's Tale

27. See *CEC*, p. 184.

28. See *L*, 4:122.

29. An acquaintance of Emerson's, the writer and lecturer Edwin Percy Whipple, tells a good anecdote testifying "to the soundness of Emerson in practical matters" and to his reputation as a man of means. Riding on the Fitchburg Railroad one day, Whipple overhead the following comments when the train stopped in Concord:

"Mr. Emerson, I hear, lives in this town."

"Ya-as," was the drawling rejoinder; "and I understand that, in spite of his odd notions, he is a man of *con-sid-er*-able propity."

See Whipple's *Recollections of Eminent Men* (Boston, 1887), pp. 125–26. On Emerson's attitude toward property and money, see Alexander C. Kern, "Emerson and Economics," *New England Quarterly* (1940), 13(4):678–96.

30. *CEC*, p. 100.

31. See Jay Leyda, *The Melville Log* (New York: Gordian Press, 1969), 1:410–12.

32. See Charvat, *Profession of Authorship*, p. 196.

33. Ibid., p. 98; *The Letters of Edgar Allan Poe*, ed. John Ward Ostrom (Cambridge: Harvard University Press, 1948), 2:369.

34. Charvat, *Profession of Authorship*, pp. 85–86.

35. *Letters*, 2:452.

36. See Harrison Hayford, "Poe in *The Confidence-Man*," *Nineteenth-Century Fiction* (December 1959), 14:207–18.

37. Walt Whitman, *Leaves of Grass and Selected Prose*, ed. Sculley Bradley (New York: Rinehart Editions, 1966), p. 89.

38. Ibid., pp. 469, 34.

39. See, for example, Michael Paul Rogin, *Fathers and Children: Andrew Jackson and the Subjugation of the American Indian* (New York: Knopf, 1975), esp. "The Mother Bank," pp. 280–95.

40. Ben Barker-Benfield, "The Spermatic Economy: A Nineteenth-Century View of Sexuality," in *The American Family in Social-Historical Perspective*, ed. Michael Gordon (New York: St. Martin's, 1973), pp. 336–72.

41. See reference notes in Barker-Benfield's essay.

42. Alex Comfort, in *The Anxiety Makers* (London: Thomas Nelson, 1967), p. 11.

43. "The Spermatic Economy," p. 339.

44. Ibid., pp. 341–42.

45. Ibid., p. 338.

46. William M. Gouge, *The Curse of Paper-Money and Banking* (London, 1833), pp. 188–96.

47. Theophilus Fisk, *The Banking Bubble Burst* . . . (Charleston, S.C., 1837), pp. 9–10.

48. Ibid., pp. 29, 30, 38.

49. *The Cantos of Ezra Pound* (New York: New Directions, 1972), p. 182.

50. Fisk, *Banking Bubble*, pp. 55–56.

51. Ibid., pp. 79–80.

52. *Proceedings of the Friends of a National Bank, at their Public Meeting, Held in Boston, Fifteenth July, 1841* (Boston, 1841), pp. 25–26, 16.

53. Ibid., p. 19.

54. Thoreau, *Walden*, ed. J. Lyndon Shanley (Princeton, N.J.: Princeton University Press, 1974), p. 297.

55. Whitney R. Cross, *The Burned-over District: The Social and Intellectual History of Enthusiastic Religion in Western New York, 1800–1850* (Ithaca, N.Y.: Cornell University Press, 1950), pp. 12–13.

56. Ibid., p. 12.

57. Ibid., pp. 268 ff.

58. Charles Grandison Finney, *Lectures on Revivals of Religion*, ed. William G. McLoughlin (Cambridge: Harvard University Press, 1960), pp. 9–10.

59. Ibid., pp. 13, 34, 60.

60. Ibid., p. l [roman].

61. See, for example, Cedric B. Cowing, "Sex and Preaching in the Great Awakening," *American Quarterly* (Fall 1968), 20(3):624–44, esp. 641 ff. Cowing cites Perry Miller's *Jonathan Edwards:* "The land was filled with enthusiasm, not just the faintings of 1740, and orgies too fantastic to be credible mounted, while the bastardy rate began to rise" (p. 172).

62. In *The Great Awakening*, ed. Alan Heimert and Perry Miller (Indianapolis, Ind.: Bobbs-Merrill, 1967), p. 231.

63. Cross, *Burned-over District*, pp. 177–78.

64. Ibid., pp. 186–87.

65. Ibid., pp. 314–15.

66. In *Native American Humor,* ed. Walter Blair (San Francisco: Chandler, 1960), pp. 317–18.

67. See William Charvat, *Emerson's American Lecture Engagements, A Chronological List* (New York: New York Public Library, 1961), pp. 27, 30.

68. Horace Bushnell, *Christian Nurture* (Hartford, Conn., 1847), pp. 102, 47, 48, 49.

69. Ibid., p. 70.

70. Ibid., pp. 71–72, 112, 114.

71. Ibid., p. 128.

72. Ibid., pp. 143, 167.

73. Marvin Meyers, *The Jacksonian Persuasion* (Stanford: Stanford University Press, 1967), pp. 166, 184.

74. *Christian Nurture*, pp. 167, 174, 184–85.

75. Ibid., pp. 220, 234, 236.

76. Cited in R. W. B. Lewis, *The American Adam* (Chicago: University of Chicago Press, 1955), pp. 68–69.

77. See Ralph Thompson, "Emerson and *The Offering for 1829,*" *American Literature* (1934), 6(2):151–57.

78. Greenberger, "The Phoenix on the Wall," p. 51.

79. See ibid., p. 53; Thurin, *Universal Autobiography*, pp. 159–60.

80. See Firkins, *Emerson*, p. 310: "It is by no means true that Emerson's later faith subsisted on the savings of his Puritanism, that he spent day by day his waning accumulations. His religion was a self-supporting enterprise, not a hoard, but capital actively employed and supplying dividends far more punctually than his precarious investments in bank stock or railways. The business, however, was of that not unusual kind which only a large initial outlay could have rendered lucrative. The lesson to the penniless is clear."

EPILOGUE

Luther

1. Mather's phrase is from the opening of *Magnalia Christi Americana*.

2. A useful general discussion of Emerson's dedication to the spirit of America is Ernest Sandeen, "Emerson's Americanism," *University of Iowa Studies* (1942), 6(1):63–118.

3. In *The American Literary Revolution*, ed. Robert Spiller (New

York: Anchor Books, 1967), p. 314. Emerson himself called Everett's Oration "the high water mark which no after tide has reached" (*JMN* 6:71).

4. The "genre of auto-American biography: the celebration of the representative self as America," is brilliantly discussed, both with reference to Emerson and in a larger context, by Sacvan Bercovitch in *The Puritan Origins of the American Self* (New Haven: Yale University Press, 1975). See esp. chapter 5, "The Myth of America."

5. Emerson considered the "reform of the Reformation" to be one of the *"peculiarities"* of his age (*JMN* 3:70). And the following passage from a journal entry of 1822 clearly suggests that he hoped to play a role in this ongoing process: "Luther and Calvin took upon themselves . . . [part of the labor of the] Reformation and some spirited servant of literature must yet devote his talents to the high purpose of leading the triumph of good principles" (*JMN* 1:151).

6. Erik H. Erikson, *Young Man Luther* (New York: Norton, 1962), p. 83.

7. *EL* 1:316, and Ralph L. Rusk, *The Life of Ralph Waldo Emerson* (New York: Scribner's, 1949), p. 151.

8. Erikson, *Young Man Luther,* p. 201.

9. See Alexis de Tocqueville, *Democracy in America,* trans. Henry Reeve (New York: Random House, 1945), 2:144: "In America I saw the freest and most enlightened men placed in the happiest circumstances that the world affords; it seemed to me as if a cloud habitually hung upon their brow, and I thought them serious and almost sad, even in their pleasures." In his journal for 1844, while speculating on the promise of America, Emerson asks: "Is not fluctuation the only abiding feature of all national character? This which gives zest to life, matter of lamentation to the aged, & of hope to the young—is not this an insuperable obstacle in the way of all rational speculation?" (*JMN* 2:256). In his own "reflections on the American identity" in *Childhood and Society,* 2d ed. (New York: Norton, 1963), p. 286, Erik Erikson suggests that "the functioning American, as the heir of a history of extreme contrasts and abrupt changes, bases his final ego identity on some tentative combination of dynamic polarities such as migratory and sedentary, individualistic and standardized, competitive and cooperative, pious and freethinking, responsible and cynical, etc."

10. Erikson, *Young Man Luther,* p. 196.

11. Oliver Wendell Holmes, *Ralph Waldo Emerson* (Boston, 1885), p. 112.

12. Cf. *CEC*, 219; *EL* 2:111; *W* 7:79.

13. Erikson, *Young Man Luther*, p. 196.

14. On Emerson's problem of "vertical" and "horizontal" see Sherman Paul, *Emerson's Angle of Vision* (Cambridge: Harvard University Press, 1952), pp. 20ff.

15. Erikson, *Young Man Luther*, p. 214.

16. Ibid., p. 214.

17. Ibid., p. 198.

Thoreau

18. Nathaniel P. Willis, *Inklings of Adventure* (New York, 1836), 1:87–90.

19. *The Writings of Henry David Thoreau*, Walden Edition (Boston, 1906), 9:141.

20. The evidence for considering Emerson's "Thoreau" as a Plutarchan attempt to create a "classical hero" is weighed by Edmund G. Berry in *Emerson's Plutarch* (Cambridge: Harvard University Press, 1961), pp. 266–67.

21. In the published version of his speech, Emerson calls Thoreau "an iconoclast in literature" (*W* 10:451), but in an earlier draft we find "he was a sans culotte in literature" (Huntington Library manuscript HM 187, p. 3).

22. See Edward W. Emerson's note in *W* 4:315.

23. Nathaniel Hawthorne, *The American Notebooks*, ed. Claude M. Simpson (Columbus: Ohio State University Press, 1972), p. 353.

24. Notebook HT (Houghton Library number 117), "Miscellaneous Notes on H. D. Thoreau," p. 19. Published here by permission of the Trustees of the R. W. Emerson Memorial Association and the Harvard College Library.

Emerson

25. On "representativeness" in Emerson's theory of great men, see John O. McCormick, "Emerson's Theory of Human Greatness," *New England Quarterly* (1953), 26(3):291–314.

26. Walt Whitman, *Leaves of Grass and Selected Prose*, ed. Sculley Bradley (New York: Rinehart Editions, 1966), pp. 469–70.

27. See *The Correspondence of Henry David Thoreau*, ed. Walter

Harding and Carl Bode (New York: New York University Press, 1958), p. 445.

28. *CEC*, p. 509.

29. See *JMN* 8:326, 382, 425–26.

30. See F. O. Matthiessen, *American Renaissance: Art and Expression in the Age of Emerson and Whitman* (New York: Oxford University Press, 1941), pp. 635 ff.

31. Whitman, *Leaves of Grass and Selected Prose*, p. 40.

32. Ibid., p. 64.

33. See W 6:209.

34. *CEC*, p. 317.

35. Whitman, *Leaves of Grass and Selected Prose*, p. 486.

36. Holmes, *Emerson*, p. 321.

37. George Santayana, *Obiter Scripta*, ed. Justus Buchler and Benjamin Schwartz (New York: Scribner's, 1936), p. 217.

38. George Santayana, *Interpretations of Poetry and Religion* (New York: Scribner's, 1900), p. 184.

39. *Obiter Scripta*, p. 216.

ACKNOWLEDGMENTS

Since I have been reading in and about Emerson for many years, and not always systematically, I fear that some of my scholarly debts may go unpaid. Apart from the specific obligations recorded in the notes, I want to express my gratitude generally to the editors of Emerson's *Early Lectures, Collected Works,* and *Journals and Miscellaneous Notebooks.* It would have been impossible for me to write this book without the benefit of their devoted labors. I am grateful to the Henry E. Huntington Library and the Harvard College Library for innumerable courtesies that facilitated the use of their collections. I also want to thank friends at Princeton University, the University of Sussex, Wayne State University, and Middlebury College for inviting me to read drafts of portions of this book. Their attention to my work—at once sympathetic and critical—was a very great help. Earlier versions of chapters, or parts of chapters, have been published in *Harvard English Studies,* volumes 4 and 8, as well as in *Forum* (University of Houston); I am grateful for permission to reprint this material. I owe a general debt to students at Harvard University over the years for listening to my ideas about Emerson and responding with their own. A representative, though inadequate, list would include Leslie Blumberg, Patricia Caldwell, Michael Gilmore, Barry Hoffman, Alex Keyssar, and the members of my freshman seminar in Emerson and Thoreau. A number of friends offered welcome advice and encouragement: Carlos Baker, Sacvan Bercovitch, Richard Bridgman, Richard Lee Francis, Justin Kaplan, Morton Paley, Vern Wagner, and

Acknowledgments

Gay Wilson Allen. James Raimes, of Oxford University Press, has guided me expertly from start to finish.

Three special debts remain. This book is dedicated to a fellow Emersonian and dear friend who has sustained me throughout this project by providing my best audience and continuing to represent my ideal of the American scholar. In addition, I owe a great deal to Sarah Preston Carleton for her unflagging interest in this book and her faith in me. Finally, I must mention my daughter Susanna, who has cheerfully and self-reliantly allowed her daddy to divide his attention between her and the subject of this book without expecting much by way of compensation. Time and again, she has brought home to me the truth of Emerson's observation that "we find a delight in the beauty and happiness of children that makes the heart too big for the body."

J.P.

INDEX

Index

Index

Index